A Jazz Lexicon

A JAZZ LEXICON

BY

Robert S. Gold

NEW YORK: ALFRED·A·KNOPF

1964

L. C. catalog card number: 63–9129

THIS IS A BORZOI BOOK,
PUBLISHED BY ALFRED A. KNOPF, INC.

FIRST EDITION

The Introduction includes a portion of "The Vernacular of the Jazz World," originally published in *American Speech*.

TO

Mitzi Ruth Haggard

Acknowledgments

I SUSPECT that my indebtedness to others is greater than it would have been had my research project been more conventional.

Undischargeable debts are owed, therefore, to a number of people, but especially to Professor Allan F. Hubbell of New York University for his lexicographical help; to Miss Mitzi Haggard for her editorial assistance; and to Mr. Leon James for help with many aspects of slang.

Mrs. Jean Stearns and Professor Marshall Stearns were extremely gracious in giving me ready access to the superb collection of the Institute of Jazz Studies, as was Mr. Robert George Reisner in permitting me to work in his jazz library, subsequently sold to Tulane University. Mr. Harold Flakser made available to me a number of rare jazz periodicals, and the staff of the Schomburg Collection of the New York Public Library introduced me to some valuable Negro source materials.

The literally hundreds of specious terms which have been circulated in jazz glossaries and slang dictionaries for the past thirty years required much weeding out, and whatever authenticity this volume possesses owes a great deal to those jazz musicians, writers, and devotees who performed that service: Danny Barker, guitarist-banjoist; Emmett Berry, trumpeter; Eubie Blake, pianist-composer; Ira Gitler, jazz critic; Gigi Gryce, alto saxophonist; Leon James, jazz dancer; Dick Katz, pianist; Jan Kindler, writer-jazz devotee; Paul Knopf, pianist; Eddie Locke, drummer; S. P. Lomax, writer-jazz devotee; Dan Morgenstern, editor of *Jazz* magazine; Tony Parenti, clarinetist; Gordon Pheil, alto saxophonist;

Robert George Reisner, jazz writer-bibliographer; Jerome Richardson, flutist-baritone saxophonist; Zutty Singleton, drummer; Hsio Wen Shih, editor of *The Jazz Review* (now defunct); John Williams, novelist-jazz biographer.

Contents

Introduction

THE STUDY of the vernacular of the jazz world is necessarily a study in sociology and social psychology as well as in linguistics. For the people who created this peculiarly American idiom did so as a result of the peculiar conditions surrounding the development of modern jazz. Hence, an understanding of their slang is hardly possible without a knowledge of how jazz grew up, who its creators were, and what kind of lives they led. Only then does the language they speak become meaningful.

It is by ignoring the sociological side of the coin that the slick magazines have been able to caricature and patronize the colorful jargon of jazz. *Life, Time, Newsweek, Collier's,* and others have made forays into the field of jazz linguistics to the amusement, if not enlightenment, of their readers. Typical is this caption from *Life,* hardly more accurate in its presentation of jazz speech than in its portrayal of college students:

> Voutians (pronounced Vowshuns) are a growing group of United States college students who are uninhibited admirers of Jazz Musician Slim Gaillard, composer of "Cement Mixer Put-ti, Put-ti," "Flat Foot Floogie with the Floy Floy." They play his records, talk his outlandish rhyming language. A pretty girl is a rootie-voutie, or viddle vop. Onions are reetie-pooties. Reeny, roony and aureenie are used as complementary suffixes (hamburgaureenie is a good hamburger).[1]

Accompanying this article are pictures illustrating the "vout handshake," a maneuver requiring a contortionist for its exe-

[1] *Life,* May 5, 1947, p. 129.

cution (a jazz musician or devotee who tried it would probably meet with serious injury).

So we have that eccentric bane of middle-class existence,
the Jazz Musician (*Life's* capitals), poisoning Our Youth
(my capitals) with nonconformist speech and greeting.
Little surprise, then, that the article provoked letters like
this:

> Sirs: Physical chastisement may be frowned upon by child
> psychologists, but it does seem a resounding whack smack
> with a snap strap on the seat meat of such ants pants as these
> Voutians would be aurightaureenie. What say, O'Day?
> Hopewell, N.J.   R. L. Scharring-Hauser[2]

Scharring-Hauser is no doubt pleased by his own clever-
ness, but his parody, unknown to him, is more of *Life* than
of the ephemeral Voutians, who doubtless vanished at the
first sign of a new diversion. The truth is that even by jazz
standards Slim Gaillard is an eccentric (but his world is
a more tolerant one, and in it, his undisciplined spoofing is
taken good-naturedly). Then, too, jazz lingo can hardly be
held responsible for university faddism, a runaway horse
that has long since departed from the stable of sanity. And,
while these shenanigans make delightful copy, one can legitimately object to the editorial irresponsibility which seizes
upon the most extravagant jazz parlance and creates the
impression that it is the norm. Such exaggerations contribute
to the classic slander—that jazz is nothing but a garish art
form and its practitioners dope addicts, and that its language
proves both points. Gilbert Seldes notes: "I have heard
Eddie Condon say that he has never heard and doesn't understand half of the jive language the hepcats are supposed
to use." [3] When a noted jazz guitarist who has "gigged
around" (worked a variety of jobs) for nearly three decades
makes an admission of this sort, it is a sign that much con-

---

[2] "Letters to the Editor," *Life*, May 26, 1947, p. 7.
[3] *The New York Times Book Review*, July 27, 1947, p. 1.

fusion abounds concerning the language of the jazz world. The air can be cleared only by studying the argot and its speakers concurrently.

Jazz had an imperceptible birth. It did not just happen one fine Louisiana night in a gin mill. It evolved from prior musical forms. In discussing the origins of jazz,

> One can no more neglect the Protestant hymn tune than the Morris dance, no more underestimate the effect of the spiritual on dozens of vaudeville circuits around the United States than the vestiges of African ceremonial in Congo Square, New Orleans. These evidences . . . make clear that New Orleans was the ineluctable starting-point for a story that is orderly for all its academic confusion, American because of its polyglot origins and development—a tapestry of impressions and expressions that becomes the richly textured history of jazz.[4]

Paralleling the "polyglot origins and development" of jazz is the strange amalgam that constitutes the language of the jazz world—the curious mixture of Negro folk expressions with the imagery of the new city life, and the blending of the two with the terms revolving about the music in which these newly freed people found even greater release:

> Jive is one more contribution of Negro America to the United States. White America perpetuated a new and foreign language on the Africans it enslaved. Slowly, over the generations, Negro America, living by and large in its own segregated world, with its own thoughts, found its own way of expression, found its own way of handling English, as it had to find its own way in handling many other aspects of a white, hostile world. Jive . . . may go way back, deep into the bowels of the Negro-American experience, back into the revolutionary times when it was necessary for the Negro to speak, sing, and even think in a kind of code. . . . Jive talk may have been originally a kind of "pig Latin" that the slaves

[4] Barry Ulanov: *A History of Jazz in America* (New York: Viking, 1952), p. 13.

talked with each other . . . when . . . in the presence of
whites. Take the word, "ofay." [5] Ninety-nine million white
Americans right now probably don't know that that means
"a white," but Negroes know it. Negroes needed to have a
word like that in their language, needed to create it in self-
defense.[6]

So we get a people in rebellion against a dominant majority, but forced to rebel secretly, to sublimate, as the psy-
chologist would put it—to express themselves culturally
through the medium of jazz, and linguistically through a
code, a jargon. But as the music developed from New Orleans marches and early Dixieland through the blues-and-
rhythm cycle and the swing era on into bop and modern,
or progressive, jazz, an immense change took place in the
life of the Negro. He became more urbanized and the life
of the streets peppered his language, and so filtered into
jazz parlance, which to this day is highly interrelated with
Negro life. Always close (though hardly by choice) to the
most squalid aspects of big-city life, the Negro assimilated
the jargon of the rackets—dope peddling, prostitution,
larceny, gambling—and the more interesting of these
terms spilled over into jazz lingo.[7] Then, too, the high frequency of Negro impressment into Southern chain gangs
was another, unhappy source of Negro slang, much as it
was a source of Negro work songs and folk songs.

The totality of his experience in America stamped the
Negro with a psychology demanding not only a unique and
rebellious music, but a unique and rebellious way of speaking:

[5] The white man was regarded as a foe. Hence, *ofay* from *foe:* in
pig Latin an initial consonant or cluster is dropped and added at the
end with an [ei] following it.

[6] Earl Conrad: Introduction to *Dan Burley's Original Handbook
of Harlem Jive* (New York, 1944), pp. 5–6.

[7] The often close connection between musicians and racketeers
(most often as employee and employer, respectively) receives ample
documentation in Mezz Mezzrow's autobiography (with Bernard
Wolfe), *Really the Blues* (New York: Random House, 1946).

Jive . . . supplies the answer to the hunger for the unusual, the exotic and the picturesque in speech. It is a medium of escape, a safety valve for people pressed against the wall for centuries, deprived of the advantages of complete social, economic, moral and intellectual freedom. It is an inarticulate protest . . . a defense mechanism, a method of deriving pleasure from something the uninitiated cannot understand. It is the same means of escape that brought into being the spirituals as sung by American slaves; the blues songs of protest that bubble in the breasts of black men and women.[8]

Like most slang, the jazz variety gains sustenance primarily from the uneducated; it is a subjective language, highly colored by the emotional reactions of its users, whose very inadequacy with the standard language prompts and inspires their linguistic inventiveness.

And like slang in general, jazz terms are relegated to the scrap heap with amazing speed, and this frequently makes their etymologies undeterminable. An example is the contradictory information given by different writers on the origin of the word describing the jazz era that grew out of swing around 1945 and evolved into modern, or progressive, jazz about 1952:

In 1939 . . . [Ella Fitzgerald] scattered around . . . an engaging tune and ended one of her phrases with the word "rebop," undoubtedly the first appearance of the first accredited name for Dizzy Gillespie's and Charlie Parker's music.[9]

Before it becomes dignified by general acceptance, let us scotch the theory that the terms *bop, bebop, rebop,* and their derivatives are onomatopoeic in origin. The jazz musician has merely adopted and assimilated the rhumba-bands' *Arriba, 'riba* (Up, up!), shouted in genuine or feigned excitement at a sudden shift in tempo. . . . *Arriba, 'riba!* has found a home in *Hey, bob a rebop! Oo bop a dah!* [1]

[8] *Dan Burley's Original Handbook,* p. 71.
[9] Ulanov: *op. cit.,* p. 252.
[1] Maurice Crane: "Bebop," *Word Study,* October, 1954, p. 6.

It was at Minton's that the word "bebop" came into being. Dizzy [Gillespie] was trying to show a bass player how the last two notes of a phrase should sound. The bass player tried it again and again, but he couldn't get the two notes. "Be-bop! Be-bop! Be-bop!" Dizzy finally sang.[2]

It is virtually impossible to resolve such a dispute, though a knowledge of jazz makes the first and third explanations more plausible than the second. Many bop phrases seem to derive from the nonsense syllables of scat-singing, q.v., which, in turn, is simply the voice imitating the sound of an instrument, the first known instance of which, so the story goes, occurred when Louis Armstrong dropped his lyric sheet in the middle of a 1926 recording date and was forced to improvise the words.

Among the more unlikely attempts to trace a word origin is this account of the phrase *get hep:*

In the 1890's . . . Joe Hep ran a saloon in Chicago. . . . Although he never quite understood what was going on, he *thought* he did, and considered himself proudly "in" on every "touch" that came off . . . and so Joe Hep's name entered the argot as an ironic appellation for anyone who thought he knew but didn't. The ironic sense has now largely disappeared from elements of the name surviving in the phrases, "to get Joe to" or "to get hep to" something. . . . The term has been sometimes corrupted [sic!] to "hip!"[3]

A more likely effort is this explanation of the origin and evolution of the word *jive:*

Jive is a distortion of that staid, old, respectable English word "jibe." In the sense in which it came into use among Negroes in Chicago about the year 1921, it meant to taunt, to scoff, to sneer—an expression of sarcastic comment. Like the tribal groups of Mohammedans and people of the Orient, Negroes

[2] Richard O. Boyer: "Bop," *The New Yorker,* July 3, 1948, p. 31.
[3] David W. Maurer: "Phrase Origins: Get Hep," *American Mercury,* May, 1947, p. 548.

of that period had developed a highly effective manner of talking about each other's ancestors and hereditary traits, a colorful and picturesque linguistic procedure which came to be known as "putting you in the dozens." Later, this was simply called "jiving" someone. Subsequently ragtime musicians picked up the term and it soon came to mean "all things to all men" . . . and since 1930 Jive has been accepted as the trade name for swing music, for the jitterbug population, and as the key to a complete new world in itself.[4]

The great difficulty in tracing jazz words to their sources stems not only from the dynamic and prolific coinage of the argot, but also from the fact that jazz terms rarely appear in those written records upon which the makers of dictionaries are necessarily so dependent. This is true to some degree, of course, of all highly colloquial language; but it is especially true of the jazz vernacular, which is generated among groups in our society least likely to record their acts and thoughts in writing.

Nonetheless, lexicographers have been all too slow in recording the more permanent jazz phrases, some of which are widely used outside the jazz world (e.g., *blow your top*). For "Negro slang expression, jazz expression, street parlance . . . have entered into the English language to stay, to root themselves, to become part of the orthodox expression of the future."[5]

The language of the jazz world is neither the language of the jazz musician nor the language of the Negro people, but a fusing of the two. It is the language spoken by jazz musicians and appreciators, giving to and receiving from the Negro people new words and phrases. It is a language that would be only partly comprehensible to Negroes not interested in jazz, or to white musicians who play "Mickey Mouse" (i.e., popular music). And it is a language which

---

[4] *Dan Burley's Original Handbook*, p. 71.
[5] Earl Conrad: "The Philology of Negro Dialect," *Journal of Negro Education*, Spring, 1944, p. 150.

has always told a great deal about the lives and attitudes of its speakers.

Time says of modern jazz: "The critics like to call it 'music of protest' . . . but the jazz style called modern does not protest against anything very much except dullness." [6] This is an obfuscation of the social roots of jazz, its creators' answer to their disenfranchisement from "highbrow" culture, just as jazz lingo is the impish rebellion of a people largely deprived of formal education.

Time's observation is less truthful than self-revealing. An almost overt hostility has from the beginning characterized jazz reportage, and the jazzman is cynically aware that he is apt to receive notoriety more for his occasional misadventures with the law than for his artistry.

The lives and attitudes of jazzmen have, of course, changed remarkably in the relatively brief history of jazz, but if there is one thing that has remained constant—*Time* and its ilk notwithstanding—it is the essential rebelliousness at the heart of both the music and the speech. This is difficult to demonstrate in the music, which is chiefly nonverbal, though a good case might be made from the lyrics of early blues and of more recent "protest" songs (*Recognition as a Man, Fables of Faubus*, etc.) and from the titles of many jazz compositions (*Gone With What Wind?, Freedom Now Suite*, etc.).

But rejection of or opposition to dominant modes of thinking and feeling *can* be found throughout the history of jazzmen's speech—for example, in his deliberate and significant reversal of the conventional connotations of terms such as *mean, dirty,* and *nasty* (all current c. 1900) and, more recently, of *bad, tough,* and *terrible*. The logic of jazz usage here lies in the Negro's awareness that conventional white morality, which countenances Negro subservience even while professing egalitarian ideals, is hypocritical and so also

6 *Time,* November 8, 1954, pp. 67, 70.

must be those terms through which the white man expresses that morality; in addition, the puritanical equation of sex with sin has reinforced the Negro's suspicion that the in-group is supremely mistaken in its judgments of good and bad, and that standard designations of disapproval have been attached to things that are, by sensible standards, perfectly good—for example, earthiness and virility. Hence, the Negro retains the standard terms of designation, but gives to these an interpretation which reverses their value.

Conversely, the favorable connotations of standard terms such as *sweet* and *square* (honest, upright) are reversed by jazzmen by the complementary logic that what the in-group might judge to be good would most likely be merely servile, genteel, or innocuous.

If anything, since the end of World War II the mood of revolt against the conventional has deepened. This is exemplified not only by the highly intricate, often esoteric, character of modern jazz, but also by the fashion in jazz slang of assigning favorable connotations to terms of mental derangement (*crazy, insane, nutty,* etc.), with its obvious suggestion of contempt for normality.

From the outset the Negro's sense of alienation intensified his need for a private vocabulary, both as a defense against hostility and as a reassurance of self-worth. *Ofay* (a white person), as already noted, is derived rather significantly from pig Latin for *foe; I feel a draft,* a relatively new expression, usually means that the Negro speaker suspects hostility or discrimination directed against him by a white; *soul brother* is an honorific phrase used of one Negro by another (it is noteworthy that the locution inevitably carries an implication that the white man's soul has been forfeited by virtue of his long-standing abuse of the Negro); *man* is a term of address to one Negro by another, meant to counteract the debilitating effects on his morale of being called "boy" by whites; etc.

Although the linguistic record is skimpy, one can safely infer from jazz history something about the extent of early jazz slang. First, since a specialized slang does not come into being all at once, it must be that much of the early jazzmen's nonstandard vocabulary consisted of general colloquialisms, Negro folk idiom, and general slang (mostly from underworld speech traditionally synonymous with the word *slang*). The development of a special vocabulary identifiable as jazz slang had to await the growth of a jazz culture which was not merely ancillary to prostitution or the rackets.

Nevertheless, certain locutions arose early either because there was no existing standard term for a phenomenon or, more frequently, because the standard term was either unknown or was too indirect for the users' taste. Special properties of the music, for example, were sometimes identified with the musicians' environment: *honkytonk, barrelhouse,* and *gutbucket* for the jazz style predominating in taverns; *tailgate* for the New Orleans trombone style, because the trombonist occupied a position in the rear (i.e., close to the tailgate) of New Orleans advertising trucks. Other characteristics of the music, in the absence of standard terms, required fresh identifiers: *blue notes* or *off notes* to describe the in-between pitch most peculiar to jazz.

The emotional content of the music gave rise to a number of terms "formed by metaphor, e.g., by the widespread practice of equating joy with height ('exultation') and grief with depth; or with the colors red and blue, or with fast and slow. Thus the quality most desired in the old blues is that it should be *low-down* or *dragging*."[7] Another early linguistic practice was the designation of rhythmic qualities by kinesthetic association: *ride, rock, roll, swing, romp, stomp,* etc. Unknown to the general public, a number of such terms (e.g., *ride, roll, rock*) derive from sexual colloquialisms, as does *jazz* itself and most probably *jitterbug* and *boogie-*

[7] Francis Newton: *The Jazz Scene* (London, 1959), pp. 290–291.

woogie; the earthiness of the music, then as now, has a linguistic equivalent in the speech of its performers.

A few terms, perhaps because of their simplicity and widespread applicability, have survived from the early jazz life. *Hip* (aware, wise, knowledgable) and *gig* (usually a jazzman's job as distinguished from other work) are two such survivors. But, for the most part, jazz parlance has a large and rapid turnover. Since one of the reasons "people talk special kinds of slang [is that] . . . they want to belong to a special group, and to exclude everyone else," [8] the jazz world has always tended to drop out of its usage such terms as are taken over by the general public. *Cat* (initially a jazzman, now anyone) and *chick* (a young woman) were widespread in the twenties and thirties; *square* (unsophisticated) and *zoot* (flashy) in the thirties and forties; *crazy* and *far out* (both superlatives) in the late forties and fifties— these are just a few of the many terms that have lost ground in jazz circles in almost direct relation to the growth of their popularity with the nonjazz public. The jazz slang speaker's aloofness is tacitly justified by his feeling that only those who are *down with the action* (aware of what is going on) should have access to the speech of those who have *paid their dues* (suffered an apprenticeship in life generally and in the jazz life in particular).

The jazzman's pain, derived in part from the frustrations that normally characterize much of contemporary life, is exacerbated by the inordinate pressure brought to bear on the creative person who must improvise—i.e., create on the spot whether he feels like it or not. The quest for release is at least partially responsible for his above-average (though generally exaggerated) addiction to drugs and his customary overindulgence in liquor and marijuana (frequently, although it is not in fact so, classified as an addictive drug by the law and in the public mind). It is inevitable, then, that

[8] Gilbert Highet: *The Anatomy of Slang*, Book-of-the-Month Club transcript of WNYC radio talk, p. 3.

there should be a considerable number of terms in jazz speech relating to drugs, drug addiction, the effects of stimulants, etc.

Another aspect of the jazz vocabulary that distinguishes it from other specialized slangs is the large number of superlatives, a consequence of a performing art that generally elicits great enthusiasm from its listeners. Currently, in response to an inspired musical performance, a jazz devotee draws from a large storehouse of terms: *crazy, nutty, insane, swinging, groovy, cooking, wailing, burning, smoking, boss, something else, out of sight,* etc. There are also a large number of escapist terms, an obvious response to the depressing realities of much of jazz and Negro life: *send me, out of this world, far out, way out, gone, cloud 9, out of sight, knock out,* etc.

A number of terms applied to human behavior are analogical extensions from properties of the music or musicians. Hence, *riff* and *lick,* originally a musical phrase or idea, are extended to mean any idea, plan, proposal, or situation. A *swinger,* initially an exciting musician, now means anyone who lives excitingly. *I don't dig the tune,* initially an admission on the speaker's part of ignorance as to the melody being played, comes to mean ignorance of whatever is happening.

Contrasting with the extravagant descriptiveness of jazz nouns, adjectives, and adverbs is the spareness of its verbs, most of which are action verbs, e.g., *blow, cook, cop, dig, jump, knock, latch on, make, pick up,* and *put down.* Their paucity forces each to carry numerous meanings, e.g., *knock:* to put down, speak, walk, loan, borrow, give, ask, exhibit, etc.

We should perhaps take note of the brief (c. 1935–c. 1940) vogue of rhyming slang in jazz which, unlike the British practice, was based generally on logical similes: e.g., *mellow like a cello; fine as wine; like the bear, I ain't nowhere* (i.e., an extension of the lumbering physical qualities of the animal to the immobilized spiritual state of a man). Although some were of the merely ebullient variety (e.g., *killer-diller:* an extraordinarily good musician or piece of music), characteristically the jazz phrases were formed by semantic association and may be contrasted with the British formations in which the meaningful word, whether slang or standard, is usually replaced by a nonsense rhyming one: e.g., *Kangaroo:* a Jew; *don't make a fuss:* a bus; *down the drains:* brains; *Colney Hatch:* a match.

Logical or not, rhyming slang and much of the older elaborateness were, during the 1940s, frozen out of the language as part of the far-reaching change in the cultural climate of jazz, a change first of all in the consciousness of the jazzman and one which had an enormous effect on his music, his speech, and his self-image. The intellectual *Putsch* of the music called *bop* was a triumph of thought over emotion, of the cerebral over the frenetic, and had a profound effect on the jazz vocabulary.

When swing reached an impasse in the early forties, a group of young Negro musicians created bop. They were rebelling not only against the dead end swing had run into, but against the old-time jazz, ragtime, and Dixieland, which they characterized as "Uncle Tom music," music appropriate to a meeker, less liberated generation of Negroes. The chief contributors to the new music were Negroes—among the more prominent Charlie Parker, Dizzy Gillespie, and Thelonious Monk. Many of the practitioners had a penchant for Mohammedanism, goatees, meerschaum pipes, berets, and shell-rimmed glasses, which seemingly was mere eccentricity or faddism, but actually was emblematic of a proudly conscious separateness.

Bop was more than music. It was the Negro's cultural declaration of independence, a further rejection of white America's conventionality, and it received encouragement by its widespread popularity in France and the Scandinavian countries. The resistance to it by the jazz traditionalists here was considerable:

> Boppers call themselves "the left wing" and their opponents "the right wing." Friends of the older music call the be-boppers "dirty radicals" and "wild-eyed revolutionaries." Boppers are proud of the men that have gone without jobs and meals rather than play music that outraged their convictions, and speak indignantly of "the underground." [9]

But occasionally, backed to the wall by monetary considerations, bopsters would make a partial concession by playing at weddings and other social functions where musical authenticity is held in low esteem. At these times, the linguistic code served a very practical function for "the underground." It enabled them to communicate their disgust to one another in a language the "citizens" could not comprehend, and through this veiled expression of contempt for the watered-down music they were playing, the situation was made somewhat more palatable to them—their feeling of self-betrayal was somewhat mitigated.

The earlier jazzman, despite his courageous musical pioneering, had been socially resigned to his substatus and, sometimes obligingly, sometimes inadvertently, reinforced the white myth of the "happy Negro." The post-World War II jazzman was equally aware of his inability to alter immediately his inferior status; nevertheless, he angrily and militantly insisted on his immediate dignity, and succeeded, at least to the satisfaction of sensitive observers, in shattering the older stereotype. Quiet, thoughtful, musically trained, socially militant, he forged a music of greater complexity, a music that distilled the purely emotional qualities of earlier jazz and mixed them with more cerebral qualities; it was a music difficult to play and difficult to follow.

Simultaneously, there entered the jazzman's speech a new

[9] Boyer: *op. cit.*, pp. 28–29.

spareness and leanness. Typically, the 1930s expression of farewell, *I'll dig you later*, became in the forties *Later!* The thirties expression of weariness or world-weariness, *beat to the socks*, yielded completely to *beat*. Some of the more widely current locutions were deliberately unintelligible, e.g., *eel-yah-dee, oopapada, oobopshebam, oobladee, oolyakoo*, all nonsense syllable words which might mean anything at all. The playful name given to the new music by its innovators, first *be-bop* and then *bop*, is a humorous manifestation of a rebellion that is essentially serious (and one which will doubtless continue for as long as the jazzman feels himself at odds with society).

The great influence of bop on jazz lingo was not so much in changing the vocabulary as in toning it down, in making it as "cool" as the music itself. Much of the earlier jazz vocabulary now seemed too elaborate to the Negro jazz-man, whose emerging self-consciousness after World War II militated against speech that would reinforce the old cari-cature of him. Jazz slang is still humorous, but not ex-travagant.

Gilbert Seldes has said:

> There are few specifications about slang . . . most people would agree on. The slang word or expression must make its meaning clear; it must add something (novelty, wit, charm) which the common word lacks; it must correspond to the natural genius of the language at the time (being . . . florid in one era, hard and short in another); it must be instinctive rather than cerebral; it must enter quickly into general con-versation.[1]

Jazz slang at its best, it seems to me, lives up to these criteria, though it assiduously avoids universality because the music and the lingo are by their very nature in revolt against the dominant culture.

No one, of course, speaks slang all of the time, and the

[1] *The New York Times Book Review,* July 27, 1947, p. 29.

knowledge and use of slang varies greatly among jazzmen; the standard language—its syntax and vocabulary—remains the base for even the slangiest of jazz speakers. Too, there are a considerable number of terms which overlap two or more specialized slangs—e.g., the "Beats," who have evolved a modest slang of their own, have imbibed much of the jazz vocabulary, though their admiration for jazz speech seems to be unrequited. Finally, as has been noted by Ortega y Gasset and others, vocabulary is not the whole of communication: nuance, inflection, gesture, and innuendo will immediately betray the speaker whose intimacy with the vocabulary does not extend to the culture itself.

A Jazz Lexicon

A & R, *adj.* [abbreviation; primarily a music trade term; current since c. 1955]   Artists and repertory man: see first 1959 quot. — 1959 *N.Y. Times,* 15 Nov., Sec. 11, p. 4M. In the recording business, A means artists; R, repertory. In a general way, an A & R man is the demiurge who selects A & R, herds the former into a studio, supervises their rendition of the latter, and edits the taped results with an engineer at his side. — 1959 *Jazz* (Hentoff & McCarthy), p. 334. Many more remain prey for . . . A & R men. — 1960 *Jazz: A Quarterly of American Music,* Winter, p. 48. So we just happen to have an A & R man with a lot of soul. — 1961 *Down Beat,* 16 Feb., p. 15. Hal McKusick brought him to the attention of Jack Lewis, then a & r head at RCA Victor.

ace, *n.* 1. [from gambling slang; cf. 1930 *American Tramp and Underworld Slang* s.v. *ace:* "dollar bill"; widely current among jazzmen since c. 1935]   See 1945 quot. — 1945 *Hepcats Jive Talk Dictionary.* s.v. *ace:* dollar bill. — 1952 *Who Walk in Darkness,* p. 13. "Can you lend me an ace?" — 1963 *Hiptionary* (caption of picture insert). Published by Simon & Schuster in September, at an $Ace.95.

    2. [by analogy with the highest of playing cards; cur-

rent c. 1940–c. 1950, rare since] See 1958 quot. —
1958 *The Book of Negro Folklore*, p. 481. *ace:* bosom
friend. — 1960 *Beat Jokes Bop Humor & Cool Cartoons*,
p. 40. The Ham's tight ace, Horatio, had brought news
of the ghost of The Big Ham. — 1962 *N.Y. Times
Magazine*, 20 May, p. 45. *ace:* a good friend, companion.

   adj. [current c. 1935–c. 1945, rare since] Possessing
importance: used of a person or thing. — 1944 *Dan
Burley's Original Handbook of Harlem Jive*, p. 133. *ace-
lane:* husband. — 1960 *Hiparama of the Classics*, p. 15.
Hip to the cool sweet groove of Liberty and solid sent
upon the Ace Lick that all Cats and Kitties, Red, White,
or Blue! are created Level, in *FRONT*.

   v.t. [cf. 1929 *American Speech*, June, "The Vocabulary
of Bums," p. 337. *"ace in:* to place yourself or a friend in
the good graces of someone"; current since c. 1935] To
help (someone), usually by getting (oneself or one's
friend) work as a musician or, less frequently, an introduction to a woman. — 1962 *Down Beat*, Jan., p. 2.
"Sis, you've aced me again."

action, *n.* [prob. from the gambling slang sense (i.e., bets);
   cf. 1960 *Dictionary of American Slang* s.v. *action:* "Activity, excitement"; cf. also its Early Modern English use
   (i.e., in the sense of sexual intercourse): c. 1607 *Pericles*,
   IV, ii. 7–9, "They with continual action are even as good
   as rotten"; current since c. 1930; see also HAPPENINGS,
   PLAY, *n.*] Any activity, but especially that relating to
   jazz and to women: see second 1944 and 1959 quots. —
   1944 *Dan Burley's Original Handbook of Harlem Jive*,
   p. 44. That Salt River action, ole man, is so un-
   glamorous. — p. 133. *action*: motivating force, issue, situation, proposition. — 1959 *Esquire*, Nov., p. 70H. *action:*
   that which is happening. — 1960 *Hiparama of the Classics*,
   p. 21. Man that Chick is puttin' down some action!!

ad lib, [from standard musical terminology (see 1949
   quot.); widely current c. 1920–c. 1935, obs. since except

historical; replaced by the standard term *improvise* and
the slang term *blow*] See 1926 quot. — 1926 *Jazz*
(Whiteman & McBride), p. 73. Perhaps I should mention that "ad lib" is a jazz musical term meaning to
improvise, to invent as you go along. — 1928 *Melody
Maker*, Dec., p. 1353. The melody is featured as an *ad
lib* solo. — 1933 *Metronome*, Dec., p. 46. If both are going
ad lib at least both are playing the down beat together.
— 1949 *Music Library Association Notes*, Dec., p. 35.
Many . . . familiar terms come direct from "longhairs"
[q.v.]—*ad lib* . . .

after hours, [refers to a practice common only c. 1925–
c. 1945, when musicians could, unpaid, play uninhibitedly
and to their own liking only at certain clubs and at
special hours, and hardly ever at their regular, paying
music jobs; rare since 1945] See note above and last
two quots. — 1942 *After Hours* (tune written by Avery
Parrish, recorded by the Erskine Hawkins Orchestra). —
1955 *Hear Me Talkin to Ya*, p. 335. There used to be an
after hours spot right off St. Nicholas Avenue. — 1959
The Horn, p. 27. "He think he earned it last night, blowing in a session after hours." — 1959 *The Permanent Playboy*, p. 243. "We would play our regular jobs until 3:00
a.m., then go to an after-hours place until around 7:00."
— 1960 *The Story of the Original Dixieland Jazz Band*,
p. 167. These enthusiastic youngsters, who were much in
demand in jazz-hungry New York, often gathered with
members of the Dixieland Band "after hours" for jam
sessions and the inevitable rounds of nocturnal revelry,
in which girl friends played no little part. Also **after-
hours,** *adj.*

alley fiddle, [see quot. for key to semantic development
—i.e., the natural association of a "primitive" style with
the attributive *alley*; primarily in the Midwest, esp. in
Chicago, where jazz bands frequently used violins, the
phrase had some currency c. 1910–c. 1925, obs. since

except historical] See quot. — 1939 *Jazzmen,* p. 18. Freddie Keppard . . . played violin in a primitive style known as "alley fiddle."

alligator, *n.* [semantic explanation in 1955 quot. seems of doubtful validity: term prob. an expanded form of *gate* q.v.; widely current only among white jazzmen c. 1935– c. 1940, obs. since except historical] See quots. — 1936 *Delineator,* Nov., p. 49. *alligator:* a non-playing swing devotee. — 1937 *This Thing Called Swing,* p. 3. *alligator:* one who's got swing rhythm but doesn't play an instrument. — 1938 *N.Y. Post,* 3 Feb., p. 15. "Now, then, the alligators, that's the swing fans, get the drift." — 1946 *Duke Ellington,* p. 178. He talked of "jitterbugs" and "alligators" — more conservatively known as swing music enthusiasts. — 1955 *Hear Me Talking to Ya,* p. 97. We'd call them alligators . . . because they were the guys who came up to swallow everything we had to learn.

all-in, *adj.* [refers to the practice in traditional jazz of *all* the instruments coming back *in* after the individual solo choruses have been played; current c. 1917–c. 1945, rare since except historical; see also RIDE-OUT, EVERY TUB, and (LET'S) GO HOME] In traditional jazz, the final chorus: see 1946 quot. — 1926 *Melody Maker,* Oct. pp. 62–63. If an "all-in" chorus has been used first, a repetition of the same movement is, of course, unnecessary. — 1940 *Swing,* Nov., p. 29. A gang of good solo . . . leading to a boisterous all-in finale. — 1941 *Gems of Jazz: Vol. III,* p. 3. The ending has . . . four bars of all-in jamming. — 1946 *The PL Yearbook of Jazz,* p. 32. Their improvisatory urge found its expression in the disjointed "Jam session," with its string of solos followed by a chaotic "all-in" chorus.

all over, See s.v. OVER.

all reat, all reet, alreet, all root, [corruptions of *all right;* cf. 1960 *Dictionary of American Slang* s.v. *all reet:* "*orig. jive use c. 1935; pop. student use c. 1940; archaic*"; see also

REET]   See 1946 quot. — 1943 *New Yorker*, 19 June, p. 15. "All reat" . . . is the rug-cutter's way of saying "all right." — 1944 *Esquire*, June, p. 170. *all root:* universally okay. — 1944 *Dan Burley's Original Handbook of Harlem Jive*, p. 44. All right, Poppa-Stoppa; all-reet, all root, all-rut. — 1946 *Big Book of Swing*, p. 124. *alreet:* O.K. — 1947 *Esquire's 1947 Jazz Book*, p. 28. *all reet:* everything is in order and you may proceed.

apple, (big), [by analogy with the shape of the world, then by synechdoche (see 1958 quot.); current since c. 1930] See 1958 quot.; for other, rare meanings, see 1938, 1944 quots. — 1938 *Cab Calloway: Hi De Ho*, p. 16. *apple:* the big town, the main stem, Harlem. — 1944 *Dan Burley's Original Handbook of Harlem Jive*, p. 133. *apple:* the earth, the universe, this planet. Any place that's large. A big Northern city. — 1946 *Really the Blues*, p. 165. As soon as we hit the Big Apple, we'll ditch the buggy. — 1950 *Gutbucket and Gossamer*, p. 26. Why should she stay in the Apple over a July weekend? — 1958 *Publication of the American Dialect Society*, Nov., p. 43. *apple* (the): New York City. Derivation obscure, but dates from the late '30's, when New York was the center of jazz in America. See also BIG APPLE.

ass, *n.* [synechdoche; prob. from Negro and/or armed forces slang; current since c. 1950] Person; self. — 1958 *Somewhere There's Music*, p. 180. "If I knew it'd kill my ass, I'd follow." — 1960 *The Jazz Word*, p. 109. "There's not really a living ass to talk to."

-assed, *suffix* [general slang emphasis additive, esp. common among jazzmen since c. 1930] Vulgar intensifier. — 1956 *Lady Sings the Blues*, p. 65. All alone in a room upstairs, snoring up a breeze and cuddling a big-assed bottle of champagne. — pp. 225–226. They slapped a high-assed old bail of seventy-five hundred dollars on us. — 1963 *Nugget*, Feb., p. 46. I've hated chicks since the day I first laid eyes on my bad-assed mother.

ax, axe, *n.* [see 1958 quot. for semantic explanation; current since c. 1950] See 1957, 1959 quots. — 1956 *Sideman,* p. 25. "You wanta make it with me tonight? Bring your ax." — 1957 *N.Y. Times Magazine,* 18 Aug., p. 26. *axe:* any musical instrument, even a piano. — 1958 *Publication of the American Dialect Society,* Nov., p. 43. *ax:* any of the solo reed or (less commonly) brass instruments. Orig. a saxophone. Fr. fancied resemblance in shape plus the abbr. *sax.* — 1959 *Esquire,* Nov., p. 70H, *ax:* instrument, horn. Extended to mean any tool of work. Example: Hemingway's ax is his typewriter. — 1960 *Jazz: A Quarterly of American Music,* Winter, p. 20. I am digging a recorded group from Canada though, with four axes.

baby, *n.* [some general slang use, but with esp. currency among jazzmen since c. 1900 as term of address for a sweetheart, since c. 1945 to anyone, regardless of sex] See 1959 quots. — 1925 *English Words & Their Background,* p. 59. *Oh, baby! Jazz baby.* — 1959 *Selected Poems,* p. 111. I asked you, baby, /If you understood. — 1959 *Newport Jazz Festival: 1959,* p. 45. *baby:* a general appellation directed at either sex. — 1960 *Hiparama of the Classics,* p. 10. "Wait a minute Babies, tell you what I'm gonna do." — 1961 *The Sound*, p. 11. "I can't make lush at all, baby," the girl said.

back, *v.t.* [extension of the standard meaning (i.e., to support); current since c. 1930; see also COMP] To provide accompaniment (for solo instruments); for its noun form, see first two quots. — 1940 *Swing*, Jan., p. 24. Everyone, however, seems happy in the rowdy backing, which gives plenty of punch to a good old barroom song. — June, p. 17. The backing is based on a riff that's been used for several other numbers lately. — 1961 *Jazz Journal*, July, p. 4. I've heard a record or two of Lang backing a singer and his harmonies and little fill-ins are really something.

back, from (way) back, *adv. & prep. phr.* [logic of its use derives from a belief in the positive correlation of worth with experience; current c. 1925–c. 1945, rare since] An intensifier (usually only implying the sense given in 1928 quot.). — 1928 *The Walls of Jericho*, p. 300. *from way back:* of extraordinary experience and skill. — 1938 *American Speech*, Dec., p. 314. *mellow back:* adjective used to describe a killer [jazz sense]. — 1944 *Dan Burley's Original Handbook of Harlem Jive*, p. 16. "That's a gasser from back." — 1952 *Flee the Angry Strangers*, p. 249. "She smoked enough for ten way-back vipers." — 1959 *Diggeth Thou?*, p. 40. The spielers were shucking some hard jive from back.

back beat, [so called because less prominent than the major accent; current since c. 1920] A secondary rhythmic accent. — 1928 *Melody Maker*, Dec., p. 1295. Back Beats! (column title). — 1948 *Metronome*, Nov., p. 28. "I'd rather use the high-hat as a back beat and break up the bass drum rhythms."

bad, *adj. & adv.* [*Dictionary of American Slang* (1960) is mistaken in characterizing the term as an "understatement" (p. 13); the term is one of several which *emphatically* reverse the standard meaning: see also HARD,

MEAN, TERRIBLE, TOUGH; cf. 1928 Negro slang listing in *The Walls of Jericho* s.v. *too bad: "marvelous";* widely current among jazzmen since c. 1945] See 1958 and first two 1959 quots. — 1957 *The Record Changer,* vol. 15, no. 2, p. 11. Something that is good is "crazy" or can be said to be "bad." — 1958 *Publication of the American Dialect Society,* Nov., p. 43. *bad:* Good. However, at times, it may mean "bad," and the listener must determine meaning fr. context, tone of voice, facial expression, etc. — 1959 *Esquire,* Nov., p. 70H. *bad:* good. Example: A bad man on flute. A superlative musician on flute. — 1959 *N.Y. Times,* 15 Nov., Sec. II, p. 2. Jazzmen often call a thing "terrible" or "bad" when they like it very much. — 1959 *Jazz: A Quarterly of American Music,* Fall, p. 294. "He's bad—he can play his ass off."

the baddest, [combination of *bad* with the tendency to form superlatives by adding the suffix *-est* (q.v.) to any word; some currency since c. 1955] The very best (usually, performer). Oral evidence only.

bad face, See s.v. FACE.

bad scene, See s.v. SCENE.

bag, [prob. by analogy with "bag of tricks"; current since c. 1958; see also GROOVE] Initially, the imaginary repository of a musician's ideas, conception, style, attack; by extension, the source of one's behavior: see 1962 quots. — 1960 *The Jazz Word,* p. 188. Man, that's really in another bag. — 1961 *Down Beat's Jazz Record Reviews,* pp. 16–17. In 1960 Pacific Jazz came to mean Les McCann and those who played out of THAT bag. — 1961 *Down Beat,* 5 Jan., p. 16. Hope shrugged and said, "But he's still in that *old* bag." — 2 Feb., p. 30. Soul is appropriately earthy, medium tempoed, and melodically a bit doubtful as to what jazz bag it belongs in. — 1962 *Jazz Journal,* March, p. 30. "Bag" is a current piece of trade jargon for hip musicians, and means something between a personal style and a body of work. — 1962 *N.Y. Times Magazine,*

20 May, p. 45. *bag:* a point of view or pattern of behavior.
ball, *n.* [prob. by analogy with the pleasure derived from
being at a ball (i.e., a formal dance); cf. 1960 *Dictionary
of American Slang* s.v. *ball:* "Some early c. 1935 Negro
jive use. Orig. popularized by bop and cool use, and
associated with jazz and avant-garde groups. Now common student and teen-age use, with less emphasis on
being unrestricted and exciting, and some general use";
see also *pitch a bitch* s.v. BITCH]   See 1938 quot. — 1938
Cab Calloway: Hi De Ho, p. 16. *have a ball:* to enjoy yourself, stage a celebration. — 1948 *Trumpet on the Wing,* p.
68. One ball we pitched got to be just too much. — 1952 *A
History of Jazz in America,* p. 351. *have a ball:* to enjoy
oneself inordinately. — 1954 *Esquire,* Nov., p. 135. "Life
was like one long ball in those days," Norvo recalls. "We
played and imbibed, played and imbibed." — 1959 *The
Holy Barbarians,* p. 52. "They sent me to Saipan, which
was even more of a ball." — 1960 *Dictionary of American
Slang,* p. 16. *have a ball:* to enjoy oneself thoroughly
and without reservations, restrictions, or inhibitions; to
have a good time.

   v.i. 1. [formed from *n.;* current since c. 1940]   See
quots. — 1942 *American Mercury,* July, p. 94. *balling:*
having fun. — 1954 *Esquire,* Nov. p. 131. In Norvo's
youth, he balled with the best . . . he drank a lot, he
experimented with the dread weed, he stayed up for long
stretches.

   2. *v.i. & v.t.* [extension of sense 1; current since c. 1940]
To engage in sexual intercourse (with). — 1959 *Easy
Living,* p. 30. "I ain't balled her yet, if that's what you're
asking." — 1960 *The Jazz Review,* May, p. 30. "Look,
sweetheart, I don't care if they're gonna ball in the
streets." — 1963 *The Realist,* June, p. 29. Is it bizarre that
married guys have to jerk off more than anyone else, because your old ladies [jazz sense] won't ball you and you
can't chippie [i.e., philander]?

ballin' the jack, [cf. 1960 *Dictionary of American Slang* s.v. *ball the jack:* "To go, move, or work very rapidly or fast. Orig. logger use, from "highballing"; current c. 1913–c. 1927, obs. since except historical] A dance in vogue c. 1913–c. 1927, consisting largely of bumps and grinds. — 1913 *Ballin' the Jack* (title of song composed by Chris Smith & Jim Burris). — 1943 *The Jazz Record*, 15 April, p. 3. In 1917 . . . there were several dances in vogue, namely: "walkin' the dog," "jazz dance," and "ballin' the jack." — 1957 *On the Road*, p. 200. "Dig the way he . . . balls that Jack."

band man, [cf. sports slang "team man" (i.e., co-operative ballplayer); some currency since c. 1935] A jazzman who excels in ensemble playing, though is not necessarily a distinguished soloist (see quot.). — 1946 *The PL Year-book of Jazz*, p. 148. King was always a "band man," playing lead and keeping fairly close to the melody, rather than a flashy soloist.

barbecue, *n.* [one of a number of food metaphors for a woman; also, according to jazzmen, the term often has a hidden reference to female genitalia; current esp. among Negro jazzmen c. 1925–c. 1945, rare since] See 1944, 1945 quots. — 1928 *Struttin' with Some Barbecue* (tune written by Lil Armstrong and Don Ray). — 1938 *Cab Calloway: Hi De Ho*, p. 16. *barbecue:* the girl friend, a beauty. — 1944 *Dan Burley's Original Handbook of Harlem Jive*, p. 133. *barbecue:* a very attractive girl. — 1945 *Hepcats Jive Talk Dictionary.* s.v. *barbecue:* beautiful girl.

bari, bary, *n.* [abbreviation; current since c. 1935] A baritone saxophone. — 1955 *Down Beat*, Sep., p. 30. It might have been Gerry on bary. — 1961 *Metronome*, Feb., p. 41. "I told her I played bari in Duke's band!"

barrelhouse, barrel-house, *n., v., & adj.* [cf. 1938 DAE, s.v. *barrelhouse:* "a cheap saloon: 1883"; also cf. 1913 Vachel Lindsay, *The Congo:* "Barrel House kings, with feet

unstable"; also see quots. for explanation of semantic
development; obs. since c. 1940 except historical] See
1949, 1952, 1956 quots. — 1913 *Memphis Blues* (song composed by Handy & Norton). I don't care what Mister
Crump don't 'low,/I'se gonna bar'l-house anyhow. — 1926
So This Is Jazz, p. 99. Trumpets and trombones . . . impart half-confidences in that semi-muffled voice aptly described by the term "barrel-house tone." — 1935 *Vanity
Fair*, Nov., p. 71. Additional synonyms for hot music are
. . . barrel-house (slang for "cheap saloon"). — 1949 *Music Library Association Notes*, Dec., p. 39. *barrelhouse:* a
style of piano playing, rhythmic, syncopated, seductive
and "blue." Term seems to have originated in relation to
the type of piano entertainment offered in cheap saloons
and in New Orleans houses of prostitution about 1910. —
1952 *A History of Jazz in America*, p. 349. *barrelhouse:*
after the New Orleans cabarets in which liquor was dis-
pensed from barrels; music that is rough and ready,
chiefly applied to Dixieland, but not exclusively. — 1956
Guide to Jazz. s.v. *barrel house:* Southern term once used
to describe small beer joints. Since the early years of the
20th century, a pianist or a small group usually playing
unpretentious but excellent jazz in the barrel houses, so
good that the word becomes a synonym for rough, spontaneous, uninhibited jazz. On piano the style is harsh and
strident . . . so it can be heard above the bedlam going
on around. Also **barrel house.**

battle, *n.* [special application of the standard sense; current c. 1915–c. 1945, very rare since except historical; see
also CUTTING CONTEST]   A musical competition, usually
between orchestras, sometimes between instrumentalists.
— 1929 Savoy Ballroom advertisement, 8 May [1962
Jazz: A History of the New York Scene, p. 198]. For this
"Battle of Jazz" the Savoy at a tremendous cost is bringing
to this city three of the south's best orchestras. — 1932
The Inter-State Tattler, 5 May, p. 10. What a battle of

music will be waged between three of the leading orchestras in New York City. — 1943 *Harlem Jazz, 1930*, p. 3. Willie "The Lion" Smith was biting cigars in half, taking his "Boston" in "piano battles" with Fats Waller. — 1946 *Esquire's 1946 Jazz Book*, p. 29. This group participated in many "battles" with the best Negro organizations. — 1958 *Jam Session*, p. 210. Or it may be "battle" wherein two similar instruments show each other their strength, friendly or unfriendly.

bear, *n.* 1. [according to jazzmen, the term derives from the nickname of a legendary New Orleans pianist, fl. 1890; cf. 1960 *Dictionary of American Slang*, p. 24. "c. 1915 pop song: 'Everybody's doin' it. Doin' what? Turkey trot. Ah, my honey, honey, I declare! It's a bear! It's a bear!' "; widely current c. 1900–c. 1925, rare since: see sense 2] See 1960 quot. — 1916 *Walkin' the Dog* (song composed by Matzan & Atteridge). But there,/it's a bear now. — 1959 *The Eddie Costa–Vinnie Burke Trio* (liner notes on LP album Jubilee 1025). "My man, Eddie Costa — he's a bear!" — 1960 *Dictionary of American Slang*. s.v. *bear*: a remarkable, first-rate person or thing; a humdinger.

2. [from the rhyming slang vogue c. 1935–c. 1940: word was rhymed with *nowhere*, q.v., and c. 1937–c. 1943 the term was usually pejorative; obs. since c. 1943] A unsuccessful or unhappy state or condition; impoverishment. —1942 *American Mercury*, July, p. 96. *the bear:* confession of poverty. — 1944 *Dan Burley's Original Handbook of Harlem Jive*, p. 60. "The other cat's playing the bear's brother." — 1959 *The Jazz Scene*, p. 292. *Jack the Bear:* nowhere [jazz sense].

beat, *n.* [see 1958 quot. for semantic development; current since c. 1900; see also TIME] See 1949, first 1952, and 1956 quots. — 1926 *Melody Maker*, Sep., p. 11. "The Charleston . . . is a fast fox-trot with an unusual beat." — 1949 *Music Library Association Notes*, Dec., p. 39. *beat:* pronounced accent, stress, or rhythm. — 1952 A

History of Jazz in America, p. 349. *beat:* jazz time; more meaningful to jazz musicians as an honorific description of rhythmic skill ("he gets a fine beat") than as a description of an underlying 2/4 or 4/4 or 6/8 or any other time. — 1952 *Music Out of Dixie,* p. 104. The music was pure New Orleans blues, slow and easy, with enough beat to punctuate it. — 1956 *Guide to Jazz* s.v. *beat:* not merely the number of beats to the bar, but the pulse created within and around those beats. — 1958 *Publication of the American Dialect Society,* Nov., p. 43. *beat:* musical rhythm, "the beat" (fr. *beat time*).

adj. [cf. 1960 *Dictionary of American Slang* s.v. *beat:* "Prob. f. 'beat-out' or 'beat-up' gen'l slang since c. 1750"; widely current among jazzmen since c. 1935; cf. its non-jazz adaptations, e.g., *beat generation, beatnik*]   See first 1939 quot. — 1938 *American Speech,* Dec., p. 314. "He looks beat." — 1939 *Jitterbug Jamboree Song Book,* p. 32. *beat:* tired, lacking anything, low in spirit. — 1939 *Jazzmen,* p. 5. He came from the beat side of town. — 1956 *Sideman,* p. 53. "I believe I'll go to bed. I'm sure beat." — 1957 *On the Road,* p. 61. He had fallen on the beat and evil days that come to young guys in their middle twenties. — p. 277. "Real beat huts, man, the kind you only find in Death Valley and much worse."

beat to the (or **one's**) **sox**, [cf. general slang intensifying phrase "from the top of my head to the tips of my toes"; widely current c. 1935–c. 1945, obs. since except historical]   Intensified form of *beat* (note: since, in jazz slang, the phr. *to the sox* is used only with *beat, adj.,* the latter should not have been omitted from the listing in the first quot.). — 1938 *American Speech,* Dec., p. 314. *to the socks:* extremely, to the nth degree. — 1939 Fortune, July, p. 78. Harlem is "beat to its socks."

beat (it) out, [shortened forms of "beat out the rhythm"; current c. 1900–c. 1945, obs. since except historical] See 1938 quot. — 1938 *Cab Calloway: Hi De Ho,* p. 16.

beat it out: play it hot, emphasize the rhythm. — 1939
Jazzmen, p. 62. "Jones, beat it out in B Flat." — 1944
Dan Burley's Original Handbook of Harlem Jive, p. 134.
beat it out: emphasize the rhythm. — 1955 *Saturday
Review,* 25 June, p. 49. I'd stand there listening to King
Oliver beat out one of those ole good-ones like "Panama."
bebop, be-bop, *n. & adj.* [see 1959 quots. for explanation of
semantic development; widely current only c. 1944–c.
1948, when it was almost completely replaced in the
speech of jazzmen by *bop;* hence, obs. since 1948 except
in print] See 1949, 1959 quots. — 1944 *Beebop Blues*
(tune by Dizzy Gillespie; spelling is unique). — 1947
Metronome, Nov., p. 38. Fats doesn't like the name
bebop. "It's just modern music . . . What they call bebop
is really a series of chord progressions." — 1949 *Music
Library Association Notes,* Dec., p. 39. *bebop:* the most
recent development in popular instrumental music, hot
jazz . . . the intricacies of African (Negro) rhythms
combined with the complexities of American and
European (white) harmony. — 1959 *Toledo* (Ohio)
Blade, 15 Feb. However, the word itself, Tamony writes,
appears in numerous forms back through the history of
jazz as early as 1928 . . . it faded away until applied to
Gillespie and his music at Minton's. — 1959 *New Yorker,*
7 Nov., p. 158. Of all the queer, uncommunicative,
secret-society terms that jazz has surrounded itself with,
few are lumpier or more misleading than "bebop." Originally a casual onomatopoeic word used to describe the
continually shifting accents of the early work of Charlie
Parker, Dizzy Gillespie, Kenny Clarke, and Thelonious
Monk, it soon became a free-floating, generic one as well,
whose tight, rude sound implied something harsh, jerky,
and unattractive. — 1961 *Ibid.,* 18 Feb., p. 127. Describing bebop in the past tense is not wholly accurate,
for it survives, in diffused shapes, in the work of almost
all modern-jazz musicians.

be-bop glasses, [current c. 1945–c. 1950, very rare since: supplanted by *shades,* q.v.] Dark (tinted) glasses. — 1956 *Sideman,* p. 121. "May have to get me a beret and some be-bop glasses."

bells, *interj.* [poss. with reference to the pleasant sound of bells, or to the name of New York City bar by that name frequented by jazzmen; according to jazzmen, term was first used in a jazz sense by Lester Young and has had some currency since c. 1940] See quots. — 1948 *New Yorker,* 3 July, p. 28. The bebop people have a language of their own . . . their expressions of approval include "Cool!", "Gone!" and "Bells, man!" — 1948 *Life,* 11 Oct., p. 139. Bebop greeting begins as Gillespie (right) hails Benny Carter with "Bells, man! Where you been?" — 1959 *Down Beat,* 30 April, p. 11. This was revelatory for Pres, who usually limited his answers to "bells" or "ding dong."

bend, *v. & n.* [see 1952 quot. for key to semantic development; according to jazzman Eubie Blake, term originates c. 1904 with Bendin' Boots Butler's manner of playing piano triplets; still current] See quots. — 1949 *Music Library Association Notes,* Dec., p. 39. *bend:* effect employed by the brass section of modern bands. It is achieved by manipulation of the lip and involves a slight upward or downward variation in pitch. — 1952 *A History of Jazz in America,* p. 350. *bending:* the process of altering pitch between notes, up or down, sometimes called "scooping pitch." — 1956 *Eddie Condon's Treasury of Jazz,* p. 214. "You must be very, *very* careful not to use the bell. Use the valves. Then what you *hit* will bend." — 1961 *Down Beat,* 13 April, p. 23. "It [jazz]'s just a tone . . . what you do to a melody . . . how you bend it."

benny, *n.* 1. [from underworld slang: cf. 1950 *Slang Today and Yesterday,* p. 423. "*benny:* an overcoat (–1905); ex *benjamin,* a coat."; current among jazzmen since c. 1920]

An overcoat. — 1944 *Dan Burley's Original Handbook of Harlem Jive*, p. 109. "Ole man, where's your benny?"

2. [from narcotics slang; some jazz use since c. 1935] Benzedrine or a benzedrine inhaler. — 1956 *Second Ending*, p. 230. "You want to crack a benny?" — 1958 *The Subterraneans*, p. 29. High on tea or benny . . . she'd walk down the street in her flip [i.e., intoxicated condition]. — 1959 *The Holy Barbarians*, p. 22. "He'd seen me go into my purse a couple of times after bennies." — 1960 *The Jazz Titans*, p. 150. *bennies:* benzedrine pills.

big apple, 1. The big town: see s.v. APPLE.

2. [current c. 1937–c. 1939] See quots. — 1937 *Life*, 9 Aug., p. 22. Copied . . . from Negroes . . . "The Big Apple" . . . a loose-hipped, free-hand combination of "truckin'" and the square dance. — 1937 *N.Y. Amsterdam News*, 4 Sep., p. 12. All the "cats" on the avenue are "breakin it up" with a new dance they call "The Big Apple," a swing square dance.

big band, [current since c. 1925] See 1960 quot. (note attrib. usage). — 1926 *Melody Maker*, Feb., p. 35. The Kit-Cat Band has again scored with "The Camel Walk," which gives the lie to those who say that a "big band" is unwieldy and not suitable for "dirt" arrangements. — 1941 *Swing*, Jan. p. 26. Teddy had a good big band last winter. — 1957 *The Book of Jazz*, p. 178. The big bands of the 1920's . . . offered very little of lasting orchestral value. — 1960 *Dictionary of American Slang*. s.v. *big band*: pertains to swing or jazz music played by a large band, usually composed of 14 to 20 men, as opposed to smaller or pick-up groups. — 1961 *The Jazz Review*, Jan., p. 8. The Basie band is the cleanest of all big bands.

big ears, See s.v. EARS.

big eyes, See s.v. EYES.

bill, *n.* [cf. 1950 *Dictionary of American Underworld Lingo* s.v. *bill*: "a one-hundred dollar note"; current among jazzmen since c. 1945]   See 1960 quot. — 1960 *Dictionary of American Slang.* s.v. *bill:* $100 bill; the sum of $100. — 1961 *The Sound,* p. 189. "You mean I only get a bill out of it?"

Bird, *n.* [see semantic explanation s.v. *Yard(bird)* for which this is the shortened form; one of the most common of the many jazz nicknames (see also LADY, PREZ, SATCH); widely current since c. 1946] Nickname for Charlie Parker (1920–1955), alto saxophonist; most musicians and critics agree that he was at once the most influential innovator and the greatest instrumentalist in the history of jazz. — 1947 *Chasing the Bird* (tune by Charlie Parker). — 1949 Birdland (famous jazz night club in New York City named for Charlie Parker). — 1955 *Hear Me Talkin to Ya,* p. 344. There was a character in town called Bird. — 1956 *Enjoyment of Jazz* (EJ402) p. 2. One can hardly name an important modern alto man, or any other modern instrumentalist who has not been influenced by "Bird." — 1956 *Sideman,* p. 274. "Made some records with Diz and Bird."

birdie, *n.* [by analogy with a bird's sound, esp. its unexpectedness; some currency since c. 1917]   See quots. — 1935 *Vanity Fair,* Nov., p. 71. Impromptu grace notes are "birdies." — 1942 *The American Thesaurus of Slang,* p. 560. *birdies:* improvised grace notes.

bit, *n.* [extension of its theater slang sense (i.e., minor part or performance); widely current since c. 1943]   See last quot. — 1956 *Sideman,* p. 275. "Gigs are hard to get so I do this bit at Macy's." — 1958 *Somewhere There's Music,* p. 69. "What's the Mister Musician bit?" — 1958 *This Week Magazine,* 28 Sep., p. 33. A "bit" is what someone does. — 1958 *American Speech,* Oct., p. 225. When, on the other hand, he *does the bit,* he is merely part of a short incident. — 1959 *The Holy Barbarians,* p. 71. "It's the old Oedipus bit, ain't it?" —

1960 *Down Beat,* 27 Oct., p. 26. Actually, the hugging bit
is the thing that bugs me. — 1960 *Dictionary of American
Slang.* s.v. *bit:* Any expected or well-defined action,
plan, series of events, or attitudes, uses, but not necessarily, of short duration . . . the role which one assumes in
a specific situation or in life. Orig. bop and cool use.
bitch, *n.* 1. [cf. 1928 *American Speech,* Feb., "Kansas University Slang," p. 218: *"bitch:* something difficult or formidable"; current among jazzmen since c. 1935, though
term, like several others (see BAD, TOUGH, HARD, TERRIBLE,
etc.) has acquired increasingly favorable connotations
since c. 1945] See note above; also, a formidable person. — 1946 *Really the Blues,* p. 19. That boy was really
a bitch. — 1955 *Hear Me Talkin to Ya,* p. 196. The depression for musicians in New York—man, it was a
bitch! — 1956 *Sideman,* p. 47. "That last road trip was a
bitch." — 1956 *Eddie Condon's Treasury of Jazz,* p. 207.
His followers, both white and Negro, often affectionately
declare that Dizzy is "it," that he is "real crazy," "a bitch,"
and "a killer."
  2. [cf. Early Modern English pejorative connotation:
c. 1605 *King Lear,* II, ii, 22. "The son and heir of a mongrel bitch"; also some general slang use, but with esp.
currency among jazzmen since c. 1935 in a less pejorative than neutral sense] A woman (note: the term does
not necessarily have a pejorative connotation). — 1956
Lady Sings the Blues, p. 80. If they had caught Pop
having a drink with a white bitch, the management
would have flipped.
  pitch a bitch, 1. [inspired by rhyming slang vogue
c. 1935–c. 1940; some currency c. 1938–c. 1945, rare
since] To cause a disturbance. — 1956 *Lady Sings the
Blues,* p. 46. Bernie pitched such a bitch up there at the
office, he finally made them pay me.
  2. [same dates as sense 1; see also BALL, *n.*] To have

an exciting party or an enjoyable evening in the company of others. Oral evidence only.

black bottom, [from general slang for Negro buttocks: cf. 1928 *The Walls of Jericho,* p. 14. "Been wantin' to spank yo' little black bottom"; current c. 1923–c. 1929, obs. since except historical] A jazz dance popular in the 1920's. — 1926 *Nigger Heaven,* p. 120. I'm dying to do the Black Bottom again with Ollie! 1934 *Metronome,* Jan., p. 30. The foxtrot . . . has outlasted . . . the Black Bottom.

blackstick, black-stick, *n. & adj.* [some currency c. 1920–c. 1940, obs. since except historical; see also LICORICE STICK] See first 1937 quot. — 1937 *This Thing Called Swing,* p. 9. *black stick:* clarinet. — 1937 *Metronome,* June, p. 26. The black-stick man gets off well on his own. — 1956 *Guide to Jazz.* s.v. *blackstick:* old-time slang for clarinet. Title of a number by Sidney Bechet recorded in 1938. Also **black stick.**

blast, *v.i.* 1. [extension of the standard meaning; some currency since c. 1930] To play loudly: refers esp. to brass instruments. — 1946 *King Oliver,* p. 6. The band's sound could fill the largest hall with nobody blasting (they never did) and no microphones. — 1956 *The Heart of Jazz,* p. 181. "I try to keep my band from blasting." — 1960 *The Story of the Original Dixieland Jazz Band,* p. 67. The bass drum was not used on this record because of its tendency to "blast."

2. [from narcotics slang; by analogy with the effect on the smoker: cf. 1958 *Southern Folklore Quarterly,* Sep., "The Anonymous Verses of a Narcotics Addict," p. 130. *"blast:* smoke, by cupping the hands and drawing deeply"; current since c. 1935] To smoke marijuana. —1952 *Go,* p. 125. "Hell, you should come along though and blast with us!" — 1958 *The Subterraneans,* p. 73. We'd been drinking French Bordeaux and blasting. —

1959 *The Naked Lunch,* p. 18. I blasted my last stick of Tangier tea. — 1960 *The Jazz Titans,* p. 151. *to blast:* to get high.

blewy, blooey, *n.* [prob. from general slang *blew* (i.e., mismanaged) and comic strip onomatopoeia for something ruined or exploded; some currency c. 1930–c. 1945, rare since; see also the more common CLAM, CLINKER, FLUFF, GOOF]. A misplayed note. Oral evidence only.

blip, *n.* 1. [etym. unknown; current c. 1930–c. 1945, obs. since except historical] See quots. — 1944 *Dan Burley's Original Handbook of Harlem Jive,* p. 134. *blip:* a nickel. — 1945 *Hepcats Jive Talk Dictionary,* s.v. *blip:* five cent coin. — 1946 *Really the Blues,* p. 114. Managers . . . would murder their own mothers for a deuce of blips. — 1956 *The Real Jazz Old and New,* p. 148. A *blip* is five cents.

2. [poss. by analogy with sense 1.: i.e., during the depression 1930's there was an esp. close relation between money and pleasure; 1960 *Dictionary of American Slang,* p. 43. "Jive use since c. 1935"; obs. since c. 1945] See first quot. — 1938 *Cab Calloway: Hi De Ho,* p. 16. *blip:* something very good. — 1944 *Dan Burley's Original Handbook of Harlem Jive,* p. 134. *blip:* very good. — 1945 *Hepcats Jive Talk Dictionary.* s.v. *blip:* superlative.

block (or **blocked**) **chord,** [from the fixed, blocklike relation of the hands to each other when playing these chords; widely current since c. 1945; see also LOCKED HANDS] See 1957 quot. — 1948 *Down Beat,* 19 May, p. 14. The final chorus is git [i.e., guitar] and block chords. — 1952 *Music Out of Dixie,* p. 180. The hunchback was working himself out of a fantastic cluster of blocked chords. — 1957 *The Book of Jazz,* p. 68. This was the "locked hands" or "block chord" style, in which the left hand moves parallel with the right, playing extra notes in the chord or duplicating the right hand's chord, instead of supplying a bass line. — 1961 *Down Beat,*

2 Feb., p. 45. With a block chord kind of feel, that's who
it suggests.

blood, *n.* [current since c. 1945]   See quots. — 1959 *Esquire*, Nov., p. 70H. *blood:* wine. — 1960 *The Jazz Titans*,
p. 151. *blood:* wine.

blow, *v.t.* 1. [metonymy: i.e., "blow smoke"; current since
c. 1935]   To smoke (marijuana): used with any of the
many analogues for *marijuana*. — 1953 *Night Light*,
p. 136. "We're all out of charge [i.e., marijuana), so I'll
dash in and get some and we'll blow one more."

2. *v.t. & v.i.* [by analogy with the method of performing on a wind instrument (for which *blow* mostly replaced *play* c. 1945): see 1958 quot.; as applied to performing on any instrument, widely current since c. 1950;
as applied to performing in any art medium or simply to
behaving, current since c. 1955]   See 1957 and 1958
quots. — 1950 *Neurotica*, Autumn, p. 46. "We just cut
out of a gone session [i.e., an exciting informal musical
performance]   and they're still blowin'." — 1955 *Solo*,
p. 107. "You've been blowing piano a long time, right?"
— 1957 *N.Y. Times Magazine*, 18 Aug., p. 26. *blow:* to
play a musical instrument, any instrument. Also to perform any act: "He blows great conversation." "She blows
scrambled eggs from endville." — 1958 *Publication of
the American Dialect Society*, Nov., p. 44. *blow:* orig. to
play a wind instrument. Generalized to performing upon
any instrument (thus, one can "blow guitar"). Probably
from fact that all solo instruments in traditional jazz are
wind instruments. — 1959 *Escapade*, Oct., p. 55. Tony
also started to blow at the Village Vanguard about this
time. — 1959 *The Holy Barbarians*, p. 26. "Are we
gonna blow some poetry, maybe?" — 1959 *Swinging
Syllables.* s.v. *blow:* to play any musical instrument, often
one which is not actually blown as bass or drums.

blow (one's) ass off, [by analogy with general slang
"work (one's) ass off"; *play* . . . current, though rare,

c. 1935–c. 1945, supplanted by blow . . . c. 1945, only slightly more common] To play music superlatively. — 1959 *Jazz: A Quarterly of American Music*, Fall, p. 294. "He's bad—he can play his ass off." — p. 295. "Cannonball, you're blowing your ass off."

blow (someone) down (or **into the ground, off the stand, out, out of the house**), [hyperbole; *blow down* and its less common variations have had some currency since c. 1935, gradually largely replacing *cut* by c. 1950; see also COOK ON 'EM, SMOKE ON 'EM]. To best (someone's) musical competition (can apply to either an instrumentalist or a group); also, less commonly, to impress favorably (the audience) with musical skill or volume (this is the sense in which the first quot. is to be taken). — 1954 *See*, Sep., p. 34. "They won't listen unless you're blowing them out of the house." — 1955 *Hear Me Talkin to Ya*, p. 25. You couldn't blow a man down with your horn. — 1956 *Lady Sings the Blues*, p. 55. He blew him out with his horn. — 1958 *Somewhere There's Music*, p. 157. "Sam got out his horn and blew them all down." — 1958 *The Horn*, p. 85 "When some goony sideman tenor can blow me off the stand." — 1961 *Down Beat*, 13 April, p. 22. "There were eight other saxophone players, and Zoot blew them all into the ground."

    blow (one's) soul, [current since c. 1957] To play music with great sincerity and passion. — 1961 *The Sound*, p. 268. "Prez blew his soul on that one, man!"

blow the gig, [general slang *blow* (i.e., to fail [at something]) + jazz slang *gig*, q.v.; current since c. 1955] To fail to appear for a one-night musical engagement; also, less commonly: to appear, but to play badly. — 1960 *Jazz: A Quarterly of American Music*, Winter, p. 32. "They're always putting *me* down for blowing the gig. I never do that. *I'm* here—it's them musicians who ain't here!" — p. 37. "He's playing beautifully now—he must feel like playing—not like that Hollywood Bowl gig. I asked him, Monk, what happened at the Hollywood Bowl? What I hear, you really blew it [i.e., the gig]!"

blow the roof off, [hyperbole; current c. 1930–c. 1940, very rare since] To play music loudly and well. — 1957 *Paris Blues,* p. 7. They let go on *Tiger Rag* . . . and they blew the roof off.

blow (one's) top, [see 1952 quot. for semantic explanation; prob. from underworld slang: cf. 1934 *The Thin Man,* p. 70. "How did I know he was going to blow his top?"; cf. also 1940 *American Speech,* Oct., "Jargon of Marihuana Addicts," p. 336. *"to blow one's top:* to become sick from excessive use of marihuana"; . . . *top* current among jazzmen since c. 1935, . . . *wig* since c. 1940, both obs. since c. 1945; see also FLIP (ONE'S) LID, FLIP, WIG] See 1938, 1952 quots.: note shift in connotation (c. 1945) from *pleasant* excitement to *unpleasant.* — 1938 *Cab Calloway: Hi De Ho,* p. 16. *blow the top:* to be overcome with emotion (delight). — 1944 *The World,* Oct., p. 33. Real jazzmen . . . work twice as hard . . . if allowed to "blow their top" in a small combination of . . . musicians who know solid jazz. — 1944 *The New Cab Calloway's Hepsters Dictionary,* [p. 4]. *blew their wigs:* excited with enthusiasm, gone crazy. — 1946 *The Jazz Record,* July, p. 9. "They sent me down South, Georgia. That was enough to make me blow my top." — 1952 *A History of Jazz in America,* p. 350. *blow one's top:* phrase expressing exasperation, enthusiasm, or insanity; synonymous with "flip one's lid," "snap one's cap" or "wig," each of which describes the process of losing the hair or skin of the head.

blow up a breeze (or **storm**), [current c. 1935–c. 1945, very rare since] To play music excitingly. — 1940 *Blowing Up a Breeze* (tune recorded by Chu Berry on Commodore C-541). — 1955 Solo, p. 25. "Mahn, but he blows up a storm." — 1957 *N.Y. Sunday News,* 6 Oct.,

p. 94. Having blown up a storm (translation: worked hard) . . . Stiles packed his ax. — 1959 *Blow Up a Storm* (title of novel).

blower, *n.* [chiefly a writers' term; some currency since c. 1955] A soloist; the hearer or reader must judge from the context whether the term is being used in a pejorative sense (a desultory *blower*), an honorific sense (an inspired *blower*), or a neutral sense (a soloing *blower*). — 1960 *Sal Salvador: The Beat for This Generation* (liner notes on LP album Decca DL 74026). Adequate space is allotted in each arrangement for one or two of the "blowers" to have their say. — 1961 *Down Beat,* 5 Jan., p. 16. He stresses that he is not referring to those who work more or less regularly in studios but to those usually referred to as "the blowers." — p. 20. It has been the blowers—and Louis, Bird, and Pres were at heart blowers—who have shown the way.

blowing room, [jazz slang *blowing* + general slang *room* (i.e., time); some currency since c. 1955; see also STRETCH OUT] Sufficient improvisational time allowed a jazzman in which to develop his musical ideas. — 1963 *Down Beat,* 20 June, p. 21. Each soloist is permitted blowing room.

blowing session, [chiefly a writers' term; some currency since c. 1955] A musical performance characterized by improvisation (rather than by arrangements), usually at a recording studio or a concert hall. — 1961 *Jazz News,* 15 March, p. 5. Nor will the prospect of another uncharted "blowing" session with Gillespie and Co. fail to attract him. — 1961 *Down Beat,* 12 Oct., p. 29. This is no helter-skelter "blowing session" although there is surely a lot of inspired blowing going on. — 1962 *Toward Jazz,* p. 88. Most of the so-called blowing sessions ("just come and blow") recorded during the past few years belong to this category. — 1962 *Jazz Monthly,* Oct., p. 25. A "blowing session" depends essentially on the strength of the soloists, for formal qualities are usually little in evidence.

blowtop, *n. & adj.* [formed from *blow (one's) top;* current c. 1935–c. 1950, very rare since] (One who is) excitable, violent, or unstable. — 1940 *Blow Top* (tune recorded by Count Basie Orchestra). — 1946 *Really the Blues,* p. 323. That's the musical mania of the blowtops. — 1952 *Flee the Angry Strangers,* p. 443. "Nobody like these blowtop hoodlum kids."

blue note, [prob. from its melancholy sound; according to jazzman Eubie Blake, current since c. 1895; see also OFF NOTE] See 1955, 1958 quots. — 1926 *Melody Maker,* April, p. 42. They are, according to the strict laws of music, "out of chord" . . . They are simply "blue" notes and sound most pleasing and effective when incorporated in a melody part. — 1947 *Frontiers of Jazz,* p. 45. Handy's interpolated minor third . . . has acquired a name of its own: "the blue note." — 1955 *The First Book of Jazz,* p. 20. These blue notes are "off notes," just a little bit flat and in between the usual notes. They most often are a somewhat flatted third or seventh note of the scale. They are impossible to show in written music, although they are sometimes indicated as flatted notes. — 1958 *Jam Session: An Anthology of Jazz,* p. 23. Louis Harap explains the "blue note" that they [the Negroes] brought into jazz: "The third and seventh of all Negro music from spirituals to hot jazz are not pitched steadily. They are, as Abbe Niles has said, 'worried,' wavering between flat and natural."

blues, *n.* [cf. 1933 OED s.v. *the blues* "(for 'blue devils'): depression of spirits, despondency. *colloq.*": first citation is 1807 W. Irving (1824) 96 "In a fit of the blues"; current among jazzmen since c. 1895] See 1949, 1956 quots. — 1905 *Jelly Roll Blues* (tune composed by Jelly Roll Morton, copyright 1915). — 1909 *Mamie's Blues* (tune composed by W. C. Handy, published 1912).

— 1939 *The International Cyclopedia of Music and Musicians,* p. 897. Though the type of Negroid song known as the "blues" probably existed in improvised form before he devoted his talents to it, it was Handy who introduced it to popular favour. The "blues" attained this popularity about 1914, just as the "rag" craze was dying out. — 1949 *Music Library Association Notes,* Dec., p. 40. *blues:* song form, style, and harmony originating with the American Negro. The "blues" form involves a 12 measure sequence instead of the 8 or 16 measure unit of popular song. The minor mode and the flatted seventh figure prominently. — 1956 *Guide to Jazz.* s.v. *blues:* a short piece of 12 bars divided into 3 sections of 4 bars each—has become standardized into a classic form both musically and with regard to the lyrics. There are variations (16 bars, etc.), but blues is then given to the style of playing. — 1959 *The Jazz Scene,* p. 95. The blues is not a style or phase of jazz, but a permanent substratum of all styles; not the whole of jazz, but its heart. — 1960 *Jazz: A Quarterly of American Music,* Winter, p. 25. By that name or by other names . . . blues were as basic to early jazz as brass bands.

bombershay, *n.* [etym. unknown; current c. 1897-c. 1917] See quot. — 1934 *Beale Street: Where the Blues Began,* p. 105. The Pasamala was a ragtime dance originated, according to Isaac Goldberg in tin pan alley, at about the same time as the bombershay, in 1898, in which the girls chanted as they danced: "Fust you do a rag, then you bombershay . . ."

bombs, *n. pl.* [so called because of the volume and suddenness with which they erupt; current since c. 1944] Unexpected bass drum accents, made an integral part of drumming by Kenny Clarke in the first years of bop (c. 1944), though occasional accidental or humorous use of them predate Clarke. — 1955 *Hear Me Talkin to Ya,*

p. 289. He taught me how to turn on what the kids now call "dropping bombs." — 1961 *Metronome*, April, p. 34. Dodds . . . underscores the work of the hornmen with "bombs" and off-beat rolls. — 1961 *The Sound*, p. 108. "That kid on drums dropped too many bombs." —1961 *The Jazz Life*, p. 37. Dropping bombs became a graphic term for the disturbing "new" drumming. — 1962 *Dinosaurs in the Morning*, p. 26. He depends on . . . the relentless use of bass-drum explosions, or "bombs."

bone, 'bone, *n.* [shortened form; some currency since c. 1917, but with wide currency only since c. 1935; see also earlier TAILGATE, SLIPHORN] See first quot. — 1942 *The American Thesaurus of Slang*, p. 559. *bone:* trombone. — 1956 *Sideman*, p. 14. "Oh, Dick's a hell of a 'bone man." — 1957 *The Book of Jazz*, p. 79. The trombone . . . contrary to popular belief as propagated by the movies, is never known among musicians by such terms as "slushpump" and "sliphorn," but is frequently known simply as a "bone." — 1961 *Down Beat*, 30 March, p. 17. "Just like Kai Winding's four 'bones and rhythm."

boo, *n.* [shortened form of *jabooby*, etym. of which is unknown; some currency since c. 1935; see also GAGE, MARY JANE, POT, TEA] See quot. — 1959 *Esquire*, Nov., p. 70H. *boo:* marijuana.

boogie, boogie-woogie, *n.* [see 1942, 1943, 1957 quots. for suggested etyms.; see 1946 quot. for beginning date] See 1944 quot.; also, now rare, as verb: to dance to the music or to have a good time (see 1955, 1960 quots.). — 1928 *Pine Top's Boogie Woogie* (tune composed by Pine Top Smith). — 1942 *American Mercury*, July, p. 94. *boogie-woogie:* type of dancing and rhythm. For years in the South, it meant secondary syphilis. — 1943 *The Jazz Record*, 15 April, p. 3. The word "boogie" was derived from our old grandmothers' use of the word meaning the devil. When the kids broke the rules in any way . . . we were told that the "Boogie man" was going to get us. The blues were considered bad music as it usually alluded to love affairs. — 1944 *Esquire,* Feb., p. 129. Boogie-Woogie is any kind of jazz or swing, solo or orchestral, generated by certain eight-to-the-bar rhythms, mostly using the twelve-measure Blues pattern for a theme. — 1946 *Harvard Dictionary of Music,* p. 378. Mention must be made of a special type of piano blues known as Boogie-Woogie, which was heard at Negro "rent parties" in Chicago in the early 1920's . . . long before it became famous in the world at large. — 1955 *Big Bill Blues,* p. 30. "Oh let's boogie, children." — 1957 *Just Jazz,* p. 13. I don't know the origin of the word "boogie woogie," but it seems obvious to me that it is onomatopoeic—it simply describes the noise that the music makes. A "boogie," of course, is a "bad girl." Brothels were called "boogie houses" in many parts of the old South. "Pitchin' boogie" was a raw term for "makin' a chick." — 1960 *Dictionary of American Slang.* s.v. *boogie:* to enjoy oneself thoroughly. Some Negro use. Also **boogie woogie.**

book, *n.* [metonymy: the repertory of arrangements are in loose book form; current since c. 1925] See first quot. — 1949 *Music Library Association Notes,* Dec., p. 40. *book:* the repertoire of a band. — 1955 *A Pictorial History of Jazz,* p. 155. Goodman set the pace here as well, by the extremely astute move of hiring Fletcher Henderson to create the foundations of his "book." — 1956 *Sideman,* p. 12. "Get down to the club an hour or so before the job, look the book over." — 1962 *Down Beat,* 21 June, p. 17. Up until now we've worked out the band's book from the old scores and in skull sessions that we hold periodically.

boot, 1. *v.i. & v.t.* [by analogy with *kick,* q.v.; some currency since c. 1930] To play (an instrument) pulsatingly, energetically, and excitingly; also, for adjective form, see last two quots.; also, for a rare noun use, see

1939 quot. — 1937 *Metronome,* Nov., p. 11. After Louis
boots, the cats truck on to their various domiciles. — 1939
Hoagy Carmichael Songs, p. 3. His is the kind of "boot"
that can only be described as "Louis Armstrong." — 1957
Down Beat, 25 July, p. 24. On *Get Happy* . . . he boots
the group, and, in turn, is booted by Candido's driving
congas. — 1960 *Down Beat Record Reviews,* p. 11. For a
happy, booting 40 minutes, you can't beat this one. —
1961 *Down Beat,* 19 Jan., p. 31. They eschew the more
recent, hard, choppy side of his personality, however, to
blow flowing booting tenor.

    2. *v.t.* [from *booted, adj.,* q.v.; some currency c. 1935–
c. 1945, obs. since; see also HIP, *v.t.*] To inform or
enlighten (someone). — 1944 *Dan Burley's Original
Handbook of Harlem Jive,* p. 15. "Let me boot you to my
play [i.e., plan]." — 1945 *Hepcats Jive Talk Dictionary.*
s.v. *boot:* clarify or understand.

booted, *adj.* [see last quot. for explanation of semantic
development (validated by jazzmen); prob. from *got
(one's) boots on,* q.v.; current esp. among Negro jazzmen c. 1920–c. 1945, very rare since; see also HIP, *adj.*]
Sophisticated; socially and/or metaphysically aware. —
1949 *Down Beat,* 28 Jan., p. 6. Another "booted" character on WJLB's assembly line of jockeys is Phil McClain
who spins an all-night record show. — 1958 *Jive in
Hi-Fi,* p. 13. It comes from a story of a fisherman warning
young fishermen never to wade in deep water without
hip boots on because they could run into trouble. So,
when you hear the words, "I'm hip" or "I'm booted" it's
said to let you know they have no fear of trouble or that
they understand what's shaking [i.e., happening].

    boots on (or **laced**), **got** (**one's**), [analogue for a state
of readiness: i.e., to have one's boots on is to be ready for
any kind of weather—hence, by extension, for any
eventuality; according to jazzmen, some currency esp.
among Negro jazzmen c. 1900–c. 1945, obs. since; see

also HIP, *adj.*, DOWN, *adj.*] See quots. — 1938 *Cab
Calloway: Hi De Ho*, p. 16. *got your boots on:* you know
what it is all about, you are a hep cat, you are wise. —
1939 *Jitterbug Jamboree Song Book*, p. 32. *got your
boots on:* know what it's all about. — 1945 *Hepcats Jive
Talk Dictionary.* s.v. *got your boots on:* hep to the jive.
bop, *n. & adj.* [See 1957, 1959 quots. for etym., first 1956
quot. for beginning date; still current with, though much
rarer than, *modern jazz;* see also HARD BOP and BEBOP]
See first 1956 quot. — 1947 *Bongo Bop* (tune recorded
by the Charlie Parker Sextet). — 1949 *Inside Be-Bop*, p.
10. Monk's place in the jazz scene, according to most
musicians in the bop movement, has been grossly distorted. — 1955 *Say*, 28 April, p. 53. They're calling him
[bop] "Modern Music" now. But he's the same cat who
was making crazy sounds back in the '40's—only the
critics didn't start cheering until he changed his name.
— 1956 *Guide to Jazz.* s.v. *bop:* originally meaningless
syllables in scat singing (as, for example, in the piece,
Hey ba ba re bop). Since about 1945 the name be bop
(re bop or today more frequently just bop) has been
applied to the new jazz: (1) the bop rhythm section
breaks the continuity of the swing, the drums constantly
introducing figures which spring from pseudo-Spanish
figures introduced from Cuba and certain Latin American
countries. — 1956 *Chicago Review*, Autumn-Winter, p.
13. The ultimate in pushing the words away, of course,
is "scat" or "bop" talk where the singer produces familiar sounds which don't make words at all. — 1957
Giants of Jazz, p. 188. The word "bop" is a contraction
of "bebop" or "rebop." The two-syllable word was
merely a way of describing the staccato two-note phrase
that became the trade-mark in its playing. — 1959 *Jazz:
A Quarterly of American Music*, Spring, p. 116. Apart
from their employment in scat, it does not appear that
rebop/bebop/bop had any widely known connotations

. . . The printed *bop!,* an onomatopoeic term, crashed off the comic pages, and has been employed colloquially since to mean *to whop, to hit, to clobber.*

v.i. [from *n.;* some currency c. 1945–c. 1950, rare since] To play in "bop" style. — 1947 *He Beeped When He Shoulda Bopped* (tune recorded by Dizzy Gillespie Orchestra). — 1962 *Down Beat,* 6 Dec., p. 23. We all started bopping.

bopper, bopster, *n.* [current c. 1945–c. 1950, rare since]   A musician who plays bop. — 1948 *New Yorker,* 3 July, p. 28. Boppers call themselves "the left wing" and their opponents "the right wing." — 1957 *American Speech,* Dec., p. 281. But occasionally, backed to the wall by monetary considerations, bopsters would make a partial concession by playing at weddings and other social functions where musical authenticity is held in low esteem. — 1963 *Down Beat,* 31 Jan., p. 24. In the '40's the boppers moved toward a less symmetrical method of construction in their improvising.

boppish, *adj.* [some currency since c. 1948]   Like bop; i.e., in that musical vein. — 1955 *The First Book of Jazz,* p. 55. Sometimes for fun, singers sing "oo-ya-koo" syllables to boppish backgrounds. — 1961 *Down Beat,* 2 Feb., p. 30. Fast, and in somewhat the same boppish groove as *Creek,* Hazel clips along with both horns shouting.

boss, *adj. & n.* [by analogy with the colloq. sense (i.e., someone of authority); some currency, esp. among Negro jazzmen, since c. 1950; very widely current since c. 1958]   Authoritative or excellent; initially, applied to jazzmen or jazz performance; by extension, applied to anyone or anything (see last quot.); as noun, one who performs authoritatively. — 1953 *Ebony,* Aug., p. 68. Bop pianists still refer to him as "the Boss Man." — 1958 *Jazz: A Quarterly of American Music,* Oct. p. 28. Those people are the Bosses. — 1959 *Gene Ammons: Boss Tenor*

(LP album Prestige PRLP7180). — 1960 *Jazz: A Quarterly of American Music* (outside back cover). Sonny Rollins the "boss of the tenor" followed his successful first CR album . . . with "The Leaders." — 1961 *Metronome*, Apr., p. 32. The arrangements by Clayton are effortless and elegant—he has always been a boss arranger. — 1961 *N.Y. Times Magazine*, 25 June, p. 39. "Man, she brews some boss stews!"

bossa nova, [see quots. for etym.; term orig. used in U.S. by jazzmen c. 1962, soon popularized] See last quot. — 1962 *Shorty Rogers and His Giants: Bossa Nova* (liner notes on Reprise LP album) The word "nova" in Portuguese, means "new." "Bossa" is a pagan word, not yet found in the dictionary. It is, however, a sincere term created to express the ability of playing well. — 1962 *High Fidelity*, Dec., p. 108. Bossa nova, the Brazilian-based music that has suddenly flooded American recording studios, is, like jazz, unsusceptible to precise definition. The term itself is translated as "the new beat" or "the new wrinkle," and the music is derived from the samba. But when one says "bossa nova," according to Charlie Byrd, the guitarist who was one of those principally responsible for launching it in this country, one refers not to a rhythm or to a melody but to "a mood, a feeling, a way of playing."

Boston, *n.* [poss. from the style originating in Boston, Mass., but according to jazzman Eubie Blake, the term derives from jazzmen's habit of referring humorously to the bass notes as being "way up North" and, subsequently, extending the verbal association to a specific Northern city; some currency c. 1917–c. 1935 when this piano style had its vogue, obs. since except historical] A piano style characterized by accented bass figures; also, the bass figures themselves. — 1943 *Harlem Jazz, 1930*, p. 3. Willie "The Lion" Smith was biting cigars in half, taking his "Boston" (accented bass figures) in "piano battles" with Fats Waller. — 1956 *Jazz: Its Evolution and Essence,* p. 213. Little by little, the drummers and then the bass players got into the habit of beating four to the bar, and at the same time pianists stopped playing exclusively Boston.

bounce, *n. & adj.* [by analogy of rhythmic accents with the bounce of a ball; current c. 1930–c. 1945, rare since; see also BUSINESSMAN'S BOUNCE] See 1937, 1952 quots.; also, for a rare verb use, see 1947 quot. — 1932 *Melody Maker,* June, p. 511. The "bounce" of the brass section . . . has degenerated into a definitely "corny" and staccato style of playing. — 1935 *Vanity Fair,* Nov., p. 71. Additional synonyms for hot music are *bounce* (indicating pronounced rhythm) . . . — 1937 *American Speech,* Feb., p. 45. *bounce:* a light-medium-fast tempo, with a light accent on the first and third beats. — 1939 *Metronome,* Dec., p. 46. Mary Lou Williams' piano helps *Andy Kirk's* band obtain a fine bounce. — 1947 *The Two Worlds of Johnny Truro,* p. 23. "Christ, all that heavy instrumentation, and it bounces, it's light as a breeze." — 1952 *A History of Jazz in America,* p. 350. *bounce:* used by some musicians, especially Duke Ellington, to describe a particularly buoyant beat.

box, *n.* 1. [see 1958 quot. for semantic explanation; current prob. since c. 1920] See 1936 quot. — 1936 *Metronome,* Feb., p. 61. *box:* piano. — 1958 *Publication of the American Dialect Society,* Nov., p. 44. *box:* a piano (undoubtedly fr. shape of upright piano and spinet, usually found in jazz night clubs). — 1959 *The Art of Jazz,* p. 101. When Yancy wasn't hired to play at a party, he might have been found in almost any joint along 31st or State Street which had a "box" on which he could practice.

2. [from its box-like shape; see 1960 quot. for beginning date; still some currency; see also GITBOX] A guitar. — 1933 *Metronome,* Aug., p. 16. Eddie was

playing the kind of banjo I wanted, but I got him to learn that "gitter box." — 1937 *American Speech,* Oct., p. 181. A "box" is any stringed instrument. — 1948 *Tremolo,* p. 115. A dark little guitar player had appeared from nowhere and he could make that old box talk, all right. — 1960 *Dictionary of American Slang.* s.v. *box:* any stringed instrument, specif. a guitar c. 1930.

3. [from its general shape; current since c. 1935] A record player. — 1937 *N.Y. Amsterdam News,* 11 Dec., p. 20. The music box, plus Tommy Dorsey, ground out "Once in a While." — 1959 *The Holy Barbarians,* p. 88. They put Mozart on the box. — 1959 *Esquire,* Nov., p. 70I. *box:* phonograph.

boxed, *adj.* [by analogy with being boxed in; some currency since c. 1955; see also HIGH, JUICED, STONED, ZONKED] Intoxicated or drugged. — 1958 *Somewhere There's Music,* p. 18. "We were sitting in the front row, so boxed that the musicians were looking at us!" — 1959 *Jazz for Moderns,* p. 20. *boxed:* stoned, circa 1959.

boy, *n.* (generally preceded by a personal pronoun, usually *my*) [orig. Negro slang, but esp. common among jazzmen c. 1925–c. 1945, very rare since because of its servile connotation, offensive to the militant post-World War II Negro: largely supplanted by *man* (with personal pronoun)] See 1928 quot.; also, one's favorite musician (see 1955 quot.). — 1928 *The Walls of Jericho,* p. 295. *boy:* friend and ally. Buddy. — 1948 *PM,* 22 Feb., p.M6, This was inscribed, "To Monk, my first inspiration. Stay with it. Your boy, Dizzy Gillespie." — 1955 *Down Beat,* 7 Sep., p. 29. O.P. is my boy; bass or cello, he's very clean, and he swings. — 1960 *Hiparama of the Classics,* p. 27. "If you do this little favor for me Lord . . . You've got yourself a Boy!!!" — 1961 *The Sound,* p. 267. "Yes, indeed-y, Roy was my boy," Red replied.

brass section, [current since c. 1925] See quots. — 1937 *American Speech,* Feb., p. 48. In the *brass section* are trumpets and trombones. — 1942 *The American The-saurus of Slang*, p. 557. *brass section:* a division of a dance band's instruments.

bread, *n.* [see 1958 quot. for explanation of semantic de-velopment; some currency esp. among Negro jazzmen since c. 1935; widely current since c. 1945; see also LOOT, GOLD] See 1958 quot. — 1939 *Jazzmen*, p. 63. Inside the low, smoky room, the musicians sweated for their bread. — 1952 *Down Beat*, 18 June, p. 15. If I had bread (Dizzy's basic synonym for loot) I'd certainly start a big band again. — 1958 *Publication of the American Dialect Society*, Nov., p. 44. *bread:* money. A double-pun — (1) "dough," (2) bread, the necessity. — 1959 *The Cool World*, p. 2. "I ain't payin that kind of bread for no iron like that."

long bread, [formed from *bread* and *long green;* cur-rent since c. 1945] Much money. — 1963 *Nugget*, Feb., p. 71. Tania's parents, and Tania, all seem to find me singularly repulsive, and will offer me pretty long bread to get out of their lives and keep my mouth shut.

small bread, [some currency since c. 1945; see also CRUMBS] See quots. — 1957 *N.Y. Times Magazine*, 18 Aug., p. 26. *crumbs:* a small amount of money. Also called small bread. — 1959 *Esquire*, Nov., p. 70I. *crumbs:* a small amount of money. Small bread. Also **light bread:** oral evidence only.

break, *n.* [an extension of the standard sense (i.e., a pause); current c. 1917–c. 1945, obs. since: replaced largely by *chorus*] See 1959 quot. — 1922 *How to Play and Sing the Blues Like the Phonograph and Stage Artists* [1962 *Jazz: A History of the New York Scene*, p. 97]. Harmony Break. —1926 *Melody Maker*, Jan., p. 31. With the exception of . . . the additional special chorus containing the violin breaks, the score used . . . is . . . identical with that issued by the publishers. — 1929 *The Musical Quarterly*, Oct., p. 611. As to what

possibilities such free-will tricks as the jazz "break" . . .
hold . . . he would be bold who would predict. — 1934
All About Jazz, p. 47. Piano "breaks" today are very
demode. — 1936 *Esquire,* June, p. 92. It was "breaks"
originally. Then it became "licks." Today it is "riffs." In
all truth hot is redundant with any of these words. —
1937 *This Thing Called Swing,* p. 8, *break:* stopping
the music for a second or two and picking it up without
missing the beat. — 1944 *This Is Jazz,* p. 24. Still another
musical device developed in jazz is the break. This is an
unaccompanied interpolation of one or two measures for
solo instrument or group of instruments. It is freely improvised. — 1959 *The Jazz Scene,* p. 290. *breaks:* open
passages in the performance when the rhythm is suspended, more generally, solo passages.

break it down, [prob. from *breakdown;* current c.
1930–c. 1937, obs. since except historical]   See quots. —
1937 *This Thing Called Swing,* p. 3. *break it down!:*
Get hot! Swing it! — 1959 *Jazz: A Quarterly of American
Music,* Fall, p. 284. "Break it down" was reported to be
Harlem's pet expression of 1933, and was synonymous
with "get hot."

break it up, [hyperbole: by analogy with dispersing a
gathering—i.e., leaving nothing more to be said or
done; current since c. 1935]   See 1938 quot. —1937
N.Y. Amsterdam News, 4 Sep., p. 12. All the "cats" on
the avenue are "breaking it up" with a new dance they
call "The Big Apple," a swing square dance. — 1938 *Cab
Calloway: Hi De Ho,* p. 16. *break it up:* to win
applause, to stop the show. — 1944 *The Jazz Record,*
Jan., p. 7. When the band really started sounding right,
Wingie broke it up and away we went to the studio.

break up, [hyperbole: by analogy with fragmenting
or dissolving (here from either a comic or thrilling
stimulus); current since c. 1940]   To convulse with
laughter; also: to excite musically. — 1956 *Lady Sings*

the Blues, p. 48. Then the house broke up. — 1959
Jazz: A Quarterly of American Music, Fall, p. 295.
Cannonball . . . breaks up. — 1959 *The Cool World,*
p. 16. George Cadmus was breaken evrybody up. [sic]
breakdown, break-down, *n.* [see first 1959 quot. for semantic development; current among jazzmen c. 1920–
c. 1940, obs. since except historical] An energetic jazz
dance originated by American Negroes and popular
among them c. 1920–c. 1935; also, the energetic music to
which it was danced; for its adjective use, see last quot.
— 1927 *Birmingham Break-down* (tune recorded by
Duke Ellington). — 1941 *Central Avenue Breakdown*
(tune recorded by the Lionel Hampton Orchestra on
Victor 26652). — 1959 *Jazz: A Quarterly of American
Music,* Fall, p. 284. A noisy, rollicking reel with the descriptive name [*breakdown*] is reported in Virginia
prior to 1820, and by the middle of the century the
word had reached currency in America and England
to denote a convivial gathering. Duke Ellington recorded "Birmingham Breakdown" in 1927; the Chocolate
Dandies cut their version in 1928. — 1959 *The Jazz Review,* July, p. 12. Breakdown music was the best for such
sets, the more solid and groovy the better.
breeze, up a, [variant of general slang phrase "up a storm";
current from c. 1935–c. 1945, rare since] Exceedingly;
to the utmost. — 1939 *Blowing Up a Breeze* (recorded
by Chu Berry on Columbia C-541). — 1946 *Really the
Blues,* p. 122. Bix cussed up a breeze. — 1956 *Lady
Sings the Blues,* p. 65. All alone in a room upstairs,
snoring up a breeze. — 1960 *Hiparama of the Classics,*
p. 30. He stated that everyone should ball up a breeze.
bringdown, bring-down, *n.* [from *bring (one) down;* current c. 1940–c. 1950, rare since; see also DRAG, *n.*] See 1944,
1952, first 1959 quots. — 1944 *The New Cab Calloway's
Hepsters Dictionary.* s.v. *bring down:* something depressing. — 1946 *Really the Blues,* p. 26. That was a

bringdown. — 1952 *A History of Jazz in America,* p. 350. *bringdown:* one who depresses. — 1959 *The Beat Generation Dictionary.* s.v. *bring-down:* joy-killer; wet blanket. — 1959 *The Naked Lunch,* p. 19. And our habits build up with the drag, like cocaine will build you up staying ahead of the C [i.e., cocaine] bring-down. Also **bring down.**

bring (one) down, [extension of the standard sense: here, to reduce *in spirit* from an exalted state to a depressed one (though very briefly, c. 1935, effect could be good or bad: see 1935, 1958 quots.); also cf. 1940 *American Speech,* Oct., "Jargon of Marihuana Addicts," p. 337. *"to bring someone down:* to calm someone when he is violent"; widely current c. 1935–c. 1950, rare since; replaced largely by *drag;* see also BROUGHT DOWN] See 1935, 1952, 1958 quots. — 1935 *His Hi De Highness of Ho De Ho,* p. 35. "That brings me down" . . . can be applied to anything that affects you strongly, whether favorably or even adversely. — 1940 *You Bring Me Down* (tune recorded by the Erskine Hawkins Orchestra on Bluebird 10756). — 1944 *The New Cab Calloway's Hepsters Dictionary,* p. 4. "That brings me down." — 1952 *A History of Jazz in America,* p. 350. *bring down:* to depress. — 1958 *Publication of the American Dialect Society,* Nov., p. 44. *bring down:* to make one feel low. (Obs.—to make one feel good—out of use since the '30's.)

broad, *n.* [see 1959 quot. for explanation of semantic development; prob. from underworld slang: cf. 1930 *American Tramp and Underworld Slang,* s.v. *broad:* "a woman, more especially one of loose morals" (note: in jazz slang, the term has no pejorative sense); also cf. 1928 *American Speech,* Feb., "Kansas University Slang," p. 218. *"broad:* a plump, shapely girl"; some general slang use, but with esp. currency among jazzmen since c. 1930, supplanted considerably by *chick* c. 1938–

c. 1952, but again widely current since c. 1952] A
woman, esp. a young woman. — 1926 *Walk That Broad*
(tune recorded by Ed Allen on Okeh 8629). — 1942
American Mercury, July, p. 88. The right broad would,
or might, come along. — 1958 *Somewhere There's Music*,
p. 35. "Jess is the craziest broad I've ever known, even
finer than that chick in New Orleans." — 1959 *Jazz: A
Quarterly of American Music*, Fall, p. 283. Usually as-
sumed to refer to the physical dimensions of a woman,
broad is more accurately a clipped form of *broad-gauge*,
and in the complex embracing *broad-minded*. After
1850-USA the interests of people were centered in rail-
roads spanning the continent. From such activity a whole
vocabulary developed. One source of concern was financ-
ing, and narrow-gauge / broad-gauge tracking was a
battle of costs versus stability and speed. *Broad-gauge*
developed extensions and association, and from the easy
grade and level of a moral judgment it was sidetracked
to an inferred physical attribute. — 1960 *Beat Jokes Bop
Humor & Cool Cartoons*, p. 56. "I told you to ease up on
this broad."

brought down, [from *bring (one) down;* current c. 1940–
c. 1950, rare since; see also the more recent DRAGGED]   See
1942 quot. — 1942 *The American Thesaurus of Slang*,
p. 581. *brought:* downcast, depressed. — 1958 *Somewhere There's Music*, p. 162. "I figured you'd be brought
down about that." — 1960 *Beat Jokes Bop Humor &
Cool Cartoons*, p. 22. "Don't be brought down 'cause you
didn't wig up this plan." — 1961 *Down Beat*, 19 Jan.,
p. 22. Then you can really get brought down. Also
brought.

brushes, *n. pl.* [short for *wire brushes* which, in turn, derives from their brush-like appearance; current since
c. 1925 when they came into use in dance bands]   See
1960 quot. — 1933 *Metronome*, Nov., p. 54. Brushes
(paragraph heading in drum instruction column). —

1948 *Tremolo,* p. 33. "The drummer maybe starts it soft with the brushes." — 1960 *Dictionary of American Slang.* s.v. *brushes:* a pair of thin drum sticks used to give the drums a soft, smooth, muted sound. Orig. jazz use; now the most common word for these items in all forms of jazz and popular music.

bruz, *n.* [short for *brother;* from common slang practice of retaining only the first syllable of a word, then substituting "z" sound for all succeeding syllables: cf. *cuz* for *cousin,* etc.; according to jazzmen, Lester Young introduced the term into jazz use c. 1935; some currency until c. 1950, very rare since]   A casual term of address to a man. — 1958 *Somewhere There's Music,* p. 35. "Romance? No, bruz, that's not my groove." — p. 73. His smiling "bubber" was equivalent to Gene's "bruz"; Mike wasn't sure he wanted to be William's brother.

bug, *v.t.* [from underworld slang: cf. 1930 *American Tramp and Underworld Slang,* s.v. *bug:* "an insane or simple-minded individual"; current since c. 1940]   See 1952, 1958 quots. — 1949 *Music Library Association Notes,* Dec., p. 40. *bug:* to be annoying. — 1952 *A History of Jazz in America,* p. 350. *bug:* to bewilder or irritate. — 1958 *Publication of the American Dialect Society,* Nov., p. 44. *bug:* to bother, especially to get one in such a state that he cannot play well. Extended to mean getting annoyed at anything. — 1960 *Hiparama of the Classics,* p. 7. The Lion was Buggin' India. — 1961 *The Sound,* p. 155. "Then, what are you buggin' me about?"

bugged, *adj.* [from *bug,* *v.t.;* current since c. 1942; see also DRAGGED, HACKED, HUNG]   Bewildered or annoyed. — 1958 *American Speech,* Oct., p. 225. *bugged:* annoyed. —1959 *San Francisco Chronicle,* 4 June, p. 35. "Them people down there must be plenty bugged if a book like this can get them so tore up."

   bugged on, [variant of *bugged;* current c. 1943–c. 1953, rare since; see also the more recent STRUNG OUT.]   Ob-

sessed with; dedicated to; exceedingly enthusiastic
about. — 1956 *Sideman,* p. 414. "Madame Luke, gonna
get her a screen test, for these art films she's bugged on."

bump, bumpty-bump, bump-the-bump, *n.* [according to
jazzman Eubie Blake, the dance originated in 1907 in
Washington, D.C.; obs. since c. 1930 except historical]
See quot. — 1928 *The Walls of Jericho,* p. 296. *bump;
bumpty-bump; bump-the-bump:* a *shout* characterized
by a forward and backward swaying of the hips.

bunny hug, [dance designations frequently refer to animal
movements: cf. CAMEL WALK, FOX TROT, TURKEY TROT;
current during the dance's vogue, 1907–c. 1927, obs. since
except historical]　A jazz dance in vogue, 1907–c. 1927:
see 1941 quot. — 1914 *Modern Dancing* [1962 *Jazz: A
History of the New York Scene,* p. 37]. Drop the Turkey
Trot, the Grizzly Bear, the Bunny Hug, Etc. — 1926 *Nigger Heaven,* p. 84. She was good at the new ones, too, the
turkey trot and the bunny hug. — 1933 *Metronome,*
July, p. 19. The Bunny-hug . . . came into popularity on
the Barbary Coast. — 1941 *Father of the Blues,* p. 226.
The Castles liked the idea and a new dance was
introduced by them which in a magazine article they
called the "Bunny hug." They went abroad and while
in mid-ocean sent a wireless to the magazine to change
the "Bunny hug" to the "Fox-trot." — 1954 *Down
Memory Lane,* p. 70. The bunny hug survived its contemporaries and made the transition to jazz.

burn, *v.i.* [by analogy with jazz slang *cook;* current since
c. 1958; see also SMOKE]　To play music intensely and
expertly; also, by extension: see 1962 quot. — 1959 *Newport Jazz Festival: 1959,* p. 45. *burn:* cook [jazz sense]. —
1959 *Paul Bryant: Burnin'* (LP album Pacific PJ–12).
— 1960 *Sonny Stitt Quartet: Burnin'* (LP album Argo
LP–661). — 1962 *N.Y. Times Magazine,* 20 May, p. 45.
burn: to do something well, quickly or efficiently.

　　v.t. [from underworld slang; cf. general slang "playing

with fire"; also cf. 1938 *Better English,* Nov., "The Language of the Jitterbug," p. 51. *"burned:* hurt"; current among jazzmen since c. 1940] To cheat. — 1958 *Somewhere There's Music,* p. 31. "The cat never burned me before." — 1959 *Esquire,* Nov., p. 70I. *to burn:* to rob.

burn (someone) for bread, [extension of *burn, v.t.* esp. current among narcotics addicts but also with some currency among jazzmen since c. 1955] See quots. — 1957 *N.Y. Times,* 25 Aug., Sec. 2, p. 8. *burn (someone) for bread:* borrow money. — 1963 *Hiptionary,* p. 18 *burn:* borrow.

business straight, get (one's), [from jazz slang *straight, adj.* 2., q.v.; some currency since c. 1935] To attend to something: see quot. — 1947 *Jive and Slang.* s.v. *I have to get my business straight:* I have something to do.

businessman's bounce, [see 1950, 1952 quots. for semantic explanation; current c. 1935–c. 1945, obs. since except historical] See 1950, 1952 quots. — 1940 *Business Man's Bounce* (tune composed and recorded by Raymond Scott). — 1950 *Lingo of Tin-Pan Alley.* s.v. *business man's bounce:* term of derision . . . Originated during the thirties, when swing music, loud and fast, was the vogue. Referred to the type of soft, smooth style in which songs were played by bands like Guy Lombardo's; it was designed to appeal to the middle-agers rather than the teen-agers. — 1952 *A History of Jazz in America,* p. 350. *businessman's bounce:* a monotonous two-beat played fast, usually by society bands, for the delectation of tired businessmen and their dance partners.

buss, buzz, *v.t.* [although *buzz* is the only form found in quots. below, several jazzmen recognized only the *buss* form, so apparently they are cognates and prob. stem from Middle English: cf. 1959 *Webster's New World Dictionary,* s.v. *buss:* "[? akin to G. (dial.) bus, kiss, or W. & Gael, *bus,* kiss, lip], [Archaic or Dial.], kiss, espe-

cially in a rough and playful manner"; some currency esp.
among Negro jazzmen c. 1935–c. 1945, obs. since except
historical]   See quots. — 1945 *Hepcats Jive Talk Dictionary.* s.v. *buzz:* kiss. — 1947 *The American Thesaurus
of Slang,* supplement, p. 9. *buzz:* to kiss.

bust (one's) **conk** (or **top**), [hyperbole; some currency
c. 1935–c. 1945, obs. since except historical]   To feel
exhilarated (see 1939 quot.); for a further, rare meaning, see 1938 quot. — 1938 *Cab Calloway: Hi De Ho,*
p. 16. *bust your conk:* apply yourself diligently, break
your neck. — 1939 *Jitterbug Jamboree Song Book,* p. 32.
bust your conk: something [sic] that will make you
enthuse. — 1946 *Really the Blues,* p. 10. Negroes and
whites side by side busting their conks. — 1955 *Hear Me
Talkin to Ya,* p. 232. We called it a "ninety-nine percent,"
one more either way would bust your top.

busted, *adj.* [hyperbole; prob. from underworld and drug
addicts slang: cf. 1958 *Southern Folklore Quarterly,* Sep.,
"The Anonymous Verses of a Narcotics Addict," p. 131,
"*busted:* arrested by the police or federal agents"; current
in jazz slang since c. 1940]   See 1948 quot. — 1948 *Metronome,* April, p. 33. You hear that such-and-such a
musician has been "busted" (arrested). — 1958 *Somewhere There's Music,* p. 143. "He got busted last week by
the local fuzz." 1958 *Jive in Hi-Fi,* p. 25. *busted:* arrested.
— 1959 *The Holy Barbarians,* p. 53. "One of them sent
her boyfriend out to have me busted."

busy, *adj.* [special application of standard term; current
since c. 1950]   Extremely energetic or supportive: said
of an accompanist, esp. a drummer. — 1962 *Jazz Journal,*
July, p. 11. Milt's a busy bass player, you must give him
credit for that. — 1962 *Down Beat,* 6 Dec., p. 30. He is
busy, but not loud.

buzz, *v.t.* See s.v. BUSS.

buzz, *n.* [prob. synesthesia—i.e., feeling represented as
sound; see quot. for dates]   See quot.; also: the begin-

nings of a thrill derived from marijuana (in this sense, oral evidence only). — 1960 *Dictionary of American Slang.* s.v. *buzz:* a thrill, a kick, a charge, a feeling of excitement, pleasure, satisfaction or the like. Since c. 1935.

buzz mute, [from its buzzing sound; current since c. 1930] See quot. — 1957 *The Book of Jazz,* p. 76. He made effective use of a strange contraption known as the "buzz mute," which sounded like the product of an illicit meeting between a trumpet and a kazoo.

C

※※※※※※※※※※※※※※

c, [abbreviation; from underworld slang: cf. 1930 *American Tramp and Underworld Slang,* s.v. *C:* "cocaine"; some currency among jazzmen since c. 1930] See 1953 quot. — 1953 *Junkie,* p. 11. *C:* Cocaine. — 1959 *Esquire,* Nov., p. 70I. *C:* cocaine. — 1959 *The Naked Lunch,* p. 19. And our habits build up with the drag, like cocaine will build you up staying ahead of the C bringdown. — p. 65. Eukodol is like a combination of junk and C.

cack, *v.i.* [etym. unknown; current since c. 1948] See quot. (note: usually, from too much stimulant) — 1959 *Newport Jazz Festival: 1959,* p. 45. *cack:* fall asleep, fall out, go under.

cake-walk, *n.* [cf. 1957 *Funk & Wagnalls New "Standard"
Dictionary,* s.v. *cakewalk:* "an entertainment originating
among Negroes of the Southern United States, in which
a cake is the prize for the most graceful walking"; current c. 1890–c. 1920, obs. since except historical despite
the fact that parts of the dance survive in other dances]
See note above and 1947 quot. — 1910 *Cake Walk*
(tune composed by Hayden & Eldridge). — 1947 *Jazzbook 1947,* p. 37. Right along with the two-step, came a
dance of American Negro origin that had a tremendous
vogue—the cake-walk. The name "cake-walk" was applied to the dance and likewise to the music for it. —
1958 *The Decca Book of Jazz,* p. 31. Both the coon song
and the cake-walk made use of syncopation, and they
were also alike in being invariably the work of white
composers, although they included material taken from
Negro sources. Also **cake walk.**
camel walk, [dance designations frequently refer to animal
movements: cf. BUNNY HUG, FOX TROT, TURKEY TROT;
current during the dance's two vogues, c. 1913–c. 1917
and c. 1940–c. 1945] A jazz dance in which shoulder
and back movements simulate somewhat those of a
camel. — 1925 *The Camel Walk* (tune recorded in
England by the Kit-Cat Band). — 1926 *Nigger Heaven,*
p. 242. Camel Walk!
canary, *n.* [from a shared activity — i.e., singing; despite
skepticism of last quot., term had some currency, esp.
among white big band musicians and jazz writers
c. 1935–c. 1945, very rare since; see also CHIRP] See
1937 quot. — 1937 *American Speech,* Feb., p. 45. *canary:*
a woman vocalist. — 1938 *Cab Calloway: Hi De Ho,*
p. 16. *canary:* girl vocalist. — 1953 *The Hot and the Cool,*
p. 48. "Where the hell do you get off blowing in here,
copping a job some poor canary could use?" — 1956
Enjoyment of Jazz (EJ410), [p. 2]. The band "canary"

was a pretty girl named Ginnie Simms. — 1956 *The Real Jazz Old and New,* p. 150. Canary or mouse for woman is just used in smart fiction about jazz.

cap, *v.t.* [prob. from Negro slang *backcap* (retort): in answering definitively, to put the lid or cap on the situation; current since c. 1940]   See 1944 quot. — 1944 *The New Cab Calloway's Hepsters Dictionary.* s.v. *capped:* outdone, surpassed. — 1952 *Who Walk in Darkness,* p. 173. "You capped me, man," he said. — 1958 *The Subterraneans,* p. 97. To cap everything . . . Adams opens the door. — 1959 *Jazz: A Quarterly of American Music,* Fall, p. 325. Mr. Pleasants . . . very fittingly caps that.

    n. **Capper:** oral evidence only.

    cap on, [extension of jazz slang *cap;* some currency since c. 1960]   To censure — 1960 *Lenny Bruce: "I Am Not a Nut, Elect Me"* (LP album Fantasy 7007). It would be different if the sharks were flagrant offenders, but, I mean, they made *one* mistake and everybody capped on them immediately.

capper, *n.* [from *cap, v.t.;* current since c. 1942]   The ultimate. — 1960 *The Jazz Review,* May, p. 30. "But dig [i.e., listen], here's the capper."

carve, *v.t.* [hyperbole; some currency c. 1920–c. 1940, obs. since except historical; see also the more common CUT] To defeat (someone) in musical competition, or simply to play better than one's contemporaries. — 1950 *Mister Jelly Roll,* p. 145. George Smith is frank to admit that Morton carved everybody.

carving contest, See s.v. CUTTING CONTEST.

cat, *n.* [semantic etym. obscure; 1946 quot. logical but of doubtful validity; most prob. shortened form of general and Negro slang *tomcat* (i.e., a female-chasing male); also poss. related to the itinerant nature of early jazzmen: cf. 1930 *American Tramp and Underworld Slang,* s.v. *cat:* "Itinerant worker . . . Possibly so called because he slinks about like a homeless cat"; see 1958 quot. for semantic development; according to jazzmen, Louis Armstrong introduced the term into jazz slang c. 1922, very widely current since]   See quots. — 1936 *Swing That Music,* p. 42. All jazz musicians from New Orleans called each other "cats" and still do. — 1937 *New Yorker,* 17 April, p. 31. Dance musicians are known as *cats.* — 1946 *Really the Blues,* p. 218. They even called each other *cats* approvingly because they wanted to be as alert and keen-sighted as an alley cat. — 1958 *Publication of the American Dialect Society,* Nov., p. 44. *cat:* orig. one who was "hep." Obsolete in this sense; now, any person. (Thus, a musician can now speak of a "square cat"— a contradiction in terms in the '30's.) — 1959 *Esquire,* Nov., p. 70I. *cat:* in the finest sense, a person who swings with life.

    catting, *part.* [prob. from general and Negro slang "tom-catting" (i.e., pursuing women), reinforced by jazz slang *cat;* some currency esp. among Negro jazzmen since c. 1925] Questing after women; also, occasionally: moving about a great deal (see note s.v. *cat*). — 1946 *Hollywood Note,* April. A hustler, he lives in Greenwich Village . . catting around Manhattan in the wake of the Ellington and Herman bands. — 1961 *The Jazz Review,* Jan., p. 7. Davis, the featured tenor soloist at the time, was "catting" with a young lady at ringside.

catch, *v.t.* [by analogy with the general meaning—i.e., the ears performing a function that is normally the hands'; some currency esp. among white jazzmen from c. 1930–c. 1940, rare since; see also DIG] To hear; to listen (to). — 1939 *Metronome,* March, p. 40. Catch those lyrics in *Don Redman's Auld Lang Syne!* — 1948 *Metronome,* Sep., p. 26. I caught them down at the Royal Roost. — 1955 *Solo,* p. 172. "Catch this Jones." — 1959 *The Horn,* p. 221. "This Kelcy Crane . . . Have you caught him yet?"

catch-up bass, [according to jazzman Eubie Blake, current from c. 1900–c. 1910, obs. since except historical] See quot. — 1940 *New Orleans Jazz,* p. 12. Thus we had, in various places from Pensacola to Dallas and from St. Louis to Chicago, such interesting names for what the left hand does (and the right hand knows it!) as . . . *catch-up bass* (a walk [q.v.] and a chord).

cents, *n. pl.* [understatement: see 1961 quot.; current since c. 1935] See 1962 quot. — 1938 *Better English,* Nov., p. 51. *two cents:* $2. — 1959 *Esquire,* Nov., p. 70I. This gig [i.e., job] pays twenty cents a night. — 1961 *The Sound* p. 157. Twenty cents meant twenty dollars; Red always spoke of dollars in amounts under one hundred as cents; perhaps it expressed his contempt for money. — 1962 *N.Y. Times Magazine,* 20 May, p. 45. *cents:* dollars.

change, *n.* [shortened form of *key change;* also standard musical term; current among jazzmen since c. 1925] See quot. — 1937 *American Speech,* Oct., p. 181. *change:* an interlude of a measure or two between choruses during which the key in which the piece is being played may be changed. (Syn. Transition.)

changes, *n. pl.* [shortened form of *Chord changes* (see 1947 quot.); some currency since c. 1920, but with wide currency only since c. 1945] See 1955, 1956, 1958 quots. — 1926 *Melody Maker,* March, p. 33. No consideration seems to be given to arranging the notes of the chords so that the fingers of a player may execute a minimum series of changes. — 1947 *N.Y. Herald Tribune,* 26 Sep. The be-bop guitar makes frequent chord "changes" within each bar and from measure to measure. — 1955 *The Encyclopedia of Jazz,* p. 346. *changes:* harmonic progression of a tune. — 1956 *Guide to Jazz.* s.v. *variations:* improvisational transformations of melody by a soloist (obs.) now "changes" since Bop revolutionized improvisation by innovating frequent key changes and many more rhythm changes than were possible in the pre-Bop era. — 1958 *Publication of the American Dialect Society*, Nov., p. 44. *changes:* the chords for whatever melody is being used as a basis for improvisation. — 1961 *Down Beat*, 16 Feb., p. 17. "For example, *Tall Polynesian* is partly modal, partly standard changes."

changes, go through (**the, all the, those, or some**) [extension of jazz slang *changes* to the realm of behavior; current since c. 1952; see also *put me through* (*some*) *changes*] To move through a progression of experiences and of emotional reactions to them. — 1962 *Down Beat*, 29 March, p. 23. Anyone who's got a white skin must be aware he's white when he looks at himself in a mirror— and because he does not get refused at a restaurant. He does not have to go through the changes that I go through.

changes, make the [formed from jazz slang *make* and jazz slang *changes;* some currency since c. 1955] To successfully perform harmonic progressions. — 1960 *Jackie McLean: Making the Changes* (LP album New Jazz 8231).

changes, put me through (**some**) [extension of jazz slang *changes* to the realm of behavior; according to jazzmen, current since c. 1952; see also *go through* (*the*) *changes*] To be subjected to a series of experiences producing a concomitant series of emotional reactions. Oral evidence only.

changes, run (**the**) [formed from jazz slang *run* and jazz slang *changes;* some currency since c. 1947, though increasingly pejorative since c. 1955 (see quots.)] See 1961 quot.: since c. 1955, term increasingly implies criticism of this practice (i.e., uninspired and mechanical reliance on the progressions as a substitute for genuine musical invention). — 1959 *Evergreen Review*, Nov.-Dec., p. 138. Silver indirectly exposed many of the adept fakers who merely "ran the changes" in familiar keys,

jumping from one chord to the next with stock phrases.
— 1961 *The Jazz Life*, p. 37. Harmonically, the modernists became so intrigued by the challenging, expanded
chordal possibilities of improvisation advanced by Charlie
Parker and his colleagues that until recently, most players
"ran changes" (improvised on the chords of a tune) instead of developing melodic variations on the theme.

channel, *n.* [extension of standard meaning (i.e., a body of
water joining two larger bodies of water); current since
c. 1945; see also the earlier RELEASE] A connecting passage between two statements of the theme: the equivalent of *bridge* in standard musical terminology. —
1951 *Down Beat*, 20 Apr., p. 18. "You know, the channel
of our theme song when I was playing with Columbus'
band in the Rendezvous 10 years ago was the channel of
Nothing But D. Best." — 1955 *The Encyclopedia of Jazz*,
p. 346. *channel:* bridge. — 1955 *Down Beat*, 19 Oct.,
p. 33. In the first chorus, he changed the channel completely for the strings.

charge, *n.* 1. [See sense 2; cf. 1934 *A Dictionary of American
Slang*, p. 6. *"charge:* a shot of dope"; also cf. *Dictionary of
American Slang*, s.v. *charge:* "General jazz use since
c. 1935; from underworld and addict use c. 1925"; rare
since c. 1950: see GAGE, POT, TEA, etc.] See 1944 quot.
— 1944 *Dan Burley's Original Handbook of Harlem Jive*,
p. 52. Charge is marijuana. — 1952 *Flee the Angry
Strangers*, p. 248. "*She's the queen of small and large,/
Ridin the sky on a ton of charge.*" — 1953 *Night Light*, p.
135. "It's a funny thing about smoking charge." — 1959
The Jazz Scene, p. 292. *charge:* marijuana.

2. [see quot.; also see note, sense 1; current since
c. 1935] See quot. — 1959 *The Holy Barbarians*, p. 172.
"Charge" and "explode" are also terms used by the head
and the hype to describe the kick of the drug at the moment of "turning on."

Charleston [from *Charleston*, S.C., its place of origin; see quots. for dates]   See 1956 quot. — 1926 *Melody Maker*, Aug., p. 7. The most popular is to play the actual Charleston rhythm. — Sep., p. 11. "The Charleston . . . is a fast fox-trot with an unusual beat." — 1956 *Guide to Jazz*, p. 59. *Charleston:* dance step done in the 1920's (recently revived) to the syncopated rhythm of two notes, one falling on the first beat of the bar and the other between the weak second beat and the strong third beat.

Charleston cymbal(s), [by association with the dance, for which they supplied part of the accompaniment; current c. 1922–c. 1932, obs. since except historical; replaced by *high hat,* q.v.]   Two cymbals (see 1927 quot.) facing each other and made to meet through pedal control. — 1927 *Melody Maker*, July, p. 697. A pair of cup cymbals or "Charleston" cymbals, as they are commonly called, hung together on a thong. — 1956 *Guide to Jazz*, p. 59. Charleston cymbals: generally called "high hat cymbals" q.v.

chart, *n.* [by analogy with standard meaning; current since c. 1955]   See 1957 quot. — 1957 *N.Y. Times Magazine*, 18 Aug., p. 26. *charts:* musical arrangements. — 1960 *Down Beat*, 9 June, p. 13. "And don't leave out Gil Fuller and John Lewis and their charts for Dizzy Gillespie's big band years ago." — 1961 *Down Beat*, 30 March, p. 29. Have you dug that album they did on all those Saxie Dowell charts? — 1962 *Down Beat*, 8 Nov., p. 38. This particular chart has a lot of places where shading would bring it out more, and I felt that the whole band played at one dynamic level.

chase (chorus), [extension of standard meaning; current since c. 1940]   See first 1959 quot.; also, for a rare verb use, see last 1959 quot. — 1942 *Gems of Jazz: Vol. 4*, p. 7. It's one of the most exciting "chase" choruses on wax. — 1949 *Down Beat*, 11 March, p. 14. *Duel* is, of course, a chase in which each tries to outdo the other by alternating first choruses, then half choruses, then four-bar phrases and so on until finally they are squalling at each other simultaneously like a couple of terrified sows. — 1958 *Publication of the American Dialect Society*, Nov., p. 44. *chase:* a 32-bar chorus divided so that two men (usually) take alternate four- or eight-bar sections. — 1959 *The Jazz Scene*, p. 289. *chase:* a series of choruses by two or more players each playing several bars in turn. — 1959 *Blow Up a Storm*, p. 39. In music, the pattern was called an answer chorus or a chase chorus . . . each of them soloing eight bars or so, and alternating. — 1959 *The Horn*, p. 34. The drummer for the house band good-naturedly chased Wing's warm-up runs with precise rim shots. — 1960 *The Jazz Review*, Nov., p. 22. And the chase fours [i.e., four-bar choruses] between Bird and Fats are thrilling indeed. — 1961 *The Sound*, p. 51. Toward the end Chuey Figueroa came in for a series of chase choruses where eight bar sections were traded back and forth between trumpet and saxophone.

cheaters, *n. pl.* [from gambling slang: cf. 1934 *A Dictionary of American Slang*, p. 318. "*cheaters:* eyeglasses"; current among jazzmen since c. 1930, largely supplanted c. 1945 by *shades*, q.v.] Dark (tinted) glasses. — 1938 *Jeepers Creepers* (tune composed by Harry Warren) "Golly gee, when you turn those peepers on,/Woe is me, got to put my cheaters on." — 1946 *Really the Blues*, p. 173. Tesch mumbled . . . cocking his sorrowful eyes over those horn-rimmed cheaters.

cheat, *v.i.* (usually in the present participle), [according to jazzmen, current since c. 1910, largely supplanted c. 1925 by *fake*] To play (music) in a tricky or illusory manner, knowing only a few basic harmonic or rhythmic variations and trying to make them fit any musical performance. Oral evidence only.

cheat on the rhythm, [see quot. for semantic explanation; current c. 1910–c. 1925, obs. since except historical] See quot. — 1947 *The Musical Digest,* July, p. 24. The changes which make up the music are felt equally in the melody and the harmony, but the most important ones are those which, in the words of the drummer Baby Dodds, "cheat on the rhythm." This quality of altering accents, with regard for and in relation to each other, is the essence of the work of New Orleans musicians.

Chicago style, [see 1958 quot.; current since c. 1927, but its use since c. 1940 is chiefly historical] See 1956, 1958 quots. — 1936 *Transatlantic Jazz,* p. 45. Bud Freeman . . . plays in the "Chicago style" (using "choppy" phrasing). — 1946 *Really the Blues,* p. 152. Four sides were made that day [i.e., a day in 1927]: *Nobody's Sweetheart, China Boy, Sugar,* and *Lisa* . . . And before the critics were through yelling their praises a new term was born—"Chicago style." — 1947 *The Two Worlds of Johnny Truro,* p. 24. They listened to Chicago. — 1956 *Guide to Jazz.* s.v. *Chicago style:* a slight departure from New Orleans style, predominating jazz during the 1920's, marked by the substitution of a tenor saxophone for a trombone in the melody ensembles and by the distinctive individual styles of its performers. — 1958 *Hi Fi & Music Review,* Aug., p. 35. There was a "Chicago style" loosely ascribed to young white musicians of the Midwest whose playing had been shaped by listening to New Orleans musicians.

chick, *n.* [cf. general slang term *chicken:* 1925 *English Words & Their Background,* p. 58. "*chicken:* girl"; also cf. 1961 *N.Y. Herald Tribune,* 12 Oct., p. 36. "Girls were known in those days [1917] as chicks"; current among jazzmen since c. 1930; see also BROAD.] See last quot. — 1937 *N.Y. Amsterdam News,* 11 Dec., p. 20. Chicks run out without a final accounting. — 1958 *American Speech,* Oct., p. 224. The cat . . . having eyes to make

the scene [i.e., wanting to go somewhere] with his chick
. . . dons his front [i.e., puts on his suit]. — 1959 *The
Holy Barbarians*, p. 20. "A chick with free-wheeling hips
and no cover charge." — 1959 *Swinging Syllables*. s.v.
chick: girl, woman, female.

chinchy, *adj.* [poss. a portmanteau word (slightly varied):
cheap + stingy; cf. 1934 *A Dictionary of American Slang*,
p. 319. "*Chinchy*: stingy"; some general slang use but
with esp. currency among jazzmen c. 1930–c. 1945, very
rare since] Stingy. — 1952 *Music Out of Dixie*, p. 71.
"I aims for the piano player to stay on the stool an' earn
his pay. Same time, I don't aim to be chinchy." — 1961
The Sound, p. 216. "What in the *world* would these
important big-time musicians want to hang around a
chinchy old uptown joint like this for?"

chirp, *n.* [by analogy (with a bird) and metonymy (with
its sound): see also CANARY; some currency since c.
1935] See quots. — 1944 *The New Cab Calloway's
Hepsters Dictionary*. s.v. *chirp*: female singer. — 1945
Hepcats Jive Talk Dictionary. s.v. *chirp*: female vocalist.

choice, *adj.* [some teen-age and general slang use, but with
esp. currency among jazzmen c. 1947–c. 1952, obs. since
except historical] Excellent. — 1958 *American Speech*,
Oct., p. 225. Among nonhipsters, the most widespread
of all hip expressions are those expressing warm approval: choice . . .

chops, *n. pl.* [dialectal English term given special application by jazzmen: cf. 1959 *Webster's New World Dictionary* s.v. *chap* "ME. *chaft*; ON. *kjaptr*, 1. a jaw. 2. a
cheek: also *chop*"; current among jazzmen since c.
1925; see also IRON CHOPS] Initially, see 1959 quot.; also,
by extension, the use a musician makes of his embouchure—i.e., his technique (see 1962 quot.). — 1939
Jazzmen, p. 141. Louis . . . daubs away with his hand-
kerchief and silently fingers the valves, while "getting

his chops set." — 1947 *Metronome*, Jan., p. 32. He might not have the chops he used to have, but his ideas are always fine. — 1954 *Satchmo*, pp. 178–179. "Every time you get mad at me the first thing you do is to try your damnedest to hit me in the chops." — 1958 *Down Beat*, 24 July, p. 14. "While it lasted, it helped musicians who weren't working because they could keep up their chops." — 1959 *Swinging Syllables*. s.v. *chops:* a musician's lips. — 1962 *Down Beat*, 27 Sep., p. 41. He's got a lotta chops, but he played way too long.

iron chops, [formed from noun above; according to jazzmen, phrase was coined by Louis Armstrong c. 1925, but it did not gain wide currency until c. 1935; still current; see also FREAK LIP] An inordinate capacity on the part of a trumpeter or a trombonist to play in the upper register and/or for long periods. — 1961 *The Village Voice*, 16 Feb., p. 13. He acknowledged playing a good deal with "Little Jazz" and credited him with having "iron chops."

chorus, *n.* [standard music term used by jazzmen in an altered sense; widely current since c. 1935] One or more thirty-two-bar (in a blues, q.v., twelve-bar) choruses played by an instrumentalist, usually with rhythmic support. — 1936 *Hot Jazz: The Guide to Swing Music*, p. 17. Tunes used in jazz generally comprise a "chorus" and a "verse," like many folk songs. Most often hot musicians use only the chorus. Hence the expression, "to take a chorus," meaning that a musician is to do a solo on the tune. — 1961 *The Jazz Review*, Jan., p. 17. Budd and Gene Ammons take the choruses on *Blowin' the Blues Away.* — 1963 *Down Beat*, 3 Jan., p. 13. Cooper got off an electrifying chorus.

-City, *suffix* [humorous superlative; according to jazzmen, first used by either Lester Young or Emmett Berry c. 1938, but has been widely current only since c. 1947] An intensifying suffix or word signifying the quintessential state of whatever precedes it: see quot. — 1960 *Hip-arama of the Classics*, p. 16. With that wild incense flyin' all over the place and that Buddha-headed moon pale Jazzmin colored flippin' the scene. It was Romance City.

clam, *n.* [poss. partly from being alliterative with its older synonym *clinker*, q.v.; more prob. shortened form of the derogatory sense of *clambake*, q.v.; current since c. 1950; see also GOOF] A misplayed note; also, for a rare verb use, see 1961 quot. — 1955 *Down Beat*, 30 Nov., p. 47. I'd say that was a band that doesn't work together regularly . . . because there were a few clams in the ensemble. — 1961 *Down Beat*, 2 Feb., p. 30. Hubbard sounds positively uncomfortable and clams in royal style at the beginning.

clambake, *n.* [by analogy with the standard sense; current c. 1930–c. 1938 in an approbative or a neutral sense, but increasingly since c. 1938 in a pejorative sense] See 1952 and first 1955 quots. — 1937 *American Speech*, Feb., p. 46. *clambake:* same as *jam session* [q.v.]. — 1938 *Cab Calloway: Hi De Ho*, p. 16. *clambake:* ad lib session, every man for himself, a jam session not in the groove. — 1949 *Music Library Association Notes*, Dec., p. 41. *clambake:* gathering of hot musicians. Also used in a derogatory sense to mean an affair that does not come off well. — 1952 *A History of Jazz in America*, p. 350. *clambake:* earlier used synonymously (and honorifically) with "jam session," later descriptive of an improvised or arranged session which doesn't come off. — 1955 *The Encyclopedia of Jazz*, p. 346. *clambake:* Originally, a jam session; currently, an unsuccessful, disorganized session. — 1955 *Hear Me Talkin to Ya*, p. 265. Everybody got kind of half-high and it ended up in a clambake.

clary, clarry, *n.* [shortened form; some currency among white jazzmen and esp. jazz writers since c. 1935] See 1942 quot. — 1942 *American Thesaurus of Slang*, p. 558.

clarry: clarinet. — 1948 *Down Beat,* 19 May, p. 13.
Pastry, by guitarist Kessel, allots two choruses to clary.
—1952 *Music Out of Dixie,* p. 187. "My clary was in
that mess."

clean, *adj.* 1. [from underworld slang: cf. 1930 *American
Tramp and Underworld Slang,* s.v. *clean:* "out of funds;
penniless"; current among jazzmen since c. 1925] See
quot. — 1960 *The Jazz Titans,* p. 152. *clean:* free from
money.

2. [by analogy with sense 1; from narcotics slang; current among jazzmen since c. 1930] See 1960 quot. —
1952 *Flee the Angry Strangers,* p. 262. She knew where
she had to go to get clean. — 1958 *Somewhere There's
Music,* p. 194. He was *clean,* in the dictionary sense and
the hipster sense. — 1960 *The Jazz Titans,* p. 152. *clean:*
not to have any narcotics on one's person or free from the
habit.

3. [current since c. 1930] Technically precise. —
1934 *Metronome,* June, p. 22. An outstandingly clean outfit with pretty tones. — 1955 *Down Beat,* 7 Sep., p. 29,
O.P. is my boy; bass or cello, he's very clean, and he
swings. — 21 Sep., p. 33. I never heard anybody play in a
higher register like that. So clean. — 1961 *Down Beat,* 13
April, p. 23. Some of Horace Silver's things sound professional to me — clean.

the scene is clean, See s.v. SCENE.

clinker, *n.* [onomatopoeic; current c. 1930–c. 1950, then
largely replaced by *clam* and *goof*] See 1958 quot.;
also, for a rare verb use, see 1948 quot.; also, by extension: any mistake (see 1961 quot.) — 1937 *Metronome,* Jan., p. 25. "Hey, you dope, watch them there
clinkers." — 1940 *Esquire,* May, p. 202. In the Crosby
band "clinkers" fall on deaf ears. — 1948 *Down Beat,*
14 July, p. 14. Though he clinkers several times on the
first slow chorus he gets off a good one. — 1958 *Publication of the American Dialect Society,* Nov., p. 44.

clinker: a missed note, or other error in playing. Largely replaced by *goof.* — 1961 *Metronome,* Feb., p. 20. This ingenuous belief that Louis Armstrong can smile away the egregious clinkers in our foreign policy is akin to having Frank Sinatra do a policy paper on Algeria.

cloud (followed by a number), *n.* [poss. by analogy with transcendent superlatives: e.g., *out of this world, far out way out;* some currency since c. 1950] See last quot. — 1956 *Sideman,* p. 120. "Oh, she's off on Cloud Seven—doesn't even know we exist." — 1959 *Down Beat,* 14 May, p. 20. "I don't like strange music, I'm not on Cloud Nine." — 1959 *Swinging Syllables,* p. 6. *Cloud Nine:* Heaven, to fly, complete contentment.

clown, *n.* [cf. its general colloquial meaning (i.e., foolish person); poss. its extension to all people reflects the jazzman's skepticism regarding humanity; current in the earlier sense since c. 1940, in the latter sense since c. 1950] As in general slang: a foolish or an ineffectual person; but also, any person (hearer must judge connotation from the context). — 1953 *Night Light,* p. 135. "Most clowns you meet are real square." — 1959 *Blow Up a Storm,* p. 71. "This clown's higher than a kite," he said. — 1959 *Diggeth Thou?,* p. 10. "Let's jive this clown into runnin' 'em around."

coast, *v.i.* [extension of standard sense; some currency since c. 1930] To play music uninspiredly: see 1936 quot. — 1936 *Stage,* March, p. 58. *coasting:* just playing notes, not socking it. — 1961 *Down Beat,* 16 Feb., p. 38. But he seems to be coasting most of the time. — 1961 *The Jazz Life,* p. 23. The man who coasts too long may retain the admiration of the critics long after he's lost the respect of other musicians.

collar the jive (or **swing**), [underworld slang *collar* (i.e., to grab) and jazz slang *jive* or *swing;* current c. 1935–c. 1945, obs. since except historical] See 1960 quot. —

1938 *Cab Calloway: Hi De Ho*, p. 16. "Do you collar this jive?" — 1946 *Big Book of Swing*, p. 124. *collar the swing:* understand swing and swing terms. — 1947 *Jive and Slang*. s.v. *collar the jive?:* understand? — 1960 *Dictionary of American Slang*. s.v. *collar the jive:* to understand and feel rapport with what is being said; to be in the know; to be hip. c. 1935 jive term.

combo, *n*. [cf. 1931 *American Speech*, Dec., "Underworld Argot," p. 107. "*combo:* combination of a safe": from the common linguistic practice of reducing a polysyllabic word to its first syllable and adding *o;* widely current in its jazz sense since c. 1935] See 1957 quot. — 1935 *Metronome*, May, p. 28. As a soft fiddle-sax combo, it clicks. — 1942 *The American Thesaurus of Slang*, p. 556. *combo:* orchestra, band. — 1949 *Music Library Association Notes*, Dec., p. 41. *Combo:* abbrev. of "combination." Refers generally to an instrumental group usually smaller than a band. — 1955 *Atlantic Monthly*, July, p. 54. The "combo," as it is called, becomes almost a term of affection. — 1956 *It's Always Four O'Clock*, pp. 106–107. I was playing with an ordinary little combo. — 1957 *The Book of Jazz*, p. 159. The term "combo," in common use for the past twenty years among jazz musicians, is usually employed to distinguish between the small group, ranging generally from trio to octet size, and the full orchestra.

come down, 1. [from narcotics slang: to reduce in spirit from a "high"; current among jazzmen since c. 1935; see also COME OFF] To sober up from the effects of narcotics or liquor. — 1959 *The Holy Barbarians*, p. 21. "But between fixes, coming down, he was one of the best sex partners I ever had."

2. [by analogy with sense 1; current among jazzmen c. 1940–c. 1950, then largely replaced by *cool it*] To stop behaving irresponsibly—i.e., as if one were "high."

— 1953 *Night Light*, p. 144. "Why don't you come down, man?" — 1959 *Music '59*, p. 80. "Come down, man," Billy said.

come off, [prob. from narcotics slang; current among jazz-men since c. 1935] To rid (oneself) of the effects of (a stimulant). — 1952 *Flee the Angry Strangers*, p. 314. But an easy charge [i.e., marijuana] to come off of.

come on, 1. [extension of standard sense (i.e., to come on stage in order to begin performing); widely current since c. 1930] To perform music, but invariably either given emphasis (indicating approval) or modified approvingly or disapprovingly (see last two quots.) — 1939 *Metronome*, April, p. 51. Bauduc . . . really comes on with some very fly and superb drumming. — 1958 *The Subterraneans*, p. 6. We hear a new young tenor-man come on. — 1958 *American Speech*, Oct., p. 225. The cat who blows well . . . is said to . . . *come on.* — 1958 *Publication of the American Dialect Society*, Nov., p. 44. *come on:* strictly, to begin a chorus, but almost always used with an approving or disparaging phrase.

2. [extension of sense 1; current since c. 1935] See 1953 quot. — 1953 *Junkie*, p. 12. *come on:* the way someone acts, his general manner and way of approaching others. — 1956 *Sideman*, p. 39. "He's a good guy . . . just comes on weird sometimes." — 1959 *The Horn*, p. 49. "I'll come on square, I'll hustle strangers, I'll hit everybody I can think of."

come on like gang busters, [variant of *come on*, sense 2; currency roughly contemporaneous with vogue of radio program *Gang Busters*, c. 1937–c. 1945, obs. since except historical] See 1944 quot. — 1942 *American Mercury*, July, p. 89. "Man, I come on like the Gang Busters." — 1944 *The New Cab Calloway's Hepsters Dictionary*. s.v. *comes on like gang busters:* playing, singing or dancing in a terrific manner. — 1952 *Flee* *the Angry Strangers*, p. 296. "Nothing can hold me down. 'Cause I'm like Gangbusters. Watch me come on."

come on strong, [variant of *come on*, sense 2; widely current since c. 1950]   To behave admirably. — 1956 *Intro Bulletin*, May, p. 5. "These cats come on so strong," a musician . . . says. — 1960 *Hiparama of the Classics*, p. 11. Now you see the Naz is comin' on so strong. — 1961 *The Sound*, p. 270. "Now let's us go see how strong this Frenchmans is gonna come on."

come on weak, [variant of *come on*, sense 2; widely current since c. 1950]   To behave reprehensibly. Oral evidence only.

come on with the come on, [nonsense phrase; current from c. 1940–c. 1944, obs. since]   An intensified approving form of *come on*, q.v. — 1942 *Jazz*, Sep., p. 26. Comin' On With the Come On (headline).

commercial, *adj.* [from jazzman's feeling that financial success and art are usually antithetical; current since c. 1925]   See 1952 quot. — 1926 *Melody Maker*, Aug., p. 35. *commercial orchestration:* one arranged for sale by the music publisher and in such a manner that it can be played by all and sundry combinations. — 1936 *Metronome*, Feb., p. 21. *commercial:* appreciated corn [jazz sense]. — 1952 *A History of Jazz in America*, p. 350. *commercial:* music or musicianship designed solely to garner money and/or fame; usually inflected with great scorn. — 1954 *Américas*, Aug., p. 31. Waller is criticized by some ultra-ultras as leaning toward the "slick" and "commercial"—two of the dirtiest words in the vocabulary of jazz.

comp, *v.i. & v.t.* [shortened form of *accompany*, poss. reinforced by *complement;* current since c. 1940]   See 1957 quot. — 1955 *Hear Me Talkin to Ya*, p. 305. Count is also just about the best piano player . . . for comping soloists. — 1956 *Enjoyment of Jazz* (EJ402), [p. 3]. Basie "comps" chords on the piano here and there. — 1957

The Book of Jazz, p. 119. The pianist and guitarist may "comp" (fill in with rhythmic punctuations and syncopation). — 1961 *Down Beat,* 5 Jan., p. 20. "You have to modify your playing with him, especially when he's comping."

con, *v.t.* [from underworld slang: orig. abbreviation of *confidence man;* also poss. reinforced by *convince;* general slang but with esp. currency among jazzmen since c. 1925] To persuade effectively; convince: see 1950 quot.; also, for a rare *v.i.* use, see 1961 quot. — 1950 *Lingo of Tin-Pan Alley.* s.v. *con:* used . . . with reference to the technique of persuasion and promotion. —1956 *Sideman,* p. 48. "Jimmy conned him into keeping him on." — 1959 *The Horn,* p. 113. For all their hipness . . . they did not notice he was conning them. — 1961 *The Sound,* p. 206. "She's seen the seamiest side of life, taken her lumps, starved, lied, stolen, conned."

connection, *n.* [from narcotics slang; some currency among jazzmen since c. 1925] See 1959 quot. — 1946 *Really the Blues,* p. 238. My friends began pestering me again about a hop connection. — 1957 *On the Road,* p. 88. The connection came in and . . . said, "Pick up, man, pick up." — 1959 *The Holy Barbarians,* p. 315. *connection:* contact man for drugs.

cook, *v.i.* [by analogy with *heat;* also cf. general slang *What's cooking?* (i.e., What's happening?), *cooking with gas* (i.e., doing something well); term had some currency, esp. among Negro jazzmen, c. 1930–c. 1940, disappeared largely from oral vocabulary c. 1940–c. 1950, reappeared c. 1950, widely current since; see also WAIL, SMOKE] See 1955 quot. — 1955 *The Encyclopedia of Jazz,* p. 346. *cook:* to play with rhythmic inspiration. — 1956 *Down Beat,* 31 Oct., p. 17. "Big Nick Nicholas had the band there . . . and it always came up cooking." — 1959 *Jazz: A Quarterly of American Music,* Spring, p. 166. We had to be playing at our absolute best, really "cooking," to reach the audience. — 1960 *The Stan Getz Quartet: The Steamer* (liner notes on LP album Verve MG V8294). Oscar Peterson . . . remarked to Granz, "My, the Stanley Steamer is certainly cooking tonight." ("cooking" is jazz jargon for someone playing exceedingly well and in a good groove at a given time.) — 1961 *The Sound,* p. 244. "Yes, yes, we gonna cook."

cook him out, [current since c. 1955; see also CARVE, CUT] To best him musically (frequently hortatory). Oral evidence only.

cook on 'em, [current since c. 1955] To play music exceedingly well (frequently hortatory). Oral evidence only.

cooker, *n.* [from *cook, v.i.;* some currency since c. 1950; see also the more common SWINGER] A musician who plays excitingly. — 1962 *Down Beat,* 13 Sep., p. 28. A hard cooker in the bop or post-bop groove he is not — he has his own slick style and stays with it. — 1963 *Down Beat,* 3 Jan., p. 25. Despite Ira Gitler's earnest notes assuring us that Garland is really a cooker, this set seems to confirm that the pianist is at his best a very able ballad player. — p. 28. This is not the hard-hitting tenor of Stitt the cooker.

cool, *adj. & interj.* [cf. earlier general colloquial *keep a cool head,* Negro slang *keep cool, fool;* term is linguistic parallel of the new post-World War II musical temper (more relaxed, cerebral, sophisticated): see first 1950 and second 1958 quots.; widely current since c. 1947; see also COOL JAZZ, UNCOOL] In addition to the several meanings in the 1948, 1952, 1955, the second 1958, and the five 1959 *Esquire* quots., this most protean of jazz slang terms also means, among other things: convenient (see third 1958 quot.), off dope (see 1956 quot.), on dope, comfortable, respectable, perceptive, shrewd—virtually anything favorably regarded by the speaker. — 1948 *New Yorker,* 3 July, p. 28. The bebop people have a language of their own . . . their expressions of approval include "cool!" — 1948 *Down Beat,* 28 July, p. 4. *cool:* some entity which, in colloquial terms, "gasses" q.v. the witness . . . an adjective describing something which impresses visibly the speaker. — 1950 *Harper's Magazine,* April, p. 93. Another reversal of the usual jazz procedure, parallelled by the Bop musician's use of "cool" instead of "hot" as a word of the highest praise, is the tendency while taking a solo to lag tantalizingly a fraction of a second behind the beat. — 1950 *Flair,* May, p. 28. Coolness . . . the word has moved into the special language of the jazz world. — 1952 *A History of Jazz in America,* p. 350. *cool:* superlative, usually reserved for sizable achievement within a frame of restraint. — 1955 *The Encyclopedia of Jazz,* p. 346. *cool:* restrained, relaxed. "Cool" is also used as an interjection meaning "fine" or "okay." — 1956 *Second Ending,* p. 215. "You don't show signs of a man who's been cool a week." — 1958 *After Hours Poetry,* p. 67. This joint is run by two ex-convicts/And a dope head./They're "cool people." — 1958 *Publication of the American Dialect Society,* Nov., p. 44. *cool:* agreeing with the generally received aesthetic standards of the modern jazzman. — 1958 *Somewhere There's Music,* p. 38. "Be cool for me too, I could ride up with you, help on the gas." — 1959 *Esquire,* Nov., p. 70H, "Do you want to go to the movies?" "It's cool with me (acquiescence)." — *Ibid.* "Do you have enough money?" "I'm cool (in good financial condition)." — *Ibid.* "Then you must be feeling lean and strong?" "I'm cool (in good shape)." — *Ibid.* "All right, let's go." "Cool." — *Ibid.* "I am moved to censure X strongly for stealing my financee." "Be cool, man." — 1959 *Jazz: A Quarterly of American Music,* Fall, p. 289. I'd like to make enough money to be cool.

cool it, [widely current since c. 1950] See both 1959 quots. — 1953 *The Hot and the Cool,* p. 13. Cool it, girl.

Nobody's interested. — 1956 *Sideman*, p. 146. "Just cool it," he told her. — 1959 *Newport Jazz Festival: 1959*, p. 45. *cool it:* to stop something, to relax, to take it easy. — 1959 *Esquire*, Nov., p. 70H. In stopping a fight or cautioning a person against losing his temper or the approach of a policeman, one can also say: "Cool it." — 1961 *Down Beat*, 5 Jan., p. 20. "Some guys say, 'Why don't you cool it the first set—take it easy?' . . . "

cool on, [current since c. 1958; see also COOL (ONE) OUT] See quots. — 1959 *Esquire*, Nov., p. 70H, "Shall I call on X and take him with us?" "I'm cooling on him (ignoring a person or subtly snubbing him)." — 1960 *The Jazz Titans*, p. 153. *cool on:* to ignore or snub (someone).

cool (one) out, [current since c. 1958; see also COOL ON] To restrain or calm (usually musically) a tendency toward overenthusiasm; by extension, to ignore, rebuke, or break off relations with (someone): in this sense, oral evidence only. — 1961 *Metronome*, Dec., p. 32. In fact, I'm of the opinion that when he is cooled out just slightly, as he is on this date, he is even a fine musician. — 1963 *Down Beat*, 20 June, p. 21. "When I had that problem with my hands in 1960, well, it was pretty frightening, even to me. Fortunately I found a doctor who could cool me out."

cooling, *adj.* [cf. underworld and general slang *cooling (one's) heels* (i.e., relaxing); note also that term is appropriately antonymous to standard term *sweating;* current since c. 1935] See quots. — 1938 *Cab Calloway: Hi De Ho*, p. 16. *cooling:* laying off between engagements, not working. — 1959 *Esquire*, Nov., p. 70H, "But aren't you supposed to play with that orchestra you have been rehearsing with?" "I'm cooling tonight (I'm refraining from playing.)." — 1960 *The Jazz Titans*, p. 153. *cooling:* unemployed.

cool jazz (or **sound**), [adapted as a generic term for a style of playing because it suggests the unemotional and unexcitable qualities which characterize that musical style; widely current since c. 1948, though the popularity of the style has waned since c. 1957; see also *West Coast jazz*] The most popular jazz style c. 1950–c. 1957, characterized by restraint, intellectuality, and a studied relaxation; its popularity has waned markedly (see first 1961 quot.) with the *cognoscenti,* though its practitioners remain legion, esp. on the West Coast. — 1949 *Inside Be-Bop,* p. 5. Lester was a radical in that he symbolized the gradual evolution from hot jazz to "cool" jazz. — 1950 *Harper's Magazine,* April, p. 93. Another reversal of the usual jazz procedure, parallelled by the Bop musician's use of "cool" instead of "hot" as a word of the highest praise, is the tendency while taking a solo to lag tantalizingly a fraction of a second behind the beat. — 1952 *A History of Jazz in America,* p. 350. *cool:* for some, synonymous with modern jazz. — 1955 *Cool Jazz From Holland* (LP album Epic LN-1126). — 1956 *Enjoyment of Jazz* (EJ410), p. 3. That was the first time [i.e., 1947] an entire section had affected the "cool" sound that was to become *the* sound of the '50's. — 1961 *Metronome,* April, p. 13. The lid was put on "cool" by hard bop. There was a search for a sound, for a *soul* sound that brought back the "group" feeling, perhaps inspired by gospel music and some aspects of rock and roll. — 1961 *The Antioch Review,* Spring, p. 58. "The temporary decline in 'cool' jazz in the early 1950's led to considerable unemployment."

cootie crawl, [cf. 1959 *Webster's New World Dictionary,* s.v. *cootie:* "Polynesian *kutu,* parasitic insect . . . (Slang), a louse"; dance designations frequently refer to animal movements: cf. BUNNY HUG, CAMEL WALK, FOX TROT; current c. 1916–c. 1920, obs. since except historical] A jazz dance popular c. 1916–c. 1926. — 1934 *Beale Street: Where the Blues Began,* p. 105. In the golden days of 1912 . . . brown beauties . . . danced the Pasamala, long before the "cootie crawl," "black bottom" and "snake hips" were thought of.

cop, *v.i.* [special application of *cop, v.t.;* some currency since c. 1945] See 1958 quot. — 1958 *Jive in Hi-Fi,* p. 25. *cop:* to get something. — 1961 *Metronome,* Dec., p. 31. All in all, this is a good record and you really ought to cop.

v.t. [cf. 1933 OED, s.v. *cop:* "*north. dialect* and *slang* (Perhaps a broad pronunciation of *cap*) . . . To capture, lay hold of": first citation is dated 1704; special applications by jazzmen widely current since c. 1935] Initially: see second 1938 quot.; latterly (as jazzmen made the term one of the more flexible and comprehensive in jazz slang): see 1958, 1959 quots. — 1938 *Metronome,* Feb., p. 24. Much swing, too, in *Harlem,* with Hodges and Williams' plunger copping most glory. — 1938 *Cab Calloway: Hi De Ho,* p. 16. *cop:* to get, to obtain. — 1952 *Flee the Angry Strangers,* p. 317. He tells me cop a walk. — 1953 *The Hot and the Cool,* p. 48. "Where the hell do you get off blowing in here, copping a job some poor canary could use? — 1956 *It's Always Four O'Clock,* p. 4. Royal and I copped Walt's car and drove down to Castle Rock. — 1958 *The Book of Negro Folklore,* p. 482. *cop:* to take, receive, understand, do. — 1959 *Newport Jazz Festival: 1959,* p. 45. *cop:* to buy, take, borrow, indulge in, or steal.

cop a nod, [jazz slang *cop* + jazz slang *nod;* some currency since c. 1940; see also the more recent *cop z's*] See quots. — 1958 *Jive in Hi-Fi,* p. 15. *to cop a nod:* to sleep. — 1961 *N.Y. Times Magazine,* 25 June, p. 39. *copping a nod:* taking a nap.

cop a plea, [from underworld slang: cf. 1950 *Dictionary of American Underworld Lingo,* s.v. *cop a plea:* "to apologize; to ask mercy"; current c. 1935–c. 1950, then largely replaced by *cop out,* q.v.] To excuse oneself, usually evasively. — 1958 *Jive in Hi-Fi,* p. 25. *to cop a* *plea:* to ask someone to listen to your story [i.e., excuse or plea]. — 1959 *The Holy Barbarians,* p. 315. *cop out:* to settle down, go conventional, in the sense of "sell out" or "cop a plea."

cop out, [from *cop a plea,* which it supplanted c. 1950] See 1955, 1959 quots. (note that the meanings are allied in that going to sleep is the supreme form of excusing oneself from company). —1955 *The Encyclopedia of Jazz,* p. 346. *cop out:* go to sleep. — 1958 *The Subterraneans,* p. 90. So I cop out, from the lot, from life, all of it, go to sleep. — 1959 *Esquire,* Nov., p. 70I. *cop out:* go to sleep. Evasiveness. Excuse. — 1960 *Down Beat,* 13 Oct., p. 6. Ralph Gleason's review of the new Ornette Coleman album (*Down Beat,* Aug. 18) was one of the grossest examples of ambiguity, copping out, padded writing and incompetency that I have ever read.

cop z's, [jazz slang *cop* + comic-strip representation of sleep; some currency since c. 1955; see also earlier COP A NOD] See first quot. — 1961 *N.Y. Times Magazine,* 25 June, p. 39. *coppin' zzzz:* taking a nap. Variant: "copping a nod." — 1963 *Hiptionary* p. 18. Nobody cops zzzz es here.

cop-out, *n.* [from phrase *cop out;* current since c. 1955] An evasion; an alibi. — 1963 *Down Beat,* 4 July, p. 30. The liner notes state, "There is much controversy as to who the sidemen were. . . ." This seems like a cop-out.

corn, *n.* [see note s.v. *corny;* some currency among white jazzmen and jazz writers c. 1930–c. 1945, very rare since] Anything, but esp. jazz, that is either dated or badly conceived: see both 1936 quots. — 1936 *Metronome,* Feb., p. 21. *corn:* rooting-tootin' 1921 vintage. — 1936 *Stage,* March, p. 58. *corn:* fake hot jazz. — 1946 *Really the Blues,* p. 32. I thought George was going to knock out some of the usual corn.

corny, *adj.* [see 1944, 1958 quots. for semantic development; also cf. 1960 *Dictionary of American Slang,* s.v. *corny:* "orig. pejorative use by musicians and theatrical folk"; some earlier general slang use, but widely current esp. among white jazzmen and jazz writers c. 1930–c. 1945, very rare since; see also TICKY] See 1952 quot. — 1932 *Melody Maker,* June, p. 511. The "bounce" of the brass section . . . has degenerated into a definitely "corny" and staccato style of playing. — 1933 *Fortune,* Aug., p. 47. *Corny* is the jazz musician's term for what is old-fashioned. — 1937 *New Yorker,* 17 April, p. 31. Dance musicians are known as *cats* and those not up on the current idioms are *corny.* — 1944 *Esquire's 1944 Jazz Book,* p. 53. To define it succinctly, corny (derived from "cornfed") means out-of-date, rustic, old fashioned. — 1952 *A History of Jazz in America,* p. 350. *corny:* stale, insipid, trite, usually the worse for age. — 1958 *Publication of the American Dialect Society,* Nov., p. 44. *corny:* non-jazz, extremely commercial music. Origin doubtful, but since it often is expanded to "corn-fed" and "corn-ball" (or may actually have been a clipped form of one of these words), I think it once meant "country" music: polkas, square dance music, etc.

corona, *n.* [etym. obscure; according to jazzman Eubie Blake, term current c. 1900–c. 1910, obs. since; see also BIRDIE] An impromptu grace note. Oral evidence only.

crack up, [by analogy with jazz slang *break up,* q.v.; some currency since c. 1950] To convulse (someone) with laughter. — 1960 *Beat Jokes Bop Humor & Cool Cartoons,* p. 56. "Where's all your hip talk, man; those way-out things you did that cracked up the house?"

crazy, *adj. & interj.* [explanation of semantic development in 1958 quot. is essentially correct, though it is doubtful that the term's creation was a reaction to criticism; more prob., since jazzmen, like most creators, greatly admire the imaginative, they are here anticipating the hostile characterization (see, for example 1939 quot., which is pre-bop); despite 1939 quot., an accidental use, widely current only c. 1945–c. 1955, rare since; see also INSANE, NUTTY] Excellent: see 1952 quot. — 1939 *Jazzmen*, p. 59. Bunk Johnson was "puffing on his cornet" in a way that made everyone "real crazy." — 1948 *Down Beat*, 28 July, p. 4. *real crazy:* a visible impression, usually meant to imply that the musician so described is playing fairly well, often even excellently. — 1948 *Metronome*, Sep., p. 16. They ain't the craziest chords, man! — 1952 *A History of Jazz in America*, pp. 350–351. *crazy:* superlative of the late forties, synonymous with "gone," "the end." — 1958 *Publication of the American Dialect Society*, Nov., pp. 41–42. Likewise, the adverse criticisms of bop were taken over almost wholesale and made into favorable ones. Such terms as *crazy* . . . used to express favorable responses to music, are adaptations of terms levelled against the bop musicians. Since they knew the music which people called "crazy" was actually good, they took over the word in a good sense. — 1959 *The Holy Barbarians*, p. 22. "If a little mayonnaise dripped onto the paper you just rubbed it into the drawing with a deft thumb—crazy, man, crazy."

crib, *n.* [cf. 1933 OED, s.v. *crib:* "*Thieves' slang:* a dwelling-house, shop, public-house, etc.": first citation is dated 1812; some currency since c. 1940; see also the more common PAD] See last two quots. — 1955 *Babs Gonzales: Dem Jive N.Y. People* (song lyrics on LP album Crazy C-OOOl-B). But every morning he's at my crib to wash up. — 1958 *American Speech*, Oct., p. 224. The cat . . . *plays on down* to her . . . crib. — 1958 *Jive in Hi-Fi*, p. 15. *crib:* house, home, or room. — 1959 *Esquire*, Nov., p. 70I. *crib:* house, apartment.

Crow Jim, [reversal of the more common term by analogy with reversal of the more common discriminatory practice; some currency esp. among white jazzmen since c. 1957]   Racial discrimination by Negroes against whites, esp. in the jazz world. — 1961 *Commonweal*, 24 March, p. 658. It was during those years of the late 1950's that I heard several white jazzmen in New York wish dolefully that they had been born Negro. In part of jazz at least, Crow Jim reigned. — 1962 *Down Beat*, 29 March, p. 24. If it were true that Crow Jim did exist, there would be no white musicians in jazz.

crumbcrusher, *n.* [some currency among Negro jazzmen since c. 1935; see also CRUMBSNATCHER]   See 1959 quot. —1959 *Esquire*, Nov., p. 70I. *crumbcrusher:* baby. — 1963 *Hiptionary*, p. 78. It must split before we cack (i.e., die) and our crumbcrushers cack.

crumbs, *n. pl.* [by analogy with jazz slang *bread,* q.v.; current since c. 1955, though some humorous and accidental use prob. since c. 1935; see also phrase SMALL BREAD S.V. BREAD]   See 1957, 1959 quots. — 1957 *N.Y. Times Magazine*, 18 Aug., p. 26. *crumbs:* a small sum of money; also called small bread. — 1959 *Esquire*, Nov., p. 70I. *crumbs:* a small amount of money. Small bread (money). — 1961 *Metronome*, April, p. 1. And the rich foundations and civic organizations are still sustaining symphony orchestras and classical music and throwing crumbs to jazz.

light crumbs, [according to jazzmen, some currency since c. 1955; see also SMALL BREAD under BREAD]   Very little money. Oral evidence only.

crumbsnatcher, *n.* [some currency among Negro jazzmen since c. 1935; see also CRUMBCRUSHER]   See 1958, 1959 quots. — 1958 *Jive in Hi-Fi*, p. 27. *a crumb snatcher:* a baby. — 1959 *Esquire*, Nov., p. 70I. *crumbsnatcher:* child. — 1960 *Beat Jokes Bop Humor & Cool Cartoons*, p. 59. The broad's old man tried to sound him that his crumb snatcher was yet too young to indulge in the marriage action.

cut, *v.i.,* See s.v. CUT OUT.

 v.t. 1. [hyperbole: see first 1959 quot.; current since c. 1920; see also CARVE, CAP] See 1937, 1952 quots. — 1937 *American Speech,* Oct., p. 182. *cut:* musicians vie with one another to see who can blow the hotter lick. The winner is said to have "cut" the loser. — 1952 *A History of Jazz In America,* p. 351. *cut:* to best a soloist or band in competition. — 1959 *The Horn,* p. 17. He would do him the honor of "cutting" him to pieces, bar by bar, horn to horn. — p. 18. For "cutting" was, after all, only the Indian wrestling of lost boyhood summers, and the trick was getting your man off balance.

 2. [from recording process of cutting grooves into a record; current since c. 1930] See 1949 quot.; also noun (though see the more common TAKE, TRACK): see 1949 quot. — 1939 *Jazzmen,* p. 19. *High Society* became a test piece which forever afterwards all aspiring clarinetists had to "cut" before they could get a job. — 1949 *Music Library Association Notes,* Dec., p. 42. *cut:* recording term used as noun and verb. A recording artist *cuts* a master and the recording executive may reject the *cut.* — 1956 *Melody Maker,* 4 Aug., p. 3. In any case, I have always been willing to cut sides with any good musician. — 1959 *The Horn,* p. 66. "That tune swings, that's sorta cute . . . Maybe I'll cut that next time."

 cut it, [extension of jazz slang *cut,* sense 1 (in the sense of something *superlative*) and jazz slang *cut,* sense 2 (in the sense of a *successful* recording); some currency since c. 1960] Usually used of a piece of music, but also of any performance or experience, to succeed. Oral evidence only.

 cut out, [see 1958 quot. for poss. explanation of semantic development; widely current since c. 1940 (the shorter form *cut,* since c. 1945) and still some currency though largely replaced by *split,* q.v., c. 1950] See 1944, 1958 quots. — 1944 *The New Cab Calloway's Hep-*

sters Dictionary. s.v. *cut out:* to leave, to depart. — 1952 *A History of Jazz in America,* p. 351. *cut* or *cut out:* to leave, to depart. — 1955 *Solo,* p. 27. "I got to cut out." — 1958 *Publication of the American Dialect Society,* Nov., p. 45. *cut:* to leave. Usually to "cut out" (cut = leave out, leave). — 1959 *The Horn,* p. 85. "I'm gonna cut this time, Baby . . . Like all I need is bus fare." — 1959 *The Naked Lunch,* p. 117. "No, we do not want to buy any used condoms! Cut!"

cutoff, *n.* [some currency since c. 1935]   Literally, a cutting off of sound by the brass section (i.e., a stop) to create a desired effect. — 1961 *Down Beat,* 19 Jan., p. 41. This is especially noticeable in the dynamics, shakes, falloffs, and cutoffs of the brass section.

cutting (or **carving**) **contest,** [hyperbole: see *cut, v.t.,* 1; see 1959 quot. for beginning date; obs. since c. 1945 except historical; see also BATTLE]   See 1956 quot. — 1955 *Hear Me Talkin to Ya,* p. 24. They used to have "cutting contests" every time you'd get on the streets. — 1956 *Guide to Jazz,* p. 73. *cutting contest:* a form of musical competition joined in by bands or individual musicians, in which audience applause determines the winner. A popular competition in the 1930's, early '40's. — 1959 "A Compendium for the Teaching of Jazz History," p. 66. In the 1910s . . . a battle of bands known as a "carving" contest was on. — 1961 *The Jazz Life,* p. 34. "We used to call them cuttin' contests . . . Like you'd hear about a very good tenor in some night spot, and I'd have to go down there and cut him."

D

dad, *n.* [preceded in jazz slang by *daddy,* q.v.; also some general and student use: cf. 1955 *American Speech,* Dec., "Wayne University Slang," p. 303. "*dad:* good friend"; more common among jazzmen since c. 1945 than *pops, papa, daddy, daddio,* q.v., though not as common as *baby,* q.v.] Term of address to a male. — 1959 *The Horn,* p. 128. "Here, dad, have a brew while I get these boys set up." — 1961 *The Sound,* p. 10. "Never mind then, dad." — 1963 *Nugget,* Feb., p. 44. The public, that means you, dad, does not respond favorably.

dada mama, [onomatopoeic; some currency since c. 1920] A drum roll: see quot. — 1934 *Metronome,* Sep., p. 64. We must distinguish between three kinds of rolls of sustentation, (1) the double stroke ("dada mama"). . . .

daddy, *n.* [from Negro slang; also some general slang use, but with esp. currency among jazzmen c. 1920–c. 1940, rare since] A male lover; also, term of address to a male lover. — 1927 *Cheatin' Daddy* (song title listed in *Columbia 1927 Race Catalogue: The Latest Blues by Columbia Race Stars,* p. 9). — 1928 *The Walls of Jericho,* p. 298. *daddy:* provider of affection and other more tangible delights. — 1959 *Selected Poems,* p. 112. My old time daddy/Came back last night. — p. 148. Keep on a-lovin' me, daddy/Cause I don't want to be blue.

daddy-o, daddy-oh, daddio, daddy, *n.* 1. [some currency since c. 1940; cf. widespread general colloquial practice of affixing "o" to a term of address; see also the more common DAD, POPS, PAPS, BABY] See first quot. — 1948 *New Yorker,* 3 July, p. 28. The bebop people have a language of their own. They call each other Pops, Daddy, and Dick. — 1949 *Music Library Association Notes,* Dec., p. 42. *daddy-o:* friend, buddy. Originated with Negro musicians. — 1959 *Selected Poems,* p. 179. He wouldn't write so/Bad that way,/Daddy-o. — 1959 *The Horn,* p. 132. "But, daddio . . . it's true." — 1961 *The Sound,* p. 210. "Yes, daddy-oh?"

2. [also some general slang use, but with esp. currency among jazzmen since c. 1940] A profound musical influence or a musical progenitor; by extension, one who is a seminal influence in any art form or in any activity (see last quot.). — 1955 *Hear Me Talkin to Ya,* p. 290. Like that Ellis Burton was the daddy of us. — 1957 *Down Beat,* 17 Oct., p. 33. That was the daddy of them all—Charlie Christian! — 1962 *Jazz Monthly,* Oct., p. 9. Jazz has always had a "daddy-o"—the only man "who could really blow"— and Parker's occupancy of this role made his publicized drug-taking very important to many young musicians. — 1962 *Dinosaurs in the Morning,* p. 17. Black introduced Rexroth as a horse wrangler and the Daddy-O of the jazz-poetry movement.

dap, *adj.* [from Negro slang; shortened form of *dapper;* current since c. 1950; for other terms which evolve from words descriptive of clothing see BOOTED, HIP, SHARP] Nattily attired (i.e., dapper); also, by extension: alert, aware, perceptive, knowledgeable, sophisticated. — 1956 *Eddie Condon's Treasury of Jazz,* pp. 303–304. "You don't say hep any more," Hampton said. "It means aware, or sharp, but you don't say it, man. The word now is *dap.* You want somebody to know a man is sharp, is au reet, you say he's dap." — 1959 *Esquire,* Nov., p. 70I, *dap:*

dapper. Sharp is obsolete. — 1960 *Beat Jokes Bop Humor & Cool Cartoons,* p. 12. Looking confused, a stranger asks a dap one, "How do I get to Carnegie Hall?"

date, *n.* 1. [shortened form of *recording date* (i.e., an appointment for the purpose of recording music); current since c. 1920] See 1935, 1937 quots. — 1924 *Variety,* 24 Sep. [1962 *Jazz: A History of the New York Scene,* p. 150]. Out west they recorded for the Gennett disks, but although less than a week on Broadway, they have had "dates" with a number of minor companies. — 1935 *Vanity Fair,* Nov., p. 38. These small bands assemble quickly at the call of a phonograph company (termed a date), assume a name for their short existence, and disintegrate after the records have been made. — 1937 *American Speech,* Oct., p. 183. *date:* this is the appointment with the recording company to appear at a certain time to record. — 1948 *Trumpet on the Wing,* p. 45. When Tommy Rockwell blew into town looking for local talent to record for Okeh, we almost drove him crazy on our date. — 1960 *The Jazz Review,* May, p. 28. Blue Mitchell, a good trumpet player and soloist, is nominally the leader of this date.

2. [extension of sense 1; current since c. 1950; see also the older GIG] A night club or concert engagement for musicians (though night club engagements are sometimes distinguished from recording sessions by being called "club dates": see 1956 quot.). — 1955 *Solo,* p. 138. "How long is this date?" — 1956 *Sideman,* p. 275. "He's giving me tips on club dates." — 1961 *Down Beat,* 19 Jan., p. 40. One afternoon a group of us did a date at a New York City college.

3. (*preceded by a possessive*), [shortened form (i.e., signifies the one who, in a recording session, is designated as leader and, therefore, under whose name the record appears); current since c. 1955] See note above. — 1959 *Jazz: A Quarterly of American Music,* Fall,

p. 291. I did a thing with "Bags" before that was a "soul" session only it was his date.

day gig, See s.v. GIG.

deuce, *n.* 1. [prob. from gambling slang; cf. 1930 *American Tramp and Underworld Slang,* s.v. *deuce:* "a two dollar bill"; current esp. among Negro jazzmen since c. 1925] See first quot. — 1945 *Hepcats Jive Talk Dictionary.* s.v. *deuce:* two dollars. — 1948 *Trumpet on the Wing,* p. 90. We did what we could to help along the merriment by selling gin under the piano, at a deuce a throw. — 1956 *Second Ending,* p. 78. "There's a fat deuce for you, Charles."

2. [extension of sense 1; current since c. 1940] See first quot. — 1944 *Dan Burley's Original Handbook of Harlem Jive,* p. 137. *deuce:* two, a pair. — 1946 *Really the Blues,* p. 114. Well, she went on for years, being robbed by stinchy managers who would murder their own mothers for a deuce of blips [i.e., two nickels]. — 1960 *Beat Jokes Bop Humor & Cool Cartoons,* p. 56. "And here hung his deuce of slobbers [i.e., lips] that drove the broads out of their hair." — p. 55. No. I won't do the cat in; not on his deuce of benders [i.e., knees].

Dick, *n.* [One of several given names made generic; some currency since c. 1945; see also JACK, JIM] See quots. — 1948 *New Yorker,* 3 July, p. 28. The bebop people have a language of their own. They call each other Pops, Daddy, and Dick. — 1953 *American Thesaurus of Slang,* p. 545. *Dick:* term of address among "bebop" players.

dicty, dickty, *adj.* [etym. unknown; from Negro slang; current esp. among Negro jazzmen since c. 1925; see also HINCTY] High-class, high-toned (frequently derisive: see first 1928 and 1959 quots.); also, for a very rare noun use, see first 1928 quot. — 1926 *Nigger Heaven,* p. 285. *dicty:* swell, in the slang sense of the word. — 1928 *The Walls of Jericho,* p. 3. Despite the objections of the dickties, who prefer to ignore the existence of so-called rats, it is of interest to consider Henry Patmore's Pool Parlor on Fifth Avenue in New York. — p. 4. Fifth Avenue's shame lies in having missed these so-called dickty sections. — 1946 *Duke Ellington,* p. 94. *The Dicty Glide,* like its adjective, a "dicty" piece, very flashy, very sophisticatedly aware of all tricks of the times. — 1959 *The Horn,* p. 180. "You gonna be one dicty nigger, now ain't you?"

dig, *v.i. & v.t.* [see 1958 quot. for poss. explanation of semantic development; also cf. 1960 *Dictionary of American Slang,* s.v. *dig:* "to study a subject diligently. *Some student use since c. 1850";* also cf. 1925 *English Words & Their Background,* p. 67. "*dig up:* get"; introduced into jazz speech by Louis Armstrong c. 1925, but widely current only since c. 1935; see also PICK UP, PUT DOWN, MAKE] See 1938 and last 1959 quots.; also: to recognize; listen to; hear (which of its many meanings is intended must be inferred from the context). — 1938 *Cab Calloway: Hi De Ho,* p. 16. *dig:* meet. — 1939 *Jitterbug Jamboree Song Book,* p. 32. *dig:* look, meet, comprehend. — 1944 *Esquire,* Feb., p. 130. *dig:* understand. — 1944 *The New Cab Calloway's Hepsters Dictionary.* s.v. *dig:* (1) meet; (2) look, see; (3) comprehend, understand. — 1947 *Frontiers of Jazz,* p. x. I dig good jazz when I hear it. — 1952 *A History of Jazz in America,* p. 351. *dig:* to understand; often to penetrate a hidden meaning, hence used of the process of intellection of the jazz initiate ("he digs!"). — 1956 *It's Always Four O'Clock,* p. 43. Frank didn't dig him at all, and he asked Walter what we saw in him. — 1956 *Sideman,* p. 117. "Plant you now and dig you later." — 1956 *Chicago Review,* Autumn-Winter, p. 15. "Dig that jive," to which Louis Armstrong could probably still lend meaning, is a similar expression used *ad nauseum* even by the hotel orchestras of the period. — 1958 *Publication of the American Dialect Society,* Nov., p. 45. *dig:* . . . (Perhaps from a sense of "getting to the bottom" of things."). — 1959 *The Holy Barbarians*, p. 77. "Anyway, I really dug this chick and I didn't want to lose her." — p. 24. "I'm not modest either, dig?" — 1959 *Swinging Syllables*. s.v. *dig*: understand; also: look, see, enjoy, like.

dig the jive, See COLLAR THE JIVE; also see last 1956 quot. s.v. DIG.

dig the play, [jazz slang *dig* + jazz slang *the play*; current c. 1935–c. 1945, rare since] See quot. — 1940 *Current History*, 7 Nov., p. 22. *Do you dig the play?*: Do you understand me?

I don't dig the scene, [from jazz slang *dig* and jazz slang *scene*; some currency since c. 1955] I don't comprehend—the situation, the environment, the music— whatever it is that is occupying my attention. Oral evidence only.

dime note, [understatement (cf. CENTS); cf. 1934 *A Dictionary of American Slang*, p. 295. "*dime*: money in general"; current since c. 1935] See 1938, 1944 quots. — 1938 *Better English*, Nov., p. 51. *dime note*: $10. — 1944 *Dan Burley's Original Handbook of Harlem Jive*, p. 137. *dime note*: ten dollar bill. — 1961 *The Sound*, p. 45. "It cost mother a double dime-note only this morning."

Dip, the (Beale Street), [according to jazzmen, the dance was almost always referred to as simply *the Dip* (which suggests the dance's movement); current c. 1912–c. 1916, obs. since except historical] Jazz dance in vogue c. 1912–c. 1916 — 1942 *Beale Street Sundown*, p. 32. They wanted to make pictures of couples doing the Beale Street Dip.

dirt (music), [by analogy with its earthiness; current c. 1920–c. 1935, obs. since except historical] "Hot," earthy, driving (jazz), characteristic of the small jazz bands c. 1920–c. 1935. — 1926 *Melody Maker*, Jan., p. 31. The former is conspicuous for an excellent hat-muted trumpet solo and some real "dirt" on the fiddle

by that super-jazz artist, Hugo Rignold. — March, p. 39.
They are full of "dirt" and everything else that's good. —
1955 *Hear Me Talkin to Ya,* p. 37. He was a great man
for what we call "dirt music."

dirty, *adj.* [one of several standard terms the connotation of which jazzmen have reversed (i.e., from bad to
good): see also BAD, MEAN, TERRIBLE, TOUGH; current
c. 1920–c. 1945, very rare since] See 1936, first 1939,
and 1959 quots. — 1926 *Melody Maker,* May, p. 48.
Fine "hot" record, with a special "dirty" piano solo. —
1929 *Jacobs' Orchestra Monthly,* June, p. 6. It [i.e., jazz]
is "hot," "dirty," maybe, at times, a little blasphemous.
— 1936 *Hot Jazz: The Guide to Swing Music,* p. 89. His
tone almost always has a pronounced rasp, the effect of
which is magnificently "dirty." — 1939 *American Jazz
Music,* p. 45. And the term "dirty" is often applied to the
general tone of certain players who favor robust, somewhat rough tone production. — 1939 *Jazzmen,* pp. 12–13.
When the orchestra settled down to the slow blues, the
music was mean and dirty. — 1959 *The Jazz Scene,* p.
116. "dirty"—instrumentally unorthodox because emotionally expressive (the word was used as a synonym for
"hot" in the 1920s).

dirty dozens, the, See s.v. DOZENS.

district, the, [see 1955 quot. for semantic explanation;
widely current c. 1910–c. 1917 when it was the geographic center of jazz, obs. since except historical] The
Storyville (q.v.) sector of New Orleans, an important
locale in the early history of jazz. — 1948 *Trumpet on the
Wing,* p. 11. But I never played in "the district." — 1955
Hear Me Talkin to Ya, p. 4. I never heard it called
Storyville . . . It was always The District—the red light
district.

Dixieland, Dixie, *n.* [see 1939 quot. for explanation of semantic development; current since c. 1916; see also NEW
ORLEANS] See 1937, 1939, 1959 quots. — 1916 Original

Dixieland Jazz Band (name of famous jazz group, which
made its first restaurant appearance on January 19, 1917).
— 1917 advertising poster [1962 *Jazz: A History of the
New York Scene*, p. 58]. Due to the expense of bringing
The Original Dixie Land Jazz Band. We are forced to
Charge a small sum of 25¢ per Person during their
Stay Only. — 1937 *American Speech*, Feb., p. 47. When
the melody of a chorus is played by a combination
of trumpet, tenor saxophone, and clarinet, it is said
to be played *Dixie*. It is voiced peculiarly in that the lead
melody is carried lower than the clarinet, which carries
a third harmony usually an octave above its normal position in a chord and always above the lead. So called after
the style of playing of the *Original Dixieland Jazz Band*,
the first great dance orchestra. — 1939 *Jazzmen*, p. 39.
Many years before, a bank in New Orleans had issued a
ten-dollar bill with the word *dix* printed in large letters
on one side. From this, the words "Dixie" or "Dixieland"
meant New Orleans, long before the word was used as a
general name for the South. This designation, in its
original sense, gave a name to hot jazz played by New
Orleans musicians. Today, it is applied more specifically
to improvised hot music as played by small five or six-
piece orchestras. — 1955 *Hear Me Talkin to Ya*, p. 402.
One great thing about Dixie . . . is its use of counter-
point. — 1956 *Guide to Jazz*. s.v. *Dixieland:* synonymous
with New Orleans or Chicago, i.e. the jazz which flourished in the 1900–1935 (pre-Swing) period. — 1959 *Jazz:
A Quarterly of American Music*, Fall, p. 273. *Dixieland:*
. . . music involving the technical idiom established by
certain players and composers, especially in New Orleans, in the second decade of this century.

do it! (or that thing!, your stuff!), [current esp. among
Negro dancers to jazz c. 1920–c. 1935, rare since]   Cries
of encouragement to either jazz musicians or dancers. —
1926 *Nigger Heaven*, p. 10. Do that thing. — 1928 *The*

Walls of Jericho, p. 299. *Do it! Do that thing! Do your stuff!:* shouts of encouragement.

dog, *n.* [prob. from Negro slang; some currency esp. among Negro jazzmen since c. 1925; for other terms in which the connotation can be either good or bad, see LOOSE, SOMETHING ELSE, WIG, WEIRD] See 1928 quot. (note, however, that the term has increasingly been used in a pejorative sense) — 1928 *The Walls of Jericho,* p. 299. *dog:* any extraordinary person, thing, or event. "Ain't this a dog?" is a comment on anything unusual. — 1961 *Swank,* July, p. 72. The *ABC* [album] is a dog, the *Impulse!* a mild winner. — 1961 *Down Beat's Jazz Record Reviews: Vol. V,* p. 210. The only real dog in the set is *Friday the Thirteenth,* a doleful, badly balanced performance.

doghouse, dog-house, *n.* [cf. 1950 *Slang Today and Yesterday,* p. 433. "*dog-house:* a bass violin (musicians—1922)"; very rare since c. 1945] See first quot. — 1925 *English Words & Their Background,* p. 45. *dog-house:* bass violin. — 1936 *Metronome,* Feb., p. 61. *dog house:* string bass. — 1936 *Esquire,* June, p. 131. What type of people get a thrill . . . out of listening to Wellman Braud "slap the doghouse"? —1960 *The Jazz Titans,* p. 20. "Doghouse" is the old slang term for the cumbersome instrument.

dog tune, [cf. teenage slang *dog* (i.e., an unattractive girl); some currency since c. 1945] See 1952 quot. — 1952 *A History of Jazz in America,* p. 351. *dog tune:* a song of questionable musical quality. — 1955 *The Encyclopedia of Jazz,* p. 346. *dog tune:* a song of no musical merit. — 1956 *The Real Jazz Old and New,* p. 149. A *dog-tune* is one that isn't very good music. — 1959 *Esquire,* Nov., p. 70I. *dog tune:* poor piece of music.

domie, domi, dommy, *n.* [shortened form of *domicile;* some currency esp. among Negro jazzmen c. 1930–c. 1940, rare since; see also CRIB, PAD] A room or apartment. — 1944 *The New Cab Calloway's Hepsters Dictionary,* p. 6. "I live in a righteous domi." — 1946 *Really the Blues,* p. 59. We headed straight for his dommy. — 1958 *Jive in Hi-Fi,* p. 15. *domie:* house, home, or room. 1959 *Diggeth Thou?,* p. 34. She cut into his dommy and helped kill the fifth.

don't take down, [according to jazzman Eubie Blake, current c. 1900–c. 1917, obs. since except historical] See quot. — 1955 *Hear Me Talkin to Ya,* p. 59. The order, "Don't take down," was a signal to everyone in the band to play all the time—no laying down the horn for a minute.

doodle, *v.i.* [prob. of sexual or scatological origin; according to jazzman Eubie Blake, some currency c. 1900–c. 1935, obs. since except historical] To play music very informally and relaxedly. — 1955 *Hear Me Talkin to Ya,* p. 164. "Get out your horn, let's doodle a little." — 1957 *Eddie Chamblee and His Orchestra: Doodlin'* (LP album Emarcy 36131).

dots, *n. pl.* [from the appearance of sheet music; some currency since c. 1920] Originally, the notes on sheet music, now also extended to the sheet music itself. — 1927 *Melody Maker,* June, p. 586. I will give you the "dots" for them. — 1958 *Teach Yourself Jazz,* p. 39. Firstly, most St. Louis musicians could read music, and were seen "carrying their 'dots' about with them."

double, *v.i. & v.t.* 1. [cf. circus slang *double in brass;* current since c. 1920 (i.e., with the advent of the *big band,* q.v.)] See 1946 quot.; also, an instrument so used: see first 1934 quot. — 1926 *Melody Maker,* Feb., p. 13. It is able to do so successfully since, owing to its musicians doubling, the combination of three fiddles, 'cello, bass, with, of course, piano, is obtained. — 1934 *All About Jazz,* p. 68. All the foregoing applies equally to clarinets and the instruments used as "doubles" by the saxophonists in the band. — p. 72. This, coupled with the "doubling" propensities of the players, allows him a huge palette of tone-colours to produce the most bizarre effects. — 1946 *Jazzways*, p. 52. Or, if a musician is able to "double," that is, play another instrument in addition to his regularly assigned one (for example, most saxophonists double clarinet, flute, etc.), he receives added compensation for that. — 1955 *A Pictorial History of Jazz*, p. 40. The excess of instruments on these bandstands indicates how much "doubling" a musician was expected to do. — 1957 *The Book of Jazz*, p. 27. "He doubled on bass and piano."

2. (occasionally with *up*), [current since c. 1925; see also DOUBLE TIME] To double the tempo; for its adjective use, see 1948 quot. — 1948 *Down Beat*, 14 July, p. 13. Ventura's doubled up tenoring on Body is some of the best that he has set down on wax. — 1950 *Mister Jelly Roll*, p. 75. As Picou saw it, jazz consisted of "additions to the bars—doubling up on notes—playing eight or sixteen for one." — 1958 *American Thesaurus of Slang*, p. 554. *double it up:* to double the tempo. — 1959 *The Horn*, p. 231. Even the doubling of the bass was distinctly audible.

double time, [variant of *double,* sense 2; current since c. 1925] See quot. — 1957 *The Book of Jazz*, p. 224. "Double time," a gambit normally associated with bop; frequent use is made of 16th notes . . . in . . . uninterrupted fashion . . . among bop soloists.

do up, [cf. Early Modern English use of *do* (i.e., of a man, to copulate): c. 1593 *Titus Andronicus*, IV, ii, "I have done thy mother"; current among jazzmen since c. 1948] To effect (something), take action with regard to (something or someone—food, music, sex, etc.); also, for a rare use (with ref. to narcotics), see first quot. — 1959 *The Holy Barbarians*, p. 24. "About the second day I was with him he offered me a fix—did I want to do up—and I said no." — 1959 *Easy Living*, p. 89. "I figure, give her

a couple days rest and then do her up right, you dig?" —
1959 *Esquire*, Nov., p. 70I. *do up, to:* term of action.
Example: let's go out and do up this club. Enjoy it to the
utmost.

down, *adj.* [from *down with it,* q.v., poss. reinforced by
general slang *down to earth;* some earlier use, but widely
current only since c. 1950] See second 1959 quot. —
1959 *Newport Jazz Festival: 1959,* p. 45. *down:* very
good. — 1959 *Esquire,* Nov., p. 70I. *down:* dirty,
earthy. Example: a down stud. A fellow devoid of pre-
tense, fundamentally honest. — 1960 *Beat Jokes Bop
Humor & Cool Cartoons,* p. 50. The old man, respected
throughout the kingdom for being a down kitty, lay but a
few weeks in his grave. — 1961 *Down Beat,* 2 Feb.,
p. 30. Collette's playing is faultless and at times he
manages to work up a "down" jazz feeling.

    adv. [poss. from general colloquial *down to his toes*
(or *socks*); current esp. among Negro jazzmen c. 1925–
c. 1945, very rare since; see also BACK, *adv.*] Extremely;
well. — 1928 *The Walls of Jericho,* p. 299. *drunk down:*
the nadir of inebriation. — 1942 *American Mercury,*
July, p. 94. *draped down:* dressed in the height of Harlem
fashion; also *togged down.*

    down with, [poss. from gambling slang *to be down*
(i.e., to have one's bet placed) and poss. from general
colloquial *down to his toes* (or *socks*); current esp.
among Negro jazzmen since c. 1935] See 1957 and
second 1959 quots. — 1944 *Dan Burley's Original Handbook of Harlem Jive,* p. 15. "I'm down with the action."
— p. 41. *Othello,* the spade stud, pops in port, "down
with it, cause he can't quit it." — p. 47. Iago is down with
the action. — 1946 *Really the Blues,* p. 369. *down with it:*
top-notch, superlative. — 1955 *Down Beat,* 5 Oct., p. 51.
I don't know who the singer is, 'cause I'm not down with
all the singers now. — 1957 *The Book of Negro Folklore,*
p. 483. *down with it:* to get acquainted with, to under-

stand. — 1959 *Diggeth Thou?*, p. 23. Let's see what's down with the deal. — 1959 *Esquire*, Nov., p. 70I. *down with something, to be:* to know something thoroughly. — 1960 *Beat Jokes Bop Humor & Cool Cartoons*, p. 57. The Ham wasn't down with the action.

   down with (one's) ax, [jazz slang *down with* + jazz slang *ax;* current since c. 1955; cf. *all over (one's) horn, get around on (one's) horn*] To be thoroughly proficient technically on one's instrument. Oral evidence only.

downhome, down-home, *adj.* [from Negro jazzman's identification of his emotional roots with the earthiness of the Southern Negro (and esp. with rural life); despite some earlier use, widely current only since c. 1950; see also FUNKY, SOUL] Earthy, honest, and unpretentious. — 1938 *N.Y. Amsterdam News*, 12 March, p. 17. The allusion to "peppermint candy" stirs almost primal emotions, hangover from the old "down home house rent strut" days. — 1959 *The Horn*, p. 85. "Maybe later pick up gigs with a downhome band." — 1960 *The Jazz Word*, p. 213. All the current terms of approbation among jazzmen —"soul," "funk," "down home"—all mean basically that if a man can play the blues from inside himself without straining to play a part, he's a legitimate jazzman. — 1960 *Down Beat*, 24 Nov., p. 18. The everchanging jazz argot is consistent in one thing: Through the years the most cogent and expressive words and terms relating to good jazz have without exception been down to earth and colorful. Jazz is not sissy music. What could be more natural than that words like "funk," "dirty" and terms like "gut-bucket" and "down home" be indigenous to it? — 1961 *Jazz Journal*, July, p. 4. That sounds "down-home" to me—that was a good one. Also **down home.**

dozens, the (dirty), [semantic development obscure: see 1960 quot.; some currency esp. among Negro jazzmen

since c. 1925 (see 1960 quot.)]   See quots. — 1928 *The
Walls of Jericho,* p. 9. For it is the gravest of insults, this
so-called "slipping in the dozens." To disparage a man is
one thing; to disparage his family is another. — 1946
Really the Blues, p. 369. *dirty dozens:* elaborate game in
which participants insult each other's ancestors. — 1955
Hear Me Talkin to Ya, p. 96. He liked to play the
"dozens" (talk about your parents and all in a joking way)
—it was a way of trying to get each other's goat. — 1960
N.Y. Citizen-Call, 30 July, p. 19. An etymologist might
be led to define "The Dozens" as the "Science of Disparaging One's Ancestors" . . . Research reveals that
the Dozens were of American slave origin and took the
place of physical assault by the "field slaves" on the more
favored "house slaves" on Southern plantations . . . It
was during the 1920's . . . that some unknown blues
pianist and singer composed an uncopyrighted tune
called "The Dirty Dozens" complete with words, which
because of their very nature never got on paper. But at
barrelhouse and buffet flat house rent parties "The Dirty
Dozens" became the rage.

draft, feel a, See s.v. FEEL A DRAFT.

drag, *n.* 1. [from the delayed, pulling movement of the
dance and the music to which it was danced: cf. 1959
quot.; current c. 1915–c. 1930, obs. since except historical, though the dance step survives in other dances;
for synonymous names, see also MOOCH, SCRAUNCH]   An
early blues style, dance and/or tempo (see 1938, 1955,
1960 quots.); also, the concomitant jazz dance, c. 1917–
c. 1935 (see 1916, 1946 quots.). — 1916 *Walkin' the
Dog* (tune). Do that slow drag 'round the hall. — 1923
Shoe Shiners Drag (tune title). — 1924 *The Chicago
Gouge* (tune, copyright 1924). Down at a Chitlin rag,/
They played a fiddlin' drag. — 1930 *Saratoga Drag*
(tune recorded on Brunswick 80038 by the Luis Russell
Orchestra). — 1938 *The Hot Jazz of Jelly Roll Morton,*

p. 7. Jelly takes . . . passages . . . returning to the essence of *slow drag,* the blues style that Jelly knew so well.
— 1946 *Big Book of Swing,* p. 124. *drag:* a dance. —
1950 *They All Played Ragtime,* p. 247. The Slow Drag
must begin on the first beat of each measure. — 1955
Hear Me Talkin to Ya, p. 123. We had only two tempos,
slow drag and the two-four one-step. — 1959 *The Jazz
Scene,* pp. 290–291. Terms for emotion were formed by
metaphor, e.g. by the widespread practice of equating
. . . grief with depth . . . thus the quality most desired in the old blues is that it should be *low-down*
or *dragging.* — 1960 *Jazz: A Quarterly of American
Music,* Winter, p. 25. By that name or by other names
("ditties," "slow drags"), blues were as basic to early
jazz as brass bands.

　2. [cf. jazz slang *drag the beat;* also cf. 1925 *English
Words & Their Background,* pp. 61–62. "If she [i.e., a
girl] is unpopular, she is . . . *a drag";* widely current
since c. 1940]　See 1960 quot. — 1946 *The Jazz Record,*
July, p. 9. "They sent me down South, Georgia. That was
enough to make me blow my top. It was a drag, Jack." —
1952 *Go,* p. 240. "It's all such a drag . . . all these rela-
tionships, hangups, conflicts." — 1959 *Esquire,* Nov., p.
70I. *drag:* an annoying person. — 1960 *Dictionary of
American Slang.* s.v. *drag:* a person, thing, event, or place
that is intellectually, emotionally, or aesthetically boring,
tedious, tiring, or colorless.

　v.t. (also, occasionally, *drug:* see 1961 quot.), [see note
in *n.,* 2; current since c. 1940]　See 1958 quot. — 1955
Down Beat, 21 Sep., p. 33. If there's anything that drags
me, it's when they put the piano up too loud in the control room. — 1958 *The Book of Negro Folklore,* p. 483.
drag: humiliate, upset, disillusion. — 1961 *Down Beat,*
19 Jan., p. 22. Something's really drugging you that
evening.

　v.i. [current since c. 1900]　In music, to fall behind

the beat. — 1953 *Night Light,* p. 223. "You're draggin'."
Also **drag the beat.**

dragged, drug(g), drugged, *adj.* [from *drag, v.t.;* current
since c. 1940; see also BROUGHT DOWN, BUGGED, HUNG]
See both 1959 *Esquire* quots. — 1946 *Really the Blues,* p.
298. I was one drugg cat. — p. 369. *drugg:* brought
down [jazz sense], depressed. — 1958 *American Speech,*
Oct., p. 225. Somewhat less frequently paired are the
synonyms for *annoyed: bugged, dragged.* — 1959 *The
Holy Barbarians,* p. 27. "Before I light up I'm drug with
. . . ten thousand things." — 1959 *Esquire,* Nov. p. 70I
dragged: depressed. Example: I'm dragged with this
scene. I'm annoyed by these surroundings. — *drugged:*
annoyed, disgusted, extremely depressed. — 1960 *Hiparama of the Classics,* p. 12. "Drag not, and Thou Shalt
not be Drug!" — 1961 *Down Beat,* 19 Jan., p. 22. There
are some moments when I do get a little drugged.

drape(s), *n.* (also *v.i.:* oral evidence only), [from standard
sense: 1959 *Webster's New World Dictionary,* s.v. *drape:*
"1. *usually in pl.* cloth hanging in loose folds"; current
since c. 1935; see also FRONT, THREADS] See 1938 and
first 1946 quots. — 1938 *Cab Calloway: Hi De Ho,* p. 16.
drape: suit of clothes, dress, costume. — 1946 *Big Book
of Swing,* p. 124. *drape:* a suit of clothes. — 1946 *Really
the Blues,* p. 41. Jack, the drapes they handed me a jungle bum wouldn't wear on weekdays. — 1952 *Park East,*
Dec., p. 31. His drapes were all crummy, his toupee was
beat.

draped, *adj.* [current since c. 1935] Attired. — 1942
American Mercury, July, p. 94. *draped down:* dressed in
the height of Harlem fashion.

drive, *n.* [special application of standard sense (i.e.,
energy); current since c. 1930] Musical power, energy,
or pulse. — 1938 *Metronome,* June, p. 21. "Mr. Gray's
band at times achieves a drive." — 1943 *Murder on the
Downbeat,* p. 27. "You can't have jazz without drive."

— 1947 *Metronome,* June, p. 16. The former [i.e., swing] bumped and chugged along like a beat locomotive; this was known in some quarters as drive. — 1951 *Down Beat,* 5 Oct., p. 12. There's a lot of drive to the rhythm section. — 1960 *The Story of the Original Dixieland Jazz Band,* p. 193. With great patience he proceeded to teach Henry . . . the idea of "drive"—when to hit hard on the downbeat, when to drop out to let the clarinet and trombone come through, how to lead into a chorus.

v.i. & v.t. [special application of a standard sense; current prob. since c. 1930] See 1952 quot. — 1952 *A History of Jazz in America,* p. 351. *drive:* to play with concentrated momentum. — 1957 *Down Beat,* 11 July, p. 19. Listening to Hamp Hawes, he'll comment, "Yeah. He plays a driving piano." — 1960 *The Story of the Original Dixieland Jazz Band,* p. 33. No one ever "drove" a band like La Rocca, and to this day his secrets of "drive"—the tricks of "blowing in" a phrase, of hitting slightly ahead of the beat, of dropping out at a critical moment—have never been equalled.

drive-notes, *n. pl.* [current c. 1930–c. 1945, obs. since] See quot. — 1935 *Vanity Fair,* Nov., p. 71. Ensemble chords that mark a transition to a new key are *drive-notes.*

drop off, See s.v. FALLOFF.

dropping bombs, See s.v. BOMBS.

drug(g), drugged, *adj.* See s.v. DRAGGED.

dues, *n. pl.* [extension of standard meaning; some currency since c. 1945, but wide currency only since c. 1955] Responsibilities; obligations. — 1946 *Good Dues Blues* (tune recorded by Dizzy Gillespie). — 1960 *Hiparama of the Classics,* p. 15. It is for us the swingin' to pick up the dues of these departed Studs.

pay (one's) dues, [extension of *dues, n. pl.*—i.e., in jazz slang, one "pays" with personal suffering instead of with money; some currency since c. 1945, but wide currency only since c. 1955] To serve an apprenticeship in life by absorbing a share of the hardships that experience brings: see 1956 quot. — 1942 *Call House Madam,* p. 292. She was mixed up later in one of the rottenest shooting messes ever staged in Hollywood, but she got away with her end of it and never paid her dues. — 1956 *Esquire,* Feb., p. 63. "Some of the commercial jazz guys think they're playing real jazz, but they aren't making it because they haven't paid their dues." (Suffering enough of the trials and tribulations of life to realize that jazz comes from the heart.) — 1960 *The Jazz Review,* May, p. 12. Paying Dues: The Education of a Combo Leader (title of article). — 1961 *The Sound,* p. 61. "I paid my dues in them big bands." — p. 62. He'd been a dues payer, too. — p. 206. "She's seen the seamiest side of life, taken her lumps, starved, lied, stolen, conned—paid her dues." — 1961 *The Jazz Life,* p. 29. "Paying dues" is the jazz musician's term for the years of learning and searching for an individual sound and style while the pay is small and irregular.

duster, *n.* [from its incidental function of dusting off chairs and benches; some currency esp. among Negro jazzmen c. 1925–c. 1945, very rare since; see also RUSTY DUSTY] The buttocks. — 1946 *Really the Blues,* p. 196. Keep on wriggling your saucy duster. — p. 369. *duster:* buttocks.

dusty butt, [some currency esp. among Negro jazzmen c. 1900–c. 1945, very rare since] See quot. — 1942 *American Mercury,* July, p. 94. *dusty butt:* cheap prostitute.

E

⟨⟨⟨⟨⟨⟨⟨⟨⟨⟨⟨⟨⟨⟩⟩⟩⟩

ear man, [general colloquial phrase but with esp. currency among jazzmen c, 1917–c. 1940, very rare since] A musicial improviser: one who doesn't read music. — 1939 *Jazzmen,* p. 190. Ammons, although strictly an "ear" man, has always been an excellent orchestra pianist.

ear music, [general colloquial phrase but with esp. currency among jazzmen c. 1917–c. 1940, very rare since; see also the more common HEAD, *adj. & n.*] Improvised music; also, for a rare adjective use, see first quot. — 1936 *Stage,* March, p. 58. *ear-music boys:* improvisers; literally those who play by ear. — 1939 *Jazzmen,* pp. 40–41. They played by note for marches and played by note at some of the more sedate balls, but had plenty of opportunity to play "ear music" at house parties, at the race track, and in "the district."

ears, *n. pl.* 1. [According to jazzmen, Lester Young was the first to apply this term in a special jazz slang sense c. 1940; still current] A desire to listen or hear. — 1960 *Jazz: A Quarterly of American Music,* Winter, p. 51. "Everybody Here's Got Ears." Also **big ears:** oral evidence only.

2. [narrowing of the standard meaning; also cf. general slang *a good ear* (*for music*); current since c. 1945] A keenly discriminating responsiveness to music. — 1958 *Nugget,* Dec., p. 42. In 1957, George Avakian, one of the notable A&R men with "ears" in the record business, decided that Miles and Gil Evans had to be reunited. — 1963 *Down Beat,* 3 Jan., p. 34. Only people with minimum preconception and maximum ears took him seriously.

East Coast (jazz), [chiefly a writers' term; some currency since c. 1955] Generic since c. 1955 for the countermovement to West Coast (i.e., *cool,* q.v.) jazz; earthy modern jazz (see also FUNK). — 1957 *New York Jazz Festival: 1957,* p. 19. The school: East Coast, "bluesy" or "funky" jazz, highlighted by such musicians as trumpeters Donald Byrd, Kenny Dorham, Art Farmer. — 1957 *Charles Mingus: East Coasting* (LP album Bethlehem BCP-6019).

eel-ya-dah, *n.* [see quot. for etym.; current c. 1945–c. 1950, rare since; see also OO-BLA-DEE] See quot. — 1949 *Music Library Association Notes,* Dec., p. 43, *eel-ya-dah:* nonsense syllables for the triplet figure common in bebop.

eighty-eight, *n.* [from number of keys on a piano; some currency esp. among white jazzmen c. 1925–c. 1945, rare since; see also BOX] See first quot. — 1942 *The American Thesaurus of Slang,* p. 559. *eighty-eight:* piano. — 1944 *Down Beat,* 15 Feb., p. 8. Nowhere can one find a more solid 88 solo. — 1949 *Down Beat,* 11 March, p. 15. Eighty-eight tinkler Allen plays most of his capitol dance dates with only himself and three rhythm. — 1959 *Evans Bradshaw Trio: Pieces of Eighty-Eight* (LP album Riverside RLP-12-296).

eighty-eighter, *n.* [some currency esp. among white jazzmen c. 1925–c. 1945, rare since] See quot. — 1949

Music Library Association Notes, Dec., p. 43. *eighty-eighter:* popular musician's term for pianist.

eight-to-the-bar, *adj.* [see 1955 quot, for etym.; some currency c. 1930–c. 1945, very rare since] Boogie-woogie (q.v.). — 1931 *Melody Maker*, May, p. 399. A fine trumpet gets going against a most modern eight-in-a-bar rhythm. — 1943 *Modern Music*, May-June, p. 235. Eight to the Bar (column headline). — 1955 *The First Book of Jazz*, p. 27. Some people started calling all boogie-woogie music the "fives." Others call it "eight-to-the-bar," because the rolling bass consists of êight eighth-notes in each bar.

end, the, [hyperbole: that point beyond which one can't go; widely current since c. 1952; see also THE MOST, SOMETHING ELSE] Superlative. — 1950 *Neurotica*, Autumn, p. 45. "Senor, this shit [i.e., narcotic] is the end!" — 1957 *On the Road*, p. 127. "That Rollo Gret is the greatest . . . Man, he's the end!" — 1958 *Somewhere There's Music*, p. 200. "I wanted to tell you I thought your singing was the end. Really nice." — 1960 *The Jazz Word*, p. 81. "Diz played with Bird's group and sounded the end." — p. 123. One of my paintings is named requiem for bird a tribute for the end alto. — 1963 *Nugget*, Feb., p. 44. I dyed it . . . to complement my end hair. — p. 46. I was blowing some jazz in the student lounge on this end Steinway.

-est, *suffix* [wide use and, consequently, rapid turnover of superlatives in jazz slang had led since c. 1950 to the affixing of *-est* to unlikely words more frequently than happens in general slang or colloquial speech] To the nth degree. — 1955 *Solo*, p. 191. "These mixed-up cats get the *gonest* chicks, I swear. — 1955 *Bop Fables*, p. 47. "She is the swingin'est, but let's take it from the top again." — p. 57. "Man," said the stranger, "they're the jumpin'est!" — 1957 *On the Road*, p. 282. "Victor is the

. . . franticest . . . cat I've ever . . . met." — 1957
New York Jazz Festival: 1957, p. 43. Al "Jazzbo" Collins
WRCA is one of the outest.

every man for himself, [general colloquialism given special
application by jazzmen; current c. 1917–c. 1940, obs.
since except historical; see also EVERY TUB] In traditional jazz, complete improvisation: no written music.
— 1955 *Hear Me Talkin to Ya*, p. 59. It was "every man
for himself," with trumpeter taking the lead and everyone else filling in the best he could.

every tub (on its own black bottom), [cf. 1952 *Invisible
Man*, p. 472. "After that it's every tub on its own black
bottom!"; nautical expression adopted by rural Southern
Negroes, then given a special application by Negro jazzmen; current c. 1917–c. 1940, obs. since except historical; see also EVERY MAN FOR HIMSELF] In traditional
jazz, complete improvisation: no written music. —
1938 *Every Tub* (tune recorded by the Count Basie
Orchestra). — 1963 *Down Beat*, 20 June, p. 26. The
"every tub on its own bottom" philosophy of a Miles
Davis unit.

evil, *adj.* [special applications of standard term; from
Negro slang; cf. 1926 *Nigger Heaven*, p. 248. "Cause
Ah's evil an' bad."; current esp. among Negro jazzmen
since c. 1935] As applied to people, see 1939 and
first 1946 quots.; as applied to nature, malign (see
second 1946 and 1957 quots.) — 1939 *Jitterbug Jamboree
Song Book*, p. 32. *evil:* in bad humor. — 1946 *Big Book of
Swing*, p. 124. *evil:* nasty. — 1946 *Really the Blues*, p.
160. This evil dim [i.e., night], as we sat around our
table at the Nest, I was still as a hoot-owl, sad and sick at
heart. — p. 197. From then on he was an evil cat. —
1956 *Eddie Condon's Treasury of Jazz*, p. 239. They for-
gave him his trespasses when Bird felt evil. — 1957 *On
the Road*, p. 61. He had fallen on the beat and evil

days that come to young guys in their middle twenties.
— 1957 *The Horn,* p. 52. "She's one of them rich, *evil*
junkies."

explosion, *n.* [from its sound; some currency since c. 1945;
see also FLARE] A loud musical chord or phrase. —
1955 *Hear Me Talkin to Ya,* p. 134. We would build up
to an explosion, then go down soft.

eyes, *n. pl.* [prob. suggested by *I Only Have Eyes for You,*
1934 song which became a jazz standard; according
to jazzmen, Lester Young was the first to use the term in
a special jazz slang sense c. 1940] A desire or inclination (for something); see 1955 quot. for special,
rare uses. — 1948 *New Yorker,* 3 July, p. 28. "Have you
eyes for a sandwich?" — 1955 *Say,* 28 April, p. 53. *historical eyes:* outdated, passé. *Hollywood eyes:* a fine
girl — 1958 *Somewhere There's Music,* p. 19. "Oh, a
girl here's got eyes to meet you." — 1959 *The Holy
Barbarians,* p. 27. "You got eyes for the scene, man."
— 1961 *The Sound,* p. 103. "It's got eyes to go, too." —
p. 174. "You always had downtown eyes."

    big eyes, [current since c. 1950] A great desire (for
something). — 1956 *Sideman,* p. 276. "I'm all happy
about it—*big-eyes.*" — 1959 *Esquire,* Nov., p. 70I. I have
big eyes to make it with this chick. — 1961 *The Sound,* p.
15. "Big eyes to scoff [i.e., eat]," Hassan said. — p. 108.
"Big eyes to hear you blow, man!"

    no eyes, [current since c. 1950] An aversion; a dis-
inclination. — 1959 *The Horn,* p. 56. "I got no eyes for
that now." — 1961 *The Sound,* p. 192. "No, no, man,
not my kick. Not kidding, Red. No eyes."

F

×◇◇◇◇◇◇◇◇◇◇◇◇◇◇◇×

face, *n.* [synechdoche; cf. 1960 *Dictionary of American Slang,* s.v. *face:* "Negro use"; some currency esp. among Negro jazzmen since c. 1940] Initially, a stranger, any anonymous individual (hence, frequently for Negroes, a white man); increasingly, any person. — 1946 *Hepcats Jive Talk Dictionary.* s.v. *face:* white man. — 1946 *Really the Blues,* p. 369. *face:* a form of greeting. — 1952 *Flee the Angry Strangers,* p. 316. "You go down and cook up some soup for the Face." — 1955 *Solo,* p. 39. "Real cool tonight!" said one face. — 1960 *The Jazz Titans,* p. 155. *face:* person, man. — 1961 *The Sound,* pp. 173–174. "Sometimes I feel I can't take it . . . me being the only white face, and all."

   bad face, [some currency esp. among Negro jazzmen since c. 1940] See quot. — 1961 *N.Y. Times Magazine,* 25 June, p. 39. *bad face:* hipster's version of Rasputin (either sex); i.e., a surly, mean, no-good cat [jazz sense].

fake, *v.i. & v.t.* [see 1958 quot. for explanation of semantic development; current c. 1915–c. 1945, less common since, primarily because modern jazz is so technically demanding that most modern jazzmen must be able to read music well: consequently, the practice now derives from choice, not from necessity] See 1937, 1958 quots.; also, by extension, to improvise or be resourceful in any situation: see 1962 quot. — 1926 *Melody Maker*, Jan., p. 20. In those days, it must be remembered, the dance band was not studied by the orchestrator as it is now, and one had to "fake" saxophone and banjo parts from those of such other instruments as were catered for in the score. — 1929 *The Musical Quarterly*, Oct., p. 623. "Faking" . . . is increasingly giving way to the printed part. — 1936 *Harper's Magazine*, April, p. 574. Thus in a typical "jam session" one instrument will lead off with a slightly modified form of the general melody, the other instruments "faking" the harmony. — 1937 *American Speech*, Oct., p. 183. *fake:* at a formal engagement, to play a piece of music without orchestration as though there were one. — 1944 *Spotlight*, Jan., p. 18. And according to what I hear played today there was enough good music "faked" in those days to last this generation of "readers" the rest of their days. — 1958 *Publication of the American Dialect Society*, Nov., p. 41. The term "fake" has been applied to improvising for a good many years. It originally implied that the player was not doing his job correctly, and possibly that he could not read music at all and thus was forced to make it up as he went along. Jazzmen, perhaps in self-defense, made the word a synonym for "improvising" and use of it implies nothing bad about a man's performance. — 1962 *Jazz Monthly*, Oct., p. 10. In a typical "bop joke" a musician passenger tells a taxicab driver who says he doesn't know how to get to a particular address: "That's all right, man, fake it."

fake book, [from *fake;* current c. 1925–c. 1945, very rare since] Any of the various books containing the basic chord progressions for many popular songs, an indispensable book for many of the dance (hotel) musicians of the 1920s and 1930s. — 1958 *American Speech,* Oct., p. 225. The . . . "fake book" . . . guides most small combos through this weary world.

faker, *n.* [from *fake;* some currency c. 1915–c. 1945, rare since except historical] See quot. — 1934 *All About Jazz,* p. 50. The early jazz drummers were nearly all "fakers," in that they could not read music.

fake fingering, See s.v. FALSE FINGERING.

fall by (or **in, out, over, up**), [understatement; current since c. 1940] See 1946, 1960 quots. — 1946 *Really the Blues,* p. 369. *fall in:* arrive. — 1953 *Night Light,* p. 141. "You'll have to fall over to the apartment sometime." — 1958 *Somewhere There's Music,* p. 34. "Why don't you fall out with your axe some night." — 1959 *The Horn,* p. 220. "I fell by here looking for a chick." — 1960 *Metronome,* Sep., p. 15. *fall by, fall in, fall up:* arrive, enter. — 1961 *The Sound,* p. 107. "Gee, I can't get over you cats falling in like this."

fall out, [see 1960 quot. for partial semantic explanation, though dating is inaccurate; current since c. 1935] Initially, see 1938 quot.; more recently, see 1959 *Esquire* quot. — 1938 *Cab Calloway: Hi De Ho,* p. 16. *fall out:* to be overcome with emotion. Ex.—"The cats fell out when he took that solo." — 1944 *Dan Burley's Original Handbook of Harlem Jive,* p. 138. *fall out:* to be aroused emotionally, to be taken by complete surprise. — 1946 *Really the Blues,* p. 369. *fall out:* be tickled to death. — 1959 *Esquire,* Nov., p. 70I, *fall out:* to leave, to sleep. Pass out from too much drugs. — 1959 *The Holy Barbarians,* p. 186. "We were down there about an hour and I kept falling out. — 1960 *Dictionary of American Slang,* p. 177. *fall out:* to be emotionally aroused; to be surprised; to "fall apart." Orig. c. 1946 bop use; now some teenage use. Prob. reenforced by the Army command "fall out" = dismissed.

falloff, drop off, [current since c. 1925] See first quot. — 1949 *Music Library Association Notes,* Dec., p. 50. *drop off:* instrumentalist begins on written note, and usually by relaxed lip pressure, slides down four or five tones, reducing volume at same time. — 1961 *Down Beat,* 19 Jan., p. 41. This is especially noticeable in the dynamics, shakes, falloffs, and cutoffs of the brass section.

false (or fake) fingering, [from improper or unconventional technique; some currency since c. 1920] A special technique for fingering a stop on a valve instrument, esp. on a trumpet, that produces certain effects (choking, etc.) which cannot be achieved conventionally. — 1926 *Melody Maker,* May, p. 29. Higher notes must be obtained by "fake" fingering and special lip pressure. — 1927 *Melody Maker,* May, p. 497. You will be required to use this fake fingering. — 1955 *Hear Me Talkin to Ya,* p. 275. He was very interested in the false-fingering ideas I was working out. — 1961 *The Jazz Review,* Jan., p. 22. *Housewarming* is a good track, with Lips showing some of the "false-fingering" that was his own and some of the strength that was his, too.

fangs, *n. pl.* [current since c. 1957; see also earlier CHOPS, LIP] For literal sense, see 1959 quots.; more generally, a musician's embouchure—the skill and power of his blowing apparatus. — 1958 *Down Beat,* 6 Feb., p. 31. The trumpet section probably includes Bernie Glow, Ernie Royal, Jimmy Nottingham, and all the guys with— to use the hip vernacular—they're saying "fangs" now instead of chops . . . a beautiful trumpet section. — 1959 *Esquire,* Nov., p. 70I. *fangs:* lips. — 1959 *Swinging Syllables.* s.v. *fangs:* teeth.

far out, [see last quot. for accurate but partial explanation of semantic development: it overlooks the fact that the other-worldliness of the term derives at least in part from the new, extreme value placed by modern jazzmen on imaginativeness (see 1958 and first 1959 quots.); current since c. 1950] Imaginative, experimental; hence, excellent. — 1956 *Esquire,* Sep., p. 79. "Far out" . . . is the new *hip,* not *hep,* term of critical approval, superseding the swing era's *hot* and the bop era's *cool.* —

1958 *Somewhere There's Music,* pp. 15–16. Mike . . .
wondered what he would play. Nothing too far out, but
a real old tune wouldn't get it either. — 1959 *The Horn,*
p. 131. "Curn, it's wild, the greatest band you've ever
had, but it'll bomb because it's too far out for the average
ginmill owner." — 1959 *Jazz Poems,* p. 7. Spend some
money on the farout cats of the fine arts. — 1959 *Jazz:
A Quarterly of American Music,* Fall, p. 284. The power
of musicians of skill to transport is verbalized in *send me*
. . . It is little wonder that swing devotees . . . on the
general observations of music as "heavenly" and "melody of the spheres," proclaimed they were sent—propelled by that centrifugal force *out of the world.* In the
1940's *far out* and *away out* became integral to bop and
cool.

fat, *adj.* [some currency prob. since c. 1935] Full-toned.
— 1958 *Somewhere There's Music,* p. 164. The clarinet
was as woody and fat as a clarinet can be. — 1961 *The
Sound,* p. 108. "And Bernie, man, I need them big fat
chords." — 1962 *Down Beat,* 30 Aug., p. 29. His fat,
warm sound comes across well on *Time.* — 1962 *Down
Beat,* 8 Nov., p. 32. Goldie has a big, fat sound, a dark,
lustrous tone.

faust, *n. & adj.* [from Faust's association in legend with the
devil: cf. 1946 quot.; from Negro slang; current esp.
among Negro jazzmen c. 1930–c. 1945, very rare since]
See quots. — 1938 *Cab Calloway: Hi De Ho,* p. 16.
Faust: an ugly girl. — 1945 *Hepcats Jive Talk Dictionary.*
s.v. *faust:* blind date. — 1946 *Really the Blues,* p. 369.
Faust: ugly (as the devil). — 1956 *The Real Jazz Old
and New,* p. 148. "Faust is not a poem, it means ugly."

fay, ofay, *n. & adj.* [from Negro slang: the most prob. etym.
(see both 1959 quots.) is that since the white man was
considered a foe, *ofay* comes from *foe:* in pig Latin an
initial consonant or cluster is dropped and added at the
end with an [ei] following it; the *fay* form, then, would

be a shortened form, but for a different suggested etym.
see 1928 quot.; current esp. among Negro musicians since
c. 1917, and fairly widespread among white musicians
as well since c. 1945; both forms of the word are still
current, *ofay* predominating before c. 1945, *fay* since;
see also GRAY] See last quot. — 1925 *The Inter-State
Tatler*, 6 March, p. 8. We hear that "Booker Red" has
three ofays on his staff. — 1928 *The Walls of Jericho*,
p. 299. *fay, ofay:* a person who, as far as is known, is white.
Fay is said to be the original term and *ofay* a contraction
of "old" and "fay." — 1945 *Music News*, 1 March, Herman's Is Finest Ofay Swing Band (headline). — 1946
Really the Blues, p. 178. The whole area was overrun
with fay gangsters. — 1959 *The Horn*, p. 89. She learned
. . . even to order coffee from an ofay waitress in a
voice that could be heard. — 1959 *Harper's Magazine*,
June, p. 75. "Ofay," the term for a white, is said by some
theorists to be pig Latin for "foe," but whatever its
etymology, the usual connotation of the word is at best
neutral and usually hostile. — 1959 *Esquire*, Nov., p.
70J. *ofay:* a white person. Sometimes shortened to fay.
Derivation: Pig Latin for foe.

feature, *v.t.* [relation, if any, to its general slang sense
(i.e., to imagine, believe, conceive of) unknown; current esp. among Negro jazzmen c. 1935–c. 1945, obs.
since] To like or approve of (something). Oral evidence only.

feed, *v.t.* [some currency since c. 1940; see also the more
common BACK, COMP] To provide a chord background
(for an instrumentalist); also *v.i.:* oral evidence only;
also, for a rare adjective use, see second quot. — 1961
The Sound, p. 108. "I mean he really feeds me good."
— p. 141. He was passing beyond the feed pianist
stage.

feel a draft, [by analogy with the discomfort; introduced
into jazz use by Lester Young c. 1945, but widely cur-

rent only since c. 1955] To feel hostility directed against one: see 1960 quot.; also, to feel that something is amiss (esp. musically): see 1961 quot. — 1957 *The Charles Mingus Jazz Workshop: The Clown* (liner notes on LP album Atlantic 1260). Mingus feels the slightest draft, sometimes even when no draft is there. — 1960 *Playboy,* Aug., p. 106. "If somebody like J.J. or Gil Evans or John Lewis is obviously not impressed by what he's doing," says a friend, "Miles feels a draft." — 1960 *Esquire,* Sep., p. 91. The term, "I feel a draft," is used by Negro musicians when there's evidence in a restaurant —or elsewhere—of Jim Crow. Ironically, white musicians who have played with Negro groups have sometimes used the same phrase in order to tell each other that they're being frozen out of the conversation or an afterhours party. — 1961 *Metronome,* Sep., p. 14. "I'm playing and all of a sudden I feel a draft. Either you should keep the trumpet going all the way or cut him sooner."

feeling, *n.* [special application of standard meaning (i.e., emotion); current c. 1935–c. 1945, rare since; see also the more recent SOUL] Emotional depth. — 1939 *Down Beat's Yearbook of Swing,* p. 25. That musician who believes only in "feeling" is sadly deluding himself. — 1940 *Swing,* Nov., p. 27. There's still a world of feeling . . . in his improvisations on this swell old tune.

feel (one's) stuff, feel it, [cf. general slang *to have the feel of (something*); some currency c. 1930–c. 1945, rare since] To be in touch with one's own creative springs; hence, to play music well. — 1938 *N.Y. Post,* 3 Feb., p. 15. If he's in the mood, we say he's in the groove, or feeling his stuff. — 1955 *Hear Me Talkin to Ya,* p. 356. He couldn't feel it.

fig, *n.* See s.v. MOLDY FIG.

fine, *adj.* [some general colloquial use but with esp. currency among jazzmen c. 1935–c. 1945, rare since] See

1960 quot. — 1938 *N.Y. Amsterdam News*, 19 Feb., p. 17. "He doesn't have to be good looking or dress so fine." — 1940 *Swing*, Jan., p. 13. "There was only one band that ever cut us down—and that was Woody's. They're fine!" — 1958 *Somewhere There's Music*, p. 35. "Jess is the craziest broad I've ever known, even finer than that chick in New Orleans." — 1958 *Jam Session*, p. 299. "We got some fine numbers. Real fine." —1960 *Dictionary of American Slang*. s.v. *fine:* pleasing; wonderful; exciting . . . *associated with bop and cool use.*

fine and mellow, [jazz slang *fine* + jazz slang *mellow;* innovated by jazz song with that title (see 1939 quot.); some currency since] Thoroughly pleasing. — 1939 *Fine and Mellow* (song recorded by Billie Holiday on Columbia C-526). — 1959 *Blow Up a Storm*, p. 19. "Sounds fine and mellow."

fine as wine, [from rhyming slang vogue, c. 1935– c. 1940, rare since] Excellent. — 1957 *American Speech*, Dec., p. 276. Jazz Lingo abounds in . . . similes, e.g., . . . *fine as wine.*

finger popper, [see 1960 quot. for explanation of semantic development; some currency esp. among white jazzmen since c. 1950; see also the older ALLIGATOR, GATE] Initially, see 1959, 1960 quots.; also, by extension, see last quot.; also, for its adjective use, see 1955 quot. — 1955 *Metronome*, July, p. 22. Lord Buckley . . . addresses this album of *classics* in *bop talk* to Hipsters, Flipsters and Finger Poppin' Daddies." — 1957 *N.Y. Times Magazine*, 18 Aug., p. 26. *Finger popper:* a cat (musician or hipster) who is swinging. — 1959 *Jazz for Moderns*, p. 20. *finger-popper:* a tune that lends itself to popping one's fingers. — 1960 *Dictionary of American Slang*. s.v. *finger popper:* literally, one who snaps his fingers; figuratively, a musician or listener who is carried away by jazz music. — 1962 *Down Beat*, 30 Aug., p. 37. But there's more things in the world besides finger-popping. — 1963

Down Beat, 9 May, p. 42. They had the whole audience stomping feet and popping fingers. —1963 *Hiptionary,* p. 72. *finger-popper:* a swinging [jazz sense] anything: play, book, meal, ball game, musician, hipster.

finger popping, See 1955, 1962 quots. s.v. FINGER POPPER.

finger style, [some currency since c. 1920] See 1957 quot. — 1926 *Melody Maker,* Jan., p. 22. There are also solos that are guaranteed to start the feet tapping and are issued for the finger style of playing in addition to plectrum style. — 1957 *The Book of Jazz,* p. 117. An innovation introduced in the Kenton band in 1947 was the incorporation, in a jazz setting, of an unamplified Spanish concert guitar, played "finger style" (without a plectrum or pick). — 1963 *Down Beat,* 28 Feb., p. 35. He plays the finger style there.

five, take, See s.v. TAKE.

fives, the, [semantic development unknown; some currency c. 1920–c. 1935, obs. since except historical] An earthy, sorrowful blues style on the piano. (Jazzmen say that this is its only meaning; hence, 1957 quot. is mistaken and 1955 quot. somewhat misleading.) — 1955 *The First Book of Jazz,* p. 27. Some people started calling all boogie-woogie music the "fives." — 1957 *Just Jazz,* p. 13. At the turn of the century, they called it [i.e., boogie-woogie] . . . "the fives." — 1959 *The Jazz Scene,* p. 130. Even the research of the jazz lovers has failed to turn many of its casually recorded pioneers into more than names, vaguely attached to a location, a blues or two, or a particular pianistic trick ("the chimes," "the rocks," "the fives," "the chains").

flagwaver, flagwaving, *n.* [by analogy with common vaudeville practice of winning applause by performing a familiar, often patriotic, tune; some currency since c. 1930] A spectacular piece of music or part of a musical performance intended to excite the listeners and win their applause; for adjective uses, see 1940, 1957 quots. — 1937 *The New York Woman*, 24 Feb., p. 29. "A flag waver" is the last chorus in which everybody goes to town ending up like a full ensemble of Valkyrie and Norse Gods. — 1940 *Swing*, Nov., p. 25. A particularly sour taste was left in my mouth by Jan's flagwaving arrangement of Rachmanioff's *Prelude in C Sharp Minor*. — 1957 *Al Cohn Quintet: Al and Zoot* (liner notes of LP album Coral CRL57171). *Just You, Just Me*, taken at a "flagwaver" tempo, closes the album. — 1959 *Jazz* (Hentoff & McCarthy), p. 262. Others . . . were . . . direct descendants of earlier "flag wavers" like *The Creeper, Birmingham Breakdown* and *Jubilee Stomp*. — 1960 *Leisure*, Dec., pp. 40–41. If you remember, the things people liked most about Benny in the old days were the Gene Krupa solos, the screaming-type solos of Harry James, the flagwaving. Also **flag waver.**

flare, flareup, *n.* [by analogy with standard meaning; current since c. 1935; see also EXPLOSION] See quots. — 1942 *The American Thesaurus of Slang*, p. 562. *flare:* to play a note with a sharp attack and hold it for extra beats gradually letting it fade away. — 1956 *Guide to Jazz*, p. 95. *flare:* a note held by a player at the end of a chorus to lead the band into a final collective improvisation. —1956 *The Real Jazz Old and New*, p. 148. The *flareup* is to build a chord.

flick, flicker(s), *n.* [earlier general slang term (*flickers*) adopted by jazzmen (usually without the *s*) c. 1940; shortened form dates from c. 1945] See 1944 quot. — 1944 *Dan Burley's Original Handbook of Harlem Jive*, p. 138. *flickers:* moving pictures. — 1946 *Really the Blues*, p. 231. To me the flickers were just a mild Minsky's on Celluloid. — 1959 *Swinging Syllables.* s.v. *flick:* movie. — 1960 *Down Beat*, 7 Jan., p. 26. I will stand by this one from here to eternity (a pretty groovy flick).

flip, *adj. & n.* [from *v.i.*; current since c. 1950] As noun, see first 1959 quot. (noun use in 1960 quot. is rare); as

adjective, exciting or excitable: hence, eccentric or unstable. — 1952 *Flee the Angry Strangers,* p. 388. "You
crazy broad. Jeez, you flip broad." — 1955 *Hear Me
Talkin to Ya,* p. 347. He's not a flip as far as business is
concerned. — 1959 *Esquire,* Nov., p. 70I. *flip:* eccentric
person. — 1959 *Aramco,* Dec., p. 9. "We blew some flip
tracks [i.e., recordings]." — 1960 *Saturday Review,* 6
Feb., p. 12. A "flip" . . . may be anything from an epi-
leptic seizure to an inner illumination.

    v.i. [shortened form of *flip (one's) lid* or *flip (one's)
wig;* current since c. 1948] See 1952, 1959 quots. —
1950 *Neurotica,* Autumn, p. 44. "If I'm not right back
don't flip." — 1952 *Life,* 29 Sep., p. 67 *flip:* to react en-
thusiastically. — 1955 *Solo,* p. 187. "Look at the Ross here
if you want to flip over a piano." — 1955 *Hear Me Talkin
to Ya,* p. 119. Everybody flipped. It was wonderful. —
1959 *Esquire,* Nov., p. 70I. To flip means to go wild. Example: He flipped over the record. He waxed enthusiastic over the record . . . Flipped can also mean going
insane.

    flip (one's) lid (or **top**), [see first quot. for semantic
explanation; current c. 1943–c. 1948 when it was largely
replaced by *flip:* see 1959 quot.] See first quot. — 1952
A History of Jazz in America, p. 351. Expressing exasperation, enthusiasm, or insanity . . . "flip one's lid"
. . . describes the process of losing the hair or skin of the
head. — 1952 *Who Walk in Darkness,* p. 47. He flipped
his wig when it was finished and they took him to a sani-
tarium. — 1953 *Night Light,* p. 160. "She's just flipping
her wig a little because she's excited." — 1959 *Esquire,*
Nov., p. 70I. Obsolete: flipped his lid or flipped his wig.
This has been shortened to just flipped.

flip side, [from the practice c. 1920–1948, when phono-
    graph records were played at 78 rpm, of recording just
    one piece of jazz music per side; some currency esp.
    among jazz writers since c. 1940, though increasingly rare

since c. 1950] The reverse and, usually, less important
side of a phonograph record. — 1949 *Down Beat*, 11
March, p. 14. The flip side (*South*) will be a shade slower
but with the same general routine. — 1959 *The Horn*,
p. 70. "What'll we do for the flip side?"

fluff, *n. & v.t.* [from entertainment (i.e., radio, theater)
slang; some currency since c. 1935; see also GOOF] A
note or phrase played incorrectly; as verb, to play a
wrong note (in this sense, oral evidence only); also, by
extension: see 1959 quot. — 1942 *The American Thesaurus of Slang*, p. 560. *fluff*: discord. — 1959 *Newport Jazz
Festival: 1959*, p. 45 *fluffed*: to be brushed off, ignored,
cast aside.

flutter, *n. & v.t.* [special application of standard meaning;
current since c. 1920] To triple- or quadruple-tongue
(the reed of any reed instrument) in order to produce a
flutter sound; also, the effect so produced. — 1926
Melody Maker, March, p. 30. Take one of the more simple figurations of the Chinese effect and play it . . . using less of the flutter tongue. — 1927 *Melody Maker*,
June, p. 541. I should be greatly obliged if you could
explain how the flutter is done on the trumpet. — 1942
The American Thesaurus of Slang, p. 561. *flutter
[-tongue]*: the effect produced by fluttering the tongue
against the mouthpiece.

fly, *adj.* [cf. 1959 *Webster's New World Dictionary*, s.v.
fly: "orig. thieves' slang"; also cf. 1930 *American Tramp
and Underworld Slang*, s.v. *fly*: "the long-established
English slang word 'fly,' designating a knowing or artful
mind"; current esp. among Negro jazzmen since c. 1900]
See 1952, 1958 quots. — 1928 *The Walls of Jericho*,
p. 156. "I got a picture o' myself lettin' any guy alone
that gets fly with my girl." — 1939 *Metronome*, April,
p. 51. Bauduc . . . really comes on with some very fly
and superb drumming. — 1952 *A History of Jazz in
America*, p. 351. *fly*: smooth; to describe looks or manner

or performance, usually the first two ("he's a fly cat").
— 1955 *Hear Me Talkin to Ya*, p. 226. Elmer Snowden
played banjo in our band, and was considered to be very
fly. — 1958 *The Book of Negro Folklore*, p. 483. *fly:*
fresh, impudent, sassy, flirtatious.

forget it, [cf. general slang meaning (i.e., never mind);
some currency since c. 1950] You don't understand me
(see quot.), or this is unparalleled (i.e., a superlative).
— 1961 *Down Beat*, 25 May, p. 24. If five stars for all
three volumes implies to you that this is a flawless set of
records, forget it.

fours, *n. pl.* [shortened form of *four bar passages;* some
currency since c. 1935, but wide currency only since
c. 1950; see also CHASE] See 1955 quot. — 1955 *The Encyclopedia of Jazz*, p. 346. *fours:* a "chase" [q.v.] in
which the soloists play four bars apiece. — 1959 *The Jazz
Review*, Jan., p. 34. After Paul's solo we have a section of
fours. — 1960 *The Jazz Review*, Nov., p. 22. And the
chase fours between Bird and Fats are thrilling indeed.
— 1961 *Down Beat*, 16 Feb., p. 36. The "fours" between
guitar and piano on . . . *I Remember You* build beautifully as they unfold.

fox, *n.* [by analogy with both the beauty and the cunning;
some currency esp. among Negro jazzmen since c. 1958
(it is, oddly, considerably predated by *foxy*)] See
1962 quot. — 1962 *N.Y. Times Magazine*, 20 May, p. 45.
fox: a beautiful girl. — 1963 *Nugget*, Feb., p. 46. There
are a whole lot of foxes in this town.

fox trot, [from common practice of designating jazz dances
by reference to animal movement (see also BUNNY HUG,
CAMEL WALK, TURKEY TROT); current since c. 1917]
Generic term for jazz (and popular) dance (and its
tempo) since c. 1917. — 1926 *So This Is Jazz*, p. 25. A
tune played doubly slow for a "toddle" is no less jazz
than when performed at its original fox-trot tempo. —
1926 *Melody Maker*, Sep., p. 7. The fox-trot still holds

sway everywhere. — 1929 *Jacobs' Orchestral Monthly,*
June, p. 6. Jazz grew up around the fox trot and is still
mainly supported by it. — 1941 *Father of the Blues,*
p. 226. They [i.e., the Castles] went abroad and while
in mid-ocean sent a wireless to the magazine to change
the "Bunny hug" to the "Fox-trot."

foxy, *adj.* [cf. 1942 *American Thesaurus of Slang,* p. 251.
"*foxy:* stylish; 'chic'"; current esp. among Negro jazzmen
since c. 1925] Beautiful (applied only to a woman). —
1959 *Esquire,* Nov., p. 70I. *foxy:* beautiful. Example:
Man, but she's foxy. — 1960 *The Jazz Titans,* p. 156.
foxy: beautiful. — 1961 *The Sound,* p. 218. I mean all
the studs in fancy duds and foxy chicks togged to the
bricks is gonna be there.

framming, *participle* [etym. obscure: poss. onomatopoeic
(i.e., with the sound of guitar chords); according to jazzmen, term had some currency c. 1900–c. 1925, obs. since
except historical] See quot. — 1959 *Jazz* (Hentoff &
McCarthy), p. 107. "The first guitar player was 'picking'
and the second was 'framming,' that is, playing chords
while the lead carried the melody."

frantic, *adj.* [extension of standard meaning; current since
c. 1940] Exciting, thrilling: see 1959, 1960 quots. —
1946 *Jazzways,* p. 51. The meaning of "jump tune" should
be clear enough from the term itself; literally, it jumps,
it's exciting or frantic, as the fan would describe it. —
1958 *The Dharma Bums,* p. 194. You never saw a more
frantic dancer. — 1959 *Esquire,* Nov., p. 70I. *frantic:*
something of wild beauty. Anything of a frenzied nature.
— 1960 *Dictionary of American Slang.* s.v. *frantic:* exciting; satisfying; wonderful.

freak, *adj.* [special application of standard meaning; current since c. 1925] Technically unusual or unorthodox.
— 1955 *Hear Me Talkin to Ya,* p. 42. We were both freak
trumpet men. — 1959 *Jazz* (Hentoff & McCarthy),
p. 241. Jonas Walker . . . was probably the first . . . to

apply the New Orleans "freak" sounds to the trombone.

n. [from *freakish*, q.v., one of several standard terms from which the pejorative connotation has been removed: because of an antipathy for the mundane, the ordinary, the conventional; current since c. 1945] One who is inordinately (not perversely) passionate (about someone or something). (Usually preceded by an adjective; where there is none, the term is short for *musician freak*: see second 1959 quot.) — 1946 *Duke Ellington*, p. 270. "I'm a train freak," Duke says. — 1956 *Lady Sings the Blues*, p. 65. She's a hat freak, that girl. — 1959 *The Holy Barbarians*, p. 39. "He looked more like one of those beachcomber Nature Boy health freaks than a real hipster." — 1959 *The Horn*, p. 112. White babies, jazz babies, freaks (as musicians called them) who attached themselves to hornmen, like camp followers, to be hurt. — 1960 *The Jazz Word*, p. 150. Called camp followers,/ they're verbally abused/but not before they're physically used/One girl follows ballplayers/her sister, sailors seek/but these chicks/are something else—they're musician freaks.

    freak lip, [current since c. 1925; see also IRON CHOPS s.v. CHOPS] See quots. — 1936 · *Metronome*, Feb., p. 21. *freak lip:* a brass man who can play three octaves for three hours at least. — 1942 *The American Thesaurus of Slang*, p. 546. *freak lip:* the ability to play high notes accurately; also strong, untiring lips.

freakish, *adj.* [current since c. 1940] Initially, and sometimes today, perverted (esp. sexually); now, usually, out-of-the-ordinary, adventuresome, stimulating. — 1956 *Lady Sings the Blues*, p. 36. But any kind of freakish feelings are better than no feelings at all. — 1958 *Somewhere There's Music*, p. 190. Everything was good, fine, swell, freakish.

freebee, freebie, freeby, *adj. & n.* [from common practice of forming a slang term by adding a rhyming syllable to a word; current among jazzmen since c. 1900]   See 1959 quot. — 1928 *The Walls of Jericho*, p. 300. *freeby:* something for nothing, as complimentary tickets to a theatre. — 1938 *Cab Calloway: Hi De Ho*, p. 16. "The meal was a freeby." — 1938 *Better English*, Nov., p. 51. *freeby:* no charge, gratis. — 1946 *Really the Blues*, p. 252. It's the brakeman who throws freebie passengers off. — 1959 *Esquire*, Nov., p. 70I. *freebee:* something for nothing, a person who always looks for free things. — 1961 *The Sound*, p. 284. "Bernie, do you recall a broadcast we did for the Armed Forces Overseas Radio Services? A freebie job."

from in front, See s.v. FRONT.

from the top (down), See s.v. TOP.

front, *n.* [cf. 1930 *American Tramp and Underworld Slang*, s.v. *front:* "a good appearance; anything designed to make a good impression"; current since c. 1940; see also DRAPE(S), THREADS, TOG]   See 1944 quot. — 1944 *The New Cab Calloway's Hepsters Dictionary.* s.v. *front:* suit of clothing. — 1956 *Tennessee Folklore Society Bulletin*, March, p. 22. *fronts:* suits. — 1958 *American Speech*, Oct., p. 224. The cat . . . dons his front.

   v.t. [See note in *n.* above; current since c. 1930]   To act as nominal head (of a band), as bandleader; also, for its adjective use, see 1952 quot. — 1937 *American Speech*, Feb., p. 46. *to front:* to serve as leader. — 1946 *Jazzways*, p. 48. Hampton was with the Les Hite Orchestra, occasionally "fronted" by Louis Armstrong. — 1952 *The Trouble With Cinderella*, p. 173. He is the "front" man, the intermediator between his band and the public. — 1955 *Hear Me Talkin to Ya*, p. 260. Fats tried fronting a big band on a southern tour. — 1961 *The Sound*, p. 45. "I gonna lay out just one more set. Chuey front it, man."

   from in front, in front, from front, out front, [prob. by analogy with sheet music, the front being the begin-

ning; current since c. 1948]   See second 1959 quot. —
1956 *Lady Sings the Blues*, p. 187. Every musician is a
friend of mine from front, we don't need any introduc-
tions. — 1959 *The Holy Barbarians*, p. 104. Sherry
McCall is beat from in front, as the bop boys of the
forties would have put it. — p. 316. *from in front:* first,
from the beginning. — 1960 *Hiparama of the Classics*,
p. 11. "My frame is bent, Naz. It's been bent from in
front!!!" — p. 15. Hip to the cool sweet groove of Liberty and solid sent upon the Ace Lick that all Cats and
Kitties, Red, White, or Blue! are created Level, in
FRONT. — 1960 *Lenny Bruce: I Am Not a Nut, Elect
Me!* (skit dialogue on LP album Fantasy 7007). I need a
little bread [i.e., money] out front.

front line, [poss. by analogy with parade positions in early
New Orleans street marches (see SECOND LINE), or poss.
simply from approximate positions on the bandstand
(see first 1959 quot.); current since c. 1950]   The featured group of instrumentalists (usually the winds) with
a small jazz band (i.e., up to eight pieces); for its adjective use, see second 1959 quot. — 1959 "A Compendium
for the Teaching of Jazz History," p. 36. Trumpets (or
cornets), trombones, clarinets, saxophones and occasionally other instruments make up the front line, a name
which doubtless grew out of the fact that they sat in a
line, in front of the rhythm section. — 1959 *The Collector's Jazz: Modern*, p. 49. Brown makes some adept
front-line uses of his bass on *Bass Hit,* Verve 8022. —
1961 *Down Beat,* 30 March, p. 17. "I've started a group
with *four* vibes players in the front line." — 1961 *The
Sound*, pp. 11–12. The Sultans were six. Three rhythms
and three horns. In the front line were a trumpet . . .
an alto saxophone and a tenor saxophone.

fruit, *v.i.* [from Negro slang; semantic development unknown; some currency esp. among Negro jazzmen
c. 1935–c. 1945, very rare since]   See 1939, 1946 quots.

— 1938 *Cab Calloway: Hi De Ho*, p. 16. *fruiting:* fickle, fooling around with no particular object. — 1939 *Jitterbug Jamboree Song Book*, p. 32. *fruiting:* fooling around. — 1946 *Really the Blues*, p. 369. *fruit:* romance playfully.

fucked up, [prob. from armed services slang meaning (i.e., badly performed or in trouble); cf. 1960 *Dictionary of American Slang*, s.v. *fucked up*: "in trouble; obsessed with a personal problem; confused; neurotic"; current among jazzmen in several senses since c. 1945; see also WASTED] In addition to the meanings in the note above: extremely drunk or high from effects of liquor, marijuana, or drugs; addicted to drugs; crippled; emotionally distraught. Oral evidence only.

funk, *n.* [see note s.v. FUNKY; also cf. 1960 *Webster's New International Dictionary*, s.v. *funk:* "cf. OF *funkier* to emit smoke . . . Offensive smell or smoke. *Now rare*"; widely current in the jazz sense since c. 1957; see also SOUL] Earthiness: see 1960 quots. — 1959 *Jazz: A Quarterly of American Music*, Fall, p. 292. You can even try to put too much "funk" in a thing. — 1959 *Jazz Poems*, p. 14. Miles Davis blowing his sophisticated funk. — 1959 *The Horn*, p. 27. All who comped with funk . . . and blew the truth. — 1960 *The Jazz Word*, p. 213. All the current terms of approbation among jazzmen — "soul," "funk," "down home"—all mean basically that if a man can play the blues from inside himself without straining to play a part, he's a legitimate jazzman. — 1960 *Down Beat*, 24 Nov., p. 18. "Funk," then, may best be described as a broad use of blue tonality.

funky, *adj. & n.* [cf. 1956 *American Speech*, Dec., p. 309. "Tobacco is said to be funked if it has become spoiled or moldy after it has been taken down, piled closely on the floor in bulk, and stripped . . . The *American Dialect Dictionary* notes that it is used only as a participle and as an adjective with the meaning of 'rotten,' 'molded.' Its earliest recorded use is from Kentucky in 1892"; also cf. 1959 *The Holy Barbarians,* p. 316: "*funky:* Old French *funicle,* terrible"; see last 1959 and 1960 quots. for etym.; also cf. what was prob. first jazz use in the old sense: Buddy Bolden's c. 1900 jazz tune *Funky Butt;* widely current since c. 1955; see also HARD BOP] As adjective, see first 1960 quot.; as noun, a jazz movement: see last 1959 quot. — 1956 *Down Beat,* 31 Oct., p. 17. "What is funky? Oh, a sort of low-down blues feeling." — 1959 *The Sound of Surprise,* p. 181. In recent years, these men [i.e., "cool" musicians] have been almost savagely ignored by the members of the "funky" or "hard-bop" school, who go at the blues with hook and claw. — 1959 *Evergreen Review,* Nov.-Dec., p. 138. The "gospel music" of Negro churches and . . . a kind of blues playing that had matured as long ago as the late twenties . . . rediscovering an *emotional* basis on which jazz could continue in the same kinds of sources from which it had originally sprung . . . And the style acquired a name, "funky"—a term borrowed from Negro argot for a certain kind of body odor. — 1960 *The Village Voice,* 3 Feb., p. 13. This term *funky,* which originally meant a pungent odor emanating from the body, has come to mean, in music, earthy and fundamental. — 1961 *Metronome,* April, p. 12. The word *funky* is taken, half a century later, to describe a return to earthy and blue tonalities.

fuzz, fuz, *n.* [from underworld slang: cf. 1930 *American Tramp and Underworld Slang,* s.v. *fuzz:* "a detective; a prison guard or turnkey. Here it is likely that 'fuzz' was originally 'fuss,' one hard to please or over-particular"; some currency esp. among Negro jazzmen since c. 1935, but wide currency only since c. 1950; see also LAW] The police. — 1952 *Flee the Angry Strangers,* p. 137. "No Law in there, baby, I can smell Fuzz from fifty yards." — 1956 *Lady Sings the Blues,* p. 33. The place was full of what they called "wayward women" in those days, and of course the vice squad fuzz. — 1956 *Sideman*, p. 275. "First thing I know, in come the fuz!" — 1958 *Somewhere There's Music*, p. 143. "He got busted [i.e., arrested] last week by the local fuzz."

gage, gauge, *n.* [semantic development unknown: cf. 1933 OED, s.v. *gage "slang:* a quart pot" (see note s.v. POT); current since c. 1935; see also MARY JANE, SHIT, TEA] See last quot. (note: the definitions in the 1945 and 1958 quots. are mistaken). — 1945 *Hepcats Jive Talk Dictionary.* s.v. *gage:* intoxicating liquor [sic!]. — 1955 *Solo*, p. 40. "You can carry about five sticks of gauge in the beard." — 1958 *American Speech*, Oct., p. 225. *gage:* narcotics. — 1959 *The Naked Lunch*, p. 81. They . . . smoke gage in cigarettes made of wrapping paper. — 1959 *Esquire*, Nov., p. 70H. *gage:* marijuana.

galloping piano (or rhythm), [from resemblance of the sound; some currency c. 1917–c. 1930, obs. since except historical] See 1937 quot. — 1937 *American Speech*, Feb., p. 46. *gallop:* a type of rhythm used in drumming, resembling the sound of a horse's gallop. — 1958 *The Jazz Review*, Nov., p. 14. The regular pianist, Turk Thomas had been with the Satisfied Five in Texas, and played what we called "galloping piano"—no equilibrium.

gang, *n.* [see 1959 quot. for semantic explanation and approx. beginning date; term largely obs. since c. 1950; see also LOT, MESS]   A great quantity (see 1959 quot.) or something of great quality—that is, excellent. — 1933 *Fortune,* Aug., p. 47. "Yeah," said the other, "he plays a gang o' horn." — 1936 *Esquire,* June, p. 132. The dark, Latin type Prima playing a gang o' horn. — 1936 *Swing That Music,* p. 1. It made a whole gang of sound, for sure. — 1955 *Hear Me Talkin to Ya,* p. 194. They worked up a gang of arrangements. — 1959 *Jazz: A Quarterly of American Music,* Fall, p. 285. In requesting a *gang of gin,* Bessie voices a use of gang in the sense of "much, several, a number" which had been developing a special sense in the gangster era of the twenties. Perhaps, as in the thirties, *gang* may have had the connotation of a medley, a number of songs or musical compositions strung together.

gang busters, come on like, See s.v. COME ON.

gappings, *n. pl.* [etym. obscure; according to jazzmen, term had some currency c. 1910–c. 1925, obs. since except historical]   Salary. — 1955 *Hear Me Talkin to Ya,* p. 8. Their tips were so great until they did not even have to touch their nightly gappings.

gas, *v.t.* [see note in *gas, n.;* current since c. 1945]   To excite or please enormously. — 1953 *The Hot and the Cool,* p. 76. And man, that was something would gas the folks back home in Lynton Bridge, Mass.! — 1959 *The Holy Barbarians,* p. 24. "He was so grateful the next day, he was just gassed." — 1960 *Jazz: A Quarterly of American Music,* Winter, p. 47. "I was THUNDERSTRUCK. I couldn't say a word. He gasses me." — 1960 *The Jazz Review,* May, p. 30. "Is Ornette Coleman gassin' everybody in the Apple or isn't he?"

gas, gasser, *n.* [by analogy with immobilizing effects of being, literally, gassed; *gasser* current since c. 1942; the shortened form, *gas,* was poss. formed directly from *gas,* *v.t.*, and has largely replaced *gasser* since c. 1957] See 1948 and last quots. — 1944 *The New Cab Calloway's Hepsters Dictionary*, p. 7. "When it comes to dancing, she's a gasser." — 1948 *Down Beat*, 28 July, p. 4. *gasser:* that instrumentalist, vocalist, arrangement, performance or 1949 convertible which is "cool," "real crazy," "half-gone" . . . which visibly impresses the speaker. — 1955 *Bop Fables*, p. 44. "It's a gasser." — 1958 *The Book of Negro Folklore*, p. 483. *gasser:* an exciting thing. — 1958 *Somewhere There's Music*, p. 29. "Be a gas when they're finished, won't it?" — 1959 *The Holy Barbarians*, p. 40. "Any sound behind poetry was a novelty, exciting, a *gas.*" — 1959 *Swinging Syllables*. s.v. *gas:* anything enjoyable, satisfying.

gate, gatemouth, gate-mouth, *n.* [See 1959 quot. for etym.; also cf. 1942 *American Mercury*, July, p. 94. "*gator-faced:* long, black face with big mouth"; current c. 1935–c. 1945, obs. since except historical; see also ALLIGATOR] See 1938, 1952 quots. — 1938 *Cab Calloway: Hi De Ho*, p. 16. *gate:* a male person (a salutation), abbr. for "gate-mouth." — 1945 *Band Leaders*, March, p. 20. Within a horn blast of Hollywood and Vine, the crossroads of Glamour-town, can be found many lairs of the hepcats —haunts of gates and ride men. — 1946 *Big Book of Swing*, p. 124. *gate:* young fellow. — 1952 *A History of Jazz in America*, p. 351. *gate:* once (and occasionally used after the swing era [i.e., 1935–1945]) synonymous with jazz musician. — 1959 *Jazz: A Quarterly of American Music*, Fall, p. 284. Louis Armstrong writes he originated the term *gate* which through the swing era was applied to musicians (*Swing That Music*, p. 77). Early in New Orleans Louis was given the nickname, "Gatemouth," an allusion to his formidable lips, teeth and general kisser . . . As gates swing, two words in the field patterned an association, which helped the currency of *gate.*

gauge, *n.* See S.V. GAGE.

gee, ghee, *n.* [from underworld slang: cf. 1934 *A Diction-*
ary of American Slang, p. 26. *"gee:* person"; also cf. 1960
Dictionary of American Slang, s.v. *gee:* "from first letter
of 'guy,' reenforced by an imitated French pronunciation"; some currency among jazzmen c. 1935–c. 1945,
obs. since] See 1939 quot. — 1939 *Jitterbug Jamboree*
Song Book, p. 32. *ghee:* a fellow, man, guy. — 1960 *Dic-*
tionary of American Slang. s.v. *gee:* a fellow; a guy.

geets, *n. pl.* [etym. unknown: see last quot. for an improb-
able one; cf. 1953 *American Speech,* May, "Carnie Talk"
p. 116. *"geetus:* money"; some currency since c. 1945;
see the more common BREAD] See 1957 quot. — 1957
N.Y. Times Magazine, 18 Aug., p. 26. *geets:* money. —
1960 *The Jazz Word,* p. 81. "I'm spendin' my hard-
earned geets." — 1960 *Dictionary of American Slang,*
p. 211. *geets:* dollars . . . that which "gets" or buys
things.

get around on (one's) horn, [special application of general slang "get around" (i.e., to be experienced, to fare
well); current since c. 1935; see also ALL OVER, DOWN
WITH (ONE'S) AX] See 1937 quot. — 1937 *American*
Speech, Feb., p. 46. *get around on a horn:* to be able to
play fast and difficult passages well. — 1942 *The Ameri-*
can Thesaurus of Slang, p. 562. *get around* (as on a
horn): play expertly. — 1950 *Metronome,* Aug., p. 16.
He sure gets around on the horn, doesn't he? . . . He
does so many little tricky things that are really not easy,
and he does them with finesse. — 1958 *Jazz: A Quarterly*
of American Music, Oct., p. 28. Whoever he is, he sure
gets around the horn. — 1961 *The Sound,* p. 252. "The
way you get around on that horn!"

get hot!, [for etym. see HOT; current c. 1925–c. 1940, obs.
since except historical or, very rare, derisive] An exhortation to a musician or musicians to play excitingly
(though note in 1956 quot. the pejorative connotation
that the phrase has taken on in its rare post-World War

II use). — 1946 *Really the Blues*, p. 141. The unhip public took over the expression "hot" and made it corny by
getting up in front of a band and snapping their fingers
in a childish way, yelling "Get hot! Yeah man, get hot!"
— 1956 *Jazz: Its Evolution and Essence*, p. 232. "Getting
hot" is relatively easy; a student band can do it as well
as anybody. Exasperated, distorted sonorities played fortissimo are generally sufficient. — 1959 *Jazz: A Quarterly
of American Music*, Fall, p. 284. "Break it down" was
reported to be Harlem's pet expression of 1933, and was
synonymous with "get hot."

get in there, [for etym. see IN THERE; some currency
c. 1935–c. 1945, obs. since] An exhortation to a musician or musicians to play excitingly. — 1938 *Cab Calloway: Hi De Ho*, p. 16. *get in there:* (an exclamation) go
to work, get busy, make it hot, give it all you've got.

get it, [current since c. 1925] To satisfy musically; also,
by extension: to be eminently satisfactory. — 1942 *Well,
Get It!* (tune recorded by the Tommy Dorsey Orchestra). — 1952 *The Record Changer*, Aug.-Sep., p. 22.
Buster says, "now let's get it." — 1958 *Somewhere
There's Music*, p. 69. "Fine, but that doesn't get it." —
1961 *The Sound*, p. 159. "Even that one night a week
gets it for me."

get off, [cf. general slang *get off the ground;* current
c. 1930–c. 1945, obs. since except historical] To improvise skillfully; also, for its rare noun form, see first 1935
quot. — 1932 *Melody Maker*, July, p. 593. There is an
abundance of trumpet-playing of the first order from the
local "get-off" man. — 1933 *Fortune*, Aug., p. 47. Returning to Trombonist Brown, he can *get off* . . .
(. . . syncopate to beat the band). — 1935 *Vanity Fair*,
Nov., p. 71. Breaks are sometimes known as *get-offs* or
take-offs. — 1935 *His Hi De Highness of Ho De Ho!*
p. 35. "A colored musician . . . says, 'Them cats is
getting off!' " — 1936 *Metronome*, Feb., p. 21. *getting*

off: really swinging. — 1947 *Frontiers of Jazz,* p. ix. The soloist is getting off.

get on, See s.v. ON.

get (one's) business straight, See s.v. BUSINESS.

ghee, *n.* See s.v. GEE.

ghost note, [by analogy with its faintness; some currency since c. 1920] On a wind instrument, a note de-emphasized in a series—that is, fingered, but barely blown; also, as a verb, to blow such a note (oral evidence only in this form). — 1927 *Melody Maker,* July, p. 695. Ghost note . . . is *barely audible.*

gig, *n.* [poss. from *gigue,* a lively dance form of Italian origin commonly used as the last movement of a suite (cf. English counterpart *jig*): from Old French *giguer;* according to jazzman Eubie Blake, bandleader James Reese Europe used the term in its jazz sense as early as c. 1905; widely current since c. 1920] Initially, see 1955 quot.; since c. 1955, see 1959 quot. (though, it should be noted, for the non-jazz job, the term is applied only to a non-jazzman; for the jazzman, the non-jazz job is a *hame* or a *day gig,* q.v.). — 1926 *Melody Maker,* Sep., p. 7. One popular "gig" band makes use of a nicely printed booklet. — 1931 *Melody Maker,* May, p. 369. Bill Henry and his orchestra were responsible for the undoubted success of half the local gigs. — 1946 *Really the Blues,* p. 370. *gig:* single engagement, club date. — 1955 *The Encyclopedia of Jazz,* p. 346. *gig:* job (esp. one-night stand). — 1959 *The Holy Barbarians,* p. 89. He returned to the bass fiddle and started making night club gigs again. — 1959 *Newport Jazz Festival: 1959,* p. 45. *gig:* a job of any kind, musical or non-.

v.i. (sometimes with *around*), [widely current since c. 1940] See 1947 quot.; also, since c. 1955: to work at any job (see also HAME). — 1947 *N.Y. Herald Tribune,* 10 March. At present he is "gigging around," a musician's term for those who take casual dates whenever they can find them. — 1952 *Music Out of Dixie,* p. 158. "I only played with him a few times, jes' giggin' aroun'." — 1955 *The Encyclopedia of Jazz,* p. 346. *gig:* to work one-night jobs.

day gig, [jazz is generally performed at night: hence, the logic of the distinguishing term; current since c. 1945; see also HAME, SLAVE] A non-jazz job reluctantly taken by a jazzman for purely monetary reasons. — 1962 *The Village Voice,* 14 June, p. 13. Shepp, Dixon, and even a leader of the advance guard like Cecil Taylor must rely on the day gig in order to survive.

gitbox, git, git-box, gitter, gitterbox, *n.* [dialectal; some currency c. 1920–c. 1945, rare since; see also BOX, 2] See 1937 quot. — 1933 *Metronome,* Aug., p. 16. Eddie was playing the kind of banjo I wanted, but I got him to learn that "gitter box." — 1936 *Metronome,* Feb., p. 61. *gitter:* guitar. — 1937 *American Speech,* Oct., p. 181. *gitbox:* guitar. — 1942 *The American Thesaurus of Slang,* p. 558. *git-box:* guitar. — 1948 *Down Beat,* 19 May, p. 14. The final chorus is git and block chords and knocked-out at that.

give (one) some skin, See s.v. SKIN.

give (out), [current c. 1930–c. 1945, obs. since except historical] To play excitingly: frequently hortatory. — 1936 *Esquire,* June, p. 92. And the singer with the outfit can do with his or her voice just what the soloist can do with his instrument, he can *give.* — 1937 *This Thing Called Swing,* p. 8. *give:* a command or plea meaning "give it all you've got, put the heat on it, go to town." — 1949 *A Wreath for Rivera,* p. 10. "Carlos steps out in a spot light and gives." — 1952 *A History of Jazz in America,* p. 351. *give* or *give out:* swing [i.e., c. 1935–c. 1945] parlance for "let yourself go." — 1955 *Hear Me Talkin to Ya,* p. 151. We would give out with such tunes as Tiger Rag.

gliss, *n.* [shortened form of technical musical term *glissando;* current since c. 1920] See 1936 quot.: in jazz, applied only to trumpet and, esp., trombone. — 1926 *Melody Maker,* March, p. 31. The aforementioned mute modifier . . . is used to get the necessary "gliss" which I have marked by means of slurs. — 1936 *Metronome,* Feb., p. 21. *gliss:* glissando. — 1942 *The American Thesaurus of Slang,* p. 561. *gliss:* glissando. — 1946 *Jazzways,* p. 31. The engineer handed them the instruction sheet and listened to Dutrey warm up with a few glisses on the long slide trombone.

go, *v.i.* [by analogy with action or movement; some currency since c. 1920 but wide currency only since c. 1947; see 1958 quot. for the term's status among musicians and fans; see also MOVE, WORK] See 1937, 1958 quots. — 1926 *Melody Maker,* Jan., p. 19. Atta-boy, let's go! — 1935 *Vanity Fair,* Nov., p. 71. Hot artists or bands that can put across their licks successfully . . . can "go." — 1937 *American Speech,* Feb., p. 46. *go:* to improvise rhythmically and expertly on a given melody. —1953 *Night Light,* p. 131. One of them was saying urgently, "Go, go." — 1958 *Publication of the American Dialect Society,* Nov., p. 45. *go:* really a fan's word, to express excitement at a particularly "swingin'" solo. Often used derisively, sometimes approvingly, by musicians. (The fan's phrase is "Go, man, go!"). — 1959 *Esquire,* Nov., p. 70I. *go:* to act with uninhibitedness. — 1959 *The Horn,* p. 144. "You can't take it away from him, that man *goes.*" — 1961 *Jazz Journal,* Feb., p. 8. Lester goes first, and how he goes.

go down, [etym. unknown; cf. 1937 *A Dictionary of Slang and Unconventional English,* s.v. *go down:* "To be accepted (by); be approved or allowed" (first citation given is from Smollett); current since c. 1940; see also SHAKING] To happen. — 1947 *Time,* 10 Feb., p. 12.

But until the groovy cats dig each other or a Webster happens by to help us pick up on what's going down, *Time* will igg [i.e., ignore] the issue. — 1956 *Lady Sings the Blues,* p. 190. In view of what went down later, who can say? — 1958 *Jazz in Hi-Fi,* p. 13. To say . . . "I dig what's going down" . . . means you are aware of the situation. — 1958 *The Book of Negro Folklore,* p. 484. *go down:* the happenings [q.v.]. — 1959 *Diggeth Thou?,* p. 43. Let me wig you to the deal that went down.

go to town, [by analogy with the excitement (i.e., of rural folk going to town); current c. 1933–c. 1943, obs. since] To play music or do anything excitingly. — 1935 *Stage,* Sep., p. 45. *go to town:* play hot. — 1935 *His Hi De Highness of Ho De Ho,* p. 35. " 'Goin' to town,' meaning to get fast and hot." — 1936 *Swing That Music,* p. 30. That phrase, "goin' to town," means cuttin' loose and takin' the music with you. — 1938 *Pic,* 5 April, p. 31. Goin' to town with a vengeance! This looks like mass murder but is only the Savoy version of hot dancing.

go home, (let's), [according to jazzmen, current c. 1925–c. 1945, obs. since except historical; see also ALL-IN, RIDE-OUT] In traditional jazz, a signal to play the final chorus. — 1959 *Jazz: A Quarterly of American Music,* Summer, p. 191. It seems such a perfect "goin' home" riff.

gold, *n.* [from underworld and general slang, but with esp. currency among jazzmen c. 1900–c. 1945, when it and *loot* were largely replaced by *bread*] Money. — 1952 *Who Walk in Darkness,* p. 12. "Can you lend me some gold?" — 1957 *On the Road,* p. 60. "All right, all right, don't drop your gold all over the place."

golden-leaf, *n.* [some currency c. 1920–c. 1945, very rare since; see also *panatella*] See 1946 quot. — 1925 *Golden Leaf Strut* (tune recorded by the Original New Orleans Rhythm Kings). — 1946 *Really the Blues,* p. 370. *golden-leaf:* the best marijuana.

gone, *adj. & interj.* [one of several terms favorably con-
noting transcendence: see also OUT OF THIS WORLD, SENT,
SOMETHING ELSE; current c. 1945–c. 1955, rare since; see
also CRAZY, NUTTY, the earlier SOLID, and the more
recent BOSS and SOMETHING ELSE] See 1946 quot. —
1946 *Really the Blues,* p. 370. *gone: out of this world,*
superlative. — 1948 *Partisan Review,* June, p. 721.
Everything was dichotomously *solid, gone, out of this
world,* or *nowhere, sad, beat, a drag.* — 1948 *New Yorker,*
3 July, p. 28. Their expressions of approval include
"Cool!," "Gone!" and "Bells, man!" — 1952 *Life,* 29
Sep., p. 67. *gone:* the tops—superlative of crazy. — 1955
Down Beat, 30 Nov., p. 47. The drummer was gone!

   real gone, [current c. 1945–c. 1955, rare since] See
1949 quot. — 1949 *Music Library Association Notes,*
Dec., p. 44. *real gone:* intensified form [of *gone*]. — 1952
A History of Jazz in America, p. 351. *gone:* superlative,
may be further qualified, such as in "real gone." —
1953 *Night Light,* p. 130. "You're so real gone, Pops."

   the gonest, [see 1954 quot.; current c. 1945–c. 1955,
rare since] See 1954 quot. — 1954 *Esquire,* Nov., p.
131. Jazz musicians and enthusiasts thrive on hyperbole,
of course; if anything is good, it's "the greatest," and if
anything is so good it's far and away ahead of everything
else, it's "the gonest." — 1957 *On the Road,* p. 60. "I
have found the gonest little girl in the world."

goof, *n. & v.i.* [cf. 1959 *Webster's New World Dictionary*
s.v. *goof:* "prob. < or akin to ME. *gofisshe, goofish,* foolish"; prob. reinforced by armed services use of *goof off*
(shun duty); also see first 1956 quot, for poss. explanation of semantic development; current among jazzmen
since c. 1943; see also CLINKER, FLUFF] See both 1952
quots.; also, to carouse (no pejorative connotation): see
1957 and first 1959 quots. — 1948 *Just Goofin'* (tune composed by Hubie Wheeler). — 1952 *Life,* 29 Sep., p. 67.

goof: to blow a wrong note, or to make a mistake. — 1952 *A History of Jazz in America*, p. 351. *goof*: to wander in attention, to fail to discharge one's responsibility (as for example, not to show up for an appointment and not to be provided with a clear excuse); in musical performance to play without much attention, to miss coming in on time, etc. — 1956 *Tennessee Folklore Society Bulletin*, March, p. 26. The verb *to goof* (to do something stupid) obviously stems from *goof balls* [i.e., barbiturates], since one might do anything under their influence. — 1956 *Sideman*, p. 20. If the band didn't all take the same route there'd be mistakes—some goofs. — 1957 *On the Road*, p. 177. Dean and I goofed around San Francisco. — 1959 *The Horn*, p. 85. "I get me some real rest, just goof a while." — p. 87. "She had heard him goof, play sour, pretend." — 1959 *Mexico City Blues*, p. 80. Goofing at the Table. — 1960 *The Jazz Review*, May, p. 37. There are a few historical goofs in the picture.

goola, *n.* [etym. unknown; according to jazzmen, term had some currency c. 1917–c. 1940, obs. since except historical; see also BOX EIGHTY-EIGHT] See quots. — 1944 *Dan Burley's Original Handbook of Harlem Jive*, p. 139. *goola*: piano. — 1953 *The American Thesaurus of Slang*, p. 550. *goola*: piano. — 1960 *Dictionary of American Slang*, p. 223. *goola*: a piano.

grass, *n.* [metonymy: marijuana derives from a weed; some currency since c. 1935; see also BOO, GAGE, POT, TEA] See quots. — 1943 *Time*, 19 July, p. 54. Marijuana may be called . . . grass. — 1959 *The Jazz Scene*, p. 292. *grass*: marijuana.

gray, grey, *n.* [from Negro slang; some currency esp. among Negro jazzmen since c. 1930; see also PINK, FAY] See 1960 quot. — 1960 *Dictionary of American Slang*. s.v. *gray*: a white person. — 1961 *The Sound*, p. 43. One of those pale, taut, overeager grays that seemed drawn in increasing numbers to the new jazz, like moths to the flame. — p. 101 "I dunno, old man, to the average colored person the average gray acts like he's in a sweat most of the time." — 1961 *Commonweal*, 24 March, p. 657. Those who retained their names and nominal church affiliations no longer, however, took any obeisance to the "greys" for granted.

grease, *n. & v.i.* [cf. 1928 *American Speech*, Feb., "Carnival Slang," p. 253. "*grease joint:* hamburger stand"; also poss. shortened from *grease one's chops*, q.v.; some currency as *v.i.* since c. 1940, as *n.* since c. 1955; see also SCOFF] See 1959 quot. — 1944 *The New Cab Calloway's Hepsters Dictionary*. s.v. *grease:* to eat. — 1959 *Jazz for Moderns*, p. 20. *grease:* food, or "to eat." — 1961 *Night Song*, p. 86. "Look, man, can we take off our things and get some grease?"

grease (one's) chops, [see note in *grease;* some currency c. 1935–c. 1945, very rare since] See 1946 quot. — 1946 *Really the Blues*, p. 370. *grease your chops:* eat. — 1950 *Gutbucket and Gossamer*, p. 19. Then the suggestion that we grease our chops was advanced.

greatest, the, [see 1954 quot.; widely current c. 1940–c. 1955, rare since; see also THE END, THE MOST] See 1954 quot. — 1946 *Jazzways*, p. 56. "Duke's the greatest" is certainly the easiest cliché tossed around swing circles. — 1954 *Esquire*, Nov., p. 131. Jazz musicians and enthusiasts thrive on hyperbole, of course; if anything is good, it is "the greatest." — 1956 *Sideman*, p. 25. "Lips is the greatest. Farther out than J.J."

green, long green, [cf. 1960 *Dictionary of American Slang,* s.v. *green:* "orig. sporting and underworld use. From 'long green' "; according to jazzman Eubie Blake, term has had some currency esp. among Negro jazzmen since c. 1900, though it has had wide currency only since c. 1950; see also BREAD, GEETS, GOLD, LOOT] See 1958 quot. — 1955 *Say*, 28 April, p. 53. *long green:* over

$1000. — 1957 *N.Y. Times Magazine*, 18 Aug., p. 26. *green:* money. — 1958 *This Week Magazine*, 28 Sep., p. 33. Money is "green" and "long green" is much money.

grey, *n.* See s.v. GRAY.

grit, *n.* [from *grits;* synechdoche: i.e., one kind of food to denote any food; according to jazz dancer Leon James, the term was introduced into jazz speech by Southern Negro musicians c. 1940; see also SCOFF] See quot. — 1962 *N.Y. Times Magazine*, 20 May, p. 45. *grit:* food.

grizzly bear, [dance designations frequently refer to animals and their movements; current during the dance's vogue, c. 1910–c. 1920, and its brief revival in 1930s, obs. since except historical] A jazz dance in vogue, c. 1910–c. 1920. — 1914 *Modern Dancing* [1962 *Jazz: A History of the New York Scene*, p. 37]. Drop the Turkey Trot, the Grizzly Bear, the Bunny Hug, etc.

groove, *n.* [from jazz slang *in the groove, groovy*, q.v.; current since c. 1940] Routine, preference, style, source of pleasure; see first 1959 quot. — 1940 *Swing*, Nov., p. 27. *Travelin'* has a sax-unison melody somewhat in the Tuxedo groove. — 1946 *Big Book of Swing*, p. 124. *a groove:* swell, good to hear. — 1954 *Jive Jungle*, p. 32. The all night "grooves" began. — 1958 *Somewhere There's Music*, p. 35. "Romance? No, bruz, that's not my groove." — 1958 *Metronome*, June, p. 18. "I play a good many fast tempos, because I feel better playing in that kind of groove." — 1959 *Esquire*, Nov., p. 70I. *groove:* category. A person's predilection. Example: Chess is his groove. — 1959 *Swinging Syllables.* s.v. *a groove:* a good scene.

v.i. & v.t. [widely current since c. 1945] See 1959 quot. — 1945 *Groovin' High* (tune written and recorded by Dizzy Gillespie). — 1959 *Esquire*, Nov., p. 70I. To groove someone means to provide them with enjoyment. Example: Her singing grooved me.

in the groove, [from the manner of making and/or playing phonograph records (i.e., with the needle in the groove of the record); widely current c. 1936–c. 1945, obs. since except historical] Excellent, esp. applied to music: see first quot.; also, by extension, excellent or sophisticated (in this sense, oral evidence only, but see first two quots.; see also IN THERE). — 1936 *Delineator,* Nov., p. 49. *in the groove:* carried away or inspired by the music; playing in exalted spirit and to perfection. — 1937 *This Thing Called Swing,* p. 8. *in the groove:* inspired playing. Swing that fairly carries away the player. A fine compliment from other members of the band— "He's in the groove tonight." — 1937 *Metronome,* May, p. 61. The band is in a groove. — 1938 *Cab Calloway: Hi De Ho,* p. 16. *in the groove:* perfect, no deviation, down the alley. — 1947 *Frontiers of Jazz,* p. 141. They simply got a great *burn* from playing *in the groove.* Also **in a groove.**

groovy, *adj.* [from *in the groove,* q.v.; current since c. 1938] See 1944, 1946, 1952 quots. — 1944 *The New Cab Calloway's Hepsters Dictionary.* s.v. *groovy:* fine. "I feel groovy." — 1946 *Really the Blues,* p. 370. *groovy:* really good, enjoyable. — 1952 *A History of Jazz in America,* p. 351. *groovy:* applied to a good swinging beat (earlier, "in the groove"). — 1953 *Night Light,* p. 154. "That dance you were doing . . . was real groovy." — 1956 *Sideman,* p. 308. "Things been real groovy!"

growl, *v.i., v.t., n., & adj.* [current c. 1925–c. 1945, very rare since except historical] See 1935, 1956 quots. — 1934 *Metronome,* Nov., p. 25. A trumpet . . . growls really effectively for a change. — 1935 *His Hi De Highness of Ho De Ho,* p. 35. "Even white musicians will say 'growl it' to a trumpet player when they are asking him to play it 'lowdown' or 'dirty.'" — 1946 *Jazzology,*

Sep., p. 32. Nanton's fame as the foremost exponent of
the "growl" trombone is known far and wide. — 1955
A *Pictorial History of Jazz*, p. 138. Seated are "growl"
trumpet star Bubber Miley (*left*) and Ellington. — 1955
Hear Me Talkin to Ya, p. 231. He used to growl all night
long, playing gutbucket on his horn. — 1956 *Guide to
Jazz*. s.v. *growl:* a deep, rough tone produced with the
lips on wind instruments in imitation of tones used by
some blues singers. — 1960 *Metronome*, Dec., p. 22.
As long as I can remember Duke Ellington, there's been
growling, right back to Bubber Miley . . . Bubber was
the first I knew to use the mute *and* the plunger.

gully-low, *adj.* [see 1939 quot. for semantic development;
some currency c. 1910–c. 1940, obs. since except his-
torical]   See 1939 quot. — 1939 *Jazzmen*, p. 12. From
barrel-houses and honky-tonks came many of the descriptive words which were applied to the music played
in them; such as . . . "gully-low," meaning as its name
implies, low as a ditch or "gully," hence "low-down." —
1946 *Really the Blues*, p. 102. They wanted to blast
every high-minded citizen clear out of his easy chair
with their yarddog growls and gully-low howls.

gutbucket, **gut-bucket**, *adj. & n.* [see 1939 and last quots.
for semantic development (the explanation in 1944 quot.
is of extremely doubtful validity); current c. 1910–c.
1940, obs. since except historical]   See 1939 and last
quots. — 1929 *New York Age*, 23 Feb. [1962 *Jazz: A History of the New York Scene*, pp. 191–192] Using a
mute, occasionally a small megaphone inserted at the
bell of his trumpet, he eschews the tin pail, hat, plunger
and other devices of the "gut bucket" player. — 1939
Jazzmen, p. 12. From barrel-houses and honky-tonks
came many of the descriptive words which were
applied to the music played in them; such as . . . "gutbucket," referring originally to the bucket which caught
drippings or "gutterings" from the barrels, later to the

unrestrained brand of music that was played by small
bands in the dives . . . — 1944 *Metronome,* Nov., p. 17.
"The word gutbucket must have stemmed directly from
Irvis's style and his use of a real bucket for a mute." —
1958 *Somewhere There's Music,* p. 73. The band played
gutbucket boogie. — 1961 *Coda,* March, p. 10. Robbins
put out some gravelly gut bucket trombone. — 1961
Esquire, May, p. 153. "Gutbucket," meaning a lowdown
type of blues (the term originated from the name of the
bucket that caught the drippings of the big, reclining
barrels from which gin was sold), perforce left its stain
on the singer as well as the music.

guts, *n. pl.* [special application of general slang meaning,
prob. reinforced by *gutbucket,* q.v.; according to jazzmen, some currency c. 1930–c. 1945, obs. since; see also
FUNK, SOUL] Earthiness (of an instrumentalist). Oral
evidence only.

gutter music, [from early (c. 1900) parade and funeral
march practice (i.e., of marching in the gutter), reinforced by jazzman's awareness of the music's disesteem
with the general public; according to jazzmen, some currency c. 1900–c. 1917, obs. since except historical] New
Orleans jazz. — 1936 *Transatlantic Jazz,* pp. 16–17. Actually, the Negro bands in New Orleans were the
originators but unfortunately no company was interested
in making records of their so-called "gutter music."

gutty, *adj.* [from *guts;* some currency c. 1930–c. 1945,
obs. since] Musically earthy. — 1939 *Blues* (Decca
Records pamphlet), p. 2. Buster Bailey's reaction can
be felt in the "gutty" clarinet tone he uses.

H [abbreviation; from underworld and narcotics slang: cf. 1934 *A Dictionary of American Slang*, p. 18. "*H:* heroin"; some currency among jazzmen since c. 1935; see also HEAVY SOUL, HORSE] See 1942 quot. — 1942 *American Thesaurus of Slang*, p. 474. *H:* heroin. — 1959 *The Cool World*, p. 43. When a guy is takin H he got to get outa the gang. — 1961 *The Sound*, p. 22. "It's not like H or M." — 1961 *Esquire*, May, p. 155. "Fat Girl," as he [i.e., Fats Navarro] was known, was dead in his twenties of tuberculosis aggravated by his bouts with the big H.

habit, *n.* [from underworld and narcotics slang: cf. 1930 *American Tramp and Underworld Slang*, s.v. *habit:* "the drug habit"; some currency among jazzmen since c. 1935] See above note. — 1952 *Flee the Angry Strangers*, p. 302. "I don't get close to a guy with a habit everybody can tell." — 1958 *Somewhere There's Music*, p. 35. "She tells me I should kick my habits and figure out what I really want out of life besides six lonely nights a week in a juice joint being ogled by the hicks and half-hispters who wonder just how *big* my habit *is*."

hacked, *adj.* [prob. by analogy with a standard meaning (i.e., chopped up); current c. 1945–c. 1955, rare since;

see also BUGGED, DRAGGED] See 1958 quot.; also, rarely, tired: see 1959, 1960 quots. — 1958 *American Speech*, Oct., p. 225. Somewhat less frequently aired are the synonyms for *annoyed: bugged, dragged, spooked, hacked,* and *hung.* — 1959 *Esquire*, Nov., p. 70I. *hacked:* tired, irritated. — 1960 *The Jazz Titans*, p. 157. *hacked:* tired, irritated.

hall, *n.* [from New Orleans practice of shortening *dance hall* to *hall:* e.g., Mahogany Hall (immortalized by Louis Armstrong's *Mahogany Hall Stomp*); some currency in a jazz sense c. 1900–c. 1940; see also JOINT, ROOM] Any place where musicians play—be it a café, a ballroom, or a concert hall. — 1960 *Down Beat*, 24 Nov., p. 6. He never left it (thereby solving the hall, gig, and transportation problems).

hame, *n.* [poss. by analogy with restraining connotation of standard meaning; current since c. 1945; see also DAY GIG, SLAVE] See 1955, 1959 quots. (1961 quot. definition is rare); also *v.i.:* oral evidence only. — 1955 *The Encyclopedia of Jazz*, p. 346. *hame:* job outside the music business. — 1959 *Esquire*, Nov., p. 70I. *hame:* a position outside the music business. — 1961 *N.Y. Times Magazine*, 25 June, p. 39. *hame:* any unpleasant job, from mowing the lawn to playing trumpet in a Mickey Mouse [q.v.] band.

hamfat, *n. & adj.* [cf. 1960 *Dictionary of American Slang,* s.v. *ham-fatter:* "An inferior, obvious entertainer . . . an actor whose subtlety is no greater than that of a Negro minstrel show. Since c. 1880"; according to jazzmen, some currency c. 1900–c. 1930, obs. since except historical] Mediocre (musician). — 1938 *N.Y. Amsterdam News*, 12 March, p. 17. The Harlem Hamfats grind out the tune on myriad Harlem piccolos [i.e., juke boxes]. — 1946 *Really the Blues*, p. 58. A lot of beat-up old hamfats . . . sang and played. — 1959 *The Country Blues*, p. 86. The singing of these little "hamfat" bands never reached the artistic intensity of men like Blind Lemon.

ham kick, [see quot. for etym.; according to jazzmen, some currency c. 1900–c. 1917, obs. since except historical] See quot. — 1939 *Jazzmen,* p. 35. One night a week, as a special added attraction, the 28 Club put on a "ham kick." A ham was hung up high, and the contest was won by the girl who could kick highest.

hang, *v.t.* [by analogy with standard meaning's connotation of immobilization; current since c. 1940; see also HUNG (UP)] To inconvenience (someone); also with *up:* oral evidence only. — 1959 *The Beat Generation Dictionary.* s.v. *hang:* delay.

happen, *v.i.* [term reflects selective or preferential attitude of the jazzman in his acknowledgement of events: cf. music trade use (1949 *Music Library Association Notes,* Dec., p. 44. "A song *happens* . . . when the preparatory work results in a successful bid for popularity"); current since c. 1945; see also SHAKING] To occur, but only if the consequence is beautiful and/or significant. — 1955 *Down Beat,* 13 July, p. 33. I don't think much of anything happens here. — 1958 *Jazz: A Quarterly of American Music,* Oct., p. 28. Well, like it's got to "funk" all the time . . . without it, nothing's happening. — 1961 *The Jazz Life,* p. 158. "A lot of musicians think the public is stupid, but the audiences know what's happening." — 1962 *Down Beat,* 8 Nov., p. 38. It sounded like they were all striving to create and get away from the standard things, but it didn't really happen.

happenings, haps, *n. pl.* [from *happen;* some currency since c. 1948; see also ACTION] Occurrences, but only those of some immediacy or significance. — 1953 *Later* (tune recorded by Ella Fitzgerald on Decca DL8149). Later for the happenings, baby. — 1958 *Jive in Hi-Fi,* p. 41. Our two friends, standing in a corner, were diggin' [i.e., observing] the happenings. — 1961 *N.Y. Times*

Magazine, 25 June, p. 39. *haps:* an event, an occurrence.
— 1963 *Down Beat,* 15 Aug., pp. 8–9. From . . . the
report on his jazz "happenings," one might reasonably
conclude that here is a man with something to say.

hard, *adj.* [one of several jazz slang terms which reverse
the standard connotation (i.e., from unfavorable to
favorable): see also BAD, MEAN, TERRIBLE, TOUGH;
current since c. 1935] See first 1938 quot. — 1938 *Cab
Calloway: Hi De Ho,* p. 16. *hard:* fine, good. Ex. — "That's
a hard tie you're wearing." — 1938 *American Speech,*
Dec., p. 314. *Beat* and *to the socks* are used in a derogatory manner, while *solid* and *hard* are more complimentary. — 1959 *Diggeth Thou?,* p. 40. The spielers were
shucking some hard jive from back. — 1962 *Down Beat,*
13 Sep., p. 28. A hard cooker in the bop or post-bop
groove he is not—he has his own slick style and stays
with it.

hard bop, [*hard* is used here in the general slang sense of
tough, virile, masculine (in opposition to what its advo-
cates and practitioners regard as sissified music — i.e.,
cool or *West Coast jazz,* q.v.); current esp. among jazz
writers since c. 1955; see also FUNKY, SOUL, and the
earlier BOP] That modern jazz or jazz style, innovated
c. 1954 on the East Coast overwhelmingly by Negro
jazzmen, which retains all of the characteristics of bop
(q.v.) but rejects the overly relaxed quality into which
it had been led esp. by West Coast jazzmen most of
whom are white; aggressive, intense modern jazz with
the tension of hot jazz reinstated: see 1957, 1959, and
last quots. — 1957 *The Book of Jazz,* p. 102. Symbolizing
a partial reaction against the ultra-cool sounds of the
late 1940's is the work of another school of tenor men,
whose style has been labeled, perhaps a little arbitrarily,
"hard bop," but might better be described as "extrovert
modern." — 1958 *N.Y. Journal-American,* 22 March. According to Sid, New York's younger jazz fans like "the

hard bop," the fast, driving jazz of men like Art Blakey and Sonny Rollins. — 1959 *Evergreen Review,* Nov.-Dec., p. 136. Jazz was not to lose its way in the temporary dead end of an increasingly tepid cool style but could find a crucial rebirth in a modified version of the bop style of the forties . . . "hard bop." — 1961 *Down Beat,* 16 Feb., p. 16. "I'm an extrovert . . . and hard bop is played by bands of extrovert people." — 1961 *Metronome,* April, p. 13. The lid was put on "cool" by hard bop. There was a search for a *soul* sound that brought back the "group" feeling, perhaps inspired by gospel music and some aspects of rock and roll.

hard bop-funky, [some currency esp. among jazz writers since c. 1957] That modern jazz style made up of two important allied styles (see HARD BOP, FUNKY). — 1959 *Evergreen Review,* Nov.-Dec., p. 140. Blakey's is only one of several rediscoveries that the by now fashionable swing to the hard bop-funky style has bought about.

hard bopper, [some currency esp. among jazz writers since c. 1957] A musician who plays hard bop. — 1960 *Jazz Monthly,* Nov., p. 29. He seems to be particularly severe on the hard boppers. — 1960 *Esquire,* Dec., p. 74. Some of the current "soul fever" being incorporated into the music of musicians who used to be called "hard boppers" is legitimately come by and is yet another way of forcefully reminding white audiences—and themselves—of a basic part of their heritage.

hard swing, hard swinging, hard-swinging, hard-driving, hard-blowing [from *hard bop,* combined with *swing, drive,* or *blow,* q.v.; some currency since c. 1955] Noun phrase: hard bop; adj.: aggressive, intense (musical attack); also, verb and adverb: see first 1960 quot. — 1958 *Down Beat,* 29 May, p. 13. If they have the right people there, perhaps they'd do some good. You know, some of the hard swinging cats from both bands.

— 1959 *Esquire,* Jan., p. 115. Our development is of the hard-swinging variety. — In the second half of the Fifties, the hard-blowing school seems to have a much bigger influence on the younger players than the soft-blowing school. — 1960 *The Jazz Review,* Nov., p. 10. My lip went bad after a year in the Earl Hines band. They swung so hard and played so much. — 1960 *Down Beat,* 24 Nov., p. 26. Bacalao maintains the same ingredients—"hard" swing, extensive solo work, by tenor and organ, and the ever-present congas and bongos. — 1961 *Metronome,* Feb., p. 30. This review is directed at the more hard-driving jazz tastes like my own.

Harlem, *n. & adj.* [named for the Negro section of New York City where the style originated; some currency c. 1930–c. 1945, obs. since except historical; see also the more common JUMP] A popular but obvious swing music style, incorporating a very pronounced rhythm and very earthy tonal qualities, c. 1935–c. 1945: see 1959 quot. — 1934 *Metronome,* Oct., p. 49. The band, its style and the vocalist is strictly Harlem. — 1947 *The Two Worlds of Johnny Truro,* p. 24. They listened to . . . Harlem. — 1959 *The Jazz Scene,* p. 112. Often vulgar and showy, this "Harlem music" (often played by non-New Yorkers) tended to commercialism.

hash, *n.* [from *hashish;* from narcotics slang; some currency among jazzmen since c. 1935] See 1960 quot. — 1960 *The Jazz Titans,* p. 157. *hash:* hashish. — 1961 *The Sound,* p. 22. " 'hash' all through them Moslem countries, man."

hassel, hassle, *n.* [cf. 1959 *Webster's New World Dictionary,* s.v. *hassle:* "? <dial. *hassle,* to breathe noisily"; from general slang, but esp. common among jazzmen since c. 1945] A difficulty, a problem, an argument; also, rare, *v.t.:* to cause a difficulty or an argument (in this sense, oral evidence only); as *v.i.:* to be in trouble or difficulty (see last quot.). — 1946 *Hollywood Note,* July,

p. 7. Jay C. Higgenbotham, Onyx Club's noted jazz trombonist, quipped, "That'll be a hassel." — 1952 *Flee the Angry Strangers,* p. 137. "Don't love me for kindness, because that's my hassel." — 1958 *The Village Voice,* 1 Oct., p. 5. Jazz musicians . . . have been temporarily brought down by life's hassels. — 1959 *The Horn,* p. 215. "Anyone makes a hassle this next set, I'll show 'em put-downs if that's all they're after." — 1959 *The Holy Barbarians,* p. 75." You *are* hassled if you haven't got loot."

hat, *n.* [obscene semantic development: i.e., an analogy is drawn between putting on a hat and mounting a woman in coitus; some currency esp. among Negro jazzmen since c. 1940] See quote. — 1963 *Hiptionary,* p. 8. *hat:* girl, chick [jazz sense], wife.

have a ball, See s.v. BALL.

have it covered, [special application of general colloquial phrase (i.e., to have something under control); current since c. 1955; see also ALL OVER, GET AROUND ON (ONE's) HORN] To play (an instrument) with great virtuosity; to do something admirably. — 1961 *Down Beat,* 17 Aug., p. 13. "This was one of the most talented youngsters I've seen come up in a long time. For his age, he really had it covered." — 1963 *Down Beat,* 9 May, p. 15. Oscar Brown Jr. really had those lyrics covered.

Hawk, *n.* [shortened form of his surname; one of the five or six indispensable nicknames in the jazz world (see also BIRD, PREZ, SATCH); although close associates frequently call him "Bean," jazz writers and fans have, since c. 1930, most often referred to him as "Hawk"] Coleman Hawkins, 1904–, tenor saxophonist, acclaimed by musicians and critics as one of the all-time great performers on his instrument. — 1935 *Metronome,* May, p. 37. "For phrasing, tone, and original ideas . . . you can't beat old Hawk!" — 1940 *Swing,* Nov., p. 28. Hawk glides along elegantly. — 1961 *The Jazz Review,* Jan., p.

16. I made some sides [i.e., records] for Victor with Hawk.
— p. 18. Budd's tone . . . was fuller, although not nearly
enough to place him as a follower of Hawk.

hawk, hawkins, *n.* [etym. unknown: poss. Hawkins was
the name of a fearsome person (poss. a New Orleans
policeman c. 1900); according to jazzmen, *hawkins* has
been current esp. among Negro jazzmen since c. 1900,
hawk since c. 1935] See 1958 quot. — 1944 *Dan Burley's
Original Handbook of Harlem Jive,* p. 44. Listen ole
man; all yon jive I have spread only has been/put down
to knock thee a Benny when/Mister Hawkins rides
his December chariot. — p. 140. *hawkins:* cold winter
wind. — 1947 *Jive and Slang.* s.v. *hawkins:* cold weather.
— 1958 *The Book of Negro Folklore,* p. 484. *hawkins:*
the wind, wintertime, cold weather, ice, snow. — 1959
Newport Jazz Festival: 1959, p. 45. *the hawk:* cold
weather. — 1959 *Esquire,* Nov., p. 70I. *the hawk:* cold
weather.

head, *adj. & n.* [from where it is "kept" (as contrasted to
"sheet" music); current since c. 1925] See 1958 quot.
— 1955 *Solo,* p. 26. "There isn't anything wrong with
blowing the way it's written, or if it's just a head arrangement, with the *mood* of the thing." — 1955
Atlantic Monthly, July, p. 55. Most of the music grew
out of fertile memories and atavistic impulses rather
than out of conscious study. "Head music" they still
call it. — 1956 *Enjoyment of Jazz* (EJ410), p. 1. At
least, there must be "head" arrangements, in which
each musician memorizes a definite part. — 1958
Publication of the American Dialect Society, Nov., p. 46.
head arrangement: a musical arrangement which is not
written down and never has been, but is known by
all the members of the ensemble. — 1959 *The Horn,* p.
193. "But maybe if we do a whole set of heads, old ones."
— 1961 *The Sound,* p. 26. "Not if I know Red. It's all
heads with this cat."

head, *n.* 1 [synechdoche; current since c. 1935; before c. 1950, preceded by an *adj.* or *prefix,* used largely alone since]   A person who uses marijuana or narcotics, etc. — 1938 N.Y. *Amsterdam News,* 2 April, p. 17. "The thousands of lushheads and 'tea' worms that are being hatched daily . . . are a peril." — 1955 *Hear Me Talkin to Ya,* p. 71. Whiskey heads are all dead. — 1955 *Solo,* p. 247. The juiceheads [i.e., drunkards: see JUICE] . . . got so fractured that they wouldn't show up for a date. — 1959 *The Horn,* p. 107. "These weird cats are blowing weird . . . and . . . everyone's a head." — 1959 *The Holy Barbarians,* pp. 171–172. When the marijuana head (vipers, we called them in the thirties) or the hype turns on, he has the feeling of setting something in motion inside himself. — 1960 *Hiparama of the Classics,* p. 7. So Mr. Rabadee . . . sent out Notices to . . . the Reed Heads, the Lute Heads, and the Flute Heads. — 1961 *The Sound,* p. 22. "Like, man, if Hitler and Mussolini had of been heads, there never would have been no Big Scuffle on the other side."

2. [metonymy and/or synechdoche; current since c. 1935] Fellatio. — 1956 *Sideman,* p. 103. "She's wild, man! Gives the craziest head!"

hear, *v.t.* [some general colloquial use, but given special application by jazzmen; some currency since c. 1925] To understand (usually, music) esthetically and/or emotionally. — 1946 *Really the Blues,* p. 318. "Yeah, I hear you." — 1961 *The Sound,* p. 55. "It took me almost a month of listening . . . before I actually heard this music." — p. 206. "It all comes out in what Red plays. It's not just a certain arrangement of notes. It's the way he hears it."

heavy, *adj.* [special applications of standard meaning (i.e., serious, profound); current esp. among Negro jazzmen since c. 1935] As in the standard sense, important or profound, but here the application is to people, ideas,

money, and music rather than to responsibilities, etc. —
1944 *Dan Burley's Original Handbook of Harlem Jive,*
p. 3. Recently, in a rather heavy article in a heavy
magazine, the *Journal of Negro Education* (Spring,
1944), I had occasion to speak of Dan Burley's work. —
1959 *Afro Magazine Section,* 3 Oct., p. E4. "Ya see,
I'm not one of those cats who is always trying to break in
on all the heavy loot." — 1961 *The Sound,* p. 190. "Baby,
this is Bernie, Bernie is a real heavy cooker on piano."
— 1963 *Down Beat,* 15 Aug., p. 31. The average human
being who understands jazz, I don't believe, could interpret this, because it's quite heavy.

heavy drums (or **drumming, beat**), [some currency since
c. 1935] See 1953 quot. — 1937 *This Thing Called
Swing,* p. 9. *mugging heavy:* soft swing with a heavy
beat. — 1940 *Swing,* July, p. 17. Very fast semi-boogie
blues in Gabriel with nasty, heavy off-beat drumming.
— 1953 *The American Thesaurus of Slang,* p. 552. *heavy
drums:* forceful drumming.

heavy soul, [jazz slang *heavy* + jazz slang *soul* (i.e.,
marijuana) = a powerful stimulant; some currency since
c. 1958; see also H, HORSE] Heroin. — 1963 *Heavy Soul*
(tune recorded by Bill English on LP album Vanguard
9127).

hemp, *n.* [cf. 1959 *Webster's New World Dictionary,* s.v.
hemp: "a drug, especially hashish made from the flowers
and leaves of this plant"; some currency among jazzmen
since c. 1935] See 1959 quot. — 1944 *Dan Burley's
Original Handbook of Harlem Jive,* p. 140. *hemp:* marijuana cigarette. — 1952 *Flee the Angry Strangers,* p. 131.
Now, smoking hemp, she let out the laughter she'd
choked back with food. — 1959 *The Jazz Scene,* p. 292.
hemp: marijuana.

hep, *adj.* [through frequently represented as jazz slang
(even jazzmen have made concessions to this popular
misapprehension: cf. *The New Cab Calloway's Hep-*

sters Dictionary), jazzmen have never used this term in
speech except derisively. Its etymology, I would suggest, is based on a Northern white hearing a Southern
Negro speak *hip* with a diphthongized vowel sound,
sounding very much like *hep* (with long vowel sound,
which is then shortened by the hearer when he in turn
speaks it).] See s.v. HIP.

hepcat, hepster, *n.* [see note in *hep*]   See s.v. HIPSTER.

hey now!, [current c. 1938–c. 1946, obs. since]   Hello. —
1946 *Hey Now, Hey Now* (song recorded on Columbia
37081).

hide beater, [from *hides;* some currency since c. 1935, very
rare since c. 1945; see also SKIN-BEATER] See 1938
quot. — 1938 *Cab Calloway: Hi De Ho,* p. 16. *hide
beater:* a drummer. — 1949 *Music Library Association
Notes,* Dec., p. 44. *hide beater:* swing and bebop term for
drummer.

hides, *n. pl.* [synechdoche; some currency since c. 1925;
see also SKINS, TUB] See 1942 quot. — 1942 *The American
Thesaurus of Slang,* p. 559. *hides:* drums. — 1961 *The
Sound,* p. 287. "Still beating his hides and winning all the
polls," Vann said.

high, *adj.* [cf. 1930 *American Tramp and Underworld
Slang,* s.v. *high:* "elevated through drink; in high
spirits"; widely current among jazzmen since c. 1917;
see also BOXED, JUICED, STONED, ZONKED] See 1939
quot. — 1928 *The Walls of Jericho,* p. 306. Not "drunk" in
the usual sense, for which the Harlemese is high. —
1935 *His Hi De Highness of Ho De Ho,* p. 36. A person
who is experiencing the exhilaration produced by a
reefer is described as "high." — 1939 *Jitterbug Jamboree
Song Book,* p. 32. *high:* intoxicated by liquor or marijuana. — 1952 *Go,* p. 110. "Sure, man, that cat's really
high on tea." — 1958 *Southern Folklore Quarterly,* Sep.,
p. 130. *high:* feeling of elation ranging from euphoria to
intoxication.

high hat, high-hat (cymbal), [from its similar collapsibility; current since c. 1932] See 1957 quot. — 1948 *Metronome,* Nov., p. 28. "I'd rather use the high-hat as a back beat and break up the bass drum rhythms." — 1956 *Guide to Jazz.* s.v. *high hat:* double cymbal operated by foot pedal. — 1957 *The Book of Jazz,* p. 126. The foot-cymbal gave way, soon after 1930, to the "high hat cymbal," two cymbals facing each other and made to meet through pedal control.

hincty, hinkty, *adj.* [etym, unknown; cf. 1934 *A Dictionary of American Slang,* p. 19. "*hinkty:* suspicious"; current esp. among Negro jazzmen c. 1930–c. 1945, rare since] See 1944, 1956 quots. — 1941 *Goin' to Chicago Blues* (tune recorded by vocalist Jimmy Rushing with Count Basie Orchestra). Well, I am hinkty and I'm lowdown too. — 1944 *The New Cab Calloway's Hepsters Dictionary.* s.v. *hincty:* conceited, snooty. — 1946 *Really the Blues,* p. 62. I had to cut loose some way, to turn my back once and for all on that hincty, kill-joy world of my sister's. — 1956 *The Real Jazz Old and New,* p. 148. Hincty is an insult, meaning snobbish. — 1958 *Somewhere There's Music,* p. 224. "Hell, I shouldn't have got so hincty."

hip, *adj.* [cf. 1930 *American Tramp and Underworld Slang,* s.v. *hip:* "wise, knowing"; last two quots. are completely mistaken about the etymology, but are much circulated (see 1944 quot.); according to jazzmen, the term has always been *hip,* never *hep* (q.v.), and it derives by analogy with having one's hip boots on (see 1938, 1958 quots.)—i.e., the way in which they protect the wearer from bad weather or dangerous currents is analogous to the way in which awareness or sophistication arms one against social perils; according to jazzmen, current since c. 1900; see also BOOTED, DOWN] See 1938, 1958, 1959, and second 1960 quots. — 1938 *Cab Calloway: Hi De Ho,* p. 16. *hip:* wise, sophisticated, anyone with boots on. — 1944 *Esquire,* Feb., p. 129. Don't believe all you read in the daily papers and the fan magazines. Very few of the terms attributed to musicians are now in use. The word "hep" is "hip" in Harlem, which is where most of this jargon originated. — 1956 *Sideman,* p. 26. "I'm hip," Bernie nodded. — 1958 *Jive in Hi-Fi.* p. 13. The correct word is "hip." It comes from a story of a fisherman warning young fishermen never to wade in deep water without hip boots on because they could run into trouble. So, when you hear the words, "I'm hip" or "I'm booted" it's said to let you know they have no fear of trouble or that they understand what's shaking [i.e., happening]. — 1959 *Toronto Telegram,* 31 March, p. 3. *hip:* equipped with enough wisdom, philosophy and courage to be self-sufficient, independent of society; able to swing on any scene [jazz slang sense]. — 1960 *The Jazz Word,* p. 149. But one who is hip/ now he's always cool/and never a flip [i.e., a frenetic person]. — 1960 *N.Y. Post,* 16 Nov., p. 50. " 'Hip,' to a musician, means up-to-date, aware, broad-minded." — 1960 *Dictionary of American Slang.* s.v. *hip:* "orig. a variant of 'hep.' " — 1961 *Encounter,* June, p. 56. Hip and hipster themselves derive from opium smoking for which the addict reclines on one hip.

v.t. [widely current since c. 1935] To advise, to tell, or to make (someone) understand. — 1944 *Dan Burley's Original Handbook of Harlem Jive,* p. 19. "Uncle is hipping a whole lot of cats as to what to do when the action gets off the track." — 1958 *The Subterraneans,* p. 90. Sand must have hipped him quietly in a whisper somewhere what was happening with the lovers. — 1959 *The Horn,* p. 130. He was always forming a new band "to hip the public." — 1959 *The Holy Barbarians,* p. 76. "Like if you don't pick up on their kick—well they try to hip you."

hipe, *n. & v.t.* See s.v. HYPE.

hipness, *n.* [some currency esp. among jazz writers since c. 1950] Modishness (with a pejorative connotation); feigned sophistication. — 1958 *Saturday Review,* 8 Feb., p. 44. Parker's line on "The Song Is You" is an anthology of "licks" still played by jazzmen striving for "hipness." — 1959 *The Horn,* p. 35. The very name conjured up a specter of a hipness he had renounced. — 1960 *The Jazz Review,* Feb., p. 9. If this is natural for you, doesn't current hipness force you into unnatural strictures?

hipped to the jive, [variant of *hip; hipped:* some currency since c. 1900, *hipped to the jive* c. 1935–c. 1945, obs. since] Aware, knowledgeable—esp., see 1938 quot.: sometimes shortened to *hipped;* also rhyming slang *hip(ped) to the tip,* c. 1935–c. 1945: oral evidence only. — 1938 *American Speech,* Dec., p. 314. *hipped to the jive:* well informed on the latest slang expressions. — 1947 *Esquire,* April, p. 76. "Are there any squares in this outfit?" "No, man, we're all hipped."

hippy, hippie, *n.* [though formed from *hip,* the term, like *hipness,* has a pejorative meaning; current since c. 1945] A would-be hipster—one who affects awareness, sophistication, wisdom, but is deficient in these qualities: see last four quots. — 1953 *Night Light,* p. 157. "Man, I really get a bellyfull of these would be hippies." — 1959 *The Village Voice,* 18 Nov., p. 13. "Imagine coming on so jaded, so epicurean, so hippie, so barbwire and fed up?" — 1959 *Swinging Syllables.* s.v. *hippy:* one who feels he is hip when in reality way in (Square). — 1959 *Jazz for Moderns,* p. 20. *hippy:* generic for a character who is supercool overblasé, so far out that he appears to be asleep when he's digging something the most. — 1960 *The Jazz Word,* p. 149. The hippy is overdone/over-hip and he ain't no fun. — 1960 *N.Y. Post,* 16 Nov., p. 50. A "hippy" in the lexicon of jazz, is a pretender to the truth of Hip. Or, in the words of Maynard Ferguson, "He's not a junkie, but he tries to act like one. He sits there in his uniform, with a blank stare and a lot of pseudo-jazz expressions in his head, and he probably doesn't understand the music, but he says, like: 'Ha, ha, John Coltrane's really saying something.' "

hipster, *n.* [from *hip;* despite definition in 1952 quot. *hepcat* was never current among jazzmen except perhaps derisively or satirically; some currency since c. 1940] One who is hip (q.v.)—a person who is knowledgeable and resourceful: see first 1959 quot. — 1952 *Life,* 29 Sep., p. 67. *hipster:* modern version of hepcat. — 1959 *Esquire,* Nov., p. 70I. *hipster:* one who is aware, as opposed to one who is a square. — 1959 *The Holy Barbarians,* p. 39. "He looked more like one of those beachcomber Nature Boy health freaks than a real hipster." — 1960 *The Jazz Word,* p. 149. The hipster is a groovy guy/colorful and laughable/he's always fallin' by.

hit, *n.* [poss. from numbers racket slang (i.e., to win); some currency since c. 1940] An amount (of anything —time, money, etc.); a puff on a cigarette (in this sense, oral evidence only). — 1960 *Hiparama of the Classics,* p. 15. Four big hits and seven licks ago, our Before daddies Swung Forth upon this sweet groovey land.

v.t. [prob. from the standard musical phrase *hit a note;* current c. 1925–c. 1945, obs. since except historical] To begin to play music: frequently hortatory. — 1939 *Jazzmen,* p. 97. "Hit it, gal." — 1944 *Chicago Documentary,* p. 6. They said, "Hit it, gal!" — 1948 *Trumpet on the Wing,* p. 20. The band would hit "Panama," "Tiger Rag," or some stomp tune. — p. 38. So he gave us the down beat and we hit it.

hit on, [poss. from the jazz slang *hit, n.;* current since c. 1948; see also SOUND] See last two quots.; also, by extension, to address oneself to (someone)—with the intent of making *any* request or asking a question. —

1959 *Diggeth Thou?*, p. 58. And right now I'm hitting on the cool young teens. — 1959 *Esquire,* Nov., p. 70I, *to hit on:* to request money or the act of love. Example: To hit on a chick means to try and get intimate with her. — 1963 *Hiptionary,* p. 18. hit on: pester, annoy; also, flirt.

hold, *v.i.* [extension of standard meaning; from narcotics slang; some currency among jazzmen since c. 1945] See 1959 quot. (note: always participial). — 1959 *The Holy Barbarians,* p. 316. *holding:* to have marijuana or any drug in your possession. — 1961 *The Sound,* p. 15. "Don't jump the light, baby, mother's holding, you know." — p. 158. He was holding just as Red had said.

holes, *n. pl.* [special application of standard meaning; some currency since c. 1950] The spaces, or intervals, between the notes played by the lead (q.v.) instrument or instruments. — 1960 *Jazz: A Quarterly of American Music,* Winter, p. 20. "What are you listening to now? . . . Jamal?" "Too many holes, man." — 1962 *N.Y. Times,* 11 Feb., Sec. 2, p. 12X. The compositions leave none of the customary holes where the jazz soloist can take over. — 1962 *Jazz Journal,* July, p. 11. Duke needs an exceptionally strong bass player. All those holes to fill, with no guitar, and even sometimes no piano.

honk, *v.i.* [onomatopoeic; some currency since c. 1930] See 1937 quot. (note its pejorative connotation in the last three quots. which derives from an overuse and consequent monotony of the effect) — 1937 *American Speech,* Feb., p. 46. *honk:* to play a note on a reed instrument in the low register with force and in a definite rhythmic pattern. Used of reed instruments only. — 1961 *Palaver,* Feb., p. 14. Shavers screams, the Hawk honks, and only Bryant and Duvivier show any real sense of proportion. — 1961 *Down Beat,* 2 March, p. 36. There is something of that honking era evident in his work. — 1961 *Metronome,* April, p. 39. It is extremely difficult to sound inventive if you are "honking" the horn.

honker, *n.* [some currency since c. 1948] Generally applied to tenor saxophonists who engage in claptrap "honking," most frequently at jazz concerts. Oral evidence only.

honkytonk, honky-tonk, *n.* [cf. 1959 *Webster's New World Dictionary,* s.v. *honky-tonk:* "prob. echoic"; current among jazzmen since c. 1900; see also BARRELHOUSE, GUTBUCKET] See 1942, 1961 quots. — 1939 *Honky Tonk Train Blues* (tune composed by Meade Lux Lewis). — 1942 *The American Thesaurus of Slang,* p. 565. *honkytonk:* primal "swing" of the style played in the bordels of New Orleans, Memphis, and St. Louis in which a free rein is given to improvising. — 1952 *Music Out of Dixie,* p. 133. "New Orleans music . . . deserved something a little better than being kicked around in the tonks and saloons." — 1955 *Hear Me Talkin to Ya,* p. 7. All along this street of pleasure there were dance halls, honky tonks, and cabarets. — 1961 *Esquire,* May, p. 153. Nor could the performer in a honky-tonk (Negro slang for gin mill) or a barrelhouse, both of which became characterizations of ragtime piano style, easily escape the tie-up. Also **honky tonk, tonk.**

hooked, *adj.* [from underworld and narcotics slang; by analogy with being caught on a hook; some currency among jazzmen prob. since c. 1935] Addicted (usually, to drugs, but not necessarily: see last two quots.). — 1946 *Really the Blues,* p. 371. *hooked:* addicted. — 1959 *The Holy Barbarians,* p. 231. A charge of heroin—the whole world is hooked. — p. 102. "It isn't genius that's got me hooked." — 1960 *Hiparama of the Classics,* p. 17. The swinging Brutus hath laid a story on you,/That Caesar was hooked for power.

hop, *n.* See s.v. LINDY HOP.

horn, *n.* [special application of standard meaning; in its more restricted sense, current since c. 1900; in its less restricted sense, widely current since c. 1945; see also

AX] See second 1937 and 1958 quots. — 1937 *Metronome*, Jan., p. 25. "Satchmo, I was only kiddin'. I'll give you your horn back!" — 1937 *American Speech*, Feb., p. 46. *horn:* any wind instrument, whether reed or brass. — 1952 *Music Out of Dixie*, p. 243. "I wanna hear that bass horn." — 1958 *Publication of the American Dialect Society*, Nov., p. 46. *horn:* any musical instrument, but especially (and originally *only*) the wind instruments. — 1959 *Jazz: A Quarterly of American Music*, Fall, p. 289. They all had so much experience in playing their horns.

horn, hornman, horn player, *n.* [see note above; current since c. 1945] A wind instrumentalist. — 1955 *Solo*, p. 52. "Take Buddy Bolden, if you will. A great horn." — 1959 *Philadelphia Afro-American*, 7 Feb. "There must be tongue, finger and thought control working simultaneously on a split-second basis for the modern hornman blowing his solo." — 1960 *Jazz: A Quarterly of American Music*, Winter, p. 33. Tenorman Charlie Rouse is one of the handful of "horn players" capable of working with Monk. — p. 46. I'm a frustrated horn player. — 1960 *The Jazz Review*, June, p. 22. There is neither the same logic nor compact emotional power to the hornmen's efforts. — 1961 *Palaver*, Feb., p. 16. Word has it that the great New Orleans hornman, Punch Miller, died in Chicago recently.

horse, *n.* [alliterative, but semantic development unknown: see first 1958 quot. for metaphoric possibility; from narcotics slang; some currency among jazzmen since c. 1935; see also H, HEAVY SOUL] See 1953 quot.— 1953 *Junkie*, p. 13. *horse:* heroin. — 1955 *Hear Me Talkin to Ya*, p. 374. Fats was a real sweet guy B.H.— before horse is what I mean. — 1958 *Oakland Tribune*, 19 Jan., p. B–15. His inner turmoil led him to heroin, the horse no one can ride. — 1958 *Somewhere There's Music*, p. 223. "Let's snort some horse." — 1960 *Beat Jokes Bop*

Humor & Cool Cartoons, p. 57. "No more arm with which to take horse?"

hot (jazz), [prob. from Negro slang: cf. 1928 *The Walls of Jericho*, p. 301. "*hot:* kindling admiration"; term orig. prob. had a sexual connotation (see 1950 quot.); widely current c. 1920–c. 1945, obs. since except historical] Initially, jazz as distinguished from popular or commercial music; since c. 1948, in writing, traditional jazz as distinguished from modern jazz (see 1936, 1956 quots.). — 1924 *Variety*, 24 Sep. [1962 *Jazz: A History of the New York Scene*, p. 149]. This "hot" septet hails from around Chicago. — 1926 *Melody Maker*, Jan., p. 31. "Jazz" enthusiasts will find their appetites thoroughly appeased by these two red-hot numbers. — April, p. 13. It is practically impossible even for the experienced dance drummer to play "hot" . . . After all, "hot" playing must be inspired. — 1929 *The Inter-State Tatler*, 9 Aug. p. 11. Such "hot" music is one reason why all roads on a Sunday afternoon lead to the Paradise. — 1936 *Esquire*, June, p. 92. *Hot* refers to a musical idiom and attitude, not to a tempo. — 1944 *Metronome*, April, p. 23. As Nappy Lamare points out, even *hot jazz* is a confusing term, because it implies that there is more than one kind of jazz music. — 1944 *Esquire's 1944 Jazz Book*, p. 26. That the popularity of hot jazz is not even more widespread may be attributed to the lack of any literature treating of hot as a special field, and also to the deadening effect of the shallow emotionalisms of sweet (popular) jazz upon the public ear. — 1946 *Harvard Dictionary of Music*, p. 377. Largely under the influence of Louis Armstrong there arose (c. 1925) the type known as "Hot Jazz" . . . as distinct from the conventional types known as "Sweet." — 1946 *Big Book of Swing*, p. 124. *hot:* torrid, loud, with solid beat. — 1946 *Really the Blues*, p. 141. This word [i.e., *swing*] was cooked up after the unhip public took over the expression "hot" and made it corny by getting up in front of a band and snapping their fingers in a childish way, yelling "Get hot! Yeah man, get hot!" — 1947 *The Two Worlds of Johnny Truro*, p. 22. "Listen to that! . . . A hot accordian!" — 1950 *They All Played Ragtime*, p. 92. The sub-title, "The Hottest Thing You Ever Saw," started a tempest among [sic] teapots, and certain women's clubs in New York complained to the Post Office Department, which ruled it obscene and unmailable. A hasty reprinting substituted the word "sweetest" for the objectionable adjective. — 1952 *Music Out of Dixie*, p. 271. "I know who's playing the hottest piano in town." — 1955 *Hear Me Talkin to Ya*, p. 45. He could play sweet and then he could play hot. — 1956 *Guide to Jazz*. s.v. *hot:* an expression current for many years to denote the warm vibrant intonations of jazz musicians and their extemporized variations on a theme. "Hot jazz" connoted real jazz as opposed to commercial music. In recent years the word has been less and less used.

hotel (style), [metonymy: style was most popular at hotel ballrooms and supper clubs; some currency c. 1925–c. 1945, rare since; see also SWEET] A soothing, musically unadventurous style of playing, popular in hotel ballrooms c. 1925–c. 1945, but scorned by jazzmen. — 1935 *Metronome*, May, p. 28. Playing in the Chez Paree doesn't give him a chance to click via his sophisticated hotel style. — 1936 *Metronome*, Feb., p. 21. *hotel:* sweet and soft. — 1937 *American Speech*, Feb., p. 47. *play hotel:* to play in a soft, smooth, controlled fashion. — 1942 *The American Thesaurus of Slang*, p. 563. *hotel:* of tempo and tone, gently, softly.

house band, [chiefly a trade term; according to jazzman Eubie Blake, current since c. 1900] A band playing more or less permanently at a particular place—theater pit, hotel ballroom, nightclub, etc. — 1959 *The Horn*, p. 34. The drummer for the house-band good-naturedly chased Wing's warm-up runs with precise rim-shots.

— 1961 *Record Research,* March, p. 9. Reams have been written about the dance bands of the acoustical era, both straight and jazz, from Prince's, Earl Fuller's, ODJB through Whiteman and beyond, but I've seen nary a word about that which, to me, is one of the most fascinating products of these times: the house band. — 1962 *Down Beat,* 4 Jan., p. 36. By now, Sims and Cohn are practically the house band at the Half Note because of their four regular engagements there each year.

house-rent party (or **stomp, strut**), See s.v. RENT PARTY.

hummer, *n.* [from underworld slang: cf. 1934 *A Dictionary of American Slang,* p. 20. "*hummer:* a false arrest"; some currency among jazzmen since c. 1950] An accidental occurrence, with either good or bad consequences. — 1959 *Esquire,* Nov., p. 70I. *hummer:* a minor mistake, something that shouldn't have happened. Example: I got busted [i.e., arrested] on a hummer.

hung, hung-up, hungup, *adj.* [by analogy with the standard term's connotation of immobilization; *hung-up* current since c. 1943, shortened form *hung* since c. 1950] See first two 1959 quots. — 1945 *Hepcats Jive Talk Dictionary.* s.v. *hung up:* mixed up. — 1952 *Go,* p. 168. "You don't know how I was hungup." — 1959 *Toronto Telegram,* 31 Mar., p. 3. *hung-up:* foolishly entangled, stalled, involved. — 1959 *Newport Jazz Festival: 1959,* p. 45. *hung up:* stood up, confused, misled, addicted. — 1959 *Louisville* (Kentucky) *Courier Journal,* 18 Oct. "I was hung," he added, in musician's argot. — 1960 *Hiparama of the Classics,* p. 19. When there ain't no place to put 'em the Poo' Cat get Hung. — 1961 *Down Beat,* 19 Jan., p. 33. The two saxophonists have a tendency to get hung for ideas, but both of them have moments of brilliance.

be (or **get**) **hung up on** (or **with**), [some currency since c. 1950; see also STRUNG OUT] To be or become obsessed with (something or someone). — 1962 *N.Y. Times Magazine,* 20 May, p. 45. *hung up:* to be obsessed

("He's hung up on Matt Dillon always shooting last.").

hustle, *v.i.* [see note in *hustler;* general slang (see last quot.) but with esp. currency among jazzmen since c. 1900] See 1944 quot.; also, by extension, since c. 1945: see last two quots.; for its adjective use, see first 1959 quot. — 1944 *Dan Burley's Original Handbook of Harlem Jive,* p. 140. *hustle:* beg, not work, to borrow, to live by one's wits or ingenuity. — 1959 *The Horn,* p. 27. "I learned *my* horn . . . in nine-piece hustling bands." — 1959 *Esquire,* Nov., p. 70J. *hustle:* to work at a job. — 1959 *The Holy Barbarians,* p. 75. Hustle is a word Itchy always uses for work, any kind of paid-for work. Notice that it is a word borrowed from whores and pimps—who, in turn, borrowed it from pedlars and door-to-door canvassers. (During the boom twenties it lost its derogatory connotations and was being used quite honorably for all selling.)

hustler, *n.* [cf. 1930 *American Tramp and Underworld Slang,* s.v. *hustler:* "a . . . street woman . . . one who 'hustles' or hurries, works quickly and in fear of detection"; also cf. 1931 *American Speech,* Dec., "Underworld Argot," p. 109. *"hustler:* illegal entrepreneur"; current esp. among Negro jazzmen since c. 1900] See first two quots. — 1944 *Dan Burley's Original Handbook of Harlem Jive,* p. 140. *hustler:* a beggar, one who refuses to work, a playboy, prostitute, lady of leisure, tramp, an illegitimate performer. — 1946 *Really the Blues,* p. 371. *hustler:* prostitute; also: anybody who makes a living by hook or crook. — 1946 *Hollywood Note,* April. A hustler, he lives in Greenwich Village . . . catting around Manhattan in the wake of the Ellington and Herman bands. — 1955 *Hear Me Talkin to Ya,* p. 12. There were cabarets and dance halls and lots of hustlers. — 1958 *The Subterraneans,* p. 94. People'll think she's a hustler.

hype, hipe, *n.* [from narcotics and underworld slang (orig. prob. from *hypodermic, hype* meant a supplier of narcotics attempting to induce a potential customer to use them); cf. 1930 *American Tramp and Underworld Slang*, s.v. *hipe:* "to cheat or short-change"; some currency among jazzmen since c. 1925; see also SHUCK] See 1959 quot.: (also *v.t.:* oral evidence only). — 1946 *Really the Blues*, p. 200. The hipe that was laid down that night was really a killer. — 1956 *Eddie Condon's Treasury of Jazz*, p. 236. "I like the people around here," he said; "they don't give you no hype." — 1959 *Esquire*, Nov., p. 70J. *hype:* deception. Example: He pulled a hype on the crowd. He fooled or cheated the crowd. — 1961 *Down Beat*, 19 Jan., p. 22. Don't let things bother you. Things like . . . hypes.

I

XXXXXXXXXXXXXXXXXXXX

icky, *adj. & n.* [see 1935 quot. for poss. etym., also poss. reinforced by the general colloquial term *hick;* some currency esp. among white jazzmen c. 1933–c. 1943, very rare since; see also SQUARE] An unsophisticated person; hence, as adjective, lacking sophistication. — 1935 *Vanity Fair*, Nov., p. 71. If the straight music is also oversweet, the term icky (a pseudo-baby-patter word, meaning "little") is frequently employed to denote this. — 1937 *Metronome*, March, p. 30. Once again I'd like to rise up in arms against the "unseen horde" of ickies who under the guise of posing as musicians and "heppers" persist in burdening us readers. — 1937 *New Yorker*, 17 April, p. 31. Dance musicians are known as *cats* and those not up on the current idioms are *corny* . . . and, if their playing is oversweet, *icky*. — 1946 *Big Book of Swing*, p. 124. *icky:* one who can't catch on to swing or swing terms. — 1948 *Tremolo*, p. 23. "What've you got that makes you cash in on the ickies?" — 1955 *Hear Me Talkin to Ya*, p. 189. I . . . grew far more excited than any of the most obnoxious ickies.

ideas, *n. pl.* [special application of standard meaning; current since c. 1930] In solo improvisation (sometimes, in composition or arrangement), musical ideas or conceptions: interesting phrases or the development of those phrases. — 1933 *Metronome*, July, p. 26. He's got the ideas, but his lip's weak yet. — 1938 *Metronome*, Feb., p. 24. Peewee Irwin exhibits some neat trumpet ideas in *Lies*. — 1947 *Metronome*, Jan., p. 32. He might not have the chops he used to have, but his ideas are always fine. — 1961 *Down Beat*, 16 Feb., p. 45. The arrangement was inventive; Michel certainly has enough ideas. — 1961 *Metronome*, April, p. 20. "Some nights I play it and ideas come, but sometimes they won't."

I'll bet you a fat man, [some general Negro slang use, but with esp. currency among Negro jazzmen c. 1932–c. 1942, very rare since] I'm quite sure (of something). — 1963 *Frontier*, June, p. 6. I'll bet you, as they say in Harlem, a fat man, that not many American children being taught American history have any real sense of what that collision was like.

I'm with you (or **him,** or a name), [some general and Negro slang use, but with esp. currency among Negro jazzmen c. 1917–c. 1945, rare since; see also CRAZY, SOLID] I approve of what you (or he) just said or did. — 1926 *Nigger Heaven*, p. 242. Buddy, I'm with you! cried Lasca. — 1962 *Down Beat*, 12 April, p. 22. "I'm with John; I'd like to know how they explain 'anti-jazz.' "

-ingest, *suffix* [common method of forming a jazz superlative since c. 1950; see also -EST] The nth degree (of whatever activity is indicated in the root verb). — 1955 *Bop Fables*, p. 47. "She *is* the swingin'est, but let's take it from the top again." — p. 57. "Man," said the stranger, "they're the jumpin'est!" — 1955 *Hear Me Talkin to Ya*, p. 217. Incidentally, that was probably one of the partyingest bands that ever was.

insane, *adj.* [one of several terms in which the standard connotation is reversed (i.e., from bad to good) through the jazzman's association of mental instability (at least, by conventional judgment) with imaginativeness; current since c. 1945; see also CRAZY, NUTTY] See 1948 quot.; also, by extension, since c. 1950: see 1959 quot. — 1948 *Down Beat*, 28 July, p. 4. *insane:* only the musical literati are addicted to (and permitted to use) this word. Pertaining to an extraordinarily dissonant conception or chorus. Applied only when the subject is "too gone," for "crazy" description. — 1952 *Park East*, Dec., p. 30. His eight tiny coursers were really insane. — 1958 *Somewhere There's Music*, p. 165. "The City's insane!" — 1959 *Esquire*, Nov., p. 70J. *insane:* very good. — 1960 *Hiparama of the Classics*, p. 22. Five Thousand Christians started to wail up the biggest breeze and most insane orchestration you ever dug.

instrumental, n. [special application of standard musical term; current as a distinguishing term during the big band era (when most bands had vocalists) c. 1930–c. 1945, rare since] See 1949 quot. — 1940 *Swing*, July, p. 17. Bob Mersey's *Blue Ink* is another slightly Whamlike instrumental. — Oct., p. 16. *Mars* is a very conventional instrumental. — 1948 *Down Beat*, 1 Dec., p. 10. We ran down three new instrumentals and a vocal for Baubles Buxon! — 1949 *Music Library Association Notes*, Dec., p. 45. *instrumental:* composition written for instrumental performance, solo or group. Also, any performance without benefit of vocal.

in there, [from *in the groove,* q.v.; widely current c. 1938–c. 1945, obs. since except historical] Of a musician, playing superbly; of anyone, possessing sophistication or wisdom; of any thing or place, exciting or interesting. — 1944 *Dan Burley's Original Handbook of Harlem Jive,* p. 104. Now, this skull [i.e., person] was in there, Jack. — 1948 *Partisan Review,* June, p. 721. *In there* was, of course, somewhereness. — 1955 *Hear Me Talkin to Ya,* p. 106. The Lincoln Gardens, of course, was still in there. — 1962 *Down Beat,* 13 Sep., p. 37. A guy playing a horn has . . . gotta get in there.

into something, (get), [current since c. 1958] In musical performance, to explore some original or interesting ideas. — 1961 *Down Beat,* 13 April, p. 43. I said to myself, "Now, at last, we're going to get into something, and then, wow, it fell apart completely." — 1961 *Dave Bailey: Gettin' Into Something* (title of LP album Epic 16011). — 1961 *Metronome,* Nov., p. 23. Gettin' into something: Dolphy and 'Trane (caption).

what are they into?, what is he into? [current since c. 1958] What musical ideas or conception are those musicians exploring? Oral evidence only.

intro, *n.* [from standard musical slang: shortened form of *introduction;* current since c. 1925] See second 1937 quot. — 1928 *Melody Maker,* Dec., p. 1353. The intro . . . is artistic as it is appropriate. — 1937 *Metronome,* May, p. 29. The latter shows off Allen on the intro. — 1937 *American Speech,* Oct., p. 181. *intro:* introduction. — 1948 *Metronome,* Sep., p. 16. After that kind of an intro you always expect them to go into *I Can't Get Started.* — 1950 *Metronome,* March, p. 25. What a strange intro! — 1955 *Sideman,* p. 32. After the intro there was a unison brass-riff.

ivories, *n. pl.* [from their component; according to jazz-man Eubie Blake, some currency c. 1900–c. 1945, very rare since] See 1926, 1942 quots.; also, the piano itself. — 1926 *American Speech,* Dec., p. 146. "Ivories" may mean . . . piano keys. — 1937 *Metronome,* March, p. 30. Teddy Wilson is on ivories. — 1942 *The American Thesaurus of Slang,* p. 559. *ivories:* piano keys. — 1946 *Really the Blues,* p. 142. That was how we got Joe Sullivan on the ivories.

    (**ivory**) **tickler, tickle (the) ivories,** [cf. 1948 *Shakespeare's Bawdy,* s.v. *tickle:* "overtly or covertly, an allusion to amorous or sexual tickling or caressing"; according to jazzman Eubie Blake, phrases based on conjoining of *tickle (r)* and *ivories* current, though not widely, c. 1900–c. 1945, obs. since except historical] (*Ivory*) *tickler:* a pianist; *tickle (the) ivories:* to play piano. — 1932 *The Inter-State Tatler,* 7 Jan., p. 8. That's where Earl Hines tickled ivories.— 1959 *The Jazz Review,* July, p. 13. He's the last of the real old-time ticklers—along with Luckey. — 1962 *Down Beat,* 16 Aug., p. 26. He had a magnificent attack . . . combined with the gaiety and sly humor that one looks for in a true "tickler."

Jack, Jackson, *n.* [cf. 1930 *American Tramp and Underworld Slang,* s.v. *Jack:* "a generic term for any tramp or other man"; *Jackson* current only c. 1938–c. 1942 (obs.

since except historical), *Jack* since c. 1935; see also Dick,
Jim] See 1938, 1952 quots. — 1938 *Cab Calloway: Hi
De Ho*, p. 16. *Jack:* name for all male friends. — 1944
Dan Burley's Original Handbook of Harlem Jive, p. 104.
Now, this skull was in there, Jack. — 1952 *A History of
Jazz in America*, p. 351. *Jack:* means of address to the
male. Also "Jim." — 1958 *Where He Went*, p. 58. "Well,
you look good, Jackson." — 1958 *After Hours Poetry*,
p. 26. But, Jack,/The place swings. — 1961 *The Sound*,
p. 210. "Hey there, Jackson!" Vann was trying to strike
the right note but it didn't come off. "Jackson" was a year
or two out of date.

Jack the bear, See s.v. NOWHERE.

jam, *n., v.i. & v.t.* [one of several food terms given a sexual
meaning by Negroes (see also BARBECUE, JELLY) and
then associated with jazz by Negro jazzmen; current c.
1930–c. 1945, rare since] See 1935, 1937, 1938, quots.
— 1935 *Stage*, Sep., p. 45. *jam:* to improvise hot music,
usually in groups. — 1937 *This Thing Called Swing*,
p. 3. *jamming:* impromptu swing, improvisation by one
player against rhythm background of other instruments.
— 1938 *Cab Calloway: Hi De Ho*, p. 16. *jam:* improvised swing music. To play such music. — 1952 *Who
Walk In Darkness*, p. 98. Decker finished his solo and
then all the musicians jammed, coming in together. —
1956 *Sideman*, p. 10. He always wanted to jam *Ol' Man
River* at a very fast tempo.

    jam session, session, [current since c. 1933, mostly
shortened to *session* c. 1945: see 1958 quot.] See 1937,
1955, 1956 quots. — 1936 *Harper's Magazine*, April,
p. 574. Thus in a typical "jam session" one instrument
will lead off with a slightly modified form of the general
melody, the other instruments "faking" the harmony. —
1937 *This Thing Called Swing*, p. 3. *jam session:* a vol-
untary gathering of swing men who play for the fun of
it, without music or leader. — 1947 *The Two Worlds of*

Johnny Truro, p. 20. "He's having a jam session." — 1955
A Pictorial History of Jazz, p. 202. "Jam session" . . .
was a highly elastic term. It could mean a group hired to
play on the night it [i.e., the night club] would otherwise be closed, it could mean added men sitting in on a
formal or informal basis, it could even mean an impromptu, odd-hours gathering at home, bar, or rented
studio—which was the original idea. — 1956 *Guide to
Jazz.* s.v. *jam session:* a gathering in a nightclub or studio
in which a group of musicians play on their own time
and improvise at length on a few numbers, usually held
after work hours [i.e., after about 3:00 a.m.]. The audience consists of a few musicians and devotees. — 1958
American Speech, Oct., p. 223. To use any form of *jam*
at what is now called simply a *session* is to brand yourself an auslander. — 1960 *The Story of the Original Dixieland Jazz Band,* p. 167. These enthusiastic youngsters,
who were much in demand in jazz-hungry New York,
often gathered with members of the Dixieland Band
"after hours" for jam sessions and the inevitable rounds
of nocturnal revelry, in which girl friends played no
little part.

jamf, See s.v. JIVE, sense 4.

JATP, [abbreviation; a writers' term only; current since
c. 1950] See quot. — 1956 *Guide to Jazz.* s.v. *JATP:*
Jazz at the Philharmonic. Title of a series of concerts
organized by Norman Granz, a form of jam session
[q.v.] on stage with only a loose format.

jazz, jass, jas, jaz, *n. & adj.* [cf. early sports slang use: 1913
San Francisco Bulletin, 6 March, p. 16. "What is the 'jazz'?
Why it's a little of that 'old life,' the 'gin-i-ker," the 'pep,'
otherwise known as the enthusiasalum"; etym. is un-
certain, but the sexual association (see 1927, 1931, 1959
quots.) is the most prob., poss. reinforced by associations
of ·speed and excitation (see 1950, 1954 quots.); etym.
in 1925 quot. is very doubtful; for dates, see 1917, 1936,

1939, 1946, 1960 quots.]   See 1958 quot. Also, note: the
term has been mostly generic for the music since c. 1917,
except during the *swing* (q.v.) era (c. 1935–c. 1945) and
the *bop* (q.v.) era (c. 1945–c. 1950) when those were
the generic terms; *jazz,* with the attributives *cool, modern,* and *progressive,* was reinstated in its honorific sense
c. 1950 (for a pejorative use, see 1944 quot.). — 1917
Victor Records (catalog advertising the world's first jazz
phonograph record, March 17, 1917). Spell it Jass, Jas,
Jaz or Jazz—nothing can spoil a Jass band. — 1925
American Mercury, Sep., p. 7. According to tradition,
jazz has taken its name from Jasbo Brown, an itinerant
Negro player along the Mississippi, and later, in Chicago
cabarets. — 1927 *The Journal of Abnormal and Social
Psychology,* April-June, pp. 14–15. Used both as a verb
and a noun to denote the sex act, it [i.e., jazz] has long
been common vulgarity among Negroes in the South,
and it is very likely from this usage that the term "jazz
music" was derived. — 1931 *Scribner's Magazine,* Nov.,
p. 461. The word jazz in its progress toward respecta-
bility has meant first sex, then dancing, then music. It is
associated with a state of nervous stimulation. — 1935
The Musical Quarterly, Jan., p. 54. Jazz is a style, not a
form, and styles can only be described, not defined. —
1936 *Harper's Magazine,* April, p. 567. The word jazz
has been used to describe every disagreeable phenomenon since the year 1916, when it came into common use.
— 1939 *Down Beat,* 1 Nov., p. 6. Back in the year 1910
. . . Schiller Cafe . . . advertising . . . sign . . . at the
very bottom . . . appeared the inspiring words: "Music
will be furnished by Jas.' Band." — 1944 *Metronome,*
April, p. 22. Some of them [i.e., swing musicians] use
the noun "jazz" to denote corn, especially those who
are opposed to the Dixieland type of music and sum
it up derogatorily with the word "jazz." — 1946 *Jazzology,* Feb., p. 6. "The word 'jazz' as a musical term,

was born in New Orleans. The Original Dixieland Jazz Band, playing at the Casino in the tenderloin district of New Orleans in 1914, first employed the term." . . . "I first heard the word 'jazz' used musically in reference to the Original Dixieland Jass Band. That was in 1913." — 1950 *N.Y. Times*, 30 June, p. 21. Dr. Bender, who joined the Princeton faculty in 1909 . . . was stumped by the word "jazz." In the three years in which he traced the word he had to write more than 500 letters before reporting that he had tracked it to the West Coast of Africa, the contact point for the slave trade with colonial America. He said that the word meant "hurry up" in the native tongue, and was first applied in the Creole dialect to mean "speed up" in the syncopated music in New Orleans. — 1954 *St. Louis Post-Dispatch*, 27 Aug. Whether spelled jass, as at first, or jas, jasz, or jaszz, as at various times, or jazz as now, "the Creoles of New Orleans used the word taken from the Negro patois and signifying *excite*, to designate a music of syncopated and rudimentary type," Lafcadio Hearn wrote. — 1958 *The Story of Jazz*, p. 282. We may define jazz tentatively as a semi-improvisational American music distinguished by an immediacy of communication, an expressiveness characteristic of the free use of the human voice, and a complex flowing rhythm; it is the result of a three-hundred-years' blending in the United States of the European and West African rhythm. — 1959 *The Jazz Scene*, p. 290. From about the same time [i.e., 1916] the term "jazz" (or jass, jaz) came to be used as a generic label for the new dance music, since few knew that it had hitherto been an African slang word for sexual intercourse. — 1960 *The Anatomy of Jazz*, p. 10. Although the word "jazz" was undoubtedly in use for a good many years before 1914, it was not until then, according to Nick La Rocca, founder of the Original Dixieland Jazz Band, that "jazz" appeared in an advertisement.

n. [general slang use, but with esp. currency among jazzmen since c. 1945; see also JIVE, sense 3, SHIT] Thing(s); nonsense. — 1953 *Night Light,* p. 153. "What do you call that jazz, alpaca or something?" — 1960 *Hiparama of the Classics,* p. 11. They want him to do this gig here, they want him to do that gig there, play the radio, do the video and all the JAZZ.

jazz (it) up, [some currency since c. 1917, though with a connotation shift c. 1940] Initially: to play jazz (see 1955 quot.); since c. 1940: to simulate a jazz feeling with the use of artificial or clichéd jazz devices (see 1958 quot.) — 1955 *Hear Me Talkin to Ya,* p. 78. I came home and started jazzing it up in Memphis. — 1958 *The Jazz Review,* Dec., p. 10. "Oscar is jazzy; he jazzes up the tune."

jazzy, *adj.* [despite the earlier 1928 quot., the term gained wide currency from the swing era (c. 1935 c. 1945) musician's association of the word *jazz* with the older traditional style of jazz, of which he disapproved (see 1944 quot.); still some currency] See 1937, 1944 quots. — 1928 *Melody Maker,* Dec., p. 1323. The trumpet was far too "jazzy." A more legato style would be a distinct improvement. — 1937 *American Speech,* Feb., p. 46. *jazzy:* outmoded, showy, ostentatious style of playing. — 1944 *Metronome,* April, p. 22. Yet most musicians use the adjective "jazzy" to denote "corny." Some of them even use the noun "jazz" to denote corn, especially those who are opposed to the Dixieland type of music and sum it up derogatorily with the word "jazz." — 1946 *Big Book of Swing,* p. 124. *jazzy:* crony. — 1952 *A History of Jazz in America,* p. 352. *jazzy:* corny. — 1958 *The Jazz Review.* Dec., p. 10. "Oscar is jazzy; he jazzes up the tune."

Jeff, *n.* [from *Jeff*erson Davis, whom Negroes disesteem; some currency among jazzmen prob. since c. 1935; see also the more neutral and more common FAY, GRAY] A white person, but esp. one who is hostile to Negroes

(hence, the definition in the 1939 quot. is inaccurate).
— 1938 *Cab Calloway: Hi De Ho* p. 16. *Jeff:* a pest, a
bore, an icky. — 1939 *Jitterbug Jamboree Song Book*,
p. 32. *Jeff:* a fellow. — 1961 *The Sound*, p. 144. "Them
Jeffs is workin' together!"

jelly (roll), *n.* [from Negro slang (see 1927 quot.); current
esp. among Negro jazzmen c. 1900–c. 1945, very rare
since] See 1927 quot. — 1919 *I Ain't Gonna Give Nobody None o' This Jelly Roll* (tune composed by Spencer
Williams and Clarence Williams). — 1927 *The Journal of
Abnormal and Social Psychology,* April-June, p. 13.
Relatively few symbols for the sex organs are found in
the blues, but these are worked to the utmost. By far
the most common of these terms is *jelly roll.* As used by
the lower class Negro it stands for the vagina, or for the
female genitalia in general, and sometimes for sexual
intercourse . . . Yet because of its decent meaning, it
passes fairly well in popular song society. — 1940 *Jelly,
Jelly* (tune recorded by Billy Eckstine). — 1942 *American Mercury,* July, p. 95. *jelly:* sex. — 1959 *The Country
Blues,* p. 83. In 1930 and 1931, Lonnie began recording
more and more blues like "I Got the Best Jelly Roll in
Town."

Jim, *n.* [some currency since c. 1940; see also DICK,
JACK] See 1952 quot. — 1952 *A History of Jazz in
America,* p. 352. *Jack:* means of address to the male.
Also "Jim." — 1955 *The Encyclopedia of Jazz,* p. 346.
Jim: form of address. — 1961 *The Sound,* p. 112. "No, no,
Jim," another disagreed. — 1963 *The Realist,* June, p. 29.
So when I see brothers and sisters that don't look alike,
that's it, Jim.

jitterbug, *n.* [see 1956 quot. for poss. etym.; also cf. 1935
His Hi De Highness of Ho De Ho! p. 35. ' "jitter
sauce,' meaning liquor, and also 'jitter bug,' meaning one
who drinks"; current c. 1936–c. 1945, now rare; see also
ALLIGATOR] See 1946, 1952 quots. — 1938 *From Spir-*

ituals to Swing (Carnegie Hall program, dated Dec. 23, 1938). But the jitterbug millions . . . have scared a lot of people away from hot jazz. — 1939 *The Kingdom of Swing*, p. 181. Mere exhibitionism, which has won the epithet of "jitterbug" as descriptive of the purely physical response that accompanies the worst phases of sensationalism by certain players. — 1946 *Duke Ellington*, p. 178. He talked of "jitterbugs" and "alligators"— more conservatively known as swing music enthusiasts. — 1950 *Metronome*, Dec., p. 20. "It's too bad the jitterbugs are gone. In those days jazz was the thing." — 1952 *A History of Jazz in America*, p. 352. *jitterbug:* a swing dancer, frantic. — 1956 *The Real Jazz Old and New*, p. 151. *Boogie woogie* used to mean the secondary stages of syphilis, and *jitterbug* a sexual reaction to music.

v.i. [general slang term, formed from *n.*, but with esp. currency among jazzmen since c. 1940] See first quot. — 1952 *A History of Jazz in America*, p. 352. *jitterbug:* to do the Lindy Hop. — 1952 *Who Walk in Darkness*, p. 101. I turned away to watch the people jitterbugging.

jive, 1. *v.t. & n.* [see first 1944 and first 1946 quots. for prob. etym.; current esp. among Negro jazzmen since c. 1920; see also THE DOZENS, PUT ON] As *v.t.*: see second 1946 quot. As noun, initially: see 1928 and second 1946 quots.; also, since c. 1935: see 1938 quot. — 1928 *The Walls of Jericho*, p. 301. *jive:* pursuit in love or any device thereof. Usually flattery with intent to win . . . this word implies . . . deceit. — 1938 *Cab Calloway: Hi De Ho*, p. 16. *jive:* (1) Harlemese speech or lingo. (2) To kid along, to blarney, to give a girl a line. — 1944 *Dan Burley's Original Handbook of Harlem Jive*, p. 71. Jive is a distortion of that staid, old, respectable English word "jibe.". . . in the sense in which it came into use among Negroes in Chicago about the year 1921, it meant to taunt, to scoff, to sneer—an expression of sarcastic comment. Like the tribal groups of Mohammedans and people of the Orient, Negroes of that period had developed a highly effective manner of talking about each other's ancestors and hereditary traits, a colorful and picturesque linguistic procedure which came to be known as "putting you in the dozens." Later, this was simply called "jiving" someone. Subsequently ragtime musicians picked up the term and it soon came to mean "all things to all men." — 1944 *Jazz Miscellany*, p. 8. If I had some money I'd stroll down the street/And jive some old broad I might meet. — 1946 *Really the Blues*, p. 215. The word jive probably comes from the old English word *jibe*, out of which came the words *jibberish* and *gibberish*, describing sounds without meaning, speech that isn't intelligible. — p. 371. *jive:* (*v.*) to kid, to talk insincerely or without meaning, to use an elaborate and misleading line; (*n.*) confusing doubletalk, pretentious conversation, anything false or phony. — 1952 *A History of Jazz in America*, p. 352. *jive:* comic speech, usually larded with ambiguous jazz terms; sometimes synonymous with "kid" ("don't jive me"). — 1955 *Solo*, p. 40. "You just play that game there without none of your jive." — 1955 *Hear Me Talkin to Ya*, p. 15. Bunk . . . would be in the nearest barroom . . . jiving some sporting women.

2. *n. & v.i.* [prob. reinforced by alliteration of *jive* with *jazz;* some currency c. 1930–c. 1945, obs. since except in jazz writing] As noun: jazz (see first 1944 quot.); as *v.i.:* see 1935 quot. — 1935 *His Hi De Highness of Ho De Ho*, p. 35. . . . "Jiving," meaning to improvise. — 1944 *Dan Burley's Original Handbook of Harlem Jive*, p. 71. Since 1930 Jive has been accepted as the trade name for swing music. — 1944 *N.Y. Times*, 23 Jan., p. 39. Attack on "Jive" Brings a Dissent (headline). — 1955 *Hear Me Talkin to Ya*, p. 104. King Oliver and I got . . . popular blending that jive together. — 1960 *Down Beat*, 9 June,

p. 15. Regarding the word jive, Wilson said, "it is nothing more than an obsolete slang term for jazz."

3. *n.* [broadening of sense 1; some currency since c. 1935; see also JAZZ, sense 2, SHIT] See 1938 quot. — 1938 *Cab Calloway: Hi De Ho,* p. 16. *jive:* stuff and things. — 1960 *Jazz: A Quarterly of American Music,* Winter, p. 36. "George Shearing copies so much jive from me."

4. **jive, jiver, jive mother-fucker, jive-ass mother-fucker, jamf** (oral evidence only for the last three), [from sense 1, in the sense of flattering, practicing deceit, "kidding"; *-ass* is an emphasis suffix here (cf. jazz slang -ASSED); *mother-fucker* (see MOTHER) a common jazz slang appellation; *jamf* is an abbreviation of *jive-ass mother-fucker* and is said to have originated with Charlie Parker; some currency since c. 1940] See 1959 quot. — 1959 *Newport Jazz Festival: 1959,* p. 45. *jive:* a zany fun-loving person; also used to describe an unscrupulous person. — 1962 *Down Beat,* 11 Oct., p. 24. "So many of the jazz cats," he said, "have become jivers. You know, the way they do it is much more important than what they do."

joint, *n.* 1. [cf. 1930 *American Tramp and Underworld Slang,* s.v. *joint:* "any hangout . . . not always a 'low resort' "; general slang but with esp. currency among jazzmen since c. 1925] See 1946 quot. — 1938 *Cab Calloway: Hi De Ho,* p. 16. *The joint is jumping:* the place is lively, the club is leaping with fun. — 1946 *Big Book of Swing,* p. 124. *joint:* entertainment place or living quarters. — 1959 *The Holy Barbarians,* p. 156. "Joint" is a place, as it is in squareville [i.e., conventional society]. — 1963 *Down Beat,* 20 June, p. 21. "You know, I like soulful joints."

2. [semantic development and relation, if any, to sense 3 unknown; some currency among jazzmen since c. 1935;

see also STICK] A marijuana cigarette (see 1960 quot.). —
1952 *Flee the Angry Strangers*, p. 171. "You got a couple
of joints to take along?" — 1958 *Nugget*, Oct., p. 51.
Everybody was sitting around puffing joints. — 1958 *The
Subterraneans*, p. 81. I remember . . . Julien, rolling
joints on the floor. — 1960 *Saturday Review*, 6 Feb., p. 12.
The marijuana is "tea." The rolled cigarette, looking very
much like a paper-wrapped toothpick, is a joint.

   3. [semantic development and relation, if any, to
sense 2 unknown; current since c. 1935] See quot. —
1959 *The Holy Barbarians*, p. 156. "Joint". . . can also
mean the penis.

jook, *n. & v.i.* See s.v. JUKE.

jug, *n.* [special application of standard meaning; also some
general and college student use, but with esp. currency
among jazzmen since c. 1900] See 1945 quot. — 1929
Knockin' a Jug (tune recorded by Louis Armstrong).
— 1945 *Hepcats Jive Talk Dictionary.* s.v. *jug:* bottle of
liquor. — 1959 *Newport Jazz Festival: 1959,* p. 45. *jug:*
a bottle of something, usually liquor.

jug band, [see last quot. for semantic development; some
currency from c. 1917–c. 1930, obs. since except histori-
cal] Any small band c. 1917–c. 1930 which used a jug or
a bottle as one of its instruments. — 1931 *Melody Maker,*
Dec., p. 1051. The only similarity I can see between this
new outfit and the jug and bottle mongers, is that each
. . . contributes something in the way of "style." — 1959
The Country Blues, p. 108. The men of the Memphis jug
bands came from the crowded neighborhoods around
Beale Street. — pp. 108–109. Roundhouse started blowing on a bottle. Everybody at the bar started shouting,
"Jug Band! Jug Band!"

juice, *n. & v.i.* [current since c. 1935; see also LUSH] See
1946 quot. — 1942 *American Mercury,* July, p. 95. *juice:*
liquor. — 1946 *Really the Blues*, p. 371. *juice:* (*n.*) liquor;
(*v.*) to drink a lot. — 1955 *Hear Me Talking to Ya,*

p. 227. . . . juice meaning any kind of firewater. — 1960
Hiparama of the Classics, p. 23. "Come on over daddy-O,
we drink up a little juice and everything be cool!" — 1961
The Sound, p. 22. "Nuthin' at all like juice, either,"
Hassan said.

juiced, *adj.* [from *juice, v.i.*; current since c. 1937; see also
BOXED, HIGH, STONED, ZONKED] See 1946 quot. — 1946
Really the Blues, p. 371. *juiced:* drunk. — 1956 *Lady
Sings the Blues*, p. 26. But he was too juiced even for
that. — 1961 *The Jazz Review*, Jan., p. 7. "If a guy comes
in juiced . . . Basie is likely to call a number on which
that guy is featured." — 1961 *The Feeling of Jazz*, p. 14.
"Who the hell needs to get juiced tonight?"

juicehead, *n.* [jazz slang *juice* + jazz slang *head, n.*; current since c. 1935] A drunkard. — 1955 *Solo*, p. 247.
The juiceheads . . . got so fractured [i.e., drunk] that
they wouldn't show up for a date.

juice joint, [jazz slang *juice* + jazz slang *joint,* sense 1; some
currency since c. 1935] A cabaret, a night club. — 1958
Somewhere There's Music, p. 35. "She tells me I should
kick my habits and figure out what I really want out of
life besides six lonely nights a week in a juice joint."

juke, jook, *adj., n. & v.i.* [cf. 1959 *Webster's New World
Dictionary*, s.v. *juke box:* "Negro Gullah jook-house, road-
house; orig., house of prostitution; akin to W. Afr. *dzug,
dzog, dzugu";* also cf. general slang *juke box,* which derives from it; current among jazzmen c. 1917–c. 1930, obs.
since except historical] As noun: a stringed-instrument
band c. 1917–c. 1930 which played at a combination road-
side inn-brothel; also, music played in that manner; as
v.i.: see 1942 quot. — 1942 *American Mercury*, July, p. 95.
jooking: playing the piano, guitar, or any musical instrument in the manner of the Jooks. — 1948 *The Record
Changer*, June, p. 6. On the folk level in New Orleans
and elsewhere in the South . . . the jazz group and the
"jook" or string band still furnish music for dancing. —

1956 *The Real Jazz Old and New,* p. 151. *Juke* . . . came
from juke house — which was once a whorehouse. —
1959 *Jazz* (Hentoff & McCarthy), p. 107. Such places
were known as "jukes," the playing was called "juking."

jump, *v.i.* [hyperbole (see 1938 quot.); current since
  c. 1935; see also SHAKE]   To be lively or animated; also:
  to dance animatedly (see first 1957 quot.); for its adjective use, see second 1957 quot. — 1938 *Cab Calloway:
  Hi De Ho,* p. 16. *The joint is jumping:* The place is lively,
  the club is leaping with fun. — 1946 *Really the Blues,*
  p. 26. The First World War was jumping then. — 1952
  Music Out of Dixie, p. 248. "You got 'em jumpin', kid,"
  Danny admitted. — 1952 *Who Walk in Darkness,* p. 25.
  "The place is beginning to jump already," Porter said. —
  1957 *On the Road,* p. 134. We all jumped to the music
  and agreed. — p. 199. They tell me it's a real jumpin
  town. — 1960 *Hiparama of the Classics,* p. 12. Now the
  fame of The Naz is jumpin'!

  adj. & n. [see note above; see first 1956 quot. for beginning date; very rare since c. 1948; see also UP-TEMPO]
  See first 1956 quot.; also, *jump band:* a band specializing
  in *jump numbers.* — 1938 *Carnegie Jump* (tune recorded
  on Columbia C-1500). — 1943 *This Is Jazz,* p. 30. You
  have left only the intolerable monotony of "jump" [riff,
  q.v.] phrases played over and over. — 1945 *Band Leaders and Record Review,* March, p. 20. Jump music, swing,
  jazz, or whatever you want to call it, jumps in the movie
  capitol, too. — 1946 *Jazzways,* p. 51. The meaning of a
  "jump tune" should be clear enough from the term itself;
  literally, it jumps . . . A "jump" treatment can be applied to almost any kind of song with success. — 1955
  Hear Me Talkin to Ya, pp. 103–104. I could hear King's
  band playing some kind of a real jump number. — 1955
  Solo, p. 203. He played everything. Ballads, jump tunes.
  — 1956 *Guide to Jazz.* s.v. *jump:* introduced about 1938
  as a synonym for "swing.". . . A *jump number:* a tune

played in a particularly bouncing rhythm affected by many bands in the late thirties. — 1956 *Second Ending,* p. 47. Jumps were always better for warm-ups than something slow and draggy. — 1956 *The Real Jazz Old and New,* p. 149. A jump band is a big and powerful jazz-band.

jump in, [hyperbole; current since c. 1940] To move into, involve oneself in (a situation). — 1960 *Beat Jokes Bop Humor & Cool Cartoons,* p. 50. "The cat did jump in soon."

jump salty, See s.v. SALTY.

junk, *n.* [from narcotics and underworld slang: 1931 *American Speech,* Aug., "Convicts' Jargon," p. 439. *"junk:* drugs"; prob. by analogy with its colloquial sense (i.e., trash); general slang but with some currency among jazz-men since c. 1935] See first 1958 quot. — 1934 *Black Mask,* Oct. "Canales has a noseful of junk a lot of the time." — 1958 *American Speech,* Oct., p. 225. *junk:* . . . meaning narcotics. — 1958 *The Subterraneans,* p. 11. "She's never had junk but only known junkies." — 1959 *Swinging Syllables. s.v. junk:* dope.

junkie, *n.* [cf. 1931 *American Speech,* Aug., "Convicts' Jargon," p. 439. *"junkie:* a drug addict"; also general slang but with some currency among jazzmen since c. 1935] See 1942 quot. — 1942 *American Thesaurus of Slang,* p. 476. *junkie:* drug addict. — 1948 *Metronome,* April, p. 33. Hanging around with 52nd Streeters you would get to know a whole new vocabulary used by the "junkies." — 1959 *Swinging Syllables. s.v. junkie:* one hooked by dope. — 1960 *The Jazz Review,* Nov., p. 22. Like Bird, he was in his later years a junkie.

K

XXXXXXXXXXXXXXXXXX

K.C., Kansas City (style), [after *Kansas City,* Missouri; current since c. 1935] A swing era (c. 1935–c. 1945) style of playing (see 1946, 1955 quots.), some elements of which survive in modern jazz. — 1938 Count Basie's Kansas City Seven (name of a jazz septet). — 1940 *Swing,* Nov., p. 28. It's getting to be a fine thing when Kansas City jump bands play kids' songs. — 1946 *Harvard Dictionary of Music,* p. 376. Passing over the somewhat lighter and less percussive "Kansas City style" of the early 1930's with its riff technique (short ostinato melodic figures by the band against which one of the instruments improvises), mention must be made of a special type of blues piano. — 1947 *The Two Worlds of Johnny Truro,* p. 24. They listened to . . . K.C. style. — 1955 A *Pictorial History of Jazz,* p. 149. They had their own way of playing in Kansas City, their own beat, and the trumpets searing through the band sound, and the spirited repetitive riffs. Some argue that there is actually no specific Kansas City "style"; but no one can claim that this town wasn't a major jazz landmark. — 1956 *Enjoyment of Jazz* (EJ401), p. 1. The Basie band . . . represents the Kansas City "school" of jazz. — p. 2. And the K.C. version of Swing was free-wheeling and flexible.

kick, *n.* 1. [semantic development unknown; from pickpockets' slang, but some currency among jazzmen since

c. 1935] See quot. — 1944 *The New Cab Calloway's Hepsters Dictionary.* s.v. *kick:* a pocket. Example: "I've got five bucks in my kick.

2. [prob. from *kicks,* q.v.: i.e., one's *kick* provides, is the source of, one's pleasure (*kicks*): widely current since c. 1940; see also GROOVE] A passion, philosophy, preference, attachment, interest, fad, vogue, style, practice, vein; also, see 1959 quot. — 1946 *The Jazz Record,* July, p. 8. "The whole jazz world was on a Hawkins kick." — 1947 *Band Leaders and Record Review,* Feb., p. 17. "I'm still on the group kick," says Buddy. — 1953 *The Hot and the Cool,* p. 38. "This domestic kick with diapers is great." — 1955 *Solo,* p. 287. "I've got to get off this kick." — 1956 *It's Always Four O'Clock,* p. 44. "Sometimes the Sauter-Finegan outfit sounds like it's trying to get off on a new kick." — 1959 *The Beat Generation Dictionary.* s.v. *kick:* current fad, hobby. — 1961 *Down Beat,* 5 Jan., p. 16. "Everybody now is on that Les McCann kick."

v.i. & v.t. 1. [prob. from standard phrase *kick it out;* from narcotics slang: cf. 1934 *A Dictionary of American Slang,* s.v. *kick the habit:* "to try to break the drug habit"; some currency among jazzmen since c. 1935] To rid oneself of (usually, a narcotics habit). — 1948 *Metronome,* April, p. 33. You hear that such-and-such a musician . . . is trying to "kick" (break the habit). — 1958 *After Hours Poetry,* p. 2. There's a thing we can't kick. — 1958 *Somewhere There's Music,* p. 35. "She tells me I should kick my habits."

2. (sometimes with *out*), [by analogy with the energy and impact; current c. 1935–c. 1945, rare since; see also BOOT, ROCK, STOMP] See first 1937 quot. — 1936 *Metronome,* Feb., p. 21. *kick out:* swing. — 1937 *American Speech,* Feb., p. 47. *kick out:* to bring out heavily the rhythm of a tune with every member of the band assisting. — 1937 *This Thing Called Swing,* p. 9. *kicking out:*

very, very free interpolation. — 1938 *Metronome*, Feb., p. 24. The reverse (*Penthouse Serenade*) kicks at a slower tempo. — 1938 *Metronome*, Aug., p. 17. "The band is kicking like mad in this one." — 1939 *Metronome*, May, p. 10. "This band of mine can sure kick me!" — p. 19. The last chorus kicks. — Artie really kicks the last two choruses of *Prosschai*. — 1961 *Down Beat's Jazz Record Reviews: Vol. V*, p. 176. The rhythm section kicks like mad all the way.

kick (it) around, [old colloquial phrase used in special sense by jazzmen c. 1935–c. 1945, rare since] To improvise music freely and relaxedly. — 1939 *Esquire*, May, p. 75. Speaking again of Swing: few tunes deserve its name till they've been "kicked around" by good performers. — 1944 *Esquire's 1944 Jazz Book*, p. 49. Benny Goodman once answered it by saying that after a musician has played a tune over and over again what can he do but "kick it around"? — 1956 *It's Always Four O'Clock*, p. 13. Lonny was tired and just kicking it around.

kick (it) off, [poss. from football slang and general slang (i.e., to begin something) but a very natural application to a jazz sense; current since c. 1917] To signal for the musicians to play by the leader's stamping his foot several times in the desired tempo; also, by extension, to begin playing (see 1956 and last quots.) — 1945 *The Jazz Record*, Nov., p. 10. Bunk "kicks off" with his heel, piano and drums pick it up and the band is off. — 1948 *Trumpet on the Wing*, p. 44. In those days I didn't know how to give a down beat with my hand, like leaders do today. We'd just kick it off on the bandstand, "One, two." — 1956 *Climax*, Summer, p. 77. The trio kicked off the next set with a modern piece. — 1957 *Concerning Jazz*, p. 16. I started to kick off the tempo. — 1957 *Giants of Jazz*, p. 75. "Okay, boys, let's kick it off in E flat."

kicks, *n. pl.* 1. [from hobo slang: cf. 1930 *American Tramp and Underworld Slang,* s.v. *kicks:* "shoes, those things with which a kick is delivered"; current among jazzmen since c. 1925] See 1959 quot. — 1958 *Somewhere There's Music,* p. 101. "She bought me these kicks," he said and held up a foot. — 1959 *Swinging Syllables.* s.v. *kicks:* shoes.

2. [poss. from narcotics slang (i.e., by analogy with the jolting effect), poss. reinforced by general slang "getting a kick out of (something)"; according to jazzmen, current since c. 1928] See 1952, 1960 quots.; also, singular form (see 1956 quot.): someone or something that is a source of pleasure. — 1937 *Metronome,* March, p. 31. Swing fans will get the biggest kicks from Swing. — 1952 *A History of Jazz in America,* p. 351. *kicks:* pleasure. — 1956 *It's Always Four O'Clock,* pp. 72–73. This Goldenson guy was a real kick. — 1959 *The Holy Barbarians,* p. 22. "I just like to take them for kicks now and then." — 1960 *Dictionary of American Slang.* s.v. *kicks:* a surge of pleasurable emotion; a thrill of enjoyment or excitement.

kill, *v.t.* [hyperbole; also some general slang use, but with esp. currency among jazzmen since c. 1935] To affect (one) powerfully and favorably. — 1938 *Cab Calloway: Hi De Ho,* p. 16. *kill me:* show me a good time, send me [i.e., jazz sense]. — 1955 *Hear Me Talkin to Ya,* p. 329. It killed me to be accepted as a regular member of the band. — 1957 *Down Beat,* 9 Jan., p. 33. Dickie Wells on trombone—he kills me. — 1958 *Down Beat,* 29 May, p. 16. Russell would have "killed" Bird, Miles says. — 1960 *The New Edition of the Encyclopedia of Jazz,* p. 478. "It's very well executed, doesn't kill me too much, but gets going nicely when he goes into the block-chords stuff." — 1961 *Jazz Journal,* March, p. 11. Clark Terry killed everybody—a biting, darting trumpet genius.

killer, killer-diller, *n.* [prob. from *kill; killer-diller* was part of the rhyming slang vogue c. 1935–c. 1940 and had slight currency; *killer* was current c. 1935–c. 1945, very rare since] Someone or something exceedingly formidable; also, by extension: a piece of music that's difficult to play (see first 1940 quot.). — 1937 *Metronome*, April, p. 55. That Zutie drummer-man is really a killer! — 1938 *Better English*, Nov., p. 51. *killer-diller:* a great thing, thrill.. — 1940 *Swing*, Jan., p. 26. *Farewell Blues* is another of those very fast killers. — 1940 *Mademoiselle*, Feb., pp. 89, 141. The Krupa band . . . is not all the killer-diller affair that a lot of people anticipated. — 1947 *Frontiers of Jazz*, p. 150. The long crashing finale—the "Killer-Diller," as Goodman calls any cumulative superlative—of the antiphonal *Sing, Sing, Sing!* — 1955 *Hear Me Talkin to Ya*, p. 227. I'm a killer with my new shepherd plaid suit. — 1960 *Metronome*, Aug., p. 18. "Man, that's a killer, isn't it?" said one of the trumpet players.

king, *n.* [general slang term for a topnotcher in any occupation, but used in special sense by jazzmen c. 1900–c. 1920, obs. since except historical; not to be confused with commercial uses in the 1920s (Paul Whiteman, King of Jazz) and the 1930s (Benny Goodman, King of Swing), etc.] A very great early (c. 1900–c. 1920) musician. (Since the trumpet was generally then the most important solo instrument, it is not surprising that this honorific title was bestowed primarily on trumpeters Buddy Bolden, Freddie Keppard, and Joe Oliver.) — 1915 advertising poster 22 April [1962 *Jazz: A History of the New York Scene*, photostat p. 35]. Contest Between the Percussion Kings. — 1946 *Jazzways*, p. 16. By 1907, Bolden had disappeared from the scene, confined to an insane asylum. But the succession of "kings" of the hot cornet showed no sign of giving out. — p. 20. Freddie Keppard was the jealous King of Jazz in 1910. — 1958 *Teach Yourself Jazz*, p. 114. The great "kings" of New Orleans took jazz groups there. — 1962 *The New Jazz Book*, p. 34. They spoke less of "King Bolden" than they did of "Kid Bolden." — p. 36. Oliver . . . was once "King of Jazz."

kitty, kitten, *n.* [prob. orig. by analogy with *cat*, q.v., poss. reinforced by the colloquial *kiddy* (i.e., a child); some currency since c. 1935; see also BABY] A young man or woman; also, by extension: any person. — 1946 *Really the Blues*, p. 194. Walking down the street, glimming [i.e., looking at] the cute kittens. — p. 372. *kitten:* very young girl. — 1956 *Lady Sings the Blues*, p. 27. I was only thirteen, but I was a hip kitty. — 1960 *Beat Jokes Bop Humor & Cool Cartoons*, p. 50. The old man, respected throughout the kingdom for being a down kitty, lay but a few weeks in his grave. — 1960 *Hiparama of the Classics*, p. 10. Look at all you Cats and Kitties out there!

knock, *v.t.* [semantic development unknown; cf. 1930 *American Tramp and Underworld Slang*, s.v. *knock:* "inform"; current since c. 1925] See individual quots. (a verb extremely protean [see first 1944 quot.] in its meanings) — 1929 *Knockin'* [i.e., consuming] *a Jug* (tune recorded by Louis Armstrong). — 1944 *Dan Burley's Original Handbook of Harlem Jive*, p. 142. *knock:* to put down, speak, walk, loan, borrow, give, ask, exhibit. — 1944 *Esquire*, June, p. 170. *knock a slave:* get a job. — 1944 *The New Cab Calloway's Hepsters Dictionary*, p. 9. "knock [i.e., give] me a kiss." — 1959 *Diggeth Thou?*, p. 40. He fell for a chick who knocked him for a deuce [i.e., borrowed two dollars from him]. — 1960 *Hiparama of the Classics*, p. 9. Knock [i.e., sew] a patch on the little Cats pants. — p. 26. The Gasser sat down to knock [i.e., write] a note on [i.e., to] Ferdinand the First.

    knock (one) out, [hyperbole; current since c. 1935; see also GAS, KILL, SEND] To please (one) greatly, to thrill (one). — 1942 *American Mercury*, July, p. 95. *knock yourself out:* have a good time. — 1947 *Band Leaders and Record Review*, Feb., p. 20. "When I heard it," Ella

Mae says, "it knocked me out." — 1950 *Metronome,* March, p. 29. "Shearing always did knock me out." — 1952 *Who Walk in Darkness,* p. 29. "Listen to . . . the big drums. It will knock you out." 1953 *Night Light,* p. 236. "It's pretty hard to be knocked out with a baby when you know its old man is bored with the whole idea." — 1957 *On the Road,* p. 202. A man who knocked himself out every evening and let the others put the quietus to him in the night. — 1960 *Jazz: A Quarterly of American Music,* Winter, p. 36. "Maybe it makes you laugh because it knocks you out."

knocked-out, *adj.* [from verb phrase; current c. 1938–c. 1946, rare since] Excellent, thrilling, superb. — 1941 *Strictly Ding-Dong,* p. 73. It had had all the dignity of a jam session, what with the staring alligators outside the church, the knocked-out musicians within. — 1948 *Down Beat,* 19 May, p. 14. The final chorus is git and block chords and knocked-out at that. — 1952 *Who Walk in Darkness,* p. 170. "You should dig that surf. It is really something. Knocked out." — 1956 *Sideman,* p. 275. "Sold knocked-out ties real cheap."

label, *n.* [metonymy: i.e., the phonograph record label bearing the recording company's name stands for the recording company; current since c. 1930] A recording company. — 1955 *Hear Me Talkin to Ya*, p. 177. I know we recorded for every label possible.

Lady, Lady Day, [one of the five or six indispensable ones of the many jazz nicknames: see also BIRD, PREZ, SATCH; see second 1956 quot. for etym.; current since c. 1940] Billie Holiday, 1915–1959; most jazz musicians and critics acclaim her as the greatest vocalist in the history of jazz. — 1942 *Travelin' Light* (Paul Whiteman Orchestra recording; vocalist listed as "Lady Day"). — 1956 *Sideman*, p. 26. "Sarah and Lady Day were both there." — 1956 *Lady Sings the Blues*, p. 59. Back at the Log Cabin the other girls used to try and mock me by calling me "Lady," because they thought I thought I was just too damn good to take the damn customers' money off the tables . . . Lester [Young] took it and coupled it with the Day out of Holiday and called me "Lady Day." — 1957 *Billie Holiday: The "Lady" Sings* (LP album Decca DL 8215). — 1958 *Melody Maker*, 18 Oct., p. 3. Lady Day is unquestionably the most important influence on American popular singing in the last twenty years. . . . The depth of Lady's singing has always rocked me.

lame, *adj. & n.* [extension of standard meaning, poss. reinforced by the similarity of sound with the earlier *lane*, q.v.; some currency since c. 1950; see also SQUARE] As adjective: unaware, unsophisticated, inexperienced; as noun: an unsophisticated, unaware person. — 1955 *American Speech*, Dec., p. 303. *Lame* is the opposite of *solid* [jazz sense]. — 1959 *Esquire*, Nov., p. 70J. *a lame:* one who doesn't know what's happening. A square [jazz sense]. — 1961 *N.Y. Times Magazine*, 25 June, p. 39. *lame:* square [jazz sense], but not beyond redemption. If you're lame, man, you can learn. — 1963 *Nugget*, Feb., p. 46. It takes a real lame stud to follow a sick-looking cat like me, with a green beard and shades into a dark alley.

lane, lain, laine, *n.* [according to jazz dancer Leon James, the term was formed by metonymy: country lanes are where many rural (i.e., unsophisticated) people live; some currency c. 1930–c. 1945, very rare since; see also LAME, SQUARE] One who is inexperienced or unsophisticated: see 1946 quot. — 1937 *Metronome*, Aug., p. 7. Nothing ever fed me up so much as that lain George Simon's review on Bunny Berigan in the July MET. — 1944 *Dan Burley's Original Handbook of Harlem Jive*, p. 52. A lamb is a lane, and a lane is a square. — 1944 *The New Cab Calloway's Hepsters Dictionary*. s.v. *lane*: a male, usually a non-professional. — 1946 *Really the Blues*, p. 372. *laine:* hick, innocent, sucker. — 1958 *Jive in Hi-Fi*, p. 30. A lane is a man not hip to jive.

latch on, [Old English term which became obsolete in standard English but survived in dialect: cf. 1954 *Webster's New International Dictionary*, s.v. *latch:* "ME. lacchen, fr AS. *læccan . . . Obs. exc. Dial.* 1. To seize; lay hold of; take; also, figuratively, to comprehend"; current among jazzmen c. 1930–c. 1945, rare since; see also PICK UP (ON)] See note above and 1938, 1958 quots. — 1938 *Cab Calloway: Hi De Ho*, p. 16. *latch on:* grab, take hold, get wise to. — 1946 *Really the Blues*, p. 372. *latch on:* get hold of. — 1948 *Trumpet on the Wing*, p. 52. One night I latched on to the screwiest job I ever had in my life. — 1958, *The Book of Negro Folklore*, p. 485. *latch on:* become aware, understand, learn.

later, *adv. & interj.* 1. [see 1957 quot.; current since c. 1950] See 1956, 1957 quots. (occasionally with *for you:* see 1961 quot.). — 1956 *Tennessee Folklore Society Bulletin*, March, p. 23. *later:* catchall word for "I'll be seeing you." — 1957 *American Speech*, Dec., p. 281. The bopster's successor, the modern jazz enthusiast, is not only moderate, but pithy. He tends to condense meanings into single words, e.g., bop and pre-bop "I'll dig you later, man" becomes simply, "Later!" — 1959 *The Horn*, p. 34. "Well, I'll cut out then . . . later, pops." — 1959 *The Holy*

Barbarians, p. 115. Angel . . . says, "Later" and leaves. — 1960 *Jazz: A Quarterly of American Music,* Winter, p. 21. Reporter: "Good night." Hippie: "Yeah, man, later." — 1961 *The Sound,* p. 14. "Later for you, bruz."

2. [extension of sense 1: figuratively, to bid goodbye to or want to be rid of someone or something; current since c. 1952] See note and 1957 quot. — 1953 *Later* (tune recorded by Ella Fitzgerald on Decca DL8149). Later for the happenings, baby. — 1957 *N.Y. Times,* 25 Aug. *Later with that, man!:* disinclination to participate in an activity or project. — 1960 *Beat Jokes Bop Humor & Cool Cartoons,* p. 54. "Aw, later for this action." — p. 61. "Cut out from thy old man, later for your name." — 1962 *Down Beat,* 22 Nov., p. 26. "Later for the music business."

law, *n.* [from underworld slang: cf. 1930 *American Tramp and Underworld Slang,* s.v. *law:* "any police authority"; also some general slang use, but with esp. currency among jazzmen since c. 1900; see also *fuzz*] See 1958 quot. — 1942 *American Mercury,* July, p. 92. "Oh, let's don't talk about the law." — 1952 *Flee the Angry Strangers,* p. 137. "No Law in there, baby, I can smell fuzz from fifty yards." — 1952 *Music Out of Dixie,* p. 302. "The law was up there this mornin'." — 1958 *The Book of Negro Folklore,* p. 488. *the law:* the police.

lay back, [prob. from general colloquial *lay back* (i.e., to stay behind); current since c. 1930; see also DRAG, *v.i.*] To fall behind the rhythm (sometimes deliberately in order to achieve a particular effect: in this sense, oral evidence only). — 1955 *Hear Me Talkin to Ya,* p. 200. Most singers . . . they're either layin' back or else runnin' away from you.

lay dead, lay up (in), [cf. 1930 *American Tramp and Underworld Slang,* s.v. *lying dead:* "in hiding"; some currency among jazzmen since c. 1935; see also COOLING] To relax, to do nothing: see 1959 quots. — 1958 *The*

Dharma Bums, p. 99. "Come and lay up in and learn to drink tea." — 1959 *Esquire,* Nov., p. 70J. *lay dead:* to wait. To stay in one place, don't move. — *lay up:* to be off the scene [jazz sense].

lay down, [extension of standard meaning (i.e., to place or set down); current since c. 1935; see also PUT DOWN, sense 1] To present, perform, or contribute (something). — 1950 *They All Played Ragtime,* p. 194. "He laid down a terrific stomp." — 1958 *Somewhere There's Music,* p. 47. "Gene must have really laid down some shuck to Barton about your playing." — 1960 *Hiparama of the Classics,* p. 10. When he laid it *down* WHAM! It stayed there! — 1960 *Down Beat,* 13 Oct., p. 23. "Those fingers have more direction and lay down better time than 90 percent working today."

lay (some) iron, [from the metal taps worn by dancers; poss. also by analogy with an earlier railroad slang term; current esp. among tap dancers, but also current to some extent since c. 1917 among jazzmen, since they frequently provided the musical accompaniment] See 1938 quot. — 1938 *Cab Calloway: Hi De Ho,* p. 16. *lay some iron:* to tap dance. Example: "Jack, you really laid some iron that last show." — 1945 *Hepcats Jive Talk Dictionary.* s.v. *lay iron:* tap dance. — 1946 *Really the Blues,* p. 212. He . . . can lay some iron, too.

lay (something) on (someone), [by analogy with standard meaning (i.e., to place on); widely current since c. 1935; see also PUT (SOMETHING) ON (SOMEONE)] To give or present or tell (something to someone). — 1942 *American Mercury,* July, p. 86. "Lay de skin on me [i.e., shake hands], pal!" — 1952 *Flee the Angry Strangers,* p. 244. "He lays some on [i.e., gives some to] his buddies." — 1952 *Music Out of Dixie,* p. 243. "If Danny or any o' the customers got any kicks they can lay 'em on me." — 1953 *Night Light,* p. 200. "Laying a story on me." — 1954 *Metronome,* Aug., p. 20. "Watch what happens when we forget to pay up, or even those terrible moments when we don't lay enough on the waiter." — 1958 *Somewhere There's Music*, p. 37. "I don't know what it is. If I did, I'd lay it on him." — 1961 *Down Beat*, 19 Jan., p. 22. It's then he lays it on you.

lay out, [prob. from general colloquial *lay* (i.e., stay), and adapted from card players' use (i.e., not to play a particular hand); current since c. 1920] To stay out of the playing (of music); also noun, see 1935 quot.; also, by extension, see 1963 quot. — 1935 *Vanity Fair*, Nov., p. 71. Extended rests are "lay-outs." — 1955 *Bop Fables*, p. 21. The commercial little pig laid out for a few bars and then moved into a prefab. — 1958 *Somewhere There's Music*, p. 178. Then Mike laid out while the guitar took a chorus. — 1959 *Jazz: A Quarterly of American Music*, Summer, p. 204. Do you like the piano player to "lay out" while you're jamming? — 1959 *The Jazz Review*, Sep., p. 10. Always leave some spaces—lay out. — 1960 *Jazz: A Quarterly of American Music*, Winter, p. 36. "Miles asked me to lay out during his solo." — 1961 *The Sound*, p. 45. "I gonna lay out just one more set." — 1963 *Hiptionary*, p. 12. *lays out:* says nothing; does not join in the action.

lay up (in), See s.v. LAY DEAD.

lazy, *adj.* [standard term given a special application by jazzmen; according to jazzman Eubie Blake, some currency since c. 1900] See 1956 quot. — 1956 *Guide to Jazz.* s.v. *lazy:* relaxed playing, devoid of any apparent effort. — 1961 *New Yorker*, 18 Feb., p. 128. Gillespie's work was an exemplary balance of extraordinary arabesque passages and lazy legato turnings.

lead, *n. & adj.* [see 1958 quot. for semantic explanation; current since c. 1925] See 1958 quot. — 1934 *All About Jazz*, p. 99. He evolved what he called a "harmony chorus," the instruments all playing harmony, with a solo lead. — 1937 *American Speech*, Feb., p. 47. It is voiced peculiarly in that the lead melody is carried lower than the clarinet. — 1940 *Swing,* Jan., p. 21. He often uses the Glenn Miller saxophone voicing with a clarinet lead. — 1955 *Down Beat,* 7 Sep., p. 29. Dizzy played lead on the last chorus. — 1956 *Sideman,* p. 9. He was playing lead sax for Matt MacNeal. — 1956 *Guide to Jazz,* p. 165. The "lead man" is the musician who leads the band or section of it. — 1957 *Giants of Jazz,* p. 26. "Play that lead, son." — 1958 *Publication of the American Dialect Society,* Nov., p. 46. *lead:* the top, or melody, part in an arrangement: therefore, the melodic line. *lead man:* one who plays the "lead" in his section of the ensemble. — 1961 *Jazz: A Quarterly of American Music,* Winter, p. 73. He was playing lead all the time on trumpet.

leader, *n.* [from *band leader;* current since c. 1935] The leader (cf. *sideman*) of a jazz band of any size. — 1926 *Melody Maker,* March, p. 4. The drummer . . . disdains the leader. — 1940 *Swing,* Nov., p. 28. It's . . . a screamer ending featuring the leader's horn. — 1960 *Jazz Street,* p. 14. There are sidemen as well as leaders in this book. — 1961 *Metronome,* Feb., p. 30. Every time he looks around he's been made *leader* again.

lead sheet, [from *lead, adj.;* current since c. 1925] See 1949 quot. — 1949 *Music Library Association Notes,* Dec., p. 46. *lead sheet:* a song as written down in its simplest form—melody line and lyric. — 1959 *The Horn,* p. 144. He picked up the lead sheet again. — 1961 *The Sound,* p. 38. "You never got around to writing out a lead sheet!"

least, *adj. & n.* [formed as antonym to *the most,* q.v.; some currency since c. 1952; see also NOWHERE] As adjective: mediocre; as noun: something mediocre. — 1955 *Bop Fables,* p. 36. "Honey, your grandma is feeling the least." — 1958 *Publication of the American Dialect Society,* Nov., p. 46. *the least:* opposite of the most. — 1959 *Swinging Syllables.* s.v. *least:* bad scene or situation.

left hand, [special application of standard phrase; current prob. since c. 1900]   A pianist's left hand; also, his skill or inventiveness with the left hand. — 1926 *Melody Maker,* Jan., p. 24. The bass, or left-hand part, is customarily the most neglected. — 1944 *Metronome,* Nov., p. 17. "Everyone wanted to treat the piano player. Drinks were lined up ten deep all night long . . . and to keep the ball rolling, the box-beater [i.e., pianist] had to reach for a drink with his right hand and keep the melody going with his left. That's how left-hands were born!" — 1959 *The Jazz Review,* July, p. 13. He . . . had a good left hand. — 1961 *The Jazz Review,* Jan., p. 26. Granted he has a great left hand, but the way he uses it detracts from his right. — 1961 *Monsieur,* April, p. 36. "That's Teddy Wilson. Listen to his left hand."

left town, [by analogy with standard meaning; some currency since c. 1900; see also QUIT THE SCENE, SPLIT THE SCENE]   Died. — 1960 *Lester Left Town* (tune written by Wayne Shorter as an elegy for Lester Young, who died in 1959).

legit, legitimate, *adj. & n.* [both the standard term and the shortened form derive from a parallel usage among theater people; some currency since c. 1925; see also LONG-HAIR]   See 1937 quot. — 1933 *Metronome,* Jan., p. 36. Naturally, the man who can play both legitimately and "hot" is the more valuable. — 1937 *American Speech,* Feb., p. 47. *legitimate, legit:* applied to other than popular music. Also applied to a musician who does not play dance music well, although he may play other music perfectly. — 1942 *The American Thesaurus of Slang,* p. 555. *legit, legitimate:* conservative musician. — 1955 *Hear Me Talkin to Ya,* p. 38. After that, I didn't play "legitimate" so much. — p. 59. He tried . . . to avoid a "legit" tone. — 1956 *Sideman,* p. 10. "Writes symphonies, you know? Legit stuff." — p. 431. "Lou says you write good legit."

less, *adv.* [one of several quantitative terms given a qualitative meaning by jazzmen (see also GANG, LEAST, THE MOST); some currency since c. 1950] Not as well. — 1959 *Jazz: A Quarterly of American Music,* Fall, p. 290. "Man, I'm playing *less.*"

let's do a set!, let's go back home!, [according to jazzmen, some currency c. 1910–c. 1930 esp. among those Negroes who danced to jazz, obs. since except historical; see also PUT US IN THE ALLEY!] Shouts of encouragement to jazz musicians c. 1910–c. 1930 to play fast, energetically and intensely. — 1959 *The Jazz Review,* July, p. 12. When they got tired of two-steps and schottisches (which they danced with a lot of spieling), they'd yell: "Let's go back home!". . . "Let's do a set!"

let's go home, See s.v. GO HOME.

let the good times roll, [according to jazzman Eubie Blake, some currency esp. among Negro jazzmen since c. 1900] Let's enjoy ourselves—drink and talk and listen to or play music. — 1948 *Let the Good Times Roll* (tune composed by Fleecie Moore and Sam Theard). — 1959 *Jazz: A Quarterly of American Music,* Summer, p. 188. This invests the whole solo with a raucous, "let-the-good-times-roll" quality. — 1960 *Hiparama of the Classics,* p. 29. He loved to hear the horns of joy blowin' that fine Jazz, plenty of juice flowin', and let the Good Times roll.

lick, *n.* 1. [prob. from its colloquial meaning (i.e., a blow): cf. 1939 *Jazzmen,* p. 60. "It was said Joe had a bad forehead wound caused by 'a lick on the haid' delivered by a wicked broomstick"; also cf. 1947 *Horn of Plenty,* p. 141. "Give it a solid lick!"; poss. reinforced by another meaning of the standard term: cf. 1938 *Cab Calloway: Hi De Ho,* p. 16. "*licking the chops:* what the cats do when they are warming up for a swing session"; widely current from c. 1930–c. 1945, obs. since except historical; see also BREAK] See second 1933 and 1938 quots. — 1932 *Melody Maker,* June, p. 509. They manage to steal a "lick" from an American record. — 1933 *Metronome*, April, p. 29. Please do not get me wrong and think I want "hot licks" to memorize in all keys. — 1933 *Fortune*, Aug., p. 47. His *licks* (musical phrases) are original to the point of being *screwy* (fantastically exciting). — 1935 *Stage*, Sep., p. 45. *licks:* hot jazz phrase. — 1936 *Esquire*, June, p. 92. The mutations of musician's slang are interesting. It was "breaks" originally. Then it became "licks." — 1938 *Cab Calloway: Hi De Ho*, p. 16. *licks:* hot musical phrases. — 1953 *Night Light*, p. 130. Al . . . hit the cymbal behind (this or some other) lick of the trumpet.

2. [extension of sense 1 (i.e., from a musical idea to any idea); current since c. 1940; see also RIFF] The idea, the plan, the situation (usually with *the*). — 1955 *Bop Fables*, p. 54. "So here's the lick. Take this beat-up bovine to market." — 1960 *Hiparama of the Classics*, p. 10. They're Pushin' The Nazz! 'Cause they wanted to dig his Lick, you see, Dig his Miracle Lick! — p. 11. He's a carpenter kitty and he's got his own lick.

licorice stick, [from its resemblance; some currency c. 1930– c. 1940, obs. since except historical; see also BLACKSTICK] See 1935 quot. — 1935 *Vanity Fair*, Nov., p. 71. *licorice stick:* clarinet. — 1942 *The American Thesaurus of Slang*, p. 558. *licorice stick:* clarinet.

lid, *n.* [cf. 1937 A *Dictionary of Slang and Unconventional English*, s.v. *lid:* "a hat, a cap . . . from ca. 1905"; current among jazzmen since c. 1935; see also SKY, WIG] Initially, see 1959 quot.; by extension, since c. 1943, the mind: see FLIP (ONE'S) LID. — 1956 *Lady Sings the Blues*, p. 20. All the big-time whores wore big red velvet hats then with bird-of-paradise feathers on them. These lids were the thing. — 1959 *Swinging Syllables*. s.v. *lid:* cap, hat.

lift, *adj. & v.t.* [by extension of standard meaning; some currency c. 1920–c. 1935, rare since] See quots. — 1927

Melody Maker, June, p. 585. This was done chiefly by
. . . placing before the original melody notes lift notes
(usually a semi-quaver in value). — 1934 *Metronome,*
Dec., p. 52. *Lift* . . . implies extra accents in certain
mensural time places . . . The "lifting" of a beat means
extra accents.

light, *adj.* [special application of standard meaning (cf.
heavy beat); some currency since c. 1935] As applied
to a rhythm instrument or instrumentalist: weakly accented, having little power; as applied to the tone of a
wind instrument or instrumentalist: thin (in this sense,
oral evidence only). — 1962 *Jazz Journal,* July, p. 11.
Duke needs an exceptionally strong bass player. . . . I
do think the man he has now . . . is a bit light for the
band.

light crumbs, See s.v. CRUMBS.

lightly and politely, [from rhyming slang vogue c. 1935–
c. 1940, very rare since] Neatly, "niftily," effortlessly,
smoothly, satisfactorily (done). — 1939 *American Jazz
Music,* p. 54. Louis Armstrong somewhere says, "lightly,
lightly and politely." — 1961 *The Sound,* p. 118. "Lightly
and po-lightly!" Red exclaimed.

light up, [cf. its general colloquial use (i.e., to light a
cigarette); some currency among jazzmen since c. 1930;
see also TURN ON] See 1938, 1946 quots. — 1938 *Cab
Calloway: Hi De Ho,* p. 16. *light up:* to smoke a reefer
or weed. — 1946 *Really the Blues,* p. 372. *light up:* smoke
marihuana. — 1953 *Night Light,* p. 136. "You light up
and you get yourself a hen and maybe shack up with
her." — 1959 *The Holy Barbarians,* p. 27. "Before I light
up I'm drug with [i.e., troubled by] the ten thousand
things."

like, *adv.* [see last quot. for humorously expressed but accurate insight into the rationale of the word; also cf.
OED "1500–20 Dunbar *Poems* xix, 19 yon man is lyke
out of his mind. 1596 Spenser *F.Q.* iv. x. 56 all looking on

and like astonisht staring"; also cf. 1960 *Dictionary of American Slang*, s.v. *like:* "reenforced by Yiddish speech patterns"; widely current since c. 1943]   See 1956, first 1958, first 1959, and last quots. — 1950 *Neurotica*, Autumn, p. 45. "Like how much can you lay on [i.e., give] me?" — 1952 *Flee the Angry Strangers*, p. 159. "I got an idea like-maybe where she is." — 1954 *Esquire*, Nov., p. 82. He is a man who laughs often, and explosively, and in this case, he flipped, or as he put it later, he like flipped (Norvo, in common with many musicians, has a great fondness for the adverb "like"). — 1956 *Tennessee Folklore Society Bulletin*, March, p. 23. *like:* filler word for pauses of uncertainty. — 1958 *Publication of the American Dialect Society*, Nov., p. 46. *like:* means little or nothing. Used to fill up gaps in the sentence. — 1958 *Nugget*, Oct., p. 51. They also tell about the hipster at the beach who got out beyond his depth and hollered to the life guard: "Like help!" — 1959 *Newport Jazz Festival: 1959*, p. 45. *like:* replaces the comma in jazz parlance. — 1959 *The Horn*, p. 85. "I'm gonna cut [i.e., leave] this time, Baby . . . Like all I need is bus fare." — 1959 *The Holy Barbarians*, p. 26. "Like I was very religious at the time." — p. 316. *like:* the theory of relativity applied to reality.

Lindy (hop), [see 1936, 1958 quots. for etym., 1937 quot. for initial date]   See 1937 quot.; also, for its *v.i.* use, see 1932 quot. — 1931 *Zit's Theatrical Newspaper*, 2 May, p. 11. The winners of the all-Harlem Lindy Hop contest . . . drew rounds of applause nightly. — 1932 *The Inter-State Tattler*, 23 June, p. 8. They . . . Lindy hopped. — 1936 *Life*, 14 Dec., p. 64. Like many another trick dance, including Trucking and the Susie Q, the Lindy Hop originated at the Savoy, was named, for good reasons, after Charles Augustus Lindbergh. — 1937 *American Speech*, Oct., p. 183. The Lindy Hop is a Negro dance which reached its present popularity during the summer of 1927. It contains elements of the previously popular Charleston and Black Bottom, and the subsequently introduced Truckin'. — 1958 *Melody Maker*, 11 Oct., p. 4. In 1927, shortly after Lindbergh's flight to Paris, he [i.e., "Shorty George" Snowden] observed a group of unusually lively dancers. "Who do you think you are, hopping around like that?" he asked — "Lindbergh?" The Lindy Hop was christened.

line, *n.* [prob. from the fact that the music, if and when written, is set down on the long parallel lines that make up the staff; current since c. 1935] A melody (and harmony); melodic (and harmonic) continuity in the building of an improvised chorus. — 1940 *Swing*, Nov., p. 27. There's . . . a lovely, smooth melodic line in his improvisations on this swell old tune. — 1958 *Saturday Review*, 8 Feb., p. 44. Parker's line on "The Song Is You" is an anthology of "licks" still played by jazzmen striving for "hipness." — 1959 *Down Beat*, 3 Sep., p. 24. This is excellent Getz, and all his talents are on display, the lyricism, the effortlessly flowing line, the subtle shifts of tone, the sudden turns and expectedly bent notes, the constant freshness. — 1960 *The Jazz Review*, Nov., p. 18. The session started slowly, confining itself, strangely yet somehow logically, to early bop lines. — 1961 *The Jazz Review*, Jan., p. 25. Red Allen is a soloist, not an ensemble improvisor; his lines are too active to be leads for this kind of polyphony. — 1961 *Down Beat*, 5 Jan., p. 36. The group has an amazing facility for twisting a familiar line to give it new and sometimes deeper interest than it had before.

liner, *n. & adj.* [chiefly jazz trade term; current since c. 1950] The back of a long-playing record cover, on which appear notes about the music and musicians. — 1955 *Saturday Review*, 15 Jan., p. 41. For the covers of these new jazz albums . . . are being covered . . . with thousands and thousands of words known as "liner

notes." — 1960 *The Jazz Word,* p. 154. They couldn't
come up with any less information than on some liners
today.

lip, *n.* [metonymy; current since c. 1930; see also CHOPS,
FANGS] See 1937 quot. — 1933 *Metronome,* July, p. 26.
He's got the ideas, but his lip's weak yet. — 1937 *Ameri-
can Speech,* Feb., p. 47. *lip:* technically embouchure.
Used in relation to the state of muscular strength of brass
instrument players' lips and their resultant ability to play
high notes accurately. — 1948 *Trumpet on the Wing,*
p. 54. I noticed that he didn't have much of a lip. — 1955
Bop Fables, p. 23. "What condition is your lip in?" — 1958
After Hours Poetry, p. 62. Where,/When a trumpeter
blows/He's got a good lip. — 1959 *Easy Living,* p. 57.
"I can't even do that until I get my lip back." — 1960
The Jazz Review, Sep.-Oct., p. 14. He didn't have it with
the lip, but he had it here, in his head. — Nov., p. 10.
My lip went bad after a year in the Earl Hines band.
They swung so hard and played so much.

Lipton's, *n.* [because jazz slang *tea* means marijuana,
a brand name of the standard sense of *tea* has become synonymous with all marijuana of poor quality—
i.e., having no more effect on the smoker than . . . ;
current since c. 1940] See note above. Oral evidence
only.

Little Jazz, [prob. from his short stature; one of the five or
six indispensable ones of the many jazz nicknames (see
also BIRD, LADY, PREZ); current since c. 1938] Roy Eldridge, 1911–, generally acclaimed by jazz musicians and
critics as one of the great trumpeters in jazz history.
— 1941 *Little Jazz* (song recorded by Gene Krupa Orchestra, featuring Roy Eldridge on trumpet). — 1956
Guide to Jazz, p. 87. *Little Jazz:* Roy Eldridge. — 1961
The Village Voice, 16 Feb., p. 13. He acknowledged playing a good deal with "Little Jazz" and crediting him with
having "iron chops" [q.v.]. — 1961 *Down Beat,* 30

March, p. 32. This could have been the best album by
Little Jazz in a long time.

locked hands, [from the fixed position of the hands in relation to one another when playing in this manner; current since c. 1945; see also BLOCK CHORD] See 1957 quot.
— 1957 *The Book of Jazz*, p. 68. This was the "locked
hands" or "block chord" style, in which the left hand
moves parallel with the right, playing extra notes in the
chord or duplicating the right hand's chord, instead of
supplying a base line. — 1959 *The Collector's Jazz: Modern,* p. 268. Shearing has run practically the entire jazz
gamut . . . through the locked hands block chords. —
1961 *Metronome,* Aug., p. 7. He often generates enough
thunder to blast off an army, and thus forces pianist Kuhn
to rely heavily on a locked-hands style.

long bread, See s.v. BREAD.

long green, See s.v. GREEN.

longhair, long-hair, *n. & adj.* [from stereotyped image of the
classical musician; chiefly teenage slang but with some
currency among jazzmen c. 1930–c. 1945, obs. since except
historical; see also LEGIT, STRAIGHT] See 1949 quot. —
1935 *Vanity Fair,* Nov., p. 71. Straight or commercial
musicians are often derisively called *salon-men* or *long-
haired* boys. — 1939 *Metronome,* Nov., p. 24. The jury
was completely longhair, however. — 1943 *Tangleweed,*
p. 174. "It ain't a song. It's a composition. Long-haired."
— 1949 *Music Library Association Notes,* Dec., p. 46.
long-hair: one who plays, appreciates, composes, or writes
about concert music.

long underwear, long-underwear (gang), [by analogy with
the cautious, conservative nature of the apparel; chiefly
teenage slang but with some currency esp. among white
jazzmen c. 1930–c. 1940, obs. since except historical; see
also HOTEL, SWEET, TICKY] See 1936 quot. — 1933 *Fortune,* Aug., p. 47. And *corny* music is what generally happens when a *sweet* band, or *long-underwear gang,* tries

to play *hot.* — 1936 *Stage,* March, p. 58. *long underwear gang:* musicians who can play only "as written." — 1937 *This Thing Called Swing,* p. 8. *long underwear gang:* a band that plays straight [jazz sense] music. — 1956 *The Real Jazz Old and New,* p. 150. *long underwear:* concert stuff.

look out!, [cf. its general colloquial meaning (i.e., "attention!"); widely current c. 1940–c. 1947, rare since] That's formidable! (esp. though not exclusively applied to music) — 1946 *Big Book of Swing,* p. 124. *look out:* expression of one's interest in ad-lib musical break. — 1960 *Stanley Turrentine: Look Out!* (LP album Blue Note BLP 4039).

loose wig, See s.v. WIG.

loot, *n.* [from underworld slang: cf. 1937 A *Dictionary of Slang and Unconventional English,* s.v. *loot:* "(*n.*) pillage, plunder"; current among jazzmen c. 1930–c. 1945 when it was largely replaced by *bread;* see also GOLD] See 1960 quot. — 1951 *Esquire,* Dec., p. 210. He must have made a nice little "taste" (meaning) the tune made quite a bit of "loot." — 1953 *Night Light,* p. 147. "He's been stealin' all his old lady's loot." — 1959 *The Naked Lunch,* p. 118. "She won't piss any more of my loot down the drain." — 1960 *Dictionary of American Slang.* s.v. *loot:* money.

lot, *adj.* [one of several quantitative words given a qualitative meaning by jazzmen (see also GANG, LEAST, THE MOST); current since c. 1935] Excellent; of great quality. — 1946 *Duke Ellington,* p. 59. "Damn," said Harry, "that's a lot of horn, that really is." — 1956 *Down Beat,* 14 Nov., p. 13. "He plays an awful lot of trumpet." — 1961 *Down Beat,* 5 Jan., p. 43. Well, I would rate it two stars for orchestral technique, for being able to handle an orchestra that size, even though it's not a lot of music. — 1961 *Jazz Journal,* April, p. 4. "What with Art and Sabu, that was a lot of drums!"

low-down, *adj.* [see 1939, 1959 quots. for semantic development; prob. reinforced by the old colloquial term: cf. 1959 *Webster's New World Dictionary* s.v. *low-down:* "colloq. mean; contemptible; despicable"; note absence of pejorative connotation in jazzmen's use of the term (one of many such: see also BAD, DIRTY, MEAN, TERRIBLE, TOUGH); according to jazzman Eubie Blake, current c. 1900–c. 1945, very rare since; see also GULLY-LOW, GUT-BUCKET, HONKYTONK] See 1934, 1939, 1960 quots. — 1926 *Sweet and Low Down* (tune recorded by Alfredo's New Prince's Orchestra). — 1928 *Variety,* Aug. [1962 *Jazz: A History of the New York Scene,* p. 198]. Witnesses state that often between two and five a.m. there were as many as 35 or 40 musicians on the stand, kidding around and giving their conception of low-down tunes. — 1939 *Jazzmen,* p. 12. From barrel-houses and honky-tonks came many of the descriptive words which were applied to the music played in them; hence, "gully-low," meaning as its name implies, low as a ditch or "gully," hence "low-down." — 1955 *Hear Me Talkin to Ya,* p. 231. Charlie Irvis could play lowdown on the trombone. — 1959 *The Jazz Scene,* p. 290. Terms for emotion were formed by metaphor, e.g. by the widespread practice of equating . . . grief with depth . . . Thus the quality most desired in the old blues is that it should be *low-down.* — 1960 *Dictionary of American Slang.* s.v. *low-down:* in jazz, slow, intense, in the manner of the blues.

lush, *n.* [cf. general slang *lush* (i.e., drunkard); also cf. 1960 *Dictionary of American Slang,* s.v. *lush:* "liquor. 1848: J. S. Farmer. Archaic since c. 1920. Reintroduced by jazzmen in the '30's"; current c. 1935–c. 1945, very rare since; see also JUICE] See 1960 quot. — 1938 *N.Y. Amsterdam News,* 2 April, p. 17. "The thousands of . . . lushheads and 'tea' worms that are being hatched daily . . . are a peril." — 1956 *Sideman,* p. 274. "Get wild enough on lush." — 1960 *Dictionary of American Slang.*

s.v. *lush:* liquor. — 1961 *The Sound,* p. 11. "I can't make [i.e., use or enjoy] lush at all, baby."

   v.i. [current c. 1935–c. 1945, rare since; see also JUICE] To drink liquor. — 1950 *Gutbucket and Gossamer,* p. 21. I hate people who don't know when to stop lushing. — 1958 *Somewhere There's Music,* p. 174. "I lush less and less the longer I'm around town."

lushed, *adj.* [current c. 1935–c. 1945, very rare since; see also BOXED, JUICED, STONED] Drunk. — 1959 *The Horn,* p. 213. "I got too lushed somewhere."

lying, *participle* [by analogy with verbal communication (see also SAY SOMETHING, TELL A STORY, TRUTH); some currency since c. 1955; see also JIVING, SHUCKING] Playing a lot of musical clichés; hence, playing music insincerely. (According to jazzmen, this is the only meaning; hence, the definitions in the quot. are inaccurate.) — 1957 *N.Y. Times Magazine,* 18 Aug., p. 26. *lying:* playing the notes as written rather than improvising on a theme; dogging it; playing with a sweet band rather than a hot one.

M, [abbreviation; from underworld and narcotics slang: cf. 1930 *American Tramp and Underworld Slang,* s.v. *M:* "morphine"; some currency among jazzmen since c. 1935] Morphine. — 1959 *The Naked Lunch,* p. 221.

Your reporter bang thirty grains of M a day and sit eight hours incrustable as a turd. — 1961 *The Sound*, p. 22. "It's not like H [i.e., heroin] or M."

mad, *adj.* [early synonym for *crazy,* q.v.; some currency since c. 1940; see also INSANE, NUTTY] Exciting, pleasurable, excellent. — 1944 *Dan Burley's Original Handbook of Harlem Jive,* p. 15. "That's mad, ole man." — 1957 *On the Road,* p. 154. We spent a mad day in downtown New Orleans.

mainstream, *adj.* [chiefly a writers' term (see 1961 quot.); some currency since c. 1955] Of music or a musician, characteristic of or belonging to a school or style of jazz that has roots in the swing (q.v.) period (see 1960 quot.) —i.e., occupying an intermediate position between the traditionalists and the modernists. — 1959 *Jazz: A Quarterly of American Music,* Spring, p. 161. It's fatuous to assess, currently with its taking place, what is mainstream jazz. — 1960 *Swing Swang Swingin': Jackie McLean* (liner notes on LP album Blue Note 4024). Swing with a capital S is a noun and besides representing an era, is used to describe a segment of jazz which has since been redubbed mainstream. — 1961 *Jazz News,* 16 Aug., p. 10. I am often labeled a "mainstream" clarinet player, but the word "mainstream" doesn't mean very much. These labels are normally manufactured by critics to bring some sort of jazz they like to the attention of more people. — 1962 *Jazz Journal,* Sep., p. 32. This is not at all wayout as one might expect, but rather in the manner of a mainstream session.

make it, [cf. 1930 *American Tramp and Underworld Slang,* s.v. *make:* "to accomplish. Much the same sense as in standard English, although applied to any object or piece of work"; widely current since c. 1948] For the commonest sense, see last two 1959 quots., but also see individual quots. (a phrase protean in its meanings) —

1950 *Neurotica,* Autumn, p. 45. "Double lock the door, George. I'm gonna make it [i.e., take narcotics] first." — 1953 *This Week Magazine,* 5 April, p. 13. "It's a kind of music I mostly can't make [i.e., enjoy]." — 1955 *Down Beat,* 28 Dec., p. 12. "Roy Kral and Jackie Cain have simply got to make it [i.e., succeed] very big." — 1956 *Sideman,* p. 25. "You wanta make it [i.e., go (somewhere) and perform] with me tonight? Bring your ax." — 1957 *On the Road,* p. 225. They went to a parking lot in broad daylight . . . and there, he claims, he made it [i.e., had sexual intercourse with her]. — 1958 *Somewhere There's Music,* p. 18. Baby and I made [i.e., used] two of those pills. — p. 47. "I made it to [i.e., arrived at] Gene's late." — 1958 *Down Beat,* 1 May, p. 20. "If the drummer doesn't make it [i.e., perform effectively], I don't know what I'm supposed to do at all." — 1959 *Toronto Telegram,* 31 March, p. 3. *make it:* cope. — 1959 *Easy Living,* p. 28. "Really? You've never made hash [i.e., smoked hashish]?" — 1959 *Afro Magazine Section,* 3 Oct., p. E4. "Me—as long as I can drag down two and a half or three beans for myself every week—I can make it [i.e., live happily, comfortably] and keep my piece [sic] of mind." — 1959 *The Holy Barbarians,* p. 54. ". . . making it! . . . getting by with as little commercial work as possible, or ideally, with no commercial work at all." — p. 78. Just good conversation is often enough to make it for [i.e., satisfy, please] me. — p. 316. *make it:* may be said of anything that succeeds. — 1959 *Newport Jazz Festival: 1959,* p. 45. *makes it:* good, acceptable. *make it:* leave, depart. — 1960 *Jazz: A Quarterly of American Music,* Winter, p. 50. I print longhand. A typewriter I can't make [i.e., use]. — 1960 *The Jazz Word,* p. 16. The mother . . . talked . . . about the old man across hall making it [i.e., having a sex affair] with Mrs. Jones' son. — p. 80. "He didn't show, I heard he made it [i.e., arrived] later." — 1961 *The Sound*, p. 11. "I can't make lush [i.e., use or enjoy liquor] at all, baby," the girl said.

make the scene, [jazz slang *make* + jazz slang (*the*) *scene;* current since c. 1950] To join or to participate in the activities of a (particular) milieu or of the world at large (see 1958 quot.). — 1958 *American Speech*, Oct., pp. 224–225. In *making the scene* one partakes in a larger tableau. (When, on the other hand, he *does the bit*, he is merely part of a short incident.) — 1959 *The Village Voice*, 28 Oct., p. 13. "So, I get up and go out and make the scene." — 1960 *Beat Jokes Bop Humor & Cool Cartoons*, p. 21. "I made the academic scene for just a week."

make (one's) love come down, [semantic development unknown; some currency esp. among Negro jazzmen since c. 1925] See last quot. — 1946 *Really the Blues*, p. 35. A woman who really knows how to sing and means it can make your love come down. — p. 372. *make your love come down:* arouse your passion.

mammy jamming, See s.v. MOTHER.

man, *n.* [from Negro slang: see last two quots.; current esp. among Negro jazzmen since c. 1920, among white jazzmen as well since c. 1940] Initially, a term of address reserved for males; since c. 1955, see second 1959 quot. — 1933 *Metronome*, Aug., p. 23. Trum's greeting was in the Negro dialect he usually employed: "Man! How is you?" — 1942 *American Mercury*, July, p. 89. "Man, I come on like the Gang Busters." — 1959 *The Holy Barbarians*, p. 26. "Like, I don't want to bug you, man." — 1959 *Toronto Telegram*, 31 March, p. 3. *man:* omnibus salutation extended to men, women, domestic animals— saves cool cat hang-up [i.e., difficulty] of remembering names. — 1959 *N.Y. Age*, 4 April. Do you know why we have always called each other "man"? Because we had to confer the mantle of age on ourselves when the white man refused to do so. To the average white person in

America, the Negro was always "boy." — 1960 *Monthly Review*, May, p. 27. He went on to explain that Negroes habitually call each other "man" in reaction to a lifetime of being addressed by white folk as "boy."

my man, [current esp. among Negro jazzmen since c. 1930, among white jazzmen as well since c. 1940] Sometimes, variant of *man* q.v. (see 1958, 1960 quots.); sometimes, my favorite (see 1953 quot.; see also MY BOY). — 1953 *Down Beat*, 11 Feb., p. 16-S. That was Frog— Ben Webster! My man! — 1958 *Somewhere There's Music*, p. 122. "How [are] you, my man?" — 1960 *The Angry Ones*, p. 113. "Do you know where I would go, my man?"

the man, [also some general and Negro slang use, but with esp. currency among Negro jazzmen since c. 1917] See 1928, 1944, 1959 quots. — 1928 *The Walls of Jericho*, p. 306. *The man:* designation of abstract authority. He who trespasses where a sign forbids is asked: "Say, biggy, can't you read the man's sign?" — 1944 *The New Cab Calloway's Hepsters Dictionary*. s.v. *the man:* the law. — 1952 *Music Out of Dixie*, p. 121. "The Man gonna git you, Johnny?" — 1959 *Jazz for Moderns*, p. 20. *the man:* the person in charge, one of authority (manager, bandleader, headwaiter, bartender, et al). Also any cat who is deserving of great respect, musically or personally. ("Miles is the Man!") — 1960 *Esquire*, Dec., p. 72. The latter reflects his listeners' daily experiences with lack of love and cash in a societal context that renews tension each morning in the trip to meet "the man" downtown.

mary jane, [poss. a pun on "marijuana" or poss. a name translated from Spanish: cf. 1947 *American College Dictionary*, s.v. *marijuana:* "t. Amer. sp.;? native word, b. with name *Maria Juana* Mary Jane"; some currency among jazzmen since c. 1950; see also BOO, GAGE, POT, TEA] See 1943 quot. — 1943 *Time*, 19 July, p. 54.

Marijuana may be called . . . Mary Jane. — 1959 *Esquire*, Nov., pp. 70H–70I. *mary-jane:* marijuana. — 1959 *Blues for Mary Jane* (song written and recorded by Stan Getz on LP album *The Steamer*, Verve MG V-8294). — 1960 *The Jazz Titans*, p. 160. *mary jane:* marijuana. — 1960 *Dictionary of American Slang.* s.v. *mary jane:* a marijuana cigarette.

master, *n.* [trade term; current since c. 1925; see also TAKE] Of the several recordings made of a particular number, the one that is deemed most successful and is, therefore, the one offered for sale to the public. — 1949 *Music Library Association Notes*, Dec., p. 42. A recording artist *cuts* [i.e., records] a master. — 1955 *Hear Me Talkin to Ya*, p. 262. The masters piled up at a truly amazing rate. — 1956 *The Genius of Charlie Parker* (liner notes on LP album Savoy MG-12014). Along with these new versions and short takes, we include some of the original masters to try to give you a more complete musical description of Charlie Parker's recording sessions and also to give you a greater insight of his work.

mean, *adj.* [one of several standard terms from which the perjorative connotation has been removed and a favorable one substituted (see also BAD, HARD, TERRIBLE, TOUGH); current since c. 1900] Initially, earthy and primitive; also, by extension, since c. 1950: see 1957 quot. — 1922 OKeh Records advertisement [1962 *Jazz: A History of the New York Scene*, p. 95]. And for mean harmony, don't overlook Handy's orchestra. — 1931 *Melody Maker*, Dec., p. 1049. (record review in brief) General remarks: Fairly mean. — 1939 *Jazzmen*, pp. 12–13. When the orchestra settled down to the slow blues, the music was mean and dirty. — 1947 *The Two Worlds of Johnny Truro*, p. 58. "Plays a mean piano." — 1954 *Ride Out*, p. 34. "Just you play me some more of that mean piano." — 1957 *N.Y. Times Magazine*, 18 Aug., p. 26. *mean:* the best, the greatest.

mellow, *adj.* [standard term used in a somewhat special sense by jazzmen c. 1935–c. 1945, rare since; see also FINE AND MELLOW] Pleasing, excellent (see 1938 quot.). — 1938 *Cab Calloway: Hi De Ho,* p. 16. *mellow:* all right, fine. — 1942 *American Mercury,* July, pp. 84–85. The stuff was there and it was mellow. — 1946 *Really the Blues,* p. 188. Somebody lays a gentle, mellow phrase on you and it's like your memory crooking its finger. — 1948 *Trumpet on the Wing,* p. 185. He thought his mellow chick . . . was dead. — 1955 *Rhythm and Blues,* Feb., p. 22. "I don't care how mellow a girl can sing." — 1960 *Hiparama of the Classics,* p. 19. ZOOM, Up go Nero, he feel mellow in-deed.

    mellow, like a cello, [from rhyming slang vogue c. 1935–c. 1940, rare since] Superlative. — 1957 *American Speech,* Dec., p. 276. Jazz lingo abounds in . . . similes, e.g., *mellow, like a cello.*

member, *n.* [by analogy of the Negro race with a formal organization; current since c. 1958; see also SOUL-BROTHER] See quot. — 1962 *N.Y. Times Magazine,* 20 May, p. 45. *member:* a Negro.

mess, *n.* [somewhat varied uses of standard meaning (i.e., a jumble or hodgepodge); some currency among jazzmen since c. 1917; see also GANG, LOT] Many; also, by extension: excellent (see 1961 quot.). — 1938 *Cab Calloway: Hi De Ho,* p. 16. *mess:* something good. Example: "That last drink was a mess." — 1952 *Music Out of Dixie,* p. 230. "I've done a whole mess of 'em." — 1959 *The Holy Barbarians,* p. 58. "I saw . . . a whole mess of old men." — 1961 *The Sound,* p. 177. "Lot of other cats blow a mess of trumpet, high notes, fast runs, and all, but Red always tells a story."

message, *n.* [prob. from revival meetings (see also RIGHTEOUS, SOUL), also prob. reinforced by analogy with verbal communication (see also SAYING SOMETHING, TELL A STORY, TRUTH); some currency since c. 1950] The feelings and attitudes communicated by music. — 1952 *Metronome*, Dec., p. 15. "I got a message from Lester," George explains. — 1957 *Down Beat*, 17 Oct., p. 15. "But who needs words, man—they'll get the message." — 1960 *The Jazz Word*, p. 33. The "message" doesn't always merit the attention. — 1961 *Metronome*, April, p. 1. The Jazz message has proven itself strong enough to capture the hearts and imaginations of the peoples all over the world. — 1963 *Down Beat*, 15 Aug., p. 31. But this thing just doesn't have any message for me.

mess around, 1. [prob. suggested by sense 2; current during the dance's vogue, c. 1920–c. 1930, obs. since except historical, though parts of the dance survive in other-named dances] A jazz dance in vogue c. 1920–c. 1930. — 1962 *Ballroom Dance*, Feb., p. 5. Leon shows it's the same Mess Around he learned years back.

2. [special application of the standard meaning (i.e., to putter around); some currency c. 1925–c. 1940, obs. since] See 1935 quot. — 1935 *His Hi De Highness of Ho De Ho*, p. 35. *messin' around:* to improvise. — 1943 *Riverboat Jazz* (Brunswick Records pamphlet), p. 4. A clarinet trio . . . then plays . . . (after the injunction "Oh, mess around!") . . . the ending.

mess with, [somewhat varied use of its general colloquial sense (i.e., to trifle with); some currency since c. 1925] To trouble (oneself) with; also, rare: to trouble (see last quot.). — 1955 *Solo*, p. 27. "And what little lady is going to mess with you?" — 1955 *Hear Me Talkin to Ya*, p. 374. The really good musicians are too smart to mess with it. — 1956 *Sideman*, p. 416. "Hell, ordinarily I'd be the last guy to mess with another guy's lovin'." — 1956 *Lady Sings the Blues*, p. 57. But anyway, this talk about a big tone messed with Lester for months.

messy, *adj.* [expressive of jazzman's association of the disordered with the complex and his admiration for them (as opposed to the ordered but shallow); current c. 1935-

c. 1945, rare since] See quot. — 1945 *Hepcats Jive Talk Dictionary.* s.v. *messy:* extraordinary.

m.f., See s.v. MOTHER.

mice, *n. pl.* [by analogy with the sounds; according to jazz-men, some currency c. 1917–c. 1930 (obs. since) esp. in Chicago, where violins were commonly part of jazz bands] Violins. Oral evidence only.

mickey, Mickey Mouse, [see 1958 quot. for semantic development; current since c. 1935] See 1947, 1958 quots. — 1946 *Duke Ellington,* p. 126. The field was overrun with "Mickey Mouse" music. — 1947 *The Musical Digest,* July, p. 25. *mickey band:* a type of popular orchestra, which plays commercial, uninspired jazz and/or swing. An orchestra like this represents the most inferior form of jazz. The species inhabits resorts and hotels for the sole purpose of furnishing music for dancing. The term "mickey," for some mysterious reason, is a shortened form of Mickey Mouse. — 1958 *American Speech,* Oct., p. 225. A *mickey* or *Mickey Mouse* band is not merely a "pop tune" band . . . but the kind of band that sounds as if it is playing background for an animated cartoon. — 1959 *Down Beat,* 14 May, p. 20. "I like mickey bands better than that." — 1961 *Metronome,* April, p. 39. Dig especially . . . Nelson's *pretty* mickey mouse tone on *The Drive.*

moan (low), [special application of standard term; some currency c. 1915–c. 1945, very rare since] To play music or sing soulfully; for its common adjective use, see 1922, 1934 quots.; for its less common noun form, see 1932 quot. — 1922 OKeh Records advertisement [1962 *Jazz: A History of the New York Scene,* p. 95]. If you crave those jazz moanin' blues, go get 'em on OKeh. — 1932 *American Speech,* April, p. 247. Clara Smith evidently deems it a mark of distinction to be known as "The World's Greatest Moaner." — 1934 *Metronome,* Jan., p. 31. It was easier to play, easier to sing and a real

moanin' low number. — 1941 *Strictly Ding-Dong*, p. 15.
"I gotta be moaning low before that gate begins to
swing." — 1954 *Basic Jazz on Long Play*, p. 43. "She was
the most powerful jazz vocalist that ever moaned the
blues."

modern jazz, [chiefly a writers' term; current since c. 1950;
see also COOL JAZZ, PROGRESSIVE JAZZ] That jazz which
embraces some or all of the harmonic and rhythmic developments innovated since c. 1945 (though the earliest
period [c. 1945–c. 1950] in modern jazz was called *bop*,
q.v.: see 1955 quot.). — 1955 *Say*, 28 April, p. 53. They're
calling him [i.e., *bop*] "Modern Music" now. But he's
the same cat who was making crazy sounds back in the
'40's—only the critics didn't start cheering until he
changed his name. — 1960 *Evergreen Review*, Nov.-
Dec., p. 124. John Coltrane seemed to want to burst
through the eight-note rhythmic ideas of Parker and
"modern" jazz. — 1961 *Commonweal*, 24 March, p. 657.
A "cool" reaction to the clawing urgency of much modern
jazz began in the late 1940's. — 1961 *Metronome*, April,
p. 12. By the 1950's "modern" jazz, as the more advanced
developments were termed, had to free itself both from
esoteric tendencies within jazz itself and from over-de-
pendence on Western European classical traditions.

moldy fig, [by analogy with the shriveled and stale associations; current since c. 1946] See 1952, first 1958,
and first 1959 quots. (sometimes shortened to *fig*). —
1948 *Collier's*, 20 March, p. 88. "The moldy figs . . . are
certain that the greatest jazz ever played . . . was
played in New Orleans in 1915." — 1952 *A History of
Jazz in America*, p. 351. *moldy fig*: a modernist's name
for an ardent admirer of Dixieland jazz. — 1958 *Publication of the American Dialect Society*, Nov., p. 46. *moldy
fig*: one who likes or plays "traditional" jazz exclusively
. . . (Refers mostly to fans, not musicians.) Often abbr.
fig. — 1958 *Somewhere There's Music*, p. 83. "Dixie Cats

and the rest of the Moldy Figs, okay for them; they don't
need to think." — 1959 *The Sound of Surprise,* p. 211.
The term "moldy fig," which is one of the aptest derogatory colloquialisms in the language, was first used in jazz
to describe those who believe that the music has been in
steady decline since around 1930. — 1959 *The Collector's Jazz: Modern,* p. 11. But this bickering was as nothing compared to the gulf that separated the adherents of
bop [q.v.] and those the boppers derisively referred to
as "moldy figs" (a term to which the unreconstructed
"figs" have now adjusted so completely that they apply it
to themselves with pride).

monkey, *n.* [cf. general slang *monkey suit* (i.e., tuxedo):
it was customary in most bands for the leader only to be
dressed in a tuxedo; some currency esp. among white
jazzmen c. 1925–c. 1940, obs. since]   See quot. — 1942
The American Thesaurus of Slang, p. 556. *monkey:* orchestra leader.

Mooch, *n.* [cf. 1950 *Dictionary of American Underworld
Lingo,* s.v. *mooch:* "to move about stealthily; to skulk";
current c. 1925–c. 1935, obs. since except historical,
though the dance survives under other names; for synonymous names, see DRAG, SCRAUNCH]   A slow, dragging
dance (see note above). — 1928 *The Mooch* (tune composed by Duke Ellington).

mood (music), [some currency since c. 1930]   Initially,
brooding, sophisticated music, most frequently associated
with the Duke Ellington Orchestra; since c. 1945, most
frequently, music that is insipid and pretentious: see
1961, 1962 quots. — 1947 *Esquire's 1947 Jazz Book,* p. 5.
The music America wanted was "mood." — 1959 *Jazz*
(Hentoff & McCarthy), p. 257. In the "blue" or "mood"
category, Duke . . . penned . . . the immortal *Mood
Indigo* of 1930. — 1961 *Down Beat,* 12 Oct., p. 32. If
"mood music" (whatever its style) is some sort of in-
nocuousness, then this is not mood music. — 1962 *Down*

Beat, 29 March, p. 26. This is, in short, no pompous "jazz suite," "concerto," or warmed-over program stuff. Nor is it "mood" jazz.

mootah, mooter, muta, mu, *n.* [etym. unknown; some currency among jazzmen since c. 1930; see also BOO, GAGE, POT, TEA] See 1943 quot. — 1943 *Time,* 19 July, p. 54. Marijuana may be called muggles, mooter . . . mu. — 1946 *Really the Blues,* p. 61. He kept waiting for a big train to pull in with a carload of muta. — 1956 *Second Ending,* p. 249. The mootah had snapped the top of his wig. — 1959 *The Jazz Scene,* p. 292. *muta:* marijuana. — 1960 *Dictionary of American Slang.* s.v. *mooter:* a marijuana cigarette.

mop, *interj.* [see 1952 quot. for prob. etym., prob. reinforced by its assonance with *bop* (q.v.); current since c. 1942] *Voila!* — 1944 *Mop Mop* (tune recorded by Coleman Hawkins on Commodore C-548). — 1945 *Hepcats Jive Talk Dictionary.* s.v. *mop:* the finale. — 1952 *A History of Jazz in America,* p. 351. *mop!:* an exclamation of wide currency in the early forties which accurately described a musical device (the final beat in a cadence of triplets, usually bringing the release of a jazz composition to an end). — 1959 *Selected Poems,* p. 221. Hey, pop!/Re-bop!/Mop! — 1959 *The Village Voice,* 28 Oct., p. 13. "I wait a while, eyes closed, and I look, mop! I'm in the bathtub, all alone."

more, *adv. & adj.* [one of several terms denoting quantity in standard speech, but used by jazzmen to denote quality (see also GANG, LESS, LOT, THE MOST); some currency since c. 1950] Better. — 1959 *The Horn,* p. 51. "I can still . . . play more tenor than them." — 1962 *Down Beat,* 26 April, p. 34. Howard McGhee was quoted recently as saying that Davis used to play "more." — 1963 *Down Beat,* 29 Aug., p. 4. Is drummer X, for example, in New York playing more drums now than drummer Y in California?

most, the, [one of several quantitative terms given a qualitative meaning by jazzmen (see also LEAST, LESS, LOT, MORE); current since c. 1950] The best. — 1954 *Ride Out*, p. 30. "That's the most horn in the world," he said. — 1954 *New Yorker*, 18 Sep., p. 30. "I'm feeling the most today." — 1961 *The Sound*, p. 102. I dig you the most that way. — 1961 *Down Beat*, 11 May, p. 35. Well, I really dig that one the most.

mother, muther, motheree, mothering, m.f., motherferyer, mother fucker, mother-fouler, mother-hugger, mother jiver, mother-lover, mother superior, mammy jammer, [all others are variants of *mother-fucker* and derive from *the dozens*, q.v.; though initially (c. 1900) an insult, the perjorative connotation is not always present since c. 1950 in this very common term; see also POPPA-STOPPA] Initially, an incestuous male; also, since c. 1950, anyone or anything that is formidable or extraordinary (see last 1959 and last two quots.). — 1946 *Really the Blues*, p. 10. A motherferyer that would cut your throat for looking. —p. 372. *mammy jamming:* incestuous obscenity. — 1948 *Trumpet on the Wing*, p. 70. "I'll be a motheree if I'll wear any damn bedpan intern's suit," I screamed. — 1952 *Invisible Man*, p. 469. "Let the mother-fouler alone." — 1955 *Solo*, p. 42. "Hell, this mother never could blow." — 1956 *Sideman*, p. 138. "That muther won't get out his knife till he sees the money." — 1956 *Lady Sings the Blues*, p. 101. A mother-hugger was a mother-hugger. — 1959 *The Naked Lunch*, p. 99. "Man, that mother-fucker's hungry," screams one of the Bearers. —p. 217. Kill the mother fucker wherever you find him. — 1959 *The Jazz Review*, Sep., p. 7. "You go and buy me a tenor saxophone and I'll play the m-f." — 1959 *Esquire*, Nov., p. 70J. *mother jiver:* someone who cons or fools. Lately has taken on affectionate meaning and even a term of praise. Example: a bad mother jiver is an excellent musician. — 1960 *N.Y. Citizen-Call*, 30 July, p. 19. Doctors, lawyers, businessmen and athletes, especially professional baseball players and jazz or cool school musicians use the term, "M . . . ," as lingual crutches. — 1960 *Hiparama of the Classics*, p. 16. Pen in hand, he was a Mother Superior. — p. 27. But The Gasser . . . made himself a connection that shook the whole Mother Peninsula!! — 1961 *The Sound*, p. 61. "I can remember 'em all, every motherin' one-night stop." — p. 106. "That's just too mother much!" — p. 132. "If I don't scoff [i.e., eat] now I'll have a mother of a headache." — p. 285. "Red really blew his mother-lovin' soul on that one." — 1961 *Metronome*, Nov., pp. 32–33. Make no mistake. Hirt is a talent. A brilliant trumpeter. Not a Miles, nor a Clark Terry. Not a jazz trumpeter. But a mother, nevertheless. — 1961 *Nobody Knows My Name*, p. 236. "But you're a tough little mother, too," he said, and referred to one of the grimmer of my Village misadventures, a misadventure which certainly proved that I had a dangerously sharp tongue, but which really didn't prove anything about my courage.

move, *v.i.* [special application of the standard term; some earlier accidental use, but widely current only since c. 1950; see also SWING, *v.i.*] To be dynamic (usually, musically). — 1955 *Down Beat*, 6 April, p. 15. The only time it does start to move is in the second chorus, with Charlie Shavers. — 1958 *Jam Session*, p. 219. "It's got to move," jazzmen say. If it doesn't "swing," it's not jazz. — 1960 *The Village Voice*, 20 Jan., p. 2. Norman swung into the obligatto [sic]. His jacket was off and he was moving. — 1961 *Down Beat*, 19 Jan., p. 3. It *moves*— like a Mardi Gras parade.

moving out, [current since c. 1955] Starting to play (jazz) dynamically, imaginatively. — 1954 *Movin' Out: Sonny Rollins with Thelonius Monk* (LP album Prestige PRL-7058). — 1961 *The Sound*, p. 99. "The Man's movin' out further than ever."

Mr. B., [not as important in jazz speech as some other nicknames (e.g., *Bird, Lady, Prez,* and *Satch[mo]*), but fairly common since c. 1943] Billy Eckstine, 1914–, jazz vocalist. — 1948 *Mr. B's Blues* (song recorded by Billy Eckstine). — 1950 *Life,* 24 April, p. 101. But Billy Eckstine, known to his fans as "Mr. B," tried this just once last week. — 1956 *Guide to Jazz,* p. 86. *Mr. B:* Billy Eckstine.

mu, *n.* See s.v. MOOTAH.

much, *adv.* [one of several terms denoting quantity in standard speech, but used by jazzmen to denote quality (see also GANG, LESS, MORE, THE MOST); current since c. 1950] Well. — 1955 *Hear Me Talkin to Ya,* p. 352. I knew Monk when he played ten times as much as he does now. — 1960 *The Jazz Review,* Nov., p. 10. They swung so hard and played so much. — 1960 *Metronome,* Dec., p. 23. He gets a big kick out of playing, but you can never tell how *much* he's going to play. — 1961 *The Sound,* p. 142. "As for Red Travers' trumpet, there just isn't anyone in the field playing as much as he is right now."

mugging heavy (or **light, lightly**), [special application of vaudeville term *mugging* (i.e., grimacing); some currency c. 1930–c. 1940, obs. since] See quots. — 1931 *"Muggin' Lightly"* (tune recorded by the Luis Russell Orchestra). — 1936 *Delineator,* Nov., p. 49. *mugging light:* swing with a light beat. *mugging heavy:* swing with a heavy beat. — 1937 *This Thing Called Swing,* p. 9. *mugging light:* soft swing. *mugging heavy:* soft swing with a heavy beat. — 1938 *Cab Calloway: Hi De Ho,* p. 16. *muggin' lightly:* light staccato swing. *muggin' heavy:* heavy staccato swing.

muggles, *n. pl.* [etym. unknown; some currency among jazzmen since c. 1925; see also BOO, GAGE, POT, TEA] See 1959 quots. — 1928 *Muggles* (song recorded by Louis Armstrong). — 1935 *His Hi De Highness of Ho De Ho,*

p. 36. They [i.e., marijuana cigarettes] are also called "muggles." — 1959 *The Holy Barbarians,* p. 77. "Muggles we called the marijuana cigarettes." — 1959 *The Jazz Scene,* p. 292. *muggles:* marijuana.

muta, *n.* See s.v. MOOTAH.

mysterious, *adj.* [special application of the standard term; some currency since c. 1950; see also WEIRD] Profound, imaginative, original (usually applied to music or to a musician). (Note: occasionally the term is used in the sense of *too* imaginative—consequently, unintelligible; this is obviously the sense in which its use in the quots. is to be taken.) — 1959 *Down Beat,* 14 May, p. 20. Sonny is no admirer of . . . musicians whose music is "too mysterious." — 1963 *Down Beat,* 15 Aug., p. 31. It was interesting . . . but it was mysterious. The average human being who understands jazz, I don't believe, could interpret this.

name, *adj. & n.* [chiefly a trade term, taken from entertainment slang; current among jazzmen since c. 1930] (A) well-known (orchestra or musician). — 1933 *Metronome,* June, p. 30. The small publishers are often more interested in "name" arrangers than big publishers. — 1936 *Stage,* March, p. 58. *name bands:* famous orchestras. — 1939 *Jazzmen,* p. 25. Robichaux's was for years the class *"name band"* of New Orleans. — 1946 *Big Book of Swing*, p. 124. *name:* well known dance band. — 1955 *A Pictorial History of Jazz*, p. 184. Teddy Wilson, a "name" after his Benny Goodman days, led various small units. — 1956 *Enjoyment of Jazz* (EJ401), p. 3. Each of the soloists is a major "name" of the Swing Era. — 1961 *Down Beat*, 30 March, p. 17. The vibist's [i.e., vibraphonist's] first "name" job came in September, 1956, when he joined the George Shearing Quintet.

nasty, *adj.* [one of several pejorative terms in standard English (see also BAD, MEAN, TERRIBLE, TOUGH) to which a favorable connotation has been given by jazzmen, according to whom the term has been current c. 1917–c. 1945, rare since] Earthy; hence, excellent. — 1940 *Swing*, July, p. 17. Very fast semi-boogie blues in Gabriel with nasty, heavy off-beat drumming. — 1955 *Hear Me Talkin to Ya*, p. 295. Martha Raye . . . got hung up listening to Lincoln's nasty beat. — 1960 *Dictionary of American Slang.* s.v. *nasty:* excellent; "wicked"; "mean."

natural, *adj.* [according to jazzmen, some currency esp. among Negro jazzmen since c. 1930] Intensifying word (as in "beat to my natural socks"). Oral evidence only.

New Orleans, [after its place of origin; current since c. 1917; see also DIXIELAND] Jazz (style) from c. 1900, which became somewhat old-fashioned with the advent of swing (c. 1935) and extremely old-fashioned with the advent of bop (c. 1945): see 1946, 1956 quots. — 1905 *New Orleans Blues* (tune composed by Jelly Roll Morton, copyright 1927). — 1922 *New Orleans Rhythm Kings* (name of jazz band). — 1946 *Disc*, Nov. "Jazz is improvising in the old New Orleans way, with the kick on the first and third beats." — 1947 *The Two Worlds of Johnny Truro*, p. 24. They listened to . . . New Orleans style. — 1947 *The Musical Digest*, July, p. 24. This quality of altering accents, with regard for and in relation to each other, is the essence of the work of New

Orleans musicians. — 1956 *Guide to Jazz*, p. 195. The New Orleans style is characterized in its rhythm by a very marked accentuation of the beat, though without any heaviness. This regular and supple stress . . . is what gives performances in the New Orleans style an easy, lazy rhythmic quality. Collective improvisation predominates in New Orleans-style playing.

new thing, the, [some currency since c. 1961] The more experimental music of the 1960s, esp. that played by such musicians as Ornette Coleman, Cecil Taylor, Eric Dolphy, and John Coltrane. — 1962 *Down Beat*, 12 April, p. 20. The anti-jazz term was picked up by Leonard Feather and used as a basis for critical essays of Coltrane, Dolphy, Ornette Coleman, and the "new thing" in general. — 1962 *Down Beat*, 5 July, p. 28. It may be that the "new thing"—if such exists—is not so new after all. — 1962 *Down Beat*, 25 Oct., p. 30. A crossbreed between the "new thing" and post-bop, this set . . . is notable on two counts.

nickel (note), [understatement; some currency esp. among Negro jazzmen since c. 1940; see also CENT, DIME] See quots. — 1944 *Dan Burley's Original Handbook of Harlem Jive*, p. 144. *nickel note:* a five dollar bill. — 1946 *Big Book of Swing*, p. 124. *nickel:* $5. — 1958 *American Speech*, Oct., p. 225. A *nickel* is five dollars.

nod, *n. & v.i.* [cf. standard meaning (i.e., of the head, to fall forward involuntarily because of drowsiness); cf. narcotics slang: 1953 *Junkie*, p. 14. *"On the nod:* full of junk"; current among jazzmen since c. 1930] See last quot. (note: there is sometimes the implication that the state is induced by narcotics: see 1958 quot.). — 1938 *Cab Calloway: Hi De Ho*, p. 16. *nod:* sleep. Example: "I think I'll cop a nod." — 1958 *Southern Folklore Quarterly*, Sep., p. 132. *nodding:* succumbing to a drug. — 1959 *Esquire*, Nov., p. 70J. *on the nod:* sleeping, usually in a standing or sitting position. — 1959 *The Naked*

Lunch, p. 22. An hour later they find the buyer on the nod in the D.S.'s chair. — 1960 *Dictionary of American Slang.* s.v. *nod:* sleep; a period of sleep.

no eyes, See s.v. EYES.

noodle, *v.i.* [etym. unknown: poss. by analogy with a standard noun meaning (i.e., a fool; ergo, *v.i.,* to fool around musically), more prob. by assonance with *doodle;* some currency since c. 1935] To play (music) in a tentative, exploratory, and sometimes desultory manner (see 1942 quot.); also, for its rare noun use, see second 1958 quot. — 1940 *Noodlin'* (tune recorded by the Willie the Lion Smith Orchestra on General 1712). — 1942 *The American Thesaurus of Slang,* p. 565. *noodle:* idle elaboration. — 1957 *Nugget,* Dec., p. 5. Every time a jazz musician noodles a passable break these days he is followed by a show of bravura on an open Underwood fingered by a jazz writer. — 1958 *High Fidelity,* Aug., p. 62. Gullin can eventually catch fire . . . but his heavy noodling constantly suffers in comparison to Rene Ofwurman's light, rolling piano. — 1958 *The Jazz Review,* Nov., p. 25. My one complaint is that Monk here allows too many of his favorite piano "noodles" (all pianists seem to have them). — 1959 *Blow Up a Storm,* p. 8. I noodled around: filling in or playing rhythm figures, and sometimes locking in harmonically with him for a phrase or break. — 1960 *The Story of the Original Dixieland Jazz Band,* p. 164. Nevertheless, Larry Shields will go down in history as the father of the "noodling" style and possessor of one of the most powerful clarinet tones on record.

nothing happens (or **shakes**), [overstatement; *nothing happening* current since c. 1940, *nothing shaking* since c. 1950; see also HAPPENINGS, SHAKING] Nothing important (usually, musically) is happening; whatever is happening is disappointing, unexciting. — 1952 *Flee the Angry Strangers,* p. 319. "Nothing's happening, Luke." —

1958 *Jazz: A Quarterly of American Music*, Oct., p. 28. Well, like it's got to "funk" all the time . . . without it, nothing's happening. — 1960 *The Jazz Word*, p. 109. "There's not really a living ass to talk to, and there's nothing shaking." — 1960 *Sal Salvador: The Beat for This Generation* (liner notes on LP album Decca DL 74026). "No matter how good your sidemen may be individually, nothing will happen if they can't play together." — 1961 *The Jazz Review*, Jan., p. 31. Mr. Barnet plays his three saxes serially . . . but otherwise there ain't nothing at all happening.

nowhere, *adj.* [by analogy of a geographic limbo with a spiritual one; widely current since c. 1935] Unhappy, lost, frustrated, undesirable, valueless, confused (see also 1946 quot.). — 1942 *American Mercury*, July, p. 86. "I ain't nowhere." — 1944 *Band Leaders and Record Review*, May, p. 59. That ickies ARE nowhere, is pointed up by an expression they frequently use. — 1946 *Really the Blues*, p. 373. *nowhere:* insignificant, broke. — 1948 *Trumpet on the Wing*, p. 10. I got to have music or I'm nowhere. — 1952 *Who Walk in Darkness*, p. 124. "Forget about them, Harry," I said. "They're nowhere." — 1955 *Solo*, p. 187. "Too many heroes is nowhere." — 1956 *Jive Jungle*, p. 31. "Aren't they the worst!" "Nowhere!" — 1960 *The Jazz Titans*, p. 161. *nowhere:* the absolute of nothing.

   like (Jack) the bear (just ain't nowhere), [part of c. 1935–c. 1940 rhyming slang vogue; some currency c. 1938–c. 1942, very rare since] See NOWHERE. — 1942 *American Mercury*, July, p. 86. "Oh, just like de bear—I ain't nowhere." — 1944 *Esquire*, June, p. 170. *like the bear, just ain't nowhere:* out of place. — 1946 *Really the Blues*, p. 372. *like Jack the Bear:* worthless, no-account, broke, insignificant.

nutty, *adj. & interj.* [colloquial variant of *crazy*, q.v.; current since c. 1950; see also INSANE, MAD] See second

1959 quot. — 1955 *Bop Fables*, p. 12. "Nutty," said the papa bear. — 1959 *Easy Living*, p. 28. "Nutty," said Wyeth. — 1959 *Newport Jazz Festival: 1959*, p. 45. *nutty:* excellent. — 1963 *Nugget*, Feb., p. 46. She had seen me around and thought that the jazz musician syndrome was kinda nutty.

O, [abbreviation; from underworld and narcotics slang; some currency among jazzmen since c. 1935]   See quots. — 1934 *A Dictionary of American Slang*, p. 28. *O:* opium. — 1958 *Southern Folklore Quarterly*, Sep., p. 137. *O:* opium.

ofay, *n.* See s.v. FAY.

off beat cymbal, [so-called because cymbal was struck on the off beat in traditional jazz; some currency c. 1917– c. 1940, obs. since; see also SOCK CYMBAL] A cymbal struck by the drummer on off beats in much traditional (pre-c. 1935) jazz. — 1936 *Metronome*, Feb., p. 61. *off beat cymbal:* sock cymbal.

off note, [from its being slightly "off" normal pitch; according to jazzman Eubie Blake, some currency since c. 1900; see also BLUE NOTE] See quot. — 1955 *The First Book of Jazz*, p. 20. These blue notes are "off notes," just a little bit flat and in between the usual notes. They

most often are a somewhat flatted third or seventh note
of the scale. They are impossible to show in written
music, although they are sometimes indicated as flatted
notes.

oldie, *n.* [formed on colloquial pattern of making a *n.* from
an *adj.* by adding *-ie, -y;* according to jazzman Eubie
Blake, current since c. 1900] See 1942 quot. — 1942
The American Thesaurus of Slang, p. 560. *oldie:* an old
tune. — 1947 *The Two Worlds of Johnny Truro,* p. 20.
"Jay dug up some 'oldies' in New Haven." — 1961 *Jazz
Journal,* May, p. 35. Another "oldie" is "Four in One,"
one of his weirdest and most angular themes in the bop
idiom.

old lady, [cf. its general colloquial meaning (i.e., wife);
current among jazzmen in a general slang meaning since
c. 1900, in an additional meaning since c. 1935] Initially, see 1960 quot.; also, since c. 1935, a mistress. —
1926 *Melody Maker,* Oct., p. 13. He [is] . . . answered
by the words "So does your Old Lady," as his better half,
emerging from her concealment, grips him by the ear. —
1959 *The Horn,* p. 134. "You guys trying to bug me with
my old lady?" — 1959 *The Real Cool Killers,* p. 18. "How
could I be mad about my old lady," Sonny argued. —
1960 *Dictionary of American Slang.* s.v. *old lady:* a wife,
esp. one's own.

old man, [cf. its general colloquial meaning (i.e., husband);
current among jazzmen in a general slang meaning since
c. 1900, in an additional meaning since c. 1935] Initially, see 1960 quot.; also, since c. 1935, a male lover. —
1957 *On the Road,* p. 203. "Her old man can come in any
hour of the night." — 1960 *Dictionary of American Slang.*
s.v. *old man:* a husband, esp. one's own.

on, *adj.* [prob. from colloquial *to be onto something* (i.e., to
be aware of something); according to jazzmen, some currency c. 1945–c. 1950, obs. since; see also DOWN, HIP]
Aware, sophisticated. Oral evidence only.

be (or **get**) **on** (**something**), [special application of colloquial use of the *prep.;* widely current since c. 1950] Under the influence of or addicted to liquor, marijuana, or narcotics. — 1955 *Hear Me Talkin to Ya,* p. 372. For an example of a guy who got on, there was Stan Getz. — 1960 *Beat Jokes Bop Humor & Cool Cartoons,* p. 11. An unkempt fellow, who is on something and almost on the nod [i.e., asleep], stumbles into a barber shop. — 1960 *The Jazz Review,* May, p. 37. He couldn't play the drums "that way" unless he were "on something." — 1961 *The Sound,* p. 20. "But let's get on first." — p. 22. "Are you on now?" Bernie wanted to know. — 1961 *Swank,* July, p. 58. By the time Bird was 25 he had been on for nearly ten years.

on the scene, See s.v. SCENE.

one-night stand, one-nighter, [see 1949 quot. for explanation of semantic development; *stand* (i.e., engagement) is borrowed from theater use; current c. 1925–c. 1945, somewhat less since] See 1949 quot. — 1939 *One Night Stand* (tune recorded by the Artie Shaw Orchestra). — 1949 *Music Library Association Notes,* Dec., p. 47. *one-nighters:* series of dates or bookings providing for one-night appearances in theatres, nite clubs, or hotel rooms. It's travel all day, perform all night—a grueling schedule. Also known as "one-night" stands. — 1961 *Night Song,* p. 100. "Sandwiches and one-night stands, blowing before some hicks who won't even know who it is they're listening to." — p. 136. "Too many o' them damn agents passin' rubber around 'cause they done spent up all the musicians' bread [i.e. money] while they out tryin' to make [i.e., to perform] one nighters six and seven hundred miles apart."

oo-bla(-dee), oo-bop-she-bam, oo(1)-ya-koo, oo-pa-pa-da (and variant spellings), [from bop singing (see first 1955 quot.); these nonsense syllable words all reflect bop (q.v.) musicians' impish irreverence for conventional

communication (linguistic as well as musical); current
c. 1945–c. 1955, rare since; see also EEL-YA-DAH] Nonsense words. — 1946 *Oo-Bop-She-Bam* (tune composed
and recorded by Dizzy Gillespie). — 1949 *In the Land
of Oo-Bla-Dee* (tune composed by Mary Lou Williams
and Milton Orent). — 1949 *Down Beat,* 20 May, p. 16.
"Let's jump!" they cried. "Give us a break, will ya!" and
"Ool-ya-koo!" — 1951 *Ebony,* Oct., p. 34. "You will thank
me for hepping [i.e., enlightening] you to this oolyakoo-
ing.". . . "Gently ease it out of casing," advises the
poobah of oo-bop-she-bam. — 1955 *The First Book of
Jazz,* p. 55. Sometimes for fun, singers sing "oo-ya-koo"
syllables to boppish backgrounds today, as Cab Calloway
in the 1930's sang "hi-de-hi-de-ho-de-hey," meaning nothing, or as Lionel Hampton sang "hey-baba-re-bop" in
1940. — 1955 *Bop Fables,* pp. 3–4. Once upon a time in
the land of Oobopshebam there lived a little girl named
Goldilocks. — p. 17. Once upon a time many years ago,
in the land of Oopoppadow, there lived three little pigs.
— 1956 *Lady Sings the Blues,* p. 207. She told him we
couldn't speak the language, she could and oo-pa-pa-da,
we needed someone to help us. — 1957 *Time,* 16 Sep.,
p. 76. Traveler from the Land of Oo-Bla-Dee. — 1959
The Horn, p. 128. "Man, loot is just around the oob-la."

oowee (and variant spellings), *interj.* [deliberately childlike exclamation; current since c. 1945] Expression of
extreme delight. — 1955 *Solo,* p. 25. "Mahn, but he blows
up a storm . . . Oooweee." — 1960 *Jazz: A Quarterly of
American Music,* Winter, p. 47. I was THUNDER-
STRUCK. I couldn't say a word. He gasses me. Ooooooooo-
weeeeee!

open (horn), [current since c. 1925] Unmuted (trumpet). — 1926 *Melody Maker,* March, p. 30. For such
occasions nothing is better suited to obtain a highly
successful result than the beautiful, sweet full tone of the
open instrument, and I advise all artistes to try a few

"open" solos. — 1942 *The American Thesaurus of Slang,* p. 563. *open:* without mechanical mutes. — 1955 *Hear Me Talkin to Ya,* p. 234. The Western style was more open . . . open horns and running chords and running changes. — 1958 *Shorty Rogers and His Giants: Shorty in Stereo* (liner notes on LP album Atlantic SC 1232). I would just like to point out . . . his jabbing, stabbing open horn solo in *Dickie's Dream.* — 1961 *Down Beat,* 13 April, p. 36. *Orbit,* the brisk opener, finds Jones blowing open horn.

open (tone), [prob. by analogy with *open (horn),* (i.e., with its full, unmuted sound); some currency since c. 1930] Full (tone). — 1942 *The American Thesaurus of Slang,* p. 563. *open:* without . . . affected tone. — 1955 *Hear Me Talkin to Ya,* p. 287. And Knight had such a great big, open tone on alto.

opener, *n.* [special application of its general colloquial meaning (i.e., that which "opens"—i.e., begins—a performance); current since c. 1935] The first chorus of a tune or the first tune of a set (q.v.). — 1949 *Down Beat,* 11 March, p. 15. *Frost* is a simple but fairly bright arrangement with a good opener. — 1961 *Down Beat,* 13 April, p. 36. *Orbit,* the brisk opener, finds Jones blowing open horn. — 1961 *Jazz Journal,* May, p. 35. The opener is one of his early pieces.

organ (chords), [see 1956 quot. for semantic development; according to jazzman Eubie Blake, some currency c. 1900–c. 1945, very rare since] See 1956 quot. — 1927 *Melody Maker,* June, p. 533. The sweetness of his sustained notes when playing his part in "organ" harmony is a sheer delight. — 1956 *Guide to Jazz,* p. 206. *organ chords:* basic chords of the blues, so called because they're the same harmonies common to most Protestant hymns.

original, *n.* [special application of standard term; current since c. 1935] A tune composed by a member of the performing troupe (as distinguished from a *standard,*

q.v.). — 1940 *Swing*, Nov., p. 27. The Will Osborne-Dick
Rogers original on the back starts with some superb reed
work. — 1949 *Down Beat*, 28 Jan., p. 14. *Goof*, an up
tempo original, tries hard but never really gets anywhere.
— 1955 *Hear Me Talkin to Ya*, p. 383. And they're recording more originals now. — 1961 *Down Beat*, 2 Feb.,
p. 30. There are three Edwards originals, used simply as
frameworks for improvisation.

other man, (the), [i.e., *not* one of us; prob. from 19th-
century Negro term *other folks;* now general Negro slang,
but according to jazz dancer Leon James, originated by
and current among Negro jazzmen since c. 1945] A
white man (frequently the storekeeper, hence the definition offered in the quot.). — 1962 *N.Y. Times Magazine*,
20 May, p. 45. *other man:* the liquor dealer.

out, *adj.* [shortened form of *knocked out*, q.v., reinforced
by *far out*, q.v.; current since c. 1942] Excellent; also,
since c. 1950: imaginative, experimental. — 1959 *Newport Jazz Festival: 1959*, p. 45. *out:* far out. — 1959 *Jazz
for Moderns*, p. 20. *out:* far out.

out (chorus), [current since c. 1925; see also ALL-IN, EVERY
TUB, LET'S GO HOME, RIDE-OUT] The final (chorus); also,
see 1937 quot. — 1937 *American Speech*, Feb., p. 47. *out:*
to finish a chorus during a jam session. The cry to the
player is, "Go on out." — 1955 *Down Beat*, 6 April, p. 15.
It's exciting, especially the out-choruses. — 1956 *Sideman*, p. 312. Matt called "Out!" and the band hit the out-
chorus. — 1961 *Down Beat*, 13 April, p. 36. Frameworks
for the blowing are in the familiar mold of stated theme,
solos in turn, and out chorus. — 1963 *Down Beat*, 20
June, p. 31. The brass section struts gloriously in the out
chorus.

out of it, [current since c. 1955] Not included in the activity or in life; not important; not participating. — 1961
Artesian, Winter, p. 23. I knew that I was a bizarre and
unacceptable character when I was a child and that I

would always be out of it. — 1962 *Down Beat*, 15 March, p. 25. And people who say this guy is better than that guy, that this guy is completely out of it—musicians don't even judge like that.

out of sight, [extension of *far out, way out,* q.v.; current since c. 1958] Extremely advanced; excellent. — 1961 *Down Beat*, 5 Jan., p. 23. "Frankly, I find some of the musicians I've encountered on the road rather ridiculous. They're like children, the way they dress, the way they talk. It seems everything is 'something else' these days. Or is it 'out of sight?' " — 1963 *Down Beat*, 20 June, p. 35. This record is out of sight.

out of (one's) skull, [jazz slang variant of general slang *out of (one's) head;* current since c. 1950; see also WIG, LOOSE WIG] Insane, or so intoxicated as to be virtually insane. — 1955 *Bop Fables*, p. 9. "You're out of your skull." — 1958 *Somewhere There's Music*, p. 33. "When it was all done one night, we got out of our skulls." — 1961 *Down Beat*, 19 Jan., p. 22. The cat . . . *finds you,* usually out of your skull in Junior's. — 1961 *Metronome*, Feb., p. 41. "Well, man, we might get out of our skulls now and then."

out of this (or the) world, out-of-this-world, [see 1959 quot. for semantic explanation; current c. 1925–c. 1945, obs. since except historical; see also GONE, OUT OF SIGHT] See 1928, 1939, 1944 quots. — 1928 *The Walls of Jericho*, p. 303. *out (of) this world:* beyond mortal experience or belief. — 1931 *The Inter-State Tattler*, 17 Dec., p. 12. Alberta Hunter . . . warbles out of this world. — 1937 *Mademoiselle*, March, p. 68. And Bunny, his eyes closed is playing out-of-this-world. — 1939 *Jitterbug Jamboree Song Book*, p. 32. *out-of-this-world:* perfection. — 1944 *The New Cab Calloway's Hepsters Dictionary.* s.v. *out of the world:* perfect rendition. — 1959 *Jazz: A Quarterly of American Music*, Fall, p. 284. The power of musicians of skill to transport is verbalized in *send me* . . . It is little wonder that swing devotees . . . on the general observations of music as "heavenly" and "melody of the spheres," proclaimed they were sent—propelled by the centrifugal force *out of the world.*

over (an instrument), be (or **get**) **(all),** [by analogy with the dexterous mobility demanded of the instrumentalist; current since c. 1955; see also GET AROUND ON (ONE'S) HORN, HAVE IT COVERED] To play (an instrument) with great virtuosity. — 1960 *The Jazz Review,* Nov., p. 12. You know how the guy got all over that alto. — 1961 *Down Beat Record Reviews,* p. 176. Sonny is all over both his horns, communicating directly and deeply. — 1961 *The Sound,* p. 47. "He gets over the piano and he knows a lot of music." — 1962 *Down Beat,* 22 Nov., p. 30. He soon falls into a series of arpeggios, which show how well he can get over his horn, but there are no sustained ideas.

o.z., [standard abbreviation for *ounce,* but not pronounced as an acronym; some currency among jazzmen since c. 1935] See 1942 quot. (usually, of marijuana) — 1942 *American Thesaurus of Slang,* p. 474. *o.z.*: ounce. — 1959 *The Horn,* p. 224. It had been something in his mind that two o.z.'s of ripe Pachuco pot [i.e., marijuana] had brought out.

P

pad, *n.* [the more common meaning was formed by synechdoche: cf. 1930 *American Tramp and Underworld Slang,*
s.v. *pad:* "bed"; widely current since c. 1935; see also
CRIB, DOMMY] A room or an apartment; also, rare: a
bed. — 1938 *Cab Calloway: Hi De Ho,* p. 16. *pad:* bed.
— 1939 *Fortune,* July, p. 170. There are reefer pads
(marijuana dens). — 1946 *Really the Blues,* p. 373. *pad:*
joint, place to enjoy yourself, bed. — 1959 *The Holy
Barbarians,* p. 26. "Young people . . . hole up in pads in
the slums and listen to jazz music." — 1959 *Esquire,*
Nov., p. 70J. *pad:* home or bed.

panatella, panatela, *n.* [by analogy with the expensive
cigar; some currency among jazzmen since c. 1935]
Top-grade marijuana. — 1956 *Lady Sings the Blues,*
p. 53. "Jimmy's got the best panatella you ever smoked
in your life." — 1959 *Panatela* (tune recorded by the
Woody Herman Orchestra on a Jazzland LP, *The Fourth
Herd*).

papa, *n.* See s.v. POPS.

paper, *n.* [according to jazzmen, current c. 1900–c. 1945,
rare since; see also CHARTS] Sheet music. Oral evidence
only.

    paper man, [according to jazzman Eubie Blake, cur-
rent c. 1900–c. 1945, rare since] See 1942 quot. (note:
by jazzmen's standards, a derisive term) — 1936 *Metro-*

nome, Feb., p. 21. *paper man:* drummer who plays only
what's written. — 1942 *The American Thesaurus of
Slang,* p. 555. *paper man:* a musician who does not improvise, but reproduces the score faithfully. — 1960 *The
Story of the Original Dixieland Jazz Band,* p. 13. For
the most part New Orleans musicians fell into three cate-
gories: (1) the "paper men" who could not play by
ear . . .

paradiddle, *n.* [onomatopoeic; current since c. 1917] A
basic drum roll. — 1934 *Metronome,* Feb., p. 47. Either
the single paradiddle or the flam paradiddle may be used
during a march step. — 1940 *Paradiddle* (tune recorded
by the Cab Calloway Orchestra on Vocalion 5467). —
1956 *Second Ending,* p. 78. "You heard a ruff. This is a
paradiddle."

party piano (style), [from origin of the piano style (see
RENT PARTY); some currency c. 1920–c. 1940, very rare
since; see also BOOGIE-WOOGIE] A boogie-woogie piano
style—i.e., eight-to-the-bar rhythm, with a twelve-measure blues pattern for a theme. — 1942 *The Jazz Record
Book,* p. 81. The "party piano" style, a growth that owes
more to oldtime blues playing than to any other one
source, was already a flourishing development in the
1930's.

Pasamala, *n.* [etym. unknown; see quot. for beginning date;
very rare since c. 1917] Jazz dance in vogue c. 1898–
c. 1917: see quot. — 1934 *Beale Street: Where the Blues
Began,* p. 105. The Pasamala was a ragtime dance originated, according to Isaac Goldberg, in tin pan alley, at
about the same time as the bombershay, in 1898, in which
the girls chanted as they danced: "Fust you do a rag,
then you bombershay—/Do a sidestep, dip, then you go
the other way,/Shoot along the line with a Pasamala,/
Back, back, back—don't you go too far!"

pay (one's) dues, See s.v. DUES.

peck, the, pecking, [by analogy with the darting, sporadic movement (see 1955 quot.); some currency since c. 1950] See 1955 quot. — 1955 *Know Your Jazz* (Vol. I), (liner notes on LP album ABC-Paramount ABC 115). Charlie Rouse plays in a fast choppy, aggressive style appropriately called "the peck." This is a rhythmic approach that actually amounts to pecking out fast melodic spurts. — 1957 *New York Jazz Festival: 1957,* p. 19. "The Peck," a highly abbreviated and syncopated variation of the ideas of Charlie Parker has been one way of stating music with profundity rather than slickness. — 1959 *The Collector's Jazz: Modern,* p. 255. Rouse . . . takes off on a tenor saxophone solo . . . playing with a strong, assertive tone and a pecking attack.

peck horn, [according to jazzmen, the term originates from the "oom-pah," pecking-like sound made by the horn; according to jazzman Eubie Blake, some currency since c. 1900] See 1942 quot. — 1942 *The American Thesaurus of Slang,* p. 558. *peck horn:* an alto horn or mellophone. — 1961 *Down Beat,* 13 April, p. 37. This set contains a good sampling of his abilities on trumpet, alto, baritone, and the oddball peckhorn.

pecking, peckin', *n.* [from the pecking-like movement of the dance; current c. 1937–c. 1945, rare since] See note above and 1944 quot. — 1938 *Pic,* 5 April, p. 29. Lindy Hop, Big Apple, Little Peach, Shag, Suzy Q, Peckin', every kind of dance ever invented is seen on the floor of the Savoy Saturday night. — 1944 *The New Cab Calloway's Hepsters Dictionary.* s.v. *pecking:* a dance introduced at the Cotton Club in 1937. — 1946 *Big Book of Swing,* p. 124. *peckin':* Dance style, jitterbug step.

    adj. See s.v. PECK, THE.

peep, *v.i.* [according to jazzmen, from Negro slang; current esp. among Negro jazzmen since c. 1940] To read music. Oral evidence only.

peep on, [according to jazzmen, from Negro slang; some currency esp. among Negro jazzmen since c. 1930] To look at. Oral evidence only.

P.I., [from first two letters of the standard term; cf. 1950 *Slang Today and Yesterday*, p. 454. "*P.I.*: a pimp (–1900)"; underworld and some general slang use, but also with some currency among jazzmen since c. 1900] See first quot. — 1955 *Hear Me Talkin to Ya*, p. 12. P.I.'s (that's what we called pimps). — p. 117. One night we saw a P.I. (one who lives and makes money from women) stabbed.

piano kid, [so called because they were usually young (i.e., in their teens); according to jazzman Eubie Blake, some currency c. 1900–c. 1917, obs. since except historical; see also the more common PROFESSOR] A pianist in any of the cabarets or brothels of New Orleans, New York, Memphis, etc., c. 1900–c. 1917. — 1947 *Frontiers of Jazz*, p. 171. His first full-time job was that of "piano kid" at Barron Wilkins' cabaret in New York.

pic, piccolo, n. [prob. corruption of *victrola; piccolo* current c. 1930–c. 1945, rare since; *pic* current since c. 1940; see also BOX, sense 3] See 1939, 1944, 1960 quots. — 1938 *N.Y. Amsterdam News*, 12 March, p. 17. The Harlem Hamfats grind out the tune on myriad Harlem piccolos. — 1939 *Fortune*, July, p. 170. A piccolo is a nickel-in-the-slot victrola. — 1944 *Dan Burley's Original Handbook of Harlem Jive*, p. 145. *piccolo:* juke box, music machine. — 1960 *The Jazz Titans*, p. 162. *pic:* a phonograph.

pick cherries, [from similarity of arm movements; current c. 1920–c. 1930, obs. since] To execute a dance step in vogue c. 1920–c. 1930; also the accompanying drum solo. — 1926 *Nigger Heaven*, p. 242. "Pull 'em down! Pick cherries!"

picker, n. [from the picking movement; according to jazzman Eubie Blake, current since c. 1900] A player or plucker of a stringed instrument (usually bass or guitar).

— 1944 *Chicago Documentary*, p. 8. "That's the bass picker from the jazz band!"

pick style, [according to jazzmen, some currency since c. 1920] Guitar-playing with a pick or plectrum, as distinguished from "finger style." Oral evidence only.

pickup, *n.* [cf. standard meaning (i.e., acceleration); current since c. 1930] Musical anacrusis — i.e., the introductory notes leading into the first note of a chorus or tune. — 1934 *All About Jazz*, p. 65. After a short passage of one or two bars, as a "pick up," the ensemble will then take the last chorus and coda. — 1956 *Sideman*, p. 150. Bernie took pickups into *Laura*.

pick-up, *adj.* [a special application of colloquial term; current since c. 1935] See last quot. — 1941 *Gems of Jazz: Vol. 3* (Decca Records pamphlet), p. 3. This unique session features one of the best all-star line-ups ever assembled for a "pick-up" band. — 1956 *Modern Jazz: A Survey of Developments Since 1939*, p. 79. The overall sound of this band, essentially a "pick-up" unit, reflects the true spirit of jazz. — 1956 *Guide to Jazz*. s.v. *pick-up band* (or *group*): a group formed of musicians who regularly play elsewhere, but who come together for a special purpose. e.g., a recording date, a broadcast, a concert, a short nightclub engagement.

pick up (on), 1. [correlative of jazz slang *put down,* q.v. (see 1956 quot.) in the sense of taking or being capable (by virtue of intelligence) of taking whatever is available; widely current since c. 1935] See 1946, 1959 quots. — 1944 *Dan Burley's Original Handbook of Harlem Jive,* p. 15. "Let me boot you to my play [i.e., inform you of my plan] and, maybe, you can pick up on the issue." — 1946 *Really the Blues*, p. 373. *pick up on:* get, take, learn. — 1956 *Sideman*, p. 291. "No, man . . . you're just not picking up what I'm putting down." — 1959 *Esquire,* Nov., p. 70]. *to pick up on:* to obtain, to find. To understand, appreciate. — 1960 *Hiparama of the Classics*, p. 8.

The snakes in the jungle picked up on the beat and came stompin' in.

2. [special application of sense 1; some currency since c. 1935] See 1946 quot. — 1946 *Really the Blues*, p. 373. *pick up on:* smoke marijuana. — 1957 *On the Road*, p. 88. The connection came in and . . . said, "Pick up, man, pick up."

piece, *n.* [special application of standard meaning; current since c. 1900; see also AX, HORN] A musical instrument. — 1933 *Metronome*, Jan., p. 34. In making stock arrangements I write for the 10-piece combination and then add the extra parts later. — 1955 *Hear Me Talkin to Ya*, p. 197. Most of the time the bands in the taxi dance halls had six or seven pieces.

pink, *n.* [also general Negro slang, but with esp. currency among Negro jazzmen c. 1900–c. 1940, rare since; see also FAY, GRAY] See 1942 quot. — 1926 *Nigger Heaven*, p. 157. Funny thing about those pink-chasers [i.e., Negroes who deliberately seek out white companions], the ofays [i.e., white people] never seem to have any use for them. — 1942 *American Thesaurus of Slang*, p. 358. *pink:* white person. — 1946 *Really the Blues*, p. 263. "You know I ain't pink and I got two strikes against me now."

pipe, *n.* [from the shape; note: *agony pipe* for clarinet and *gobble pipe* for saxophone, both listed in several glossaries of the 1930's, are, according to jazzmen, specious; some slight currency esp. among white jazzmen since c. 1935; see also PLUMBING] Any wind or reed instrument: see quots. — 1936 *Metronome*, Feb., p. 61. *pipe:* sax. — 1942 *The American Thesaurus of Slang*, p. 558. *pipe:* clarinet. — 1955 *Say*, 28 April, p. 53. *pipe:* a trumpet. — 1957 *N.Y. Times Magazine*, 18 Aug., p. 26. *pipe:* a saxophone.

   big pipe, [some currency since c. 1955; see also BARI] See quot. — 1959 *Jazz for Moderns*, p. 21. *big pipe:* baritone sax.

small pipe, [some currency since c. 1955] See quot. —
1959 *Jazz for Moderns*, p. 21. *small pipe:* alto saxophone.

pitch a ball, See s.v. BALL.

pitch a bitch, See s.v. BITCH.

play, *n.* [from gambling and underworld slang: cf. 1929
The Dain Curse (New York: Permabooks reprint, 1961),
p. 124. " 'That's the wrong play,' I said"; poss. also reinforced by the football term; current since c. 1930] The
plan, scheme, proposal, idea. — 1944 *Dan Burley's Original Handbook of Harlem Jive*, p. 15. "Let me boot you
to my play and, maybe, you can pick up on the issue." —
1946 *Really the Blues*, p. 63. Now-or-never was the play.

play a part, [from the standard theater phrase; some general slang use, but esp. current among jazzmen since
c. 1935] To assume a personality; to pretend to be a
particular social type. — 1960 *The Jazz Word*, p. 213. If
a man can play the blues from inside himself without
straining to play a part, he's a legitimate jazzman.

play it cool, [from jazz slang *play a part* and jazz slang *cool;*
some currency since c. 1947] See first 1959 quot. —
1954 *Confidential*, Sep., p. 19. "Man, I tried to play it
cool," Erskine said. — 1959 *The Beat Generation Dictionary.* s.v. *play it cool:* be cautious, be smart. — 1959
Selected Poems, p. 234. I play it cool/And dig all jive. —
1961 *The Sound*, p. 23. "That's where you have to play
it cool."

play (one's) ass off, See s.v. BLOW (ONE'S) ASS OFF.

play on the line, [according to jazzmen, some currency c.
1900–c. 1917, obs. since except historical] To play music in the various cafés and/or brothels c. 1900–c. 1916
along New Orleans' main entertainment street, Basin
Street. — 1947 *Jazz Forum*, April, p. 5. The expression
"playing on the line" indicates the essentially migrant
and transient thrusts of the journeyman rag players.

play (someone) down, [current c. 1930–c. 1945, obs. since
except historical; see also BLOW (SOMEONE) DOWN,

CARVE, CUT] To defeat in musical competition (see CUT-
TING CONTEST). — 1955 *Hear Me Talkin to Ya*, p. 25.
Bands in those days . . . play each other down.

play that thing, [see jazz slang *thing;* current c. 1925–c.
1940, very rare since] To play that music, to play that
instrument: frequently, hortatory (see first quot.). —
1948 *The Record Changer*, June, p. 6. Appeals to "play
that thing" might not be necessary then. — 1948 *Trumpet
on the Wing*, p. 100. Man, he could really play that thing.

plenty, *adj.* [one of several quantitative terms given a
qualitative meaning by jazzmen (see also LESS, MORE,
MUCH); according to jazzman Eubie Blake, current c.
1900–c. 1940, obs. since] Excellent. — 1933 *Fortune*,
Aug., p. 47. Mr. Brown plays plenty trombone. — 1941
So It Doesn't Whistle, p. 53. When they want to say a
man's good, they say he plays plenty sax or plenty
drums.

plumbing, *n.* [from the shape; some currency esp. among
white jazzmen since c. 1930; see also PIPE] See 1942
quot. — 1935 *Vanity Fair*, Nov., p. 71. *plumbing:* trumpet. — 1942 *The American Thesaurus of Slang*, p. 558.
plumbing: wind instruments. — 1951 *Cosmopolitan*, July,
p. 85. Hap said, "You with the plumbin', what's your
name?" — 1955 *Vogue*, 15 Sep., p. 124. Kai Winding and
J. J. Johnson (above) pair their spruce, understated
trombones ("just plumbing") against a backing of bass,
drums, and piano.

pod, *n.* See s.v. POT.

poke, *n.* [prob. by analogy with *hit,* q.v.; some currency
among jazzmen since c. 1940] A puff (of marijuana).
— 1956 *Sideman*, p. 274. He exhaled, "sure you don't
want a poke?"

pop, *adj. & n.* [from *popular;* chiefly trade term but with
some currency among jazzmen since c. 1930; see also
STANDARD] See first 1956 quot. — 1933 *Metronome*,
Dec., p. 31. Pop songs will go along with modern music.

— 1940 *Swing*, Jan., p. 24. These two pops didn't inspire
Benny to any miracles of orchestration. — 1956 *Guide to
Jazz*. s.v. *pop:* a popular number, a tune enjoying a success with the large public. If it stands the test of time it
becomes a "standard." — 1956 *Chicago Review*, Autumn-
Winter, p. 6. There was a time when jazzmen did not
play "pop" tunes. — 1959 *Jazz: A Quarterly of American
Music*, Spring, p. 172. Excluding rock and roll, pop music is a lot better off because of jazz than in the past. —
1961 *Down Beat*, 2 Feb., p. 30. There are three Edwards
originals, used simply as frameworks for improvisation
. . . and one pop standard.

 v.i. [semantic development unknown; current esp.
among Negro jazzmen since c. 1940] To pay someone
else's way; to treat. — 1960 *The Angry Ones*, p. 179. "I'll
take the afternoon off and pop to a show." — 1961 *The
Sound*, p. 188. "You pop for all this?"

poppa, *n.* See s.v. POPS.

poppa-stoppa, poppa-stopper, poppa-loppa *n.* [from common practice of insulting someone by characterizing him
as incestuous (see THE DOZENS); some currency since c.
1935; see also MOTHER] One who commits sexual acts
with (one's) father; also, an intimate term of address. —
1944 *Dan Burley's Original Handbook of Harlem Jive*,
p. 44. All right, Poppa-Stoppa. — 1952 *Invisible Man*,
p. 420. "What brand you drinking tonight, Poppa-Stopper?" he said. — 1960 *The Jazz Word*, p. 16. "You, my
audience, are a bunch of poppaloppers."

popping, *participle* [by analogy with suddenness and sharp-
ness of the sounds; some currency esp. among Negro
jazzmen since c. 1935] Playing (music) with power
and precision. — 1935 *His Hi De Highness of Ho De Ho*,
p. 35. "That brass sure is popping."

pops, poppa, *n.* [cf. general colloquial use: 1925 *English
Words and Their Background*, p. 59. "Expressions . . .
circulating in the year 1920. . . . : *Sweet Papa!*"; accord-

ing to jazzmen, Louis Armstrong introduced jazz slang use of *pops* c. 1922; rare since c. 1945; see also BABY, JACK, JIM] Although occasionally used as a nickname for Louis Armstrong (see 1959 quot.) and for Sidney Bechet, for the most common use, see 1938 quot. — 1938 *Cab Calloway: Hi De Ho,* p. 16. *pops:* salutation for all males. — 1946 *Big Book of Swing,* p. 124. *pops:* male. — 1955 *Solo,* p. 187. "Too many heroes is nowhere. Right, pops?" — 1959 *The Jazz Scene,* p. 294. Nobody who plays with Louis Armstrong ever calls him *Satchmo* or *Satchelmouth,* a label much fancied for advertising purposes. He is merely called Pops. — 1961 *Metronome,* Feb., p. 60. Jazz . . . is . . . an art in which a musician can become known as "Pops" by the time he is 22 or even at 18. — 1961 *The Sound,* p. 25. "And you know one thing, Poppa?"

pork chop (music), [prob. from jazzman's approval of both; according to jazzmen, current c. 1900–c. 1917, obs. since; see also BARRELHOUSE, GULLY-LOW, LOWDOWN] Slow, earthy blues music. Oral evidence only.

pot, pod, *n.* [poss. because frequently grown in window-sill flower pots; widely current since c. 1940; see also BOO, GAGE, MARY JANE, TEA] See second 1959 quot. — 1952 *Flee the Angry Strangers,* p. 133. "We'll smoke pod and everything." — 1959 *The Holy Barbarians,* p. 21. "Every user I know calls it pot." — 1959 *The Jazz Scene,* p. 292. *pot:* marijuana. — 1962 *Monthly Review,* Oct., p. 332. Further, there are cultural and social subdivisions: the jazz hippies, the folk-niks, the pot heads [i.e., users].

potato man, [see quot. for semantic explanation; some currency c. 1900–c. 1917, obs. since except historical] See quot. — 1961 *Show Business Illustrated,* 5 Sep., p. 133. To plug the gaps, he put together marching bands of ten or twelve men that included three or four nonplaying but horn-carrying stand-ins. They were called "potato men" because the bells of their instruments were stuffed with potatoes to make sure that no disturbing sounds came out of them.

pots (are) on, (all) the, [metaphoric extension of *cook*, q.v.; current since c. 1955; see also BURN, POPPING, SMOKE] The music is exciting, thrilling. — 1960 *The Paul Horn Quintet: Something Blue* (liner notes on LP album Hifijazz J615). When the quintet drives, it drives hard, and there is hard cooking all the way. Or, as they say in the trade, "All the pots are on." — 1961 *N.Y. Times Magazine,* 25 June, p. 39. *the pots are on:* the joint's jumping; all the musicians are cookin'. — 1961 *The Village Voice,* 23 Nov., p. 15. A wildly exuberant drummer named Sam Woodyard . . . kept yelling: "Let's put the pots on!"

powerful, *adj.* [according to jazzmen, standard term was given special application by and has had some currency esp. among Negro jazzmen since c. 1900; see also BOSS, HARD, STRONG, TOUGH] Sometimes, possessed of a strong embouchure (see 1946 quot.); usually, formidable as a musician or as a person. — 1946 *Jazzways,* p. 31. Joe Oliver was so powerful he blew a horn out of tune every two months. — 1959 "A Compendium for the Teaching of Jazz History," p. 61. All the musicians who heard Bolden play agreed that he "couldn't read a note and he played the most powerful [cornet] of all time." — 1960 *Metronome,* Dec., p. 23. Cootie Williams, he was a powerful man.

Pres, President, *n.* See s.v. PREZ.

press roll, [some currency since c. 1917] A kind of drum roll. — 1939 *American Jazz Music,* p. 53. . . . a "press roll," one of the many rhythmic patterns which have been used by jazz drummers for years. — 1955 *Hear Me Talkin to Ya,* p. 44. He had a press roll that one very seldom hear nowadays.

pretty, *adj.* [pejorative connotation applied to standard term reflects jazzman's disdain for that which is merely

superficially esthetic; some currency since c. 1917; see
also COMMERCIAL, SWEET] Ornate, pretentious, deficient in earthiness or simplicity (applies to music only;
note: the term may also be used in a neutral or even
favorable sense, so that the connotation must be determined from the context). — 1926 *Jazz* (Whiteman & Mc-
Bride), p. 242. "Nuh, Suh, I jes' can't play that 'pretty
music' that you all play. And you fellers can't never play
blues worth a damn." — 1939 *The Kingdom of Swing*, p.
178. There is no member of a prominent swing band who
could not if he were asked, or felt the inclination, "play
pretty." — 1960 *Jazz Scene 2* (liner notes on LP album
on Epic LA 16001). Thus, though at times Jamal
plays "pretty" piano, he is a real innovator. — 1961
Metronome, April, p. 39. Dig especially . . . Nelson's
pretty mickey mouse [i.e., saccharine] tone on *The
Drive*.

Prez, Pres/President, [see first 1956 quot. for etym.; one
of the five or six indispensable of the many jazz nicknames (see also BIRD, LADY, SATCH); current since c.
1942] Lester Young, 1909–1959, tenor saxophonist, acclaimed by musicians and critics as one of the all-time
great performers on his instrument. — 1949 *Inside Be-
Bop*, p. 5. Known today as "Pres," the president of the
tenor sax men, Lester was first heard of when he replaced Coleman Hawkins in the Fletcher Henderson
band in 1934. — 1954 *Life*, 17 Jan., p. 46. Called "The
Prez" by other saxophone players, Lester Young (left)
was one of the early experimenters with his frenetic off-
the-beat style of "cool" jazz. — 1955 *Down Beat*, 30 Nov.,
p. 47. I was listening to Pres all the way. — 1956 *Lady
Sings the Blues*, p. 59. When it came to a name for Lester, I [i.e., Billie Holiday] always felt he was the greatest . . . So I started calling him the President. It got
shortened to Prez. — 1956 *Jazz: Its Evolution and Essence*, pp. 116–117. His influence . . . is evident . . . in

the work of a whole group of young saxophonists who regard the "President" as their spiritual father. — 1959
Jazz: A Quarterly of American Music, Summer, p. 184.
"Pres" had none of the qualifications for being a successful leader.

professor, prof, *n.* [poss. from the fact that they also gave
piano lessons, or poss. as term of mock respect; according
to jazzmen, current c. 1900–c. 1917, obs. since except historical; see also PIANO KID] A pianist in a brothel or
carbaret, c. 1900–c. 1916. — 1939 *Jazzmen,* p. 24. "My
prof. was a Mexican." — 1950 *They All Played Ragtime,*
p. 270. The spotlight on the "professors" is dimmer and
the tips that support them smaller. — 1955 *Hear Me
Talkin to Ya,* p. 53. The sporting houses needed professors.

progressive jazz, [chiefly a writers' term; current since c.
1950; see also COOL JAZZ, MODERN JAZZ] That jazz
which embraces some or all of the harmonic and rhythmic developments innovated since c. 1945 (though the
earliest period [c. 1945–c. 1950] in progressive jazz was
called *bop,* q.v.): see 1960 quot. — 1952 *Mademoiselle,*
Dec., p. 121. All that was *really* new in bop was absorbed
by progressive jazz (Stan Kenton, et al.), which was
nothing more than the continuation of swing. — 1956
Guide to Jazz, p. 42. *cool* or *progressive jazz:* a logical
development of bop. — 1956 *Enjoyment of Jazz* (EJ410),
p. 2. Thousands of ears were attracted to and condi-
tioned to the modern, "progressive" jazz idiom by his
[i.e., Kenton's] highly-provocative fare. — 1960 *Dictionary of American Slang.* s.v. *progressive jazz:* jazz music
based on chord progressions, rather than on a melody.

pull one's coat, [common attention-getting device; though
now general Negro slang, the term originated among jazzmen c. 1935] See quot. — 1962 *N.Y. Times Magazine,*
20 May, p. 45. *pull one's coat:* to bring to someone's attention.

punch, *n.* [cf. 1934 *A Dictionary of American Slang*, p. 383. "*punch:* energy, vigor, enthusiasm"; some currency in special sense among jazzmen since c. 1925; see also DRIVE] Musical impact, energy, vigor. — 1926 *Melody Maker*, Sep., p. 49. The lyrics in these measures have a particular significance, or what is called "punch." — 1940 *Swing*, Jan., p. 24. Everyone, however, seems happy in the rowdy backing, which gives plenty of punch to a good old barroom song. — 1957 *Giants of Jazz*, p. 25. "Ump! Listen to 'im play that 'Panama.' What a punch!" — 1961 *Down Beat*, 16 Feb., p. 36. The clear, crisp, punching trumpet of Marsala adds more of this same quality.

push, *n. & v.i.* [according to jazzmen, current c. 1920–c. 1935, rare since] A strong rhythmic accompaniment; to provide such an accompaniment (usually participial). — 1959 *Jazz* (Hentoff & McCarthy), p. 36. Dixieland was a "pushing" style. — p. 299. It was a drum style that implied . . . a "push" behind the improviser. — 1961 *The Jazz Review*, Jan., p. 26. The subtlety of his work is conspicuously absent, and there is a quality of obvious pushing rather reminiscent of Buddy Rich.

v.t. [from underworld slang; current among jazzmen since c. 1935] To sell or promote (something—frequently, narcotics). — 1946 *Really the Blues*, p. 373. *push:* sell, handle, purvey. — 1959 *Esquire*, Nov., p. 70J. *push:* sell drugs. — 1959 *The Holy Barbarians*, p. 25. "He was pushing heroin to other musicians." — 1960 *Hiparama of the Classics*, p. 10. They're Pushin' The Nazz [i.e., Jesus]!

push the beat, [according to jazzmen, current c. 1920–c. 1935, rare since] To play with a strong, pulsating beat. — 1961 *New Yorker*, 23 Sep., p. 103. But Beiderbecke lacked Young's tricks and simply pushed the beat before him.

pusher, *n.* [narcotics slang, but with some currency among jazzmen since c. 1930] A seller of narcotics. — 1943 *Time,* 19 July, p. 54. He is known to his clients as a "pusher." — 1948 *The American Language: Supplement II,* p. 681. A peddler is a *pusher.* — 1959 *The Naked Lunch,* p. 226. In 1920s a lot of Chinese pushers [i.e., narcotics sellers] found The West so unreliable, dishonest and wrong . . . when an Occidental junky came to score [i.e., buy narcotics], they say, "No glot . . . Clom Fliday . . ." — 1960 *Beat Jokes Bop Humor & Cool Cartoons,* p. 60. The cat went on the wagon, got rid of his pusher, and even went to church once.

put-down, *n.* [formed from *put down,* sense 2.; current since c. 1942] An adverse criticism, a squelch, an insult. — 1959 *The Horn,* p. 215. "Anyone makes a hassle this next set, I'll show 'em put-downs if that's all they're after."

put down, 1. [correlative of jazz slang *pick up,* q.v.; from sense of setting something down or presenting it; current since c. 1935; see also *lay down*] See 1944 quot. — 1944 *Dan Burley's Original Handbook of Harlem Jive,* p. 145. *put down:* say, perform, describe, do. — 1953 *Down Beat,* 11 Feb., p. 16–S. Those old masters have really put something down, and it'll be a long, long time before those basic sounds change. — 1955 *Hear Me Talkin to Ya,* p. 69. Now I haven't got no other way to go but . . . put my music down. — 1956 *Sideman,* p. 24. "What you putting down, man?" — p. 291. "No, man . . . you're just not picking up [i.e., understanding] what I'm putting down." — 1957 *On the Road,* p. 134. "Listen will you to this old tenor man blow his top . . . tell the story and put down real relaxation." — 1959 *The Holy Barbarians,* p. 67. "The party people didn't like me or the ideas that I put down."

2. [from sense of reducing something in status or from setting it down and leaving it there (i.e., discarding it); some 19th century, and poss. earlier, British use; widely

current among jazzmen since c. 1940] See 1958 quot.; also, to quit or reject. — 1953 *Night Light,* p. 135. "You really ought to put school down." — 1955 *Hear Me Talkin to Ya,* p. 381. I heard a guy last week . . . putting a musician down. — 1957 *Paris Blues,* p. 10. "Then stop trying to put him down." — 1958 *American Speech,* Oct., p. 225. When someone puts you down he criticizes you unfavorably. — 1959 *The Holy Barbarians,* p. 102. "I put that scene [i.e., domesticity] down when I got divorced." — 1960 *Down Beat,* 10 Nov., p. 45. Maybe as far as swinging jazz is concerned this might not mean very much, but . . . it's a wonderful piece of music, and I couldn't put it down.

put on, [from *put (one) on;* some currency since c. 1955] An act of deception; a joke; a subterfuge. — 1961 *The Jazz Life,* p. 18. At the Savoy, I learned, I think, to recognize the "put on."

put (one) on, [Early Modern English phrase that survived in dialectal English: cf. 1611 *The Winter's Tale,* II, i. "You are abused and by some putter-on/That will be damned for't"; widely current since c. 1940] See 1958, 1959 quots. — 1948 *Trumpet on the Wing,* p. 119. Eddie Miller and the boys used to put me on for bringing atomizers on these dates. — 1958 *American Speech,* Oct., p. 225. When a hipster *puts* someone *on* he is pulling his leg (perhaps putting him on a stage to be laughed at). — 1959 *Esquire,* Nov., p. 70J. *put on:* to make fun of, or ridicule without the victim being aware of it. — 1961 *The Jazz Review,* Jan., p. 13. You might be putting yourself on. — 1961 *Down Beat,* 5 Jan., p. 43. I think he was putting on the Viennese composers, and it was marvelous.

put (something or someone) on (someone), [from the sense of putting someone into contact with something or someone; current since c. 1935; see also LAY (SOMETHING) ON (SOMEONE)] To present (something or someone) to (someone). — 1960 *Hiparama of the Classics,* p. 10. But,

I'm gonna put a Cat on you, who was the Sweetest, groov-iest . . . Cat that ever Stomped on this Sweet Green Sphere. — p. 11. The Naz was in a bind so he put it on a couple of his Buddy-Cats. — 1961 *Down Beat*, 5 Jan., p. 16. "If any of them who read this think I'm jivin', let 'em look me up, and I'll put some music on 'em."

put us in the alley!, [according to jazzmen, some currency esp. among those Negroes who danced to jazz c. 1910– c. 1925, obs. since except historical; see also LET'S DO A SET!, LET'S GO BACK HOME!] A shout of encouragement to jazz musicians c. 1910–c. 1925 to play fast, energetically, and intensely. — 1959 *The Jazz Review*, July, p. 12. When they got tired of two-steps and schottisches (which they danced with a lot of spieling), they'd yell: . . . "Now, put us in the alley!"

queen, *n.* [cf. 1960 *Dictionary of American Slang*, s.v. *queen*: "some student use since c. 1915"; not to be con-fused with its general slang sense (i.e., a male homosex-ual): cf. 1959 *The Naked Lunch*, p. 184. "Carl saw some-thing ignoble and hideous in the queen's spayed animal brown eyes"; current among jazzmen c. 1930–c. 1945, rare since; see also FOX] See 1938 quot. — 1938 *Cab Callo-way: Hi De Ho*, p. 16. *queen*: a beautiful girl. — 1946

Big Book of Swing, p. 124. *queen:* frantic [jazz slang sense] chick. — 1952 *Park East,* Dec., p. 30. My queen in her scanties and I in my robe,/Had just fixed our wigs for a long winter's load. — 1958 *Jive in Hi-Fi,* p. 15. *fine queen:* a pretty woman or one in her late teens or early 20's.

quit the scene, [general Negro slang *quit* (cf. song title *Hit Me But Don't Quit Me* by George Williams and Bessie Brown, listed in *Columbia 1927 Race Catalogue: The Latest Blues by Columbia Race Stars*) + jazz slang *(the) scene;* current since c. 1950; see also CUT OUT, SPLIT, SPLIT THE SCENE] To leave; also, by extension: to die (see also LEFT TOWN, SPLIT THE SCENE): in this sense, oral evidence only. — 1955 *Hear Me Talkin to Ya,* p. 248. Ma had quit the scene. — 1955 *Babs Gonzales: Babs' Celebrity Party* (lyrics on LP album Crazy C-0001-A). It was nab [i.e., a policeman] and the super tellin' us we had to quit the scene.

race (music or **records),** [see 1959 quot.: chiefly a trade term, and one which reflects the separateness of white and Negro jazz markets (see 1960 quot.) during the pre-Swing (i.e., pre-c. 1935) era, a schism which has been gradually closing; some currency among jazzmen c. 1920–

c. 1940, obs. since except historical; see also RHYTHM AND
BLUES]   See 1949, 1960 quots. — 1927 *Columbia 1927
Race Catalogue: The Latest Blues by Columbia Race
Stars* (title of record company catalogue). — 1935 *Vanity
Fair,* Nov., p. 71. Negro bands play *"race music"* (a curious euphemism spread by phonograph companies). —
1946 *Really the Blues,* p. 164. These guys . . . hit them
with the real race music. —1949 *Music Library Association Notes,* Dec., p. 49. *race:* type of song whose characteristics are difficult to define but which is supposed to
appeal particularly to Negro audiences. Such songs are
modern derivatives of old *blues* songs in subject matter,
harmony, rhythm and form. Trade papers also classify
certain performers as race artists and their recordings are
race records. "Billboard" recently substituted "rhythm
and blues" for race. — 1958 *Jam Session,* p. 275. In the
twenties and thirties, rhythm and blues was called "race
music." — 1959 *The Country Blues,* p. 47. Ralph Peer
was trying c. 1920 to think of a catalog title for his
new records, and rather than calling them "Negro" records, decided on "Race" records, and the name lasted. —
1960 *Dictionary of American Slang.* s.v. *race music:* a
simple form of jazz based on the blues, usually with a
melancholy or sometimes religious theme, a heavily accented beat, etc. Because such music, during the 1920's
and 1930's was issued by the recording companies on
records informally known as "race records," intended
primarily for sale to Negroes.

rag, *n. & adj.* [prob. from *ragged:* see note s.v. *ragtime;*
see 1956 quot. for dates]   See 1956, 1960 quots. —
[1895] *Harlem Rag* (tune composed c. 1895). — 1899
Maple Leaf Rag (tune composed by Scott Joplin). —
1916 *Variety,* 25 Aug., p. 8. Ash . . . is seen daily on the
streets playing rag dance numbers. — 1926 *Harper's
Magazine,* April, p. 579. Just how is the typical "rag"
built? — 1939 *The International Cyclopedia of Music*

and Musicians, p. 896. Nearly all the good "rag" composers were pianists. — 1947 *The Two Worlds of Johnny Truro,* p. 24. They listened to rags and stomps, to fox trots and marches. — 1956 *Guide to Jazz.* s.v. *rag:* a form of piano piece, generally 16 bars, which flourished in the late 19th century and until c. 1928, and which was, though initially a piano piece, transcribed for bands as well. — 1960 *Dictionary of American Slang,* p. 417. Strictly speaking, rag preceded jazz and was distinct from it, being mostly written music.

v.i. & v.t. [formed from the *n.* and contemporaneous with it] See 1939 quot. — 1936 *Harper's Magazine,* April, p. 570. "Ragging," "gut-bucketing," and all the rest are names for the *hot* performance which is the heart and soul of jazz. — 1939 *Jazzmen,* p. 43. To "rag" a tune was to syncopate it. — 1952 *Music Out of Dixie,* p. 59. They ragged it and rocked it in joyous abandon.

ragmen, *n.* [from *rag* and contemporaneous with it] A jazzman, c. 1900–c. 1916. — 1947 *Frontiers of Jazz,* p. 107. I used to hear . . . Buddie Canter, Josky Adams . . . what we call "ragmen" in New Orleans.

rag-time, ragtime, *n. & adj.* [see 1957 quot. for prob. etym.; dates are contemporaneous with those of *rag,* q.v.] See 1958 quots. — 1908 *New York Age,* 5 March [1962 *Jazz: A History of the New York Scene,* p. 43]. "The Maple Leaf Rag" . . . was the first ragtime instrumental piece to be generally accepted by the public. — 1912 *The Autobiography of an Ex-Coloured Man,* p. 100 [New York: Hill & Wang reprint, 1960]. American musicians, instead of investigating rag-time, attempt to ignore it, or dismiss it with a contemptuous word. — 1931 *Zit's Theatrical Newspaper,* 2 May, p. 11. If you want to hear a great ragtime singer step yourself up to the Club Calais and get a load of Lillian Barnes. — 1939 *The International Cyclopedia of Music and Musicians,* p. 896.

Though ragtime was sometimes played by larger combinations of instruments, the piano retained a dominant influence over its structure and phraseology. — 1950 *They All Played Ragtime,* p. 210. The date was 1896, the place . . . a New York vaudeville theatre. It was "jig-piano" then. Not until a year later was the music christened "ragtime." — 1957 *The Book of Jazz,* p. 58. Perhaps this apparently ragged rhythmic imbalance (leading to the spontaneous development of the term "ragtime") . . . — 1958 *The Decca Book of Jazz,* p. 29. Ragtime was the hot music of the first ten years of this century. — p. 34. It was not until 1897 that the name "ragtime" was invented to describe the new syncopated piano style that was developing among the Missouri pianists.

ragtime shuttle, [according to jazzman Eubie Blake, current c. 1900–c. 1917, obs. since except historical] A ragtime drum break or figure. — 1960 *The Story of the Original Dixieland Jazz Band,* p. 33. Some of his breaks . . . like . . . the "ragtime shuttle" have never been duplicated.

raise sand (or **cain**), [cf. 1934 *A Dictionary of American Slang,* p. 385. *"raise cain:* to create a disturbance; *raise sand:* to make a disturbance"; according to jazzmen, given a special application by them c. 1930–c. 1945, obs. since except historical] See quot. (note: usually achieved by playing music excitingly) — 1946 *Really the Blues,* p. 374. *raise sand:* make a fuss, create a stir.

rank, *adj.* [prob. from standard meaning (i.e., offensive in smell); also cf. 1930 *American Tramp and Underworld Slang,* s.v. *rank:* "poor; worthless; disagreeable"; current esp. among Negro jazzmen since c. 1925] Nasty, disagreeable; also, see 1959 quot. — 1937 *Metronome,* Aug., p. 7. "In my opinion, a great many readers of *Met* are the rankest sort of ickies." — 1959 *Esquire,* Nov., p. 70J. *rank:* stupid.

v.t. [prob. from armed forces slang *pull rank on some-one* (i.e., to subordinate someone); some currency esp. among Negro jazzmen since c. 1925; see also PUT DOWN, sense 2.]   See 1946 quot. — 1938 *Cab Calloway: Hi De Ho,* p. 16. *rank:* to lower. — 1945 *Hepcats Jive Talk Dictionary.* s.v. *rank:* to criticize. — 1946 *Big Book of Swing,* p. 125. *rank:* to find fault. — 1960 *Down Beat,* 7 Jan., p. 29. I'm not ranking either of these two excellent writers.

ratamacue, *n.* [onomatopoeic; some currency since c. 1925] A drum figure. — 1934 *Metronome,* Feb., p. 47. The rata-macue is somewhat more difficult than the paradiddle.

ready, *adj.* [prob. by analogy with *hip* and *booted,* q.v.: i.e., if one's hip boots are on, he is ready for any kind of weather, and, by extension, for any eventuality; current c. 1930–c. 1945, rare since]   See 1935 quot. — 1935 *His Hi De Highness of Ho De Ho,* p. 35. "When an individual or a piece of music is high class or greatly admired, we indicate it by saying, 'He's ready!' or 'That's ready!'" — 1944 *The New Cab Calloway's Hepsters Dictionary.* s.v. *ready:* 100 percent in every way. Example: "That fried chicken was ready." — 1958 *Jam Session: An Anthology of Jazz,* p. 91. This time he was *ready,* so to speak, for it was on this second sojourn that he started to impress his musical contemporaries. — 1960 *The Teddy Edwards Quartet: Teddy's Ready!* (LP album Contemporary S 7583).

rebop, re-bop, *n.* [see 1957 quot. for etym.; reinforced by popular Lional Hampton tune recorded 1946, *Hey-Baba-Rebop;* some currency among jazzmen c. 1945–c. 1947, but never as common as and soon completely supplanted by *bebop* and *bop*]   Early term for that highly technical and cerebral modern jazz innovated c. 1945 more commonly called *bop,* q.v. — 1946 *Disc,* Nov., "Re-bop is four-beat music, but it's too complicated." — 1947 *Esquire's 1947 Jazz Book,* p. 26. To play "re Bop" one has

to have mighty good, strong chops [jazz sense]. — 1956
Eddie Condon's Treasury of Jazz, p. 191. The center of
attention seemed to be a new kind of jazz, successively
known as "Rebop," "Bebop," and finally just plain "bop."
— 1957 *Giants of Jazz*, p. 188. The word "bop" is a contraction of "bebop" or "rebop." The two-syllable word was
merely a way of describing the staccato two-note phrase
that became the trademark in its playing. Also **re bop.**

reefer, *n.* [see 1959 quot. for poss. etym.; some currency
among jazzmen c. 1925–c. 1940, obs. since except historical; see also BOO, GAGE, MARY JANE, POT, TEA] See 1938
quot. — 1931 *Reefer Man* (tune recorded by Don Redman). — 1933 *Chicago Defender*, 2 Dec., p. 5. The
humble "reefer," "the weed," the marijuana, or what have
you by way of a name for a doped cigarette has moved to
Park Ave. from Harlem. — 1935 *His Hi De Highness of
Ho De Ho*, p. 36. A person who is experiencing the exhilaration produced by a reefer is described as "high." —
1938 *Cab Calloway: Hi De Ho*, p. 16. *reefer:* marijuana
cigaret. — 1959 *Jazz: A Quarterly of American Music*,
Fall, p. 285. "Smokin' Reefers" was a title in *Flying Colors*
produced on Broadway in 1932, where a stick retailed for
five cents . . . The word *reefer* is an Anglicization of *gri-
fo* . . . Along the border it indicates a drunkard, and by
extension one under the influence of any soporific.

reefer man, [some currency c. 1925–c. 1940, obs. since except historical] See 1935 quot. — 1931 *Reefer Man*
(tune recorded by Don Redman). — 1935 *His Hi De
Highness of Ho De Ho*, p. 36. A "reefer man" is a peddler
who bootlegs these cigarets.

reet, *adv. & adj.* [*all right* corrupted to *all reet*, q.v., then
shortened to *reet*; current c. 1935–c. 1945, very rare
since] As *adv.*: all right, yes; as *adj.*: excellent, nifty.
— 1942 *American Mercury*, July, p. 85. So Jelly got his
zoot suit with the reet pleats. — 1944 *Metronome*, Jan.,

p. 12. Anita O'Day, the gal with the reet beat in her voice. — 1956 *Eddie Condon's Treasury of Jazz,* p. 447. "Reet," the trombonist told him.

release, *n.* [prob. in sense of a liberty taken from the major theme; current since c. 1930; see also the more recent CHANNEL] See 1959 quot. — 1936 *Hot Jazz: The Guide to Swing Music,* p. 18. Also called, quite poetically, "the release." — 1956 *Guide to Jazz.* s.v. *release:* describes the phrase "B" in themes of the A,A,B,A sequence. — 1959 *Webster's New World Dictionary.* s.v. *release: in jazz music,* the third group of four measures in a common form of sixteen-bar chorus, which supplies a bridge between repetitions of the melody.

rent party (or **stomp, strut**), (**house**), [Negro general slang, but with esp. currency among Negro jazzmen c. 1920–c. 1940, obs. since except historical] See first 1955 quot. — 1925 *The Inter-State Tattler,* 6 March, p. 8. It would be extremely cruel to the South American amateurs if they had to pick up Harlem by the sounds of house rent parties. — 1938 *N.Y. Amsterdam News,* 12 March, p. 17. The allusion to "peppermint candy" stirs almost primal emotions, hangover from the old "down home house rent strut" days. — 1946 *Harvard Dictionary of Music,* p. 378. *Boogie-Woogie* . . . was heard at Negro "rent parties" in Chicago in the early 1920's. — 1955 *A Pictorial History of Jazz,* p. 127. The music . . . is probably best described by turning to its basic setting during the '20's, the raucous, colorful "rent party." This rather widespread phenomenon . . . originally was literally a device for rounding up the rent money by crowding as many friends as possible into an apartment and having them pay for an evening of food, drink and entertainment. This specific purpose may have been ignored before long, but the parties became a staple item at, seemingly, every flat that boasted a piano in working condition. — 1955 *Hear Me Talkin to Ya,* pp. 210–211. Joe . . . would bash at numerous functions and house-rent stomps along Carlisle and John Streets. — 1957 *Giants of Jazz,* p. 71. "Rent parties" too became the rage in the early twenties. Admission ranged from thirty-five cents to half a buck, for which the guest received a plate of pig's feet and potato salad or an order of chitlins. But the prime attractions were the piano players.

rhythm and blues, rhythm-and-blues, r&b, [from its dominant components; current c. 1935–c. 1945, rare since; see also the earlier RACE (MUSIC)] See 1955, 1956 quots. (note: *rhythm and blues* grew out of race music and grew into rock 'n roll: see first 1961 quot.) — 1955 *The Encyclopedia of Jazz,* p. 347. *rhythm-and-blues* (or *r&b*): a type of harmonically, rhythmically and melodically simple popular music or jazz, originally intended for a Negro audience. — 1956 *Guide to Jazz.* s.v. *rhythm-and-blues:* singing style characterized by a very heavy, emphatic boogie bass accompaniment. — 1961 *The Jazz Review,* p. 24. Rhythm and blues or rock 'n roll has been a whipping boy for almost as long as it has enjoyed popular success. — p. 30. At least r&b went back to feeling rather than an idea about feeling.

rhythm section, [current in special sense since c. 1925] See 1937 quot. (Note: in a small group, the guitar is frequently omitted; in a large group, the following instruments may also occasionally serve as rhythm instruments: vibraphone, celeste, bongo and conga drums.) — 1937 *American Speech,* Feb., p. 48. In the *rhythm section* are drums, piano, bass, guitar. — 1942 *The American Thesaurus of Slang,* p. 557. *rhythm section:* a division of a dance band's instruments. — 1949 *Down Beat,* 11 March, p. 15. Allen plays most of his Capitol dance dates with only himself and three rhythm. — 1961 *The Sound,* pp. 11–12. The Sultans were six. Three rhythms and three horns.

ricky-tick(y), *adj.* See s.v. TICKY.

ride, *n. & adj.* [by analogy with the rhythmic movement; according to jazzmen, current c. 1922–c. 1945, very rare since; see also CHORUS, SOLO]   An improvised solo chorus. — 1940 *Swing*, Jan., p. 25. The other side is *Bugle Call Rag* at ride tempo. — 1949 *Ebony*, June, p. 41. "When Willie plays a ride solo, he is better received than anyone else in the band." — 1956 *Second Ending*, p. 63. "You give him all the hot rides."

v.i. & v.t. [by analogy with the rhythmic movement; cf. 1959 *The Jazz Scene*, p. 16n. " 'Riding,' 'rocking' and 'rolling' are words applied both to the railroad and to coitus"; cf. also its Early Modern English use (i.e., in a sexual sense): c. 1599 *Henry V*, III, vii, 53–54. "You rode . . . your French hose off"; according to jazzmen, current c. 1922–c. 1945, very rare since; see also GROOVE, SWING] See first 1938 and 1952 quots. — 1933 *Metronome*, July, p. 28. He [i.e., the drummer] "rides" the band. — 1936 *Metronome*, Feb., p. 61. *ride:* swing with a bit more physical force. — 1938 *Cab Calloway: Hi De Ho*, p. 16. *ride:* to swing, to keep perfect tempo in playing or singing. — 1938 *Metronome*, Feb., p. 25. "When they ride, you can't help getting a lift." — 1952 *A History of Jazz in America*, p. 352. *ride:* to swing, esp. in the last chorus or section. — 1956 *Second Ending*, p. 57. They rode into the sock chorus like a storm cloud of marauders.

v.t. [some currency since c. 1930]   To play music inspiredly and pulsatingly (with *it*). — 1937 *This Thing Called Swing*, p. 8. *Ride it!:* Take it! Give it the works! Put out, boy. — 1954 *Ride Out*, p. 24. "On those passages that belong to you, go right on and ride it out."

ride cymbal [current since c. 1925; see also SOCK CYMBAL]   A medium-sized single cymbal, part of a jazz drummer's standard equipment. — 1961 *The Sound*, p. 42. And the magic sound he had on the ride cymbal was there.

— 1962 *Dinosaurs in the Morning,* p. 26. He depends on
. . . the ride cymbal.

ride man, [from *ride, n.;* current c. 1922–c. 1940, obs. since
except historical] An improvising soloist. — 1935
Vanity Fair, Nov., p. 38. *Ride-men* is a term applied to
the improvisers of these licks. — 1937 *This Thing Called
Swing,* p. 3. *ride man:* the player whose improvisations
during a piece set the lead for the rest of the swingers.
— 1945 *Band Leaders and Record Review,* March, p. 20.
Within a horn blast of Hollywood and Vine, the
crossroads of Glamour-town, can be found many lairs of
the hepcats—haunts of gates and ride men.

ride-out, *n. & adj.* [from *ride n. + out,* in the sense of
exit; current since c. 1925] See 1958 quot. — 1939 *Metronome,* May, p. 19. *Pussy Willow* has a great ride-out.
— 1954 *Ride Out,* p. 27. They were struck by a violent
wave of sound, the ride-out finish of "China Boy."
— 1958 *Publication of the American Dialect Society,*
Nov., p. 46. *ride-out:* the final chorus of an arrangement.
— 1962 *Jazz Monthly,* Oct., p. 24. *Folk Forms* is reduced
to a short bass solo, a short drum solo and a ride-out.

ridiculous, *adj.* [one of several terms reflecting the
jazzman's fondness for the bizarre, eccentric, or unconventional (see also CRAZY, INSANE, NUTTY, SOMETHING
ELSE); current since c. 1935] See 1960 quot. — 1959
Jazz: A Quarterly of American Music, Summer, p. 209.
His technique is ridiculous! — 1960 *The Jazz Word,*
p. 143. To a jazzman . . . *ridiculous* is wonderful.

riff, *n. & adj.* [etym. unknown; according to jazzmen,
some currency since c. 1917, but widely current only
since c. 1935] See 1946, 1949 quots. — 1936 *Esquire,*
June, p. 92. The mutations of musician's slang are interesting. It was "breaks" originally. Then it became "licks."
Today it is "riffs." — 1946 *Harvard Dictionary of Music,*
p. 378. *riff* technique: short ostinato melodic figures by
the band sometimes against which one of the instruments

improvises. — 1948 *Down Beat*, 14 July, p. 15. Its final riff chorus spots a repetitive phrase that every small jobbing band from here to Keokuk has used since 1934. — 1949 *Music Library Association Notes*, Dec., p. 50. *riff:* musical phrase usually developed by musicians, rather than composers, and taking an identifiable form. Riffs occasionally become basis of pop songs just as folk motifs serve as symphonic themes. — 1958 *The Story of Jazz*, p. 199. The repeated phrases which the brass and reed sections threw back and forth became known as "riffs," and "riffing" developed as a fine art. — 1959 *The Horn*, p. 35. Soloing on some copybook riff, he played clear, original things.

    v.i. [according to jazzmen, some currency since c. 1917, but widely current only since c. 1935] To play a riff (see *n.*): see last quot. — 1936 *Harper's Magazine*, April, p. 570. "Swing," "riffing" . . . and all the rest are names for the hot performance which is the heart and soul of jazz. — 1958 *The Story of Jazz*, p. 199. The repeated phrases which the brass and reed sections threw back and forth became known as "riffs," and "riffing" developed as a fine art.

riff, *n.* [by analogy with **riff,** *n. & adj.* (i.e., from the initial sense of a musical phrase that in repetition becomes characteristic, the meaning is extended to anything which through repetition becomes familiar or habitual); current since c. 1940; see also LICK, PLAY] See note. — 1944 *Dan Burley's Original Handbook of Harlem Jive*, p. 150. *wrong riff:* the wrong thing—either by words or action. — 1952 *Who Walk in Darkness*, p. 90. "I've found a new riff . . . Bicycling." — 1959 *Diggeth Thou?*, p. 34. So after he had sounded and she had dug his riff,/she cut into his dommy and helped him kill the fifth. — 1959 *San Francisco Chronicle*, 4 June, p. 35. "None of that trash about how them black rabbits sing and dance all the time and are light on their feet and how they look alike, you know, that old-time riff."

right, *adj.* [some general slang use, but with esp. currency among jazzmen since c. 1925] In good form, musically. — 1928 *The Walls of Jericho,* p. 304. *right:* somewhat in excess of perfection. — 1956 *Down Beat Jazz Record Reviews: 1956,* p. 109. She's absorbingly right on these sides. — 1958 *After Hours Poetry,* p. 31. When Lester is "right"/All others pale.

right ahead, See s.v. STRAIGHT AHEAD.

righteous, *adj.* [see 1956 quot. for semantic development; according to jazzmen, current esp. among Negro jazzmen c. 1900–c. 1945, rare since] Genuine; authentic: see first 1944 quot. — 1937 *Mademoiselle,* Oct., p. 71. He plays righteous clarinet; no razzle-dazzle, but tremendous warmth and expressiveness. — 1944 *The New Cab Calloway's Hepsters Dictionary.* s.v. *righteous:* splendid. — 1944 *Dan Burley's Original Handbook of Harlem Jive,* p. 25. You could hear Joe Hipp spieling that righteous ad lib. — p. 41. Desdemona, the righteous wren, is stashed in her lilywhites. — 1956 *The Heart of Jazz,* p. 67. . . . "that righteous New Orleans stuff." This persistent use of an adjective associated with religion, and especially with Judaism and Christianity, can be explained most naturally as a reflection of a conspicuously religious character in the music. — 1961 *The Sound,* p. 112. "The man ain't cut a righteous hunk of wax yet."

right hand, [special application of standard phrase; current since c. 1900 though, for reasons of pianistic technique, less current than *left hand,* q.v.] A pianist's right hand; also: his skill or inventiveness with the right hand. — 1940 *New Orleans Jazz,* p. 12. The left hand does (and the right hand knows it!) . . . a New Orleans *hop scop.* — 1960 *Jazz: A Quarterly of American*

Music, Winter, p. 35. The crowded cult devoted to blinding up-tempo right hand bedazzlement simply holds no allure for him. — 1961 *The Jazz Review,* Jan., p. 26. Granted he has a great left hand, but the way he uses it detracts from his right.—1961 *Metronome,* April, p. 32. This sensation of tonality is fashioned by the fusion of many wonderful elements: a rich left hand, lagging yet leaping, coupled with a right hand that can seem to do no wrong.

rigor mortis, rig city, rigville, [by analogy with the moribund stiffening; according to jazzmen, current since c. 1955] The situation (often, the music or the music business) is bad: either (1) there is very little work for jazz musicians, or (2) there are very few customers in a night club, or (3) the musician is playing badly or, after starting his solo chorus well, is losing his inspiration and is slipping into musical clichés. (Oral evidence only for the second and third senses.) — 1961 *Night Song,* p. 47. "B" couldn't record because the war was on. Rigor Mortis.

rimshot, rim-shot, *n.* [from the part of the drum on which it is sounded and its sound; current since c. 1930] See 1937 quot. — 1937 *American Speech,* Feb., p. 48. *rimshot:* the noise made by striking the rim and head of a snare drum simultaneously. — 1959 *The Horn,* p. 34. The drummer for the house band good-naturedly chased Wing's warm-up runs with precise rim-shots. — 1961 *The Sound,* p. 12. The drummer . . . sounded a rim shot.

rip, *n.* [poss. from *ripple* or simply a special application of a standard meaning; current since c. 1925] See 1949 quot. — 1933 *Metronome,* Jan., p. 34. The rip is produced by short and quick glissando up to the tone, attacked sforzando and cut off quickly. — 1949 *Music Library Association Notes,* Dec., p. 50. *rip:* modern effect used by reed and brass instruments. Instrumentalist begins

on a note, four or five notes below particular note he is
shooting for, and leaps quickly up to written note,
which he hits hard and staccato.

ripped, *adj.* [hyperbole: emotional analogy with physical
fragmentation; some old general slang use, but reintroduced by and current esp. among Negro jazzmen
since c. 1958; see also TORE UP] Distraught; grief-
stricken. Oral evidence only.

roach, *n.* [prob. by analogy with its smallness; current
among jazzmen since c. 1935] See 1946 quot. — 1938
Cab Calloway: Hi De Ho, p. 16. *roach:* butt of a partially
smoked reefer cigaret. — 1943 *Time,* 19 July, p. 54.
When he has smoked a reefer down to a half-inch butt
. . . it is known . . . as a "roach." — 1946 *Really the
Blues,* p. 374. *roach:* small butt from a cigarette of
marijuana. — 1959 *The Holy Barbarians,* p. 110. Did
you say you had a roach stashed away [i.e., hidden]
somewhere?

rock, *v.i. & v.t.* [see 1927 quot. for semantic explanation;
also cf. 1959 *The Jazz Scene,* p. 16*n.* " 'Riding,' 'rocking'
and 'rolling' are words applied both to the railroad and
to coitus"; current since c. 1900; see also BOOT, GROOVE,
SWING, WAIL] To move or do (something) im-
pressively—usually, applied to dancing, to coition or, in
its most common sense since c. 1935, to musical performance: see second 1938 quot.; also, rare, noun: see
first 1952 quot. — 1926 *Sugar Foot Stomp* (song copyright by Melrose Music Publishers). When they start
dancin'—Stompin' and prancin'—the dance called the
sugar foot stomp. Let your doggies romp. Rock your
mama like a cradle. — 1927 *The Journal of Abnormal
and Social Psychology,* April.-June, p. 15. The majority of
the expressions in the blues relating to the sex act are
sung from the point of view of women and are mostly
concerned with the quality of the movements made by
the male during coitus . . . "My man rocks me with one

steady roll." Here the woman boasts of the steady movement with which her man executes the act. — 1938 *Metronome,* July, p. 21. Harry James' *Lullaby in Rhythm* really rocks. — 1938 *Cab Calloway: Hi De Ho,* p. 16. *rock me:* send me, kill me, move me with rhythm. — 1939 *American Jazz Music,* p. 45. It may be powerful and driving . . . which, in jazz slang, might be said to "rock the joint." — 1952 *Music Out of Dixie,* p. 245. "I want that steady rock." — 1952 *Flee the Angry Strangers,* p. 46. "Who did you rock this week?" — 1956 *The Real Jazz Old and New,* p. 149. *To rock* is to jump and swing. — 1957 *On the Road,* p. 176. The big booming beat begins and everybody starts rocking. — 1961 *Jazz Notes,* Feb.-March, p. 39. "I don't remember anyone who could 'rock' a Kenilworth audience before."

roll, *v.i. & v.t.* [see note s.v. *rolling bass:* also cf. 1959 *The Jazz Scene,* p. 16n. " 'Riding,' 'rocking' and 'rolling' are words applied both to the railroad and to coitus"; according to jazzmen, current c. 1910–c. 1945, rare since] To play a particular pianistic figure with the left hand (see ROLLING BASS). — 1925 *Steady Roll Blues* (tune composed by George Bates and Mel Stitzel). — 1937 *Roll 'Em* (tune composed by Mary Lou Williams). — 1955 *Hear Me Talkin to Ya,* p. 291. "Roll for me— come on, roll 'em, Pete."

rolling bass (or **piano**), [see 1957 quot. for semantic explanation; according to jazzmen, current c. 1910–c. 1945, rare since] A bass foundation provided by the pianist's left hand (see 1957 quot.). — 1940 *New Orleans Jazz,* p. 12. Thus we had, in various places from Pensacola to Dallas and from St. Louis to Chicago, such interesting names for what the left hand does . . . as . . . *rolling bass.* — 1946 *Metronome,* Oct., p. 25. Trumpet with modern riffs, and Hodes with that rolling piano. — 1957 *Just Jazz,* p. 15. The "rolling" bass was an attempt to recreate the sound of train wheels.

romp, *v.i.* [special applications of standard meaning (i.e., to play or frolic in a lively, boisterous way); according to jazzmen, current c. 1917–c. 1945, rare since]   To play jazz or dance (figuratively, see 1946 quot.) to jazz. — 1926 *Sugar Foot Stomp* (tune copyright by Melrose Music Publishers). When they start dancin'—Stompin' and prancin'—the dance called the sugar foot stomp. Let your doggies romp. — 1944 *Salute to Fats Waller* (Carnegie Hall program for April 2, 1944). "I'm telling you, we used to really 'romp.'" — 1946 *Really the Blues,* p. 73. Romance began to romp all over the Inn. — 1961 *Metronome,* Aug., p. 7. We entered as Stan was finishing a set with a romping "52nd Street Theme."

room, *n.* [special application of the standard term; prob. from comparative smallness of modern jazz clubs (i.e., "listening rooms" with no dance floors: cf. earlier *hall*); current since c. 1955]   A night club. — 1963 *Nugget,* Feb., p. 46. While not as cool [i.e., safe] as blowing jazz in some hip room, I find that monetary rewards are considerably better and more consistent in rolling people.

roost, *n.* [analogical extension of standard meaning; current c. 1945–c. 1955, rare since; see also CRIB, DOMMY, and esp. PAD]   See 1946 quot. — 1946 *Really the Blues,* p. 374. *roost:* home — 1958 *The Book of Negro Folklore,* p. 486. *roost:* crib, pad [both in jazz sense].

rubber, *n.* [synechdoche: the rubber of the tires = the automobile; current c. 1935–c. 1950, rare since; see also SHORT, WHEELS]   See quots. — 1944 *Dan Burley's Original Handbook of Harlem Jive,* p. 146. *rubber:* automobile. — 1946 *Really the Blues,* p. 374. *rubber:* automobile. — 1947 *Jive and Slang.* s.v. *rubber:* automobile.

rugcutter, rug cutter, *n.* [see 1942 quot. for etym.; current in its initial sense c. 1925–c. 1935, current in its modified sense c. 1935–c 1945, obs. since except historical]   See 1942 quot. — 1936 Cootie Williams and His Rug-Cutters (name of small performing jazz group). — 1938 *N.Y.*

Amsterdam News, 2 April, p. 17. "The thousands of . . . rugcutters . . . that are being hatched daily . . . are a peril." — 1941 *Strictly Ding-Dong,* p. 6. "I'm a rugcutter." — 1942 *American Mercury,* July, p. 96. *rugcutter:* originally a person frequenting house-rent parties [q.v.], cutting up the rugs of the host with his feet; a person too cheap or poor to patronize regular dance halls; now means a good dancer. — 1944 *Dan Burley's Original Handbook of Harlem Jive,* p. 95. Cop a trot, you rugcutters. — 1946 *Duke Ellington,* p. 181. "Rug Cutter" was one of Harlem's terms for a jitterbug, a technically skillful dancer, fast on his feet and "hip" (in the jazz or swing know).

run away, [standard phrase given special application; according to jazzman Eubie Blake, current since c. 1905] To move rhythmically, sometimes harmonically (see last quot.), ahead (of the other players). — 1955 *Hear Me Talkin to Ya,* p. 200. Most singers . . . they're either layin' back or else runnin away from you. — 1961 *The Jazz Review,* Jan., p. 7. Guitarist Freddie Greene, annoyed by Payne's tendency to rush the beat, kept a long stick on stand with which he poked the drummer when the beat began to run away. — 1961 *The Sound,* p. 38. "He's a helluva chord man, Red. Even you won't be able to run away from him there."

run down, [cf. entertainment slang *run through* (i.e., to rehearse) and standard phrase *run down* (i.e., to read through rapidly); current since c. 1935] To perform, usually in rehearsal, a piece of music, usually arranged (i.e., not improvised); also, for its rare noun form, see second 1959 quot. — 1948 *Down Beat,* 1 Dec., p. 10. We ran down three new instrumentals and a vocal for Baubles Buxon! — 1959 *Blow Up A Storm,* p. 19. I distributed the parts and we ran it down. — p. 31. "Okay. Let's give it a rundown. Once." — 1960 *The Jazz Review,* Nov., p. 12. When we rehearsed an arrangement that no

one had seen before, we'd run it down once or twice. —
1961 *The Sound*, p. 10. Bernie struck a rich chord and
began running the tune down in his immaculate post-
Teddy Wilson style.

running changes, [standard term *running* (i.e., successive)
+ jazz slang *changes;* some currency since c. 1920] A
sequence of key changes. — 1955 *Hear Me Talkin to Ya,*
p. 234. The Western style was more open . . . open
horns and running chords and running changes.

running wild [special application of general slang term
(i.e., acting with abandon); some currency c. 1920–c.
1940, obs. since] Playing music excitingly, skillfully and
uninhibitedly. — 1922 *Running Wild* (tune written by
A. Harrington Gibbs). — 1939 *Jazzmen*, p. 136. Louis,
"running wild," regularly tied the show at the Metropoli-
tan Theatre in a knot.

run the changes, See s.v. CHANGES.

rusty dusty [*dusty* prob. from *duster*, q.v., *rusty* a humorous
rhyming modifier; some currency, chiefly sustained by
the Count Basie recording (see 1942 quot.), c. 1940–c.
1945, obs. since] The buttocks. — 1942 *Harvard Blues*
(song recorded by Count Basie Orchestra, vocal sung by
Jimmy Rushing). Mama, get up off your big fat rusty
dusty. — 1945 *Rusty Dusty Blues* (tune composed by
J. Mayo Williams).

S

❬❬❬❬❬❬❬❬❬❬❬❬❬❬❬

salty, *adj.* [prob. by analogy with the brashness of seamen just come ashore; from Negro slang: cf. 1928 *The Walls of Jericho*, p. 304. *"salty dog:* stronger than *dog";* see also EVIL, WRONG] See 1938 and second 1946 quots. — 1938 *Cab Calloway: Hi De Ho,* p. 16. *salty:* angry, ill-tempered. — 1946 *Really the Blues,* p. 69. Ray and Fuzzy were salty with our unhip no-playing piano player. —p. 374. *salty:* sour, hostile, unpleasant. — 1952 *Who Walk in Darkness,* p. 67. "Why do you have to get so salty when people want to have fun?"

jump salty, [jazz slang *jump* (i.e., to be animated) + jazz slang *salty;* current since c. 1935] See 1946, 1962 quots. — 1938 *N.Y. Amsterdam News,* 26 Feb., p. 17. Let's sound a high C on the post office man whose Girl Friday is "jumpin' salty." — 1946 *Really the Blues,* p. 371. *jump salty:* turn sour or hostile. — 1962 *N.Y. Times Magazine,* 20 May, p. 45. *jump salty:* to become petulant, angry.

Sand, *n. & v.t.* [by analogy with standard meaning (i.e., to sand [a piece of wood]); orig. a c. 1900 Negro vaude-ville dance step; current c. 1938–c. 1945, rare since] A jazz dance step popular esp. in Harlem, c. 1938–c. 1945.

— 1946 *Really the Blues*, p. 230. And from the old folks'
shuffle to the Suzie Q and Sand, wasn't none of them
steps new to grandpa.

sassy, *adj.* [special application of the general colloquial
term; according to jazzmen, some currency esp. among
Negro jazzmen c. 1935–c. 1942, obs. since] Lively
(esp. as applied to musical performance). Oral evidence
only.

Satch, Satchmo, [see 1946 quot. for etym.; one of the five
or six indispensable ones of the many jazz nicknames
(see also Bird, Lady, Prez); current since c. 1925; see
also Pops] Louis Armstrong 1900–, trumpeter, generally
acclaimed by jazzmen and critics as one of the great
figures in jazz history. — 1937 *Metronome*, Jan., p. 25.
"Satchmo, I was only kiddin'. I'll give you your horn
back!" — 1942 *The American Thesaurus of Slang*, p. 557.
Satch: Louis Armstrong. — 1946 *Jazzways*, p. 29. It
wasn't long before hangers-on at the Lincoln Gardens
bandstand caught on to the fact that Louis answered to
"Satchelmouth." The trademark stuck, but it was shortened to "Satchmo," because that was easier to say. —
1955 *Hear Me Talkin to Ya*, p. 97. We called him Dipper-
mouth. Satchmo was unheard of then.

sax, *n.* [general colloquial term, but with esp. currency
among jazzmen since c. 1920; see also AX, HORN] A
saxophone (soprano, alto, tenor, or baritone); also, see
1942 quot. — 1926 *Melody Maker*, March, p. 4. Then, for
a certainty, you have heard some bad saxes! — 1937
Metronome, March, p. 31. Don't miss the sax figures in
the last chorus of *Bridge.* — 1942 *The American Thesaurus of Slang*, p. 556. *sax:* saxophonist.

sax section, [current since c. 1925] See quots. — 1937
American Speech, Feb., p. 48. In the *sax section* are
reed instruments. — 1942 *The American Thesaurus of
Slang*, p. 557. *sax section:* a division of a dance band's
instruments.

saying nothing (or **something**), [by analogy with verbal communication (see also TALK, TELL A STORY); some earlier use of *say* in a jazz sense: cf. 1955 *Hear Me Talkin to Ya*, p. 260. "From those evenings I know what he was trying to say"; nevertheless, widely current only since c. 1958] See first 1959 and 1960 quots. (*saying nothing* is, of course, the antithesis of *saying something*); also, for its nonparticipial form, see last 1961 quot. — 1959 *Jazz for Moderns*, p. 21. *saying something:* producing something of value: ("That cat is saying something!" This could pertain to a good musician, actor, driver, shoemaker, etc.). — 1959 *Jazz: A Quarterly of American Music*, Summer, p. 201. He'd say, "he ain't sayin' nothin'." — 1960 *The Jazz Titans*, p. 164. *saying something:* contributing something interesting in a musical solo or in any endeavor. — 1961 *The Jazz Review*, Jan., p. 6. Basie is also an admirer of Martin Luther King: "Like the cats would put it, he's *saying* something." — 1961 *Down Beat*, 5 Jan., p. 38. He spends too much time mumbling around, looking for something to say. — 1962 *Bird: The Legend of Charlie Parker*, p. 20. It seems that, when he first heard Charlie's music and expressed his opinion to Parker, he said, "You ain't sayin' nothin' on your horn."

scare, *v.t.* [reflecting jazzman's irreverence for conventional attitudes and modes of feeling (the implication here being that the listeners will be awakened to some terrible [hence, unsettling] aspects of their own natures and/or to the startling possibilities of beauty in the world); reinforced by the group of words which associates impact with negative attributes (i.e., *bad, mean, tough, terrible*); current since c. 1948] To impress, to excite, to startle delightfully (by playing music with originality and skill): see note above. — 1959 *Down Beat*, 5 March, p. 19. "When Nick settles down on his instrument and begins to find his own personality, he's

going to scare everybody to death." — 1960 *Playboy*,
Aug., p. 109. "I have almost always been able to predict
what Miles is going to play. Yet," the musician concedes,
"every once in a while, he does scare everybody." —
1961 *The Sound*, p. 141. "You gonna scare a lot of folks
now, man."

scarf, *n.*, *v.i.* & *v.t.* See s.v. SCOFF.

scat, scat-singing, scat-chorusing, *adj.* *n.* & *v.i.* [onomato-
poeic (i.e., *scat* was one of the more common nonsense
sounds made in the early practice of this form); see first
1955 and last quots. for further etym.; current since
c. 1926] See 1946 and last quots. — 1935 *Metronome*,
April, p. 54. Cab scats through this pair in his best Harlem manner. — 1935 *Stage*, Sep., p. 46. *scat-chorusing*:
a hot chorus, generally vocal. — 1946 *Harvard Dictionary
of Music*, p. 377. Negroes . . . produced an important
figure in the Negro trumpet virtuoso and "scat" singer
(i.e., interpolation of nonsense syllables and other peculiar vocal effects), Louis Armstrong. — 1955 *Hear Me
Talkin to Ya*, p. 108. And it's true about the scat-singing
story. That's really the way it started. Louis Armstrong
forgot the words and just sang sounds. — p. 109. Louis
forgot the lyrics and started scattin'. — 1956 *Chicago
Review*, Autumn-Winter, p. 13. The ultimate in pushing
the words away, of course, is "scat" or "bop" talk where
the singer produces familiar sounds which don't make
words at all. — 1956 *Guide to Jazz*. s.v. *scat*: doubletalk;
originally a succession of meaningless syllables sung to
fill in when a vocalist can't remember the lyrics of a
song, or simply "for the hell of it." Innovated acciden-
tally by L. Armstrong in 1926, but since c. 1945, it
has become an integral part of jazz, the voices on occasion duplicating the sound of an instrument or imitating instrumental phrasing, though the more traditional
jazz use of voice, singing song lyrics, has not been dis-
carded.

scene, (on) the, [standard term given special application, and reflecting perhaps the jazzman's sense of the playlike artificiality of life; some currency since c. 1925, but widely current only since c. 1945] See first 1959 quot. — 1926 *Melody Maker,* Sep., p. 61. Since "Nelly Kelly's Cabaret" came on the scene, it's put fresh kick into dancing. — 1946 *Jazzways,* p. 16. By 1907, Bolden had disappeared from the scene, confined to an insane asylum. — 1959 *Jazz for Moderns,* p. 21 *scene:* center of activity for musicians, where they play or gather. ("See anybody on the scene?") A superfluous word to describe further a person, place, thing or happening. ("Have eyes for the Chinese food scene?" Or: "Let's split [i.e., leave], man, I don't dig this scene."). — 1959 *Esquire,* Jan., p. 112. I listen to everybody I get a chance to hear, but there's not much new on the scene. — 1959 *The Holy Barbarians,* p. 40. "Something was happening on the poetry scene in Venice West." — 1960 *Hiparama of the Classics,* p. 7. Everytime India got a little extra Supply in the cupboard the Lion went ZOOM—snapped it up and swooped the scene [i.e., left]. — 1960 *Beat Jokes Bop Humor & Cool Cartoons,* p. 21. "I made [i.e., was a part of] the academic scene for just a week." — 1961 *Down Beat,* 16 Feb., p. 14. It is true that for years, the name George Russell meant little to anyone not closely associated with the jazz scene. — 1961 *Jazz Journal,* March, p. 16. "They were just trying out that recording scene in the nightclubs, then."

    bad scene, [current since c. 1955] See 1963 quot. — 1956 *Somewhere There's Music,* p. 179. "It was a bad scene." — 1963 *Hiptionary,* p. 18. *bad scenes:* places or situations fraught with danger.

    the scene is clean, [some currency c. 1948–c. 1955, very rare since] I have a job (i.e., in music). — 1955 *Say,* 28 April, p. 53. *is the scene clean?:* are you working?

scoff, scarf, *n., v.i. & v.t.* [cf. 1930 *American Tramp and Underworld Slang,* p. 165. "*scoff:* to eat. *scoff:* food . . . Orig. Scottish, 'scaff,' food of any kind, it became English nautical slang as 'scoff,' and the earliest written Am. use appears to be in Flynt's *Tramping with Tramps,* 1893 ('Scoff's always more plenty than money.')"; for earliest use of the verb, 1960 *American Speech,* Dec., p. 310, cites Chapter 15 of Herman Melville's *White Jacket* (1850): "Quick, men, quick; bear a hand and scoff away."; widely current among jazzmen since c. 1935; see also GREASE] See second 1944 and 1959 quots. — 1942 *American Mercury,* July, p. 88. "Talking about *me* with a beat chick scoffing a hot dog!" — 1944 *Dan Burley's Original Handbook of Harlem Jive,* p. 102. It's finer than the beans you scarf in the Navy! — p. 146. *scarf, scoff:* food, meat, dinner. — 1946 *Really the Blues,* p. 195. I scoffed back double helpings and yelled for more. — 1956 *It's Always Four O'Clock,* p. 43. What is Romanoff's? Just a place where you scoff. — 1959 *Newport Jazz Festival: 1959,* p. 46. *scarf:* to eat. — 1959 *Swinging Syllables.* s.v. *scoff:* eat.

score, *n. & v.i.* [by analogy with standard use of term in card playing and sports; from underworld slang: cf. 1938 *Dictionary of Slang and Unconventional English,* s.v. *score:* "to gain (a success)"; also cf. 1950 *Dictionary of American Underworld Lingo,* s.v. *score:* "anything secured by skill or craftiness"; current among jazzmen since c. 1935] As *v.i.:* to obtain something pleasurable or advantageous (most often, a woman, marijuana, or narcotics); as noun: that which is obtained or the source from which it is obtained. — 1952 *Flee the Angry Strangers,* p. 368. "Who's got [i.e., paying for] the next score, Harry Sticks? Nobody has any gold." — 1956 *It's Always Four O'Clock,* p. 8. Wishy-washy babes . . . don't know their own minds; I score big with them. —

1958 *Somewhere There's Music,* p. 19. So they went out
on the street and scored for some fair pot [i.e., mari-
juana] and came back. — 1960 *Beat Jokes Bop Humor &
Cool Cartoons,* p. 23. "I scored with an ancient apothe-
cary, and here it is." — 1961 *Down Beat,* 2 Feb., p. 17.
"When did you last score?" Dederich asked. — 1963
Nugget, Feb. p. 55. This score I met out here, he got me
that job.

scraunch, *n.* [etym. unknown; current c. 1915–c. 1930, obs.
since except historical though the dance survives under
other names; for synonymous names, see DRAG, MOOCH]
A slow, dragging dance (see note above). — 1943 *The
Jazz Record,* 15 April, p. 3. In 1917 . . . there were
several dances . . . resembling the rhumba or "scraunch."

scream, *n. & v.i.* [some currency since c. 1930] As *v.i.:* to
play a wind instrument (esp. a trumpet) in the upper
register and with great volume; as noun: the effect produced by such playing. — 1933 *Metronome,* Jan., p. 34.
A scream is produced somewhat the same way as the
rip, only in the rip the note is cut off shortly, but in the
scream it is held. — 1960 *Leisure,* Dec., pp. 40–41. If
you remember, the things people liked most about Benny
in the old days were the Gene Krupa solos, the screaming-type solos of Harry James. — 1961 *Palaver,* Feb.,
p. 14. Shavers screams, the Hawk honks, and only Bryant
and Duvivier show any real sense of proportion. — 1962
Jazz: A History of the New York Scene, p. 200. "Each
section answering the other in 'screams' (chords) was
the feature of 'Tiger Rag.' "

screamer, *n.* 1. [according to jazzmen, some currency since
c. 1935; see also FREAK LIP, IRON CHOPS] A trumpeter
who specializes in high notes. Oral evidence only.

2. [some currency esp. among white jazzmen since
c. 1940] An orchestration featuring the brass section,
usually very high in volume. — 1940 *Swing,* Nov., p. 28.
It's another riff tune . . . plus (or minus) a screamer

ending featuring the leader's horn. — 1948 *Down Beat,*
1 Dec., p. 13. *Minor* is a screamer but not without change
of pace.

scuffle, *n. & v.i.* [special application of the standard term
(i.e., to struggle or fight in rough confusion); current
among jazzmen since c. 1935] See 1939, first 1946, and
1959 quots.; also, by extension: any hardship. — 1939
American Jazz Music, pp. 172–173. At the bottom of the
economic pile are those musicians who have nothing
which could accurately be called a job but are taking
whatever one-night stand happens along; this is called
"scuffling." — 1946 *Really the Blues,* p. 280. Well, I
really had to scuffle for a while. — p. 374. *scuffle:* struggle to get along. — 1946 *Jazzways,* p. 26. Often the first
jobs were "scuffling"—any sort of work, just to keep
going. — 1958 *Somewhere There's Music,* p. 136. "Three's
a scuffle." — 1959 *Esquire,* Nov. p. 70J. *to scuffle:* to be
down and out. — 1960 *Jazz Street,* p. 33. Eddie Condon
scuffled through the streets and dives before he became
owner of his own club, now on New York's East Side. —
1962 *Bird: The Legend of Charlie Parker,* p. 19. All of a
sudden Bird started "52nd Street Theme," which is a
very fast tune. Jones was skuffling [sic] all the way
through, playing on instinct rather than ability.

second ending, [so called because it continues beyond the
restatement of the theme (which should then be the
first ending); current since c. 1925] That passage (after
the second eight bars) which leads into the bridge passage. — 1956 *Second Ending* (title of novel). — 1959
Blow Up a Storm, p. 9. "A lady gave it to me because she
liked my second endings."

second line, [cf. standard phrase *front line;* current since
c. 1900, though the practice largely ceased c. 1915]
See quots.; also, for its rare *v.i.* use, see 1954 quot. —
1939 *Jazzmen,* p. 27. The funerals and parades always
had a "second line" which consisted of the kids who

danced along behind. — 1954 *Satchmo,* p. 24. I was "second lining"—that is, following the brass bands in parades. — 1955 *Hear Me Talkin to Ya,* p. 30. I was a "second-line" kid. That meant I'd follow the big bands down the streets, and . . . carry their cases while they played. — 1955 *The First Book of Jazz,* pp. 30–31. Always following these marching bands on the streets would be a horde of children, dancing along, some playing on their own homemade instruments, keeping time with the music. These youngsters were called the "second line."

section, *n. & adj.* [special application of a standard term; current since c. 1925] See 1959 quot. — 1955 *A Pictorial History of Jazz,* p. 103. Those two men added were both saxophone players; the total of three, instead of a single clarinetist, made a "section." That of course is one of the key words, one of the fundamentals of big-band music. — 1959 *The Jazz Scene,* p. 9. *section:* coherent group of instruments in a band, e.g., the brass, reeds, rhythm. — 1961 *Jazz Monthly,* Feb., p. 17. Which one are you going to play section parts with?

see, *v.i.* [narrowing of general sense; current from c. 1930–c. 1945, rare since] See quot. — 1958 *Publication of the American Dialect Society,* Nov., p. 47. *see:* to read music.

   see around a corner, [by analogy with the difficulty and power of doing so; according to jazzmen, some currency c. 1935–c. 1945, rare since] To read music expertly. Oral evidence only.

send, *v.t.* [see 1959 quot. for an explanation of its semantic development; widely current c. 1933–c. 1948, rare since; see also GAS, KILL, KNOCK (ONE) OUT] See 1938, 1946 quots.; also, for a rare *v.i.* use, see 1935 quot. — 1935 *Vanity Fair,* Nov., p. 71. Hot artists or bands that can put across their licks successfully are *"senders"; they "send."*

— 1936 *Metronome,* Feb., p. 61. *send me:* inspire me. — 1938 *Cab Calloway: Hi De Ho,* p. 16. *send:* to arouse the emotions (joyful). — 1946 *Big Book of Swing,* p. 125. *send:* to move emotionally. — 1947 *Frontiers of Jazz,* p. 64. He has that rare quality of being able to send himself. — 1959 *Jazz: A Quarterly of Music,* Fall, p. 284. The power of musicians of skill to transport is verbalized in *send me.*

sender, *n.* [current c. 1934–c. 1944, obs. since; see also KILLER] A musician or, by extension, any person of excellence: see 1935, 1942 quots. — 1935 *Vanity Fair,* Nov., p. 71. Hot artists that can put across their licks [i.e., musical phrases] successfully are *"senders."* — 1937 *This Thing Called Swing,* p. 3. *senders:* a phrase that sets the boys off. Sometimes a reference to the man who starts the band swinging. — 1942 *American Mercury,* July, p. 96. *sender:* he or she who can get you to go, i.e., has what it takes. Used often as a compliment: "He's a solid sender!"

session, *n.* 1. See s.v. JAM SESSION.

2. [special application of standard meaning; current since c. 1940; see also DATE] See first 1959 quot. — 1940 *Swing,* Jan., p. 25. *Horn* is from an earlier session. — 1959 *The Jazz Scene,* p. 10. *session:* unit of time for recording (e.g. "on the next session six sides were cut"); more generally, any unit of time in which musicians play several pieces. — 1959 *Swinging Syllables.* s.v. *session:* a recording date.

set, *n.* 1. [special application of standard term; current since c. 1925] See 1956, 1959 quots.; also, since c. 1958, an LP record (since its time length is roughly equal to that of a night club set): see 1960, 1961 quots. — 1955 *Solo,* p. 159. Between sets at Fack's Jaeger found himself alone. — 1956 *Guide to Jazz.* s.v. *set:* twenty or thirty minute session in a night club after which the band rests.

Between sets either another group will play or the juke box is in operation or there is silence. — 1959 *The Jazz Scene*, p. 10. *set*: set of pieces played by musicians followed by a rest or by the end of the session. — 1960 *The Jazz Review*, May, p. 22. Everyone, even those who have had reservations about Coltrane, should hear this set. — 1961 *Down Beat*, 16 Feb., p. 36. The only real drag about this set is the fact that the pieces are stretched out far beyond the group's ability to do anything with them.

2. [prob. less from sense 1 than from the old underworld term *set up*: 1960 *Dictionary of American Slang*, s.v. *set up*: "to provide or give someone whisky or food . . . since c. 1870"; current esp. among Negro jazzmen since c. 1935] See quots. — 1959 *Newport Jazz Festival: 1959*, p. 46. *set*: a party. — 1962 *N.Y. Times Magazine*, 20 May, p. 45. *set*: an intimate party.

set-ending, *n.* [current since c. 1935] A short musical passage, usually of from four to sixteen bars, played at the end of a set—i.e., a short musical theme or signature. — 1958 *Somewhere There's Music*, p. 178. They blew a set-ending.

set up, [shortened form of standard phrase (i.e., to set up the music stand, chairs, etc.); according to jazzmen, current since c. 1900] To get things in readiness for a band that is about to perform (see note). — 1959 *The Horn*, p. 128. "Here, dad, have a brew while I get these boys set up." — 1961 *Metronome*, April, p. 14. Milt Hinton was snapping pictures, and Gene Krupa was setting up.

shades, *n. pl.* [by analogy with the function (i.e., to keep the sun out); current since c. 1950; see also BEBOP GLASSES] See first quot. — 1958 *American Speech*, Oct., p. 225. *shades*: dark glasses. — 1958 *Nugget*, Oct., p. 51. "I been thinkin' about these shades (dark glasses), man. Believe I'll get me a pair of contact shades." —

1960 *The Village Voice*, 13 Jan., p. 13. "One cat comes in, he's got good, dark shades on."

shag, *n.* 1. [cf. 1890 *A Dictionary of Slang, Jargon, and Cant*, s.v. *shag:* "From provincial shake"; also cf. 1937 *A Dictionary of Slang and Unconventional English*, s.v. *shag:* "a copulation . . . *v.t.* To coit (with a woman)"; some currency c. 1900–c. 1917, obs. since except historical] A crude, earthy type of blues c. 1900–c. 1917 (see quot.). — 1939 *Jazzmen*, p. 30. Then there were always the blues, some, such as "the shags," of the meanest sort.

2. [relation, if any, to sense 1 unknown; current c. 1937–c. 1940, obs. since except historical] See 1954 quot. — 1938 *N.Y. Amsterdam News*, 26 Feb., p. 17. Let's do the Shag in broad daylight so all can see. — 1939 *Fortune*, July, p. 170. The nightly fifty-cent ecstasy of shag and stomp at the Savoy. — 1939 *Jazzmen*, p. 197. In spite of being lame, he could probably win a "shag" contest. — 1954 *Down Memory Lane*, p. 131. The shag is a fast, nervous, hopping dance, performed in time to a strongly accentuated rhythm. — 1955 *Hear Me Talkin to Ya*, p. 266. The jitterbugs are cooling off, and the shag is no more.

shake, *n. & adj.* [from the vibratolike shakiness of the sound; cf. its standard musical sense (i.e., trill); current among jazzmen in an altered sense since c. 1925] See 1956 quot. — 1933 *Metronome* Jan., p. 34. The glissando and the shake may be used in either hot or sweet arrangements. — 1956 *Guide to Jazz*. s.v. *shake:* a note executed with particularly pronounced vibrato, almost a trill, esp. by trumpets and trombones, particularly to link one chorus to another or at the beginning of a phrase. — 1959 *Jazz: A Quarterly of American Music*, Summer, p. 263. She helps to recreate . . . an altissimo "shake" finale riff. — 1961 *The Feeling of Jazz*, p. 20. I been diggin' that boogie-woogie, with them poundin' eight beats to the bar in the left hand and the tremolo and the shakes . . . with their right hand.

shake, *v.i. & n.* [from body-shaking movements of the dance; according to jazzman Eubie Blake, current c. 1900–c. 1930, obs. since except historical]   A jazz dance popular c. 1900–c. 1930; as *v.i.*: to dance the shake; also, as adjective, applied to the music (see 1935 quot.) to which the shake was danced, a sensual Oriental style of jazz. — 1923 *Sobbin' Blues* (song copyright by Melrose Music Publishers). It sure has got 'em shakin' down in Dixieland. — 1935 *Vanity Fair,* Nov., p. 71. Negro bands play *"race music"* (a curious euphemism spread by phonograph companies), and the savagery of their rhythm calls forth the terms *"shake music"* and *"jungle music."* — 1940 *Jelly Roll Morton's New Orleans Memories,* p. 8. Visitors would propose that one of the girls dance in the nude, or wearing merely stockings and shoes, and the dance—also called "The Shake"—was done on a piece of board about three feet square. — 1956 *Lady Sings the Blues,* p. 51. They came to the Cotton Club—a place Negroes never saw inside unless they played music or did the shakes or shimmies.

shake it, shake that thing, shake 'em out, [see 1927 quot. for explanation of semantic development; according to jazzmen, current c. 1917–c. 1935, rare since]   To dance: frequently hortatory. — 1926 *Nigger Heaven,* p. 249. Shake 'em out! went the cry. — 1926 *Shake That Thing* (tune recorded on Brunswick-Cliftophone 3069). — 1927 *The Journal of Abnormal and Social Psychology,* April-June, p. 16. "Shake it," "shake that thing" . . . Ostensibly they refer to dancing, but they are really Negro vulgar expressions relating to coitus. — 1948 *The Record Changer,* June, p. 6. On records of the 1920's, one way to loosen things up before rigor mortis sets in completely might be to get out on the floor and "shake that thing." —

1961 *The Jazz Review*, Jan., p. 24. The crowd is stamping their feet and hollering, "shake that thing."

shake (oneself) apart, [hyperbole; according to jazzmen, some currency c. 1917–c. 1940, very rare since] To dance, laugh or cry heartily. — 1956 *Lady Sings the Blues*, p. 179. When we got to her car she wheeled around the corner, then stopped and began to shake herself apart.

shake up, *v.t.* [by analogy with the physical act; current since c. 1953] To unsettle, to profoundly trouble (note: past participle is always *shook*, never *shaken*, frequently without *up*: see 1955 quot.). — 1955 *American Speech*, Dec., p. 304. *shook*: emotionally upset. — 1957 *Down Beat*, 17 Oct., p. 33. That kind of shook me up. — 1958 *Jive in Hi-Fi*, p. 27. [*I'm all*] *shook up*: you can't seem to cope with it. — 1958 *Somewhere There's Music*, p. 69. "It would shake Sam up . . . I started blowing full time." — 1959 *San Francisco Chronicle*, 4 June, p. 35. "It might shake up the whole joint and probably lower the real estate values." — 1960 *The Village Voice*, 20 Jan., p. 2. "Come on, Norman, say something," Glick exhorted. "Shake up the squares."

shaking, *participle* [by analogy of movement with life; current since c. 1953; see also HAPPENING] Happening, esp., of importance. — 1958 *Jazz in Hi-Fi*, p. 13. They understand what's shaking. — 1959 *San Francisco Chronicle*, 4 June, p. 35. "Okay," I said, "hip me to [i.e., tell me] what's shakin'." — 1961 *Down Beat*, 13 April, p. 50. There's *something* shakin' in that town—even if it ain't Dixieland.

sharp, *adj.* [poss. from connotation of incisiveness, or poss. from *sharper* (i.e., dishonest gambler), but stressing the sense of shrewdness and minimizing the sense of dishonesty; cf. general and teenage slang *sharpie* (i.e., one who is well-groomed and flashily attired) which derives from this term; current among jazzmen c. 1925–

c. 1945, somewhat less since; see also DAP, FLY, HIP]
Sophisticated, as reflected by wit or attire, or both: see
first six quots. — 1928 *The Walls of Jericho*, p. 305.
sharp: striking; "keen." A beautifully dressed woman is
"*sharp out of this world.*" —1938 *Better English*, Nov.,
p. 151. *sharp:* neat and tricky, high class dame, a looker.
—1946 *Really the Blues*, p. 374. *sharp:* alert, dressed
well, keen-witted. — 1952 *A History of Jazz in America*,
p. 353. *sharp:* hip [jazz sense]. — 1955 *The Encyclopedia of Jazz*, p. 347. *sharp:* smart. — 1955 *Solo*, p. 256.
"Five chicks and sharp cats . . . getting ready to juice."
— 1956 *Sideman*, p. 243. "You're a pret-ty sharp cat,
aren't you?" — 1957 *On the Road*, p. 61. He liked to dress
sharp. — 1959 *The Holy Barbarians*, p. 137. Their clothes
were sharp.

shimmy, shimme-sha-wabble, shim-sham-shimmy, *n. & v.i.*
[see 1927 quot. for etym.; see 1917, 1959 quots. for
beginning date; obs. since c. 1935 except historical] See
1939, 1959 quots.; as *v.i.,* to do the dance. — 1917
Variety, 30 Nov. The opening number was programmed
as a combination of "Strutters' Ball," "Shimme-Sha-
Wabble," and "Walking the Dog." — 1919 *I Wish I
Could Shimmy Like My Sister Kate* (song). — 1927
The Journal of Abnormal and Social Psychology, April-
June, p. 16*n*. A note on "shake the shimmy" . . . Che-
mise is pronounced "shimmy" by most Negroes and a
great many whites in the South. In its original meaning
it described the effect produced when a woman made a
movement or did a dance step which caused her breasts
to shake. This caused her "shimmy" to shake. — 1938
Cab Calloway: Hi De Ho, p. 16. *shim-sham-shimmy:* a
dance introduced at the Cotton Club. — 1939 *American
Jazz Music*, p. 109. "Shimmy" dancing—shoulder-and-
body shaking— . . . started soon after the "jazz" fad.
— 1959 *Jazz: A Quarterly of American Music*, Fall, pp.
284–285. The *shimmy* was introduced about the end of

World War I. In the Zeigfield Follies of 1919 vocalists proclaimed that "The World Is Going Shimmy Mad" and "You Can't Shake Your Shimmy on Tea." Ameliorated and no longer a sensation the Shim-Sham-Shimmy was introduced at the Cotton Club in 1930.

shit, n. 1. (occasionally, esp. when used in an exclamatory or other emphatic sense, the vowel is lengthened: see last quot.), [scatological analogy in general slang use, but with esp. currency among jazzmen in certain related senses since c. 1900] Stuff (i.e., in the sense either of essence or of nonsense)—frequently, music (concerning which the connotation can be favorable or unfavorable). — 1956 Eddie Condon's Treasury of Jazz, pp. 238–239. Trumpeter Howard McGhee once said, "Whoever the musician is who plays with him, he feels he's playing shit next to what Bird is putting down [i.e., performing]." — 1959 Jazz: A Quarterly of American Music, Fall, p. 294. Cats stand on the corner and talk that shit. — 1960 Jazz: A Quarterly of American Music, Winter, p. 38. "Look, man, if you don't think I can play your shit, you get somebody you think can!" — 1961 The Sound, p. 159. "Why, man, they got cats—the organization that bust people's arms and mash up your teeth, rough shit like that." — 1961 Night Song, p. 89. "Tell me about jazz and American art and how us niggers did it. Sheeeeeeeeeet!"

2. [special application of sense 1; some currency among jazzmen since c. 1935; see also BOO, GAGE, POT, TEA] Marijuana or narcotics. — 1950 Neurotica, Autumn, p. 45. "Senor, this shit is the end [i.e., marvelous]!" — 1956 Sideman, p. 282. "You oughta smoke some shit." — 1958 Southern Folklore Quarterly, Sep., p. 132. Usually "junk" and "shit" also mean heroin. — 1959 The Naked Lunch, pp. 65–66. Eukodol is like a combination of junk and C [i.e., cocaine]. Trust the Germans to concoct some really evil shit.

shootin' the agate, [semantic development unknown; according to jazzmen, current c. 1900–c. 1917, obs. since except historical] A dancelike walk popular in New Orleans and Memphis street parades c. 1900–c. 1917: see quot. — 1948 *The Record Changer,* June, p. 10. He would walk with a cake walkish strut and "drive them chicks wild." This was called "shootin' the agate."

short, *n.* [poss. because it was considered the shortest way to get places; current since c. 1945; see also RUBBER, WHEELS] See 1955 quot. — 1955 *American Speech,* Dec., p. 305. *short:* automobile. — 1958 *Somewhere There's Music,* p. 39. "Fine short, but dirty. Let's wash it this weekend." — 1960 *Down Beat,* 7 Jan., p. 26. Then when they get there, a corny gig, a cup of coffee, back in the short and on from Roanoke to Tabor City, N.C.

shout, *n., adj., v.i., & v.t.* [See second 1939, 1950, 1956 quots. for explanation of semantic development; current in various jazz senses since c. 1920] See first 1955 and 1956 quots.; initially, where the music was sung and played (see 1928 quot.): obs. — 1928 *The Walls of Jericho,* p. 305. *shout:* ball; prom. — 1939 *Blues* (Decca Records pamphlet), p. 3. The Fourth chorus is virtually a "shout" vocal with the fire and gusto of a real spiritual. — 1939 *American Jazz Music,* pp. 46–47. An example is the "shouting" of the brass choir with "Count" Basie's piano solo in *Sent For You Yesterday.* — 1950 *They All Played Ragtime,* p. 188. "The true 'shout' takes place on Sundays or on 'praise' nights through the week." — 1955 *A Pictorial History of Jazz,* p. 127. Stomping variations of rags, known as "shouts," were the show-pieces most often used in competition; they were ideally suited to be heard over the normal rent party din. — 1955 *Hear Me Talkin to Ya,* p. 43. And he could shout a tune. — 1956 *Guide to Jazz.* s.v. *shout:* a style of singing the blues in a penetrating, shouting tone, usually in the spirit of gospel-singing. "James P. Johnson and Fats Waller are 'shout pianists' and Tommy Ladnier a 'shout trumpet.'" — 1957 *Giants of Jazz,* p. 25. "Listen to 'im play that 'Panama.' What a punch! Nobody can shout a tune like Papa Joe!" — 1961 *Down Beat,* 13 April, p. 43. He . . . is great. He just shouts all the time.

shouter, *n.* [current since c. 1925] One who sings the blues in shout style (see 1956 quot. s.v. SHOUT). — 1955 *Hear Me Talkin to Ya,* p. 245. She was certainly recognized among blues singers—a shouter, they called her.

shuck, *n., v.i. & v.t.* [poss. originated as a euphemism for *shit,* or from the general colloquial *shucks* (i.e., something valueless); some currency esp. in the Midwest and on the West Coast; see also JIVE] See last 1959 quot. (note: the quality of insincerity is common to all uses of the word). — 1958 *Somewhere There's Music,* p. 91. "Mike shucked it up so much that Guy Lombardo might have liked it." — p. 163 "I know about double negative too, but that's a lot of shuck." — 1959 *Diggeth Thou?,* p. 40. The spielers were shucking some hard jive from back. — 1959 *The Holy Barbarians,* p. 25. "I didn't shuck the customers enough to please the crook who was running the car lot." — 317. *shuck:* as a noun, a falsehood, deception, fraud; as a verb, to deceive, swindle, or defraud. — 1961 *Down Beat,* 5 Jan., p. 16. "If I put some of my music in front of them they're shucking and jivin'."

shuffle, *adj. & n.* [see 1956 quot. for explanation of semantic development; current since c. 1917] See 1940, 1949, 1956 quots. — 1925 *River Boat Shuffle* (tune composed by Hoagy Carmichael, Irving Mills and Dick Voynow). — 1940 *Swing,* June, p. 13. The typifying characteristic of the Savitt band is its "shuffle rhythm," which is distinguished . . . by its . . . 4/4 jazz time. It gets its shuffle from the piano's push in the treble. — 1949 *Music Library Association Notes,* Dec., p. 51. *shuffle rhythm:* mode of playing a popular song, which involves breaking each measure into eighth notes. Four eighth notes in treble of piano follow successively the four eighth notes in bass, which moves step-wise or in arpeggio form. Rhythm is adaptable for orchestra as well as piano, and is used effectively with certain songs. — 1955 *Hear Me Talkin to Ya*, p. 21. They played the shuffle beat on the snare drum. — 1956 *Guide to Jazz.* s.v. *shuffle:* a dance created in the South, later applied to a boogie-woogie type rhythm, slow and strongly syncopated. — 1961 *The Jazz Review*, Jan., p. 31. Someone told you about Jonah Jones and shuffle rhythm.

side, *n.* [from the usual pre-1948 practice of recording one piece of music per side of a record; widely current c. 1930–c. 1950, somewhat less current since: see the more recent TRACK] See 1959 quot. — 1937 *Metronome*, March, p. 31. It's the wonder that Victor is issuing so many sides by this band. — 1949 *Down Beat*, 28 Jan., p. 14. With Herman sides being dished out in such small quantities, it is more than depressing to run up against such an unexciting side. — 1959 *The Jazz Scene*, p. 10. *side:* side of an old 78 rpm. record. — 1961 *Down Beat*, 19 Jan., p. 40. Four sides. LP? That came later, and you didn't say "track" then.

sideman, *n.* [cf. general slang *front* (*man*): i.e., leader; current since c. 1930] See 1942 quot. — 1937 *American Speech*, Feb., p. 48. *side-man:* a musician who is not featured. — 1942 *The American Thesaurus of Slang*, p. 555. *side man:* any musician in the band except the leader. — 1959 *The Horn*, p. 34. He . . . was a good, disciplined sideman. — 1961 *Jazz Street*, p. 14. There are sidemen as well as leaders in this book.

sing, *v.i.* [vocalic analogy; some slight currency since c. 1925] See 1939 quot. — 1939 *American Jazz Music*, p. 44. The jazz players "sang" with their instruments, played them with personal, expressive inflections variable between robust roughness and pure, bodiless lyricism. —

1947 *Frontiers of Jazz,* p. 167. "He doesn't make it sing like Bix." — 1963 *Down Beat,* 15 Aug., p. 32. Jefferson's creamy, sentimental alto [saxophone] . . . has [its] own way of "singing."

single, *n.* 1. [chiefly entertainment trade (i.e., night clubs and booking agencies) slang, but with some currency among jazzmen since c. 1935] A performer working alone—usually, a singer with only piano accompaniment or a pianist. — 1938 *The American Language,* p. 585. "Why don't you air her and do a single?" — 1957 *Down Beat,* 11 July, p. 19. "Personally, I like playing as a single." — 1961 *Metronome,* April, p. 46. Red Allen . . . has disbanded his group and is working as a single.

2. [chiefly recording trade slang, but with some currency among jazzmen since c. 1935] Initially: a single 78 rpm record (as distinguished from an album containing a set of records); since c. 1950: a 45 rpm record (as distinguished from a 33 rpm LP; in this sense, oral evidence only). — 1940 *Mademoiselle,* June, p. 131. The best single of the month is Barney Bigard's *Lost in Two Flats.*

single-line, single line, [current since c. 1935] Of music, played in a sequence or pattern of single notes (as distinguished from chords). — 1958 *Lennie Tristano* (liner notes on LP album Atlantic 1224). In *These Foolish Things,* it is the splendidly long line that Lee plays, Lennie's reflective musing, now single-line, now in block chords, and a finish together that puts a glistening coda on both their backs. — 1960 *The Jazz Review,* June, p. 23. The fast right-hand single lines are similar.

single-string, single-note, *adj.* [standard musical term, but with esp. currency among jazzmen as a distinguishing term since the innovations of Charlie Christian c. 1940, which had the effect of re-establishing the guitar as a solo instrument instead of merely an accompanying one] See 1942, 1949 quots. — 1942 *The American Thesaurus* *of Slang,* p. 562. *single-string work:* picking melodies on the guitar in adding to rhythmic chords. — 1949 *Inside Be-Bop,* p. 6. The single-note solo style was a complete departure from the pattern of solos in chords established by Carl Kress, Dick McDonough and the other conventional jazz guitarists. — 1959 *Jazz* (Hentoff & McCarthy), p. 289. He might speak of . . . Christian's "single-string" technique.

sit in [prob. by analogy with card playing slang; also cf. 1934 *A Dictionary of American Slang,* p. 394. *"sit in:* to take part; to be present"; widely current since c. 1930] See 1936, 1937, 1942 quots. — 1936 *Delineator,* Nov., p. 49. *sitting in:* when an outside musician drops in by invitation to play with a swing band or group. — 1937 *This Thing Called Swing,* p. 9. *sitting in:* playing by invitation with a band of which the musician is not a member. Also joining in a jam session. — 1937 *American Speech,* Oct., p. 184. *sit in:* to take a few licks [jazz slang sense] with another band . . . without pay. — 1942 *The American Thesaurus of Slang,* p. 566. *sit in:* of an outside musician, to drop in by invitation to play with "swing" band or group without pay. — 1959 *Somewhere There's Music,* p. 57. "Why not sit in a set or two." — 1959 *The Horn,* p. 6. Edgar Pool had been inveigled to sit in with the house group.

sixteens, the, [according to jazzman Eubie Blake, some currency c. 1900–c. 1917, obs. since except historical] A pianistic device of rolling sixteenth notes in the bass (quot. is, therefore, inaccurate). — 1957 *Just Jazz,* p. 13. At the turn of the century, they called it [i.e., boogie-woogie] . . . "honky tonk" . . . "rolling bass" . . . or "the sixteens."

skiffle (band), [etym. unknown; according to jazzman Eubie Blake, current c. 1900–c. 1914, obs. since except historical] A band c. 1900–c. 1914 consisting primarily of rhythm instruments and playing in a shuffle rhythm

style; for a rare adjective form, see 1961 quot. — 1957
Sing Out!, Spring, p. 30. In the first decade of the 20th
Century, these New Orleans boys called themselves a
"Skiffle" band. — 1961 *The Jazz Review*, Jan., p. 26. This
recording seems to recreate the skifflish sounds of The
Mound City Blues Blowers and similar groups.

skin, give (or **slip**) (**one**) **some,** [synechdoche; current
c. 1938–c. 1948, rare since]   Slap the palm of my hand
with the palm of yours (or vice versa) as a greeting or
farewell or because one of us approves of what the
other just said or did (see 1939, 1944, 1946 quots.). —
1939 *Jitterbug Jamboree Song Book*, p. 33. *slip me some
skin:* congratulate me. — 1942 *American Mercury*, July,
p. 86. "Gimme some skin!" — 1944 *The New Cab Calloway's Hepsters Dictionary.* s.v. *gimme some skin:*
shake hands. — 1946 *Big Book of Swing*, p. 125. *skin:*
handshake. — 1955 *Bop Fables*, p. 38. "Baby," he said,
grinning affably, "gimme some skin." —1962 *Down Beat*,
19 July, p. 49. The French horn player tries some very
adventurous things, and . . . that's a hard instrument
. . . so I've got to give him skin for it.

skins, *n. pl.* [synechdoche; current since c. 1925; see also
HIDES, TUBS]   See 1942 quot. — 1926 *Melody Maker*,
March, p. 32. The Skin Game (title of column on drumming instruction). — 1942 *The American Thesaurus of
Slang*, p. 559. *skins:* drums. — 1944 *Dan Burley's Original Handbook of Harlem Jive*, p. 147. *skins:* drums. —
1952 *Music Out of Dixie*, p. 161. "He kin sure work them
skins." — 1959 *Holiday for Skins* (title of LP album
Blue Note 4004).

skin-beater, *n.* [from *skins;* some currency c. 1935–c. 1945,
very rare since; see also HIDE BEATER]   See 1937 quot. —
1937 *This Thing Called Swing*, p. 9. *skin-beater:* drummer. — 1940 *Swing*, Jan., p. 11. How about a bit of
Drummer Krupa and the other good "skin-beaters"! —
1943 *A Curtain of Green*, p. 257. "Where that skin

beater?"—wanting drums. — 1944 *Dan Burley's Original Handbook of Harlem Jive*, p. 147. *skin-beater*: drummer.

sky (piece), [from its lofty position on the head; some currency since c. 1935]   See 1944 quot. — 1944 *The New Cab Calloway's Hepsters Dictionary*. s.v. *sky piece*: hat. — 1957 *N.Y. Times Magazine*, 18 Aug., p. 26. *sky*: a hat. — 1958 *American Speech*, Oct., p. 224. The cat . . . dons his . . . *skypiece*. — 1963 *Hiptionary*, p. 78. The hang up [i.e., predicament] is a tight sky crushing our konks [i.e., heads].

slam, slammer, *n*. [metonymy: by association with the banging shut of the door(s); see 1946 quot. for longer form which is the key to semantic development; also see last quot. for orig. source and dates]   For an occasional sense, see 1944 quot.; for the usual sense, see 1959 quot. — 1944 *The New Cab Calloway's Hepsters Dictionary*. s.v. *twister to the slammer*: the key to the door. — 1946 *Really the Blues*, p. 371. *house of many slammers*: jail. — 1952 *Flee the Angry Strangers*, p. 358. "I'm hip what you was doin wit Ange while I was in the slammer." — 1959 *The Holy Barbarians*, p. 318. *slam, slammer*: jail. — 1960 *Dictionary of American Slang*. s.v. *slammer*: a door. Jive use c. 1935 . . . Old underworld use.

slap, *v.i. & v.t.* [see 1956 quot. for key to semantic development; according to jazzmen, *slap* has been current since c. 1915, coupled with *doghouse*, q.v., since c. 1922]   See 1934, 1956, 1959 quots. — 1931 *Melody Maker*, Dec., p. 1029. Slapping, too, becomes next to impossible with a high bridge. — 1934 *A Dictionary of American Slang*, p. 171. *slap the dog house*: to pluck the strings of a bass viol. — 1936 *Esquire*, June, p. 131. What type of people get a thrill out of an orchestra that knows its way to town, out of listening to an expert bass player like Wellman Braud "slap the doghouse." — 1956 *Guide to Jazz*. s.v. *slap*: pluck (the bass string so that it hits against the neck of the bass producing a slapping effect). —

1959 *The Jazz Scene,* p. 289. *slapping:* pizzicato playing.

slap-tongue, *v.i. & adj.* [some currency since c. 1925]   See 1942 quot. (for its adjective use, see 1963 quot.); also, *v.t.:* oral evidence only. — 1942 *Amerian Thesaurus of Slang,* p. 563. *slap-tongue:* to strike the tongue against the mouthpiece. — 1963 *Down Beat,* 3 Jan., p. 20. Even his first solo with Henderson, a clownlike, slap-tongue effort, presaged important things to come.

slave, *v.i. & n.* [special application of standard term; widely current c. 1935–c. 1945, somewhat less since; see also DAY GIG, HAME]   To work (*not* in music): see 1938 quot.; as noun: a job outside the jazz world. — 1938 *Cab Calloway: Hi De Ho,* p. 16. *slave:* to work, whether arduous labor or not. — 1944 *Dan Burley's Original Handbook of Harlem Jive,* p. 147. *slave:* to work. — 1944 *Esquire,* June, p. 170. *knock a slave:* get a job. — 1958 *Jive in Hi-Fi,* p. 15. *to collar a slave:* to get a job.

slide, *n.* [from sliding effect produced by it; according to jazzmen, some currency since c. 1925; see also GLISS, SMEAR]   See 1959 quot. — 1959 *The Jazz Scene,* p. 289. *slide:* glissando. — 1961 *The Feeling of Jazz,* p. 29. They're too involved with making sensuous sounds with all those vibratos and slides and slurs.

sliphorn, slip-horn, *n.* [from slipping movement of the slide part of trombone; according to jazzman Eubie Blake, some currency c. 1900–c. 1945, very rare since except to distinguish the slide trombone from the valve trombone (see 1957 quot.); see also BONE, TRAM]   See 1925 quot. — 1925 *English Words & Their Background,* p. 45. *sliphorn:* trombone. — 1956 *Sideman,* p. 198. "Message here for 'Tex the sliphorn player!'" — 1957 *Melody Maker,* 4 May, p. 6. Wilbur himself was somewhat subdued, using both sliphorn and valve, but what he did was pleasant trombone. — 1958 *Where He Went,* p. 53. I've never heard a trombone called a "slip-horn."

slow drag, See s.v. DRAG.

slush pump, *n.* [prob. from the great amount of spittle that collects in the slide part; some currency (see last quot.) esp. among white jazzmen c. 1935–c. 1945, obs. since except historical; see also BONE, SLIPHORN, TRAM] See 1942 quot. — 1942 *The American Thesaurus of Slang,* p. 559. *slush pump:* trombone. — 1943 *Barefoot Boy with Cheek,* p. 90. "Awful fine slush pump . . . you ought to dig that." — 1960 *Dictionary of American Slang.* s.v. *slush pump:* trombone. Some jazz use, mostly synthetic c. 1935.

small bread, See s.v. BREAD.

smear, *n.* [from the extending or spreading of the sound produced; current since c. 1925; see also GLISS, SLIDE] See 1959 quot. — 1933 *Metronome,* Jan., p. 34. A smear is produced by first playing a tone a trifle flat. — 1944 *New Yorker,* 1 July, p. 29. "Someone may advocate extending a note or cutting it off. The sax section may want to put an additional smear on it." — 1958 *N.Y. Daily News,* 4 March. Yet, says Father O'Connor, "a conviction has gotten around that a jazz theme supports and girds a seamy tale of human failure, moral or physical. A muted trumpet, a breathy sax, a high trombone smear— these express (in media such as movies and TV) that human area in which a will decides to commit a wrong, a sin, to misuse a freedom." — 1959 *The Jazz Scene,* p. 289. *smear:* glissando.

smoke 'em out (or **on 'em**), [by analogy of excitement with heat (see also BURN, COOK); according to jazzmen, current since c. 1952] To play music excitingly, pulsatingly. Oral evidence only.

snake hips, [from common practice of designating jazz dances by reference to animal movements or parts of the body (see also BUNNY HUG, CAMEL WALK, FOX-TROT, TURKEY TROT); some currency esp. in New York City and Baltimore c. 1915–c. 1930, obs. since except historical] Jazz dance in vogue c. 1915–c. 1930 esp. in New

York City and Baltimore. — 1931 *Snake Hips* (tune recorded by the Blue Rhythm Boys). — 1934 *Beale Street:
Where the Blues Began,* p. 105. In the golden days of
1912 . . . brown beauties . . . danced the Pasamala,
long before the "cootie crawl," "black bottom" and "snake
hips" were thought of.

sock chorus, [see 1936 quot. for key to its semantic development (i.e., it is the last chorus that generally receives the heaviest emphasis); according to jazzmen,
current c. 1920–c. 1945, rare since]   See first two quots.
(note: phrase generally applies to pre-1945 jazz) —
1936 *Delineator,* Nov., p. 49. *sock chorus:* last chorus of
an arrangement. — 1937 *This Thing Called Swing,* p. 9.
sock: emphasis, usually referring to the last chorus. —
1937 *Metronome,* March, p. 31. The full sock chorus of
the reverse hits you between the eyes. — 1956 *Second
Ending,* p. 57. They rode into the sock chorus like a
storm cloud of marauders.

sock cymbal, [so called because in much pre-1945 jazz it
was the vehicle of the heaviest accents; current since c.
1920]   A fairly large single cymbal. — 1936 *Metronome,*
Feb., p. 61. *off beat cymbal:* sock cymbal. — 1944 *Met-
tonome,* July, p. 31. "Dizzy has a phobia about drummers
who play sock cymbals," reports drummer Jackie Mills.
— 1953 *Night Light,* p. 130. Problems were posed . . .
between one clap of the sock cymbal and the next. —
1959 *Jazz: A Quarterly of American Music,* Fall, p. 275
Suspended cymbals are used very little, most often only
at the end of a piece, "sock" or "hi-hat" cymbals are not
used at all.

sock it (out), [from the sense of giving a heavy accent;
some currency c. 1916–c. 1945, very rare since]   See
1933, 1935 quots.: frequently hortatory (see 1955 quot.).
— 1927 *Melody Maker,* July, p. 697. Sock out your last
chorus on that, my friends. — 1933 *Fortune,* Aug., p. 47.
Returning to Trombonist Brown, he can get off, *swing it,*

sock it . . . (all of which mean syncopate to beat the band). — 1935 *Vanity Fair*, Nov., p. 71. Hot artists or bands that can put across their licks [i.e., musical phrases] successfully . . . can "sock it." — 1939 *Jazzmen*, p. 12. Bolden was "socking it out." — 1955 *Hear Me Talkin to Ya*, p. 81. "Blow it, kid. Sock it out."

sock rhythm (or **style**), [from the pronounced rhythmic accents; some currency c. 1920–c. 1945, obs. since except historical] See 1942 quot.: also, that style of playing. — 1934 *A Dictionary of American Slang*, p. 171. *sock rhythm:* rhythm that enables special use of drums, tuba, or piano. — 1939 *Jazzmen*, p. 50. He had what might be described as a "sock" style, "blowing in" phrases with little bursts of sound and riding the melody. — 1942 *The American Thesaurus of Slang*, p. 560. *sock rhythm:* an emphasized syncopated rhythm.

solid, *adj. & adv.* [see 1954 quot. for prob. semantic origin; according to jazzmen, Louis Armstrong was the first to habitually use the term in a jazz sense c. 1920; widely current c. 1935–c. 1945, very rare since; see also CRAZY, GROOVY] See 1938, 1954, 1960 quots. — 1928 *Melody Maker*, Dec., (insert). He is a complete master, and a "solid" man. A great artist on the cymbal. — 1938 *Cab Calloway: Hi De Ho*, p. 16. *solid:* great, swell, okay. — 1938 *Metronome*, June, p. 40. I'd like to put in my own little, personal plug for that really solid man . . . Ray McKinley. — 1938 *American Speech*, Dec., p. 314. *solid:* extremely, to the nth degree. — 1953 *Night Light*, p. 137. "That's all there is to it. Solid?" — 1954 *Social Forces*, Dec., p. 179. Because of the importance of solid rhythm, the term "solid" came to be applied to anything good or desirable or approved by the jazzman. — 1956 *Chicago Review*, Autumn-Winter, pp. 14–15. Appearing suddenly in the song, "Soli-tudy," with its echo of "solid" . . . makes fun of the degraded pseudo-jazz lyrics of a period when everything was "solid." — 1960 *Dictionary of American Slang.* s.v. *solid:* . . . often used as a one-word reply to a statement.

solid sender, [jazz slang *solid* + jazz slang *sender,* frequently used in combination c. 1936–c. 1941, obs. since except historical] Someone (often, a musician) or something (often, music) that provides excellent entertainment. — 1938 *Metronome,* April, p. 26. "A really solid sender is the third record from the right in my collection." — 1940 *Current History,* 7 Nov., p. 22. *solid sender:* O.K.

something else (or **different**), [see first three quots. for explanation of semantic development; widely current since c. 1957] See first three quots. (note: usually applied to something or someone in a favorable sense, but also occasionally in an unfavorable sense) — 1959 *Jazz for Moderns,* p. 21. *something else:* a phenomenon so special it defies description. — 1959 *Esquire,* Nov., p. 70J. *something else:* so good that it is in a category by itself. — 1960 *The Jazz Titans,* p. 109. Musicians say of Earl "Bud" Powell that "he's somethin' else," in the sense that he's in a class by himself. — 1961 *Metronome,* March, p. 24. Pleasant as this had been, what was to come was something else. — 1962 *Down Beat,* 7 June, p. 39. That rhythm section was something different. The band was swinging.

soul, *n. & adj.* 1. [see second 1959, 1961 quots. for explanation of semantic development; despite 1946 quot., widely current only since c. 1955; see also FEELING] See 1958, first two 1959, and first three 1960 quots. — 1946 *Ebony,* Sep., p. 34. He uses a bewildering technique and his playing is full of what jazzmen refer to as "soul." — 1958 *Down Beat,* 20 March, p 30. Mingus is sensitive, powerful, lyrical, and several other adjectives which make up the feel of the much abused word *soul.* — 1959 *Jazz for Moderns,* p. 21. *soul:* an inborn quality of authenticity. The opposite of mechanical. Almost beyond

description. — 1959 *New York Jazz Festival* (vol. 3),
p. 18. (Most of the critics fifteen years ago were convinced the modernists had sold their blue souls for Me-
phistophelian technical wizardry and that their music
accordingly was "cold, cerebral, and mechanical.") The
soul of which Horace Silver speaks is used in a secular
sense, but several of the younger jazzmen are happily
tracing their music back to such pre-jazz sources as spiritual and gospel singing. . . . "What is 'soul' in jazz? It
comes from within; it's what happens when the inner
part of you comes out." — 1959 *Harper's Magazine*,
June, p. 75. The frequency with which "soul" has entered
into the conversation of young Negro jazzmen is reflected in some of the titles of their works—"Soul Brothers," "Soulville," "Soul-O Blues," "Plenty, Plenty Soul."
— 1959 *Jazz: A Quarterly of American Music*, Fall,
p. 291. I thought it was a very good date. It was a "soul"
session. — 1960 *Down Beat*, 24 Nov., p. 18. "Soul" simply
means heart and conviction, an unconscious feeling for
jazz roots that emerges in a musician's playing and
makes it authentic. — 1960 *The Jazz Word*, p. 213. All
the current terms of approbation among jazzmen—
"soul," "funk," "down home"—all mean basically that
if a man can play the blues from inside himself without
straining to play a part [i.e., assume a personality not
his own], he's a legitimate jazzman. — 1960 *Metronome*,
Dec., p. 19. *Soul* is an intangible, indefinable element,
and all the great swingers have got it; it's a special kind
of beat really . . . somebody's beat is a little stronger
than another's. — 1960 *Esquire*, Dec., p. 74. Some of the
current "soul fever" being incorporated into the music of
musicians who used to be called "hard boppers" is legitimately come by and is yet another way of forcefully
reminding white audiences—and themselves—of a basic
part of their heritage. — 1961 *Commonweal*, 24 March,

p. 658. It's called "soul music" because its practioners
have incorporated some of the backbeat, rhythms, and
exclamatory melodic lines of Negro gospel music. — 1963
Down Beat, 20 June, p. 21. By the end of 1961, it was
evident that "soul" as a movement had been corrupted,
suffocated, and killed.

    2. *n.* [special application of sense 1: because it is
valued highly; current since c. 1957; see also MARY JANE,
SHIT] See quot. — 1959 *Esquire*, Nov., pp. 70H–70I.
soul: marijuana.

    heavy soul, See s.v. HEAVY.

soul brother, [special use of *soul* in combination, further
reflecting its gospel music origin; current esp. among
Negro jazzmen since c. 1957] A fellow "soul" musician
(see SOUL); also, frequently, when used by a Negro
jazzman: another Negro jazzman or another Negro. —
1959 *Jazz: A Quarterly of American Music*, Fall, p. 291.
It's one of those type LPs. I had all "soul brothers." It's
on Riverside. I used "Bags" (Milt Jackson), Percy Heath,
Wynton Kelly and Art Blakey.

soul food, [special use of *soul* in combination; current esp.
among Negro jazzmen since c. 1957] Tasty food, esp.
Southern style cooking. Oral evidence only.

sound, *n.* 1. [special application of standard term; current
since c. 1945] Literally, the "sound" of a performing
group—its distinguishing melodic, harmonic and rhythmic qualities, its conceptual approach to music. — 1948
Metronome, June, p. 15. Woody's new band gets a very
fine sound. — 1949 *Long Island Sound* (song recorded
by Stan Getz on June 21, 1949) [Note: the title is a pun
on the word.]. — 1955 *Hear Me Talkin to Ya,* p. 383.
They're not trying so much any more for a "new sound."
— 1958 *Jazz: A Quarterly of American Music,* Oct.,
p. 28. Who else but Basie gets that SOUND, man.
— 1961 *Metronome,* April, p. 13. There was a search for

a sound, for a *soul* sound that brought back the "group" feeling, perhaps inspired by gospel music and some aspects of rock and roll.

2. [analogical extension of sense 1; current since c. 1960] See quot. — 1963 *Hiptionary*, p. 56. *his sound:* his message [jazz sense], his doctrine.

v.t. & v.i. [cf. c. 1605 *King Lear*, I, ii, "Hath he never before sounded you in this business?"; also cf. general slang phrase *sound (someone) out;* widely current among jazzmen since c. 1950] To speak (to): see first two 1959 quots. — 1958 *Somewhere There's Music*, p. 82. "She probably wants to sound you herself when the scene's cool." — 1958 *Nugget*, Oct., p. 51. "I didn't sound at all." — 1959 *The Holy Barbarians*, p. 318. *sound:* to voice an opinion, recite a poem, or inquire. — 1959 *Esquire*, Nov., p. 70J. *to sound on:* to ask someone for something. — 1959 *Diggeth Thou?*, p. 34. So after he had sounded and she had dug his riff,/She cut into his dommy and helped him kill the fifth. — 1960 *Beat Jokes Bop Humor & Cool Cartoons*, p. 54. When Ham sounded on her, she was convinced. — 1961 *The Jazz Review*, Jan., p. 9. We are very good friends, but I stopped seeing her when stories got back to my daughters, and they sounded on me. — 1961 *The Sound*, p. 58. "All I want from you is to sound him for me."

sounds, *n. pl.* [metonymy; current since c. 1950] See first quot. — 1959 *Swinging Syllables*. s.v. *sounds:* music, usually jazz, as "Cool Sounds." — 1959 *Aramco*, Dec., p. 9. "Then we split for the pad, but no more sounds." — 1961 *The Sound*, p. 122. The railroad flat always vibrated softly with the cool sounds.

spade, *n. & adj.* [by analogy with the black suit in playing cards; very old general slang term (cf. 1934 *A Dictionary of American Slang*, p. 38. "*spade:* a very dark Negro"), but widely current among white jazzmen since c. 1935; see also SOUL BROTHER] See 1946 quot.; for evidence of

its non-derogatory jazz use, see first 1959 quot. — 1933
Metronome, Aug., p. 16. "The blues those spades put in
my ear was great stuff for it." — 1946 *Really the Blues,*
p. 375. *spade*: Negro. — 1952 *Who Walk in Darkness,*
p. 61. "These spade intellectuals really think they've
made it." — 1959 *The Holy Barbarians,* p. 318. *spade cat*:
Negro. The holy barbarians, white and Negro, are so far
beyond "racial tolerance" and desegregation that they no
longer have to be polite about it with one another. —
1959 *Life,* 30 Nov., p. 116. "Beat talk," a narrow and
repetitive argot mostly stolen [sic] from jazz musicians, narcotics addicts and prostitutes . . . substitutes
"Spade" for Negro.

spasm band, [from the fitful nature of the music; current
c. 1900–c. 1917, obs. since except historical]   See 1956
quot. — 1941 *Observer-Kaleidoscope,* Nov., p. 11. "Stale
Bread" Lacoume, white race track tout . . . organized a
"spasm" band, playing on instruments made of junk pile
material. — 1955 *Hear Me Talkin to Ya,* p. 53. A lot of
bad bands, that we used to call "spasm" bands, played
any jobs they could get in the streets. — 1955 *A Pictorial
History of Jazz,* p. 20. Emil Lacoume, nicknamed "Stale
Bread" . . . played zither, piano, banjo and guitar, and
led various "spasm" bands consisting of such home-made
instruments as cheese-box banjo and soap-box guitar. —
1956 *Guide to Jazz.* s.v. *spasm band*: small street band,
the instruments of which are objects not usually used for
making music, e.g., suitcase for drums, wine jug for tuba,
etc. Flourished when jazz was simpler, more primitive.
— 1959 *The Sound of Surprise,* p. 196. A spasm band
(washboard, bones, harmonica, and washtub bass)
rattled along with all the force of a quilting bee.

special, *n. & adj.* [limited use of the standard meaning;
current c. 1925–c. 1935, when it was largely replaced by
original, q.v.]   See 1937 quot. — 1926 *Melody Maker,*
Nov., p. 10. There is a lot of money to be made at this

"special arrangement" game. — 1936 *Metronome*, Feb., p. 61. *special:* an original arrangement. — 1937 *American Speech*, Feb., p. 48. *special:* an exclusive arrangement, belonging to one band only.

speed up, [special application of standard phrase; some currency since c. 1900] To increase the tempo of the music. — 1948 *The Record Changer*, June, p. 6. Jelly Roll Morton's demonstration, on a Library of Congress record, of ragtime "speeding up," is a good example of what happens when the functional controls cease to operate.

spitvalve, *n.* [according to jazzman Eubie Blake, current since c. 1900] The slide part of the trombone, in which the player's saliva collects; also sometimes: the corresponding part of a trumpet or of a baritone saxophone. — 1956 *Sideman*, p. 20. Many of the pages were smeared where drops from spitvalves had fallen and wetted the ink.

split, *v.i.* [prob. derives from the sense of separating self from place; widely current since c. 1950 when it largely supplanted *cut* (*out*), q.v.] See last quot. — 1956 *Sideman*, p. 294. "But that's why the cat split." — 1959 *The Real Cool Killers*, p. 15. "Split!" one of the Arabs hissed. — 1959 *Swinging Syllables*. s.v. *split:* leave.

split the (or **that**) **scene,** [from jazz slang terms *split* and *scene;* widely current since c. 1952; see also LEFT TOWN, QUIT THE SCENE] To remove oneself from a place, circumstance, or situation; also, by extension: to die (in this sense, oral evidence only). — 1956 *Sideman*, p. 272. "Naw, man — I split that scene." — 1956 *Tennessee Folklore Society Bulletin*, March, p. 23. *split the scene:* to leave. — 1958 *Jive in Hi-Fi*, p. 27. In slang if you say "split the scene," it means a situation is in progress and your better judgment tells you to leave or stay clear. — 1961 *Metronome*, April, p. 1. Making a fast buck and splitting the scene is the order of the day.

spot, *n.* [prob. shortened form of colloquial *night spot* (i.e., night club); current among jazzmen since c. 1915; see also JOINT] A night club. — 1944 *Metronome,* Nov., p. 18. "The Hollywood was quite a spot." — 1955 *Hear Me Talkin to Ya,* p. 45. Freddie Keppard was playin' in a spot across the street. — 1955 *Bop Fables,* p. 6. "The Three Suns must be working this spot." — 1956 *Enjoyment of Jazz* (EJ410), p. 3. "We've proved you can swing and still play commercial spots, like the Statler."

spots, *n. pl.* [from the appearance of sheet music; according to jazzmen, some currency since c. 1920; see also DOTS] See 1937 quot. — 1935 *Vanity Fair,* Nov., p. 71. Notes are *"spots."* — 1937 *American Speech,* Feb., p. 48. *spots:* the notes on sheet music. — 1942 *The American Thesaurus of Slang,* p. 559. *spots:* the notes on sheet music. — 1948 *Dead Ringer,* p. 28. "I can learn to play the spots."

square, *n. & adj.* [see 1958 and first 1959 quots. for poss. explanation of semantic origin, though more prob. the term stems from colloquial *on the square* and/or the underworld slang *squarejohn* (both taken in the sense of honesty and trustworthiness based solely on innocence or naivete: see 1945, 1946 quots.); some currency among jazzmen since c. 1925, wide currency since c. 1935; see also NOWHERE, UNCOOL, UNHIP] See 1945, 1946, 1958, 1959 quots. — 1938 *Cab Calloway: Hi De Ho,* p. 16. *square:* an un-hip person. — 1945 *Hepcats Jive Talk Dictionary.* s.v. *square:* a hard-working unromantic person. — 1946 *Really the Blues,* p. 375. *square:* unenlightened person, a working man, an orthodox follower of the rules. — 1956 *Sideman,* p. 141. "Man, I wanta be *square* . . . settle down some place." — 1958 *Publication of the American Dialect Society,* Nov., p. 47. *square:* not in accordance with the jazzman's aesthetic standards. Probably comes from steady 1–2–3–4 rhythm without variation. Many musicians, while saying the

word, will make a motion similar to the band director's indication for 4/4 time — the hand moves in a
square for the four beats. — 1959 *N.Y. Times Magazine,*
5 April, p. 81. In the late Nineteen Twenties, an old word
acquired a new meaning in the American language. The
word was "square," and the world of jazz blew it into
everyday usage. . . . A square was someone who did
not understand their style of music . . . a square peg in
their musical circles. — 1959 *The Horn,* p. 33. The
mechanical objections of the square: the man who was
captive in a world of regular hours, transportation diffi-
culties and lean thoughts.

stand, one-night, See s.v. ONE-NIGHT.

standard, *n.* [from its achieving the status of a fixed part
of the jazz repertory; current since c. 1930] See 1937
and last quots. — 1937 *American Speech,* Oct., p. 184.
standard: a number whose popularity has withstood the
test of time. — 1955 *Hear Me Talkin to Ya,* p. 383. You
don't have to just hang a tune on the changes of a standard. — 1956 *Second Ending,* p. 45. "I figured we should
start buying some standards." — 1956 *Guide to Jazz,*
p. 256. *standard:* a number which has stood the test of
time and found a permanent place in the repertory of
jazz performers.

stash, stache, *n.* [formed from *v.t.;* current since c. 1935;
see also PAD] See 1946 quot.; also: that which is hidden
(see last quot.)—frequently, liquor or marijuana. —
1946 *Really the Blues,* p. 375. *stash:* house, bed, hiding-
place. — 1952 *Flee the Angry Strangers,* p. 440. "Nobody
suppose to know my stash, nobody." — 1958 *The Book
of Negro Folklore,* p. 487. *stash:* a place. — 1958 *Somewhere There's Music,* p. 32. "I didn't want to bring out
the stash while Dog was here."

v.t. [cf. 1959 *Webster's New World Dictionary,* s.v.
stash: "prob. a blend of *store* and *cache*"; from underworld slang: cf. 1930 *American Tramp and Under-*

world Slang, s.v. *stash:* "to hide"; current among jazzmen since c. 1930]   See 1944, 1946 quots. — 1944 *The New Cab Calloway's Hepsters Dictionary.* s.v. *stache:* to file, to hide away, to secrete. — 1946 *Really the Blues,* p. 375. *stash:* to hide or put away. — 1956 *Sideman,* p. 134. "Maybe he's got a chick stashed someplace." — 1952 *Park East,* Dec., p. 30. The boppers were stashed real cool in their pads [jazz sense]. — 1959 *The Naked Lunch,* p. 95. The Beagle has stached the heroin in a lottery ticket.

v.i. 1. [special application of *v.t.:* i.e., to put oneself away, to secure oneself (in sleep); current since c. 1935] See quot. — 1946 *Really the Blues,* p. 375. *stash:* to go to sleep.

2. [prob. extension of sense 1 or of the *n.* (i.e., to assume a place for oneself); current since c. 1940]   See 1944, 1958 quots. — 1944 *The New Cab Calloway's Hepsters Dictionary,* p. 14. *stashed* [sic]: to stand or remain. — 1958 *The Book of Negro Folklore,* p. 487. *stash:* to stand; to stand arrogantly — 1960 *Beat Jokes Bop Humor & Cool Cartoons,* p. 50. "He stashes around that battlement until the cock crows, then he splits [i.e., leaves]."

stay inside, [in the sense of not going outside of what is essential; according to jazzmen, current since c. 1930] A bandleader's command to the orchestra to dispense with the introduction and the verses and to play only the choruses. Oral evidence only.

stick, *n.* 1. [from its shape (see also BLACK-STICK, LICORICE STICK); according to jazzmen, current c. 1920–c. 1945, very rare since; see also CLARY]   See 1936 quot. — 1935 *His Hi De Highness of Hi De Ho,* p. 35. "The clarinet player, when he takes a soaring break, is 'getting off on a stick.'" — 1936 *Metronome,* Feb., p. 61. *stick:* clarinet. — 1948 *Capitol News,* Feb., p. 7. Swedish Stick Star Wins L. A. Acclaim (headline). — 1948 *Tremolo,* p. 25.

"Say, Miss, who's that guy came in with you playing that stick now?"

2. [from its resemblance to a (very small) stick; current since c. 1935; see also REEFER, TEA] See 1946, 1958 quot. — 1938 *Cab Calloway: Hi De Ho*, p. 16. *stick:* a reefer cigaret. — 1946 *Really the Blues*, p. 375. *stick of tea:* cigarette of marijuana, — 1958 *Southern Folklore Quarterly*, Sep., p. 135. *sticks:* marijuana cigarettes. — 1959 *The Horn*, p. 7. He . . . lit up a stick of tea with the piano man. — 1959 *The Holy Barbarians*, p. 78. Rolling their sticks of tea, they looked like a ring of kindergarteners.

sticking?, are you, [semantic development unknown: perhaps phrase derives from sense of having the tenacity to continue struggling for subsistence; according to jazzmen, some currency since c. 1925] See 1951 quot.; also: are you working? are you succeeding? — 1941 *Are You Sticking?* (tune written by Duke Ellington, recorded by his orchestra on June 5, 1941). — 1951 *Esquire*, Dec., p. 210. Then I asked Zoot, "are you stickin?" (meaning) "Have you any money on you at the moment?????" — 1952 *Flee the Angry Strangers*, p. 213. "How are you, Luke; you sticking?"

sticks, *n. pl.* [shortened from of standard *drumsticks;* current since c. 1900] See 1942 quot. — 1926 *Melody Maker*, Sep., p. 56. The tambourine is . . . played with the sticks. — 1933 *Metronome*, Oct., p. 51. Playing with the sticks widely separated on the head of the snare drum is a common fault. — 1942 *The American Thesaurus of Slang*, p. 559. *sticks:* drumsticks. — 1952 *Music Out of Dixie*, p. 161. "Put them sticks in his hands."

stiffin' 'n' jivin', [*stiffin'* prob. from general and underworld slang (i.e., failing to pay or tip someone), *jivin'* in the jazz slang sense of deceiving; according to jazzmen, some currency c. 1935–c. 1945, very rare since] See quot. — 1957 *N.Y. Times Magazine*, 18 Aug., p. 26.

stiffin 'n' jivin': showing off or blowing high with lots of sound effects but not much musicianship.

stock, *adj. & n.* [in sense of a (music publisher's) store or supply; current since c. 1925]   See 1935 quot. and see note above. — 1933 *Metronome,* Jan., p. 34. In making stock arrangements I write for the 10-piece combination and then add the extra parts later. — 1935 *Vanity Fair,* Nov., p. 71. "*Stock*" arrangement are the conventional ones made by publishers and sold generally. — 1936 *Metronome,* Feb., p. 61. *stock:* the publisher's arrangement. — 1937 *American Speech,* Feb., p. 48. *stock:* an arrangement bought from a publishing house. — 1942 *The American Thesaurus of Slang,* p. 561. *stock:* a conventional published arrangement.

stomp, *n., adj. & v.i.* [from a dialectal form: see 1950, 1955, 1956 quots.; current among jazzmen c. 1900–c. 1945, very rare since except historical]   As noun: see 1940, 1950 quots.; as adjective, applied to music: lively and danceable; as *v.i.:* to dance (to jazz) in a lively manner. — 1906 *King Porter Stomp* (tune composed by Jelly Roll Morton, copyright 1924). — 1926 *Sugar Foot Stomp* (song copyright 1926 by Melrose Music Corp.). When they start dancin'—Stompin and prancin'—the dance called the sugar foot stomp. — 1936 *Stomping at the Savoy* (song composed by Chick Webb, Benny Goodman, and Edgar Sampson). — 1940 *Swing,* June, p. 24. Fundamentally there are two types of jazz—blues and stomps . . . Stomp tunes are gay; blues are mournful. — 1942 *American Mercury,* July, p. 96. *stomp:* low dance, but hot man! — 1948 *Trumpet on the Wing,* p. 20. The band would hit "Panama," "Tiger Rag," or some stomp tune. —1950 *They All Played Ragtime,* p. 166. The term "stomp," used to designate a hot number of dynamic rhythm, was derived in New Orleans from the stomping of bare feet in the Bamboula and the the Congo. — 1952 *Mademoiselle,* Dec., p. 120. And the great era of the stomp was the twenties. — 1955 *The Atlantic Monthly*, July, p. 55. The "stomp" grew out of their [i.e., the Negroes'] own primitive folk dances. — 1956 *Guide to Jazz*. s.v. *stomp:* Originally a synonym for "stamp" . . . and is very nearly synonymous with "swing" [jazz sense].

   stomp off, [variant of *kick off,* q.v.; according to jazzman Eubie Blake, some currency since c. 1910] To kick the floor in rhythm several times with the heel of the shoe as a signal for the musicians to start playing. — 1925 *Stomp Off, Let's Go* (tune recorded by the Savoy Orpheans). — 1960 *Hiparama of the Classics*, p. 8. Mr. Rabadee, The All Hip Petrillo stomped off a Leapin' Beat and all these Four Acres of Musicians Began to *WAAIL!!* — 1960 *The Story of the Original Dixieland Jazz Band*, p. 68. For this reason LaRocca was not allowed to "stomp off" his band in the usual fashion. — 1961 *Artesian*, Winter, p. 33. They stomped off the solid beat/lifted up their horns/and blew it out.

stoned, *adj.* [by analogy with the immobility; some general and teenage use, but esp. common among jazzmen since c. 1945; see also BOXED, HIGH, JUICED, ZONKED] See 1952 quot.; for verbal use, see last quot. — 1952 *Life*, 29 Sep., p. 67. *stoned:* drunk, captivated, ecstatic, sent out of this world. — 1956 *Sideman*, p. 213. I want to be blind, I want to be stoned, I want to be high. — 1958 *Somewhere There's Music*, p. 19. Unless Gene was stoned and exaggerating when he wrote. — 1959 *The Holy Barbarians*, p. 85. He was stoned out of his mind with pot [i.e., marijuana]. — 1959 *Jazz: A Quarterly of American Music*, Fall, p. 290. I heard Phineas Newborn play *I'll Remember April* two Mondays ago at The Five Spot and he completely stoned me.

stone out, [variant of *stoned;* some currency since c. 1946] To fall asleep or become unconscious from an excess of a stimulant. — 1952 *Flee the Angry Strangers,* p. 139. "I don't want to stone out."

stop chorus, stop time (chorus), [from the practice of all but stopping the rhythm accompaniment; current since c. 1920] See 1942, 1944, 1956 quots. — 1929 *The Musical Quarterly,* Oct., p. 611. As to what possibilities such free-will tricks as the jazz "break," stop-time, the harmony chorus, an exaggerated syncopation, etc., hold for the development of musical form beyond jazz itself, he would be bold who would predict. — 1942 *The American Thesaurus of Slang,* p. 561. *stop chorus:* a chorus in which the orchestra plays only one note in every one or two measures as a background for a tap dancer or other soloists. — 1943 *Riverboat Jazz* (Brunswick Records pamphlet), p. 7. Note particularly his trumpet played against "stop time" chords, a familiar Armstrong device. — 1944 *This Is Jazz,* p. 24. Another phenomenon peculiar to jazz is the stop-time chorus. This is a solo chorus for any instrument of the band (including rhythm instruments) or even for voice, played with no accompaniment except a periodic pulsing accent by the other instruments generally on the first beat of every measure or alternate measures. — 1956 *Guide to Jazz.* s.v. *stop chorus:* a chorus in which a soloist is not accompanied by the rest of the band with any continuing rhythm; the band plays chords on the first beat of the bar every two bars and the soloist plays alone in between. *stop time:* the same, but usually pertaining only to the rhythm section, — 1957 *Giants of Jazz,* p. 33. In "Cornet Chop Suey," he introduced the daring device known as the "stop-chorus."

story, *n.* [special application of its colloquial sense (i.e., a lie or a fib); also a special use of an archaic sense (i.e., history); current among jazzmen since c. 1935] One's excuse, explanation, condition, situation, ruling passion, philosophy, or history (note: one of the more protean nouns): see both 1944 quots. — 1940 *What's Your Story Morning Glory?* (tune recorded by the Jimmie Lunceford Orchestra). — 1944 *Dan Burley's Original Handbook of Harlem Jive,* p. 150. *What's your story?:* How are things, what excuse do you have, what do you want? — 1944 *The New Cab Calloway's Hepsters Dictionary.* s.v. *What's your story?:* what do you want, what have you got to say for yourself, how are tricks, or what excuse can you offer. Example: "I don't know what his story is." — 1952 *Flee the Angry Strangers,* p. 16. "That's *your* story." — 1952 *Who Walk in Darkness,* p. 66. "What's his story? Is he a fruit [i.e., homosexual] or something?" —1955 *Hear Me Talkin to Ya,* p. 361. If you walked in without your horn, they'd say, "What's your story?" — 1961 *The Sound,* p. 206. "It all comes out in what Red plays. It's not just a certain arrangement of notes. It's the way he hears it. His story." — 1961 *Jazz News,* 2 Aug., p. 13. But the fact is that Lester was irritated with people like, say, Allen Eager, because, as he put it, they "aren't telling their own story; part of their story is mine."

Storyville, *n.* [cf. 1938 *The French Quarter,* pp. 430, 433. "Alderman Sidney Story['s] . . . measure set aside an area in the French Quarter wherein prostitution was to be permitted but not actually legalized. . . . By the middle of 1898 the movement had been completed, and the new district, popularly known as Storyville, much to Aderman Story's disgust, was operating full blast under the sheltering shadow of the law"; see 1960 quot. for dates; see also THE DISTRICT] See 1960 quot. — 1946 *Really the Blues,* p. 375. *Storyville:* the old tenderloin district of New Orleans. — 1955 *Hear Me Talkin to Ya,* p. 4. I never heard it called Storyville . . . It was always The District—the red light district. — 1960 *Dictionary of American Slang.* s.v. *Storyville:* the famous New

Orleans legalized brothel district from 1896–1917, where many of the early jazz musicians first played and introduced jazz music. Some jazz use; not common.

straight, *adj.* 1. [prob. from standard meaning (i.e., undeviating); current since c. 1920; see also COMMERCIAL, LEGITIMATE, SWEET] See 1935, 1956 quots. — 1926 *Melody Maker*, Feb., p. 15. His father was . . . one of the finest "straight" saxophonists in the world.— March, p. 2. "Straight" musicians apparently are piqued because their art is temporarily losing its grip. — 1934 *All About Jazz*, p. 66. Listen to the tune played "straight," or as written. — 1935 *Vanity Fair*, Nov., p. 38. There are two kinds of jazz, *straight* (or *sweet*) and *hot. Straight* jazz, as its name implies, reproduces the composer's score faithfully. — 1948 *Trumpet on the Wing*, p. 26. Then we would play it straight. — 1956 *Jazz: Its Evolution and Essence*, pp. 129–130. Both "straight" jazz and "sweet" music, which are commercial products, make use of a sonority and a melodic and harmonic language that are exaggeratedly sugar-coated. — 1958 *Somewhere There's Music*, p. 16. He blew a straight introduction. — 1958 *Melody Maker*, 19 April, p. 7. "Marian Anderson the straight singer?" — 1961 *Record Research*, March, p. 9. Reams have been written about the dance bands of the acoustical era, both straight and jazz, from Prince's Earl Fuller's, ODJB through Whiteman and beyond.

2. [special application(s) of standard meaning (i.e., properly arranged); current since c. 1935] Satisfactorily situated or taken care of—e.g., financially secure, physically comfortable, happy, drunk, sober: see last 1959 quot. — 1946 *Really the Blues*, p. 163. We'll be straight with ourselves. — 1952 *Flee the Angry Strangers*, p. 190. "I want to be straight when I see the kid." — 1957 *On the Road*, p. 155. "Everything is straight between us at last." — p. 165. All the papers were straight. — 1959 *Easy Living*, p. 90. "You don't want a

slug, huh?" "No thanks. I'm straight." — 1959 *The Jazz
Review*, Sep., p. 7. I was born in Woodville, Mississippi,
because my mother went back to the family; so after I
was straight, everything was cool, she took me back to
New Orleans. — 1959 *Esquire*, Nov., p. 70J. *straight:* in
good shape. — 1960 *The Jazz Review*, Sep.-Oct., p. 14.
He was straight at this time—saved his money and
everything.

    n. [since it arises to distinguish the ordinary cigarette
from the marijuana cigarette, the term prob. derives
from the once general slang, now standard, *adj.* con-
noting legality and conventionality: cf. 1930 *American
Tramp and Underworld Slang*, s.v. *straight:* "honest";
current since c. 1937] See note above and quots. —
1959 *Esquire*, Nov., p. 70J. *a straight:* an ordinary cigarette. — 1960 *Saturday Review*, 6 Feb., p. 12. *straight:*
a regular cigarette.

straight (or **right**) **ahead**, [special application of standard phrases: from sense of moving forward undevi-
atingly; cf. early instructional use: 1926 *Melody Maker*,
Jan., p. 24. "The first time 'have a shot at it'; go straight
ahead; don't go back, no matter if it sounds wrong as
soon as you have struck the notes"; both current since
c. 1955, *straight ahead* much the more common of the
two] To play music in a continuously exciting manner:
frequently hortatory. — 1959 *Jazz: A Quarterly of
American Music*, Fall, p. 293. "But Specs is so thorough,
he can play in tempo." "Plays right ahead." — 1961 *The
Sound*, p. 51. Very simple and straight ahead. — 1961
Dave Newman: Straight Ahead (LP album Atlantic
1366).

straighten, *v.t.* [special application of standard term: cf.
jazz slang *straight* (*adj.*, sense 2) and jazz slang
twisted; current since c. 1935; see also HIP (*v.t.*)] See
1959 quot. (note: definition in first quot. is accurate but
restricted). — 1946 *Really the Blues*, p. 375. *straighten:*

pay up, straighten out a debt. — 1959 *Esquire,* Nov.,
p. 70J. *straighten someone:* to give a person the real
truth or genuine article. To provide a person with what
he needs. — 1960 *Hiparama of the Classics,* p. 8. They
straightened the nanny goats. — p. 9. "Straighten me,
'cause I'm Ready."

Street, The/Swing Street (or **Alley**), [from its importance
to jazzmen during the Swing era (i.e., c. 1935–c. 1945);
current c. 1937–c. 1949, obs. since except historical] In
New York City, 52nd Street between 5th and 7th Avenues (but esp. between 5th and 6th), where small jazz
night clubs flourished c. 1935–c. 1948, when they were
reconverted into conventional night clubs. — 1943 *Metronome,* July, p. 12. We head towards Swing Alley, better
known as 52nd between Sixth and Fifth Avenues. — 1948
Metronome, April, p. 16. Even today, when you leave a
musician and say "See you on The Street tonight" he
doesn't have to ask you which street you mean. But soon
maybe he will. — 1955 *Hear Me Talkin to Ya,* p. 359.
Young musicians and veterans were playing the new music on The Street. — 1955 *A Pictorial History of Jazz,* p.
185. The year is 1939, a time when Red and Higgy were
often to be found on New York's "Swing Street" — 52nd
Street in the late thirties and early forties . . . "Swing
Street" they called it.

stretch out, [special application of standard phrase; current since c. 1955] To play music over a period of time
sufficiently long to permit a successful exploration of
one's theme. — 1961 *Down Beat,* 25 May, p. 39. The
vibes player really stretched out on that one. — 1961 *The
Jazz Life,* p. 41. In more and more clubs, the audience
expects the experimenting and "stretching" out to be
done during working hours for *them,* and not later for
musicians only. — 1962 *Down Beat,* 5 July, p. 35. I heard
this group in person, at the Village Gate, and they
stretched out. — 1963 *Down Beat,* 29 Aug., p. 30.

Some of these things are so short that nobody has a chance to stretch out and blow on it.

stride (piano), [from common practice of designating jazz styles and techniques by kinetic terms (see also MOVE, RIDE, STROLL, WALK): see 1958 quot.; current since c. 1925]   See 1956, 1958 quots. — 1935 *His Hi De Highness of Ho De Ho*, p. 35. But "gut tempo" and "stride tempo" usually are intelligible only to our own musicians. — 1944 *Dan Burley's Original Handbook of Harlem Jive*, p. 148. *striding:* playing ten key stretches in bass on piano. — 1944 *Metronome*, Nov., p. 17. "Alberta Simmons, from down in the Jungles, could beat the average man's 'striding.'" — 1955 *A Pictorial History of Jazz*, p. 135. Willie the Lion Smith . . . is the only man continuing in the "stride piano" tradition of the '20's. — 1956 *Guide to Jazz.* s.v. *stride:* a piano style much in use by soloists about 1930, characterized by a chord on the weak beats alternating with a bass note on the strong beats. — 1958 *The Collector's Jazz: Traditional and Swing*, p. 22. A propulsive style which has been labeled "stride piano" because of the striding effect produced by the left hand hitting a single note in the first and third beats and a chord of three or four notes on the second and fourth beats. — 1960 *Jazz Scene 2* (liner notes on LP album Epic LA 16001). Bryant's bass, at times, utilizes the "stride" made famous by Fats Waller. — 1961 *The Jazz Review*, Jan., p. 26. Teddy Wilson may use stride figures, but they do so more discreetly.

stroll, *v.i.* [special application of standard meaning (i.e., to wander off); according to jazzmen, term was introduced as an exhortation by Roy Eldridge (see LITTLE JAZZ) c. 1938, current ever since; see also LAY OUT]   Of the pianist, to refrain from playing (so that the bass and drums exclusively can play together). — 1959 *Jazz: A Quarterly of American Music*, Summer, p. 204. Oh, periodically I like the piano player to stroll. . . . He'll stroll, then he comes back in and he plays a little more.

strong, come on, See s.v. COME ON.

struggle, *v.i.* [special application of standard term; according to jazzman Eubie Blake, some currency c. 1900–c. 1935, obs. since] To play music or dance badly. Oral evidence only.

strung out, [by analogy with its connotation of immobility (see also HUNG UP), poss. from standard sense of *strung* (i.e., tied), poss. reinforced by *hamstrung* and/or *highstrung;* current since c. 1950] Obsessed with, immobilized by, completely preoccupied with something (most often, a woman or narcotics). — 1960 *The Jazz Review,* Nov., p. 8. Unfortunately it was at this period he acquired the "monkey" [i.e., narcotics addiction] and frequently was strung out. — 1962 *N.Y. Times Magazine,* 20 May, p. 45. *hung up:* to be upset, worried, obsessed, addicted ("He's hung up on Matt Dillon always shooting last"). Going out of vogue in favor of *strung out.*

strut, strutter, strut (one's) stuff, [see last quot. for explanation of semantic development and for beginning date; obs. since c. 1935 except historical; see also STUFF] To dance: frequently hortatory; *strutter:* one who dances. — 1900 *The Blackville Strutters' Ball* (song composed by Bert Williams). — 1917 *Variety,* 30 Nov. The opening number was programmed as a combination of "Strutters' Ball," "Shimme-Sha-Wabble," and "Walking the Dog." — 1926 *Nigger Heaven,* p. 242. Some one cried, "Strut your stuff, Lasca!" — 1928 *The Walls of Jericho,* p. 305. *strut one's stuff:* shout of encouragement. — 1959 *Jazz: A Quarterly of American Music,* Fall, p. 283. The strut of the turkey gobbler was too familiar not to become a figure of speech. The general sense of the metaphor is in earliest English, of course, but here it takes coloration from Bert Williams' 1900 "The Blackville Strutters' Ball," "Strut, Miss Lizzie," the title and song of the 1922 all-Negro revue, and "The Darktown Strutters' Ball."

Through the 1920's there were so many "struts" the phrase *strut your stuff* became colloquial.

stud, *n.* [cf. 1960 *American Speech*, Feb., p. 78. "The strong sexual meaning the word *stud* has had . . . cannot fail to suggest *studhorse*, of which it is a shortened form"; current from c. 1938–c. 1945, somewhat less common since] See 1944 quot. — 1944 *Dan Burley's Original Handbook of Harlem Jive*, p. 148. *stud:* a man, male. — 1959 *The Real Cool Killers*, p. 13. "Oh, that's them" the driver said, cooling off as quickly as a showgirl on a broke stud. — 1960 *Hiparama of the Classics*, p. 10. "I'm gonna take all twelve of you Studs and Straighten you all at the same time." — 1963 *Nugget*, Feb., p. 46. Sometimes these studs in expensive evening attire actually start chasing me.

stuff, *n.* [also general colloquial use, but with esp. currency in particular senses among jazzmen since c. 1925; cf. 1948 *Shakespeare's Bawdy*, s.v. *stuff:* "marrow or semen"; see also JIVE, SHIT] As in general colloquial usage: anything, but esp.: see 1928, 1942, 1953 quots. Also: marijuana (see first 1956 quot.) or narcotics (see 1955 quot.). — 1928 *The Walls of Jericho*, p. 305. *stuff:* talent. — 1929 *The Musical Quarterly*, Oct., p. 606. Indeed, many of its contemporaries there be who execrate the "stuff" [i.e., jazz] as inebriate, doggerel, degenerate, ghoulish, vulturine, etc. — 1934 *All About Jazz*, p. 66. The trumpet player is allowed to "do his stuff" [i.e., display his talent]. — 1942 *The American Thesaurus of Slang*, p. 561. *stuff:* any playing or arranging. — 1953 *The American Thesaurus of Slang*, p. 552. *stuff:* one's playing technique. — 1955 *Hear Me Talkin to Ya*, p. 374. He had remained off the stuff [i.e., narcotics]. — 1956 *It's Always Four O'Clock*, p. 48. "Have you fellows got any stuff [i.e., marijuana]?" — 1956 *Sideman*, p. 10. "Writes symphonies, you know? Legit stuff."

suitcase, *n.* [because if frequently served as drums in *spasm bands,* q.v.; some currency c. 1935–c. 1945, obs. since except historical] See quot. — 1937 *This Thing Called Swing,* p. 9. *suitcase:* drums.

Susie Q, Suzie Q Suzy-Q, [see 1944 quot. for beginning date; term obs. except historical since c. 1941, though parts of the dance survive in other dances] A jazz dance: see note above and 1944 quot. — 1939 *Jazzmen,* pp. 27–28. When the big band "went crazy" after the funeral, the kids cut up with their primitive version of the "Susie Q" and danced the "shudders." — 1944 *The New Cab Calloway's Hepsters Dictionary.* s.v. *Susie-Q:* a dance introduced at the Cotton Club in 1936. — 1946 *Really the Blues,* p. 230. And from the old folks' shuffle to the Suzie Q and Sand, wasn't none of them steps new to grandpa. — p. 375. *Suzie-Q:* a Negro dance. — 1954 *Down Memory Lane,* p. 137. The Savoy developed the Lindy, shim-sham, Suzy-Q and others to their most extreme phases.

sweat, in a, [some currency esp. among Negro jazzmen since c. 1950; see also UNCOOL] Frenetic, nervous, anxious. — 1961 *The Sound,* p. 101. "I dunno, old man, to the average colored person the average gray acts like he's in a sweat most of the time. Hung up. Uncool."

sweet, *adj. & n.* [see both 1956 quots. for key to semantic development; largely a writers' term (see MICKEY, TICKY, which are more common among jazzmen); current c. 1928–c. 1945, obs. since except historical; see also HOTEL (STYLE)] See 1933, 1946, 1952, 1956 quots. — 1933 *Fortune,* Aug., p. 47. He is decidedly not a *sweet* trombonist—he doesn't play sentimentally with lots of vibrato. — 1934 *All About Jazz,* p. 69. "Hot" numbers will have "hot" codas, "sweet" numbers "sweet" endings, etc. — 1944 *Esquire's 1944 Jazz Book,* p. 26. That the popularity of *hot* jazz is not even more widespread may be attributed to the lack of any literature treating of *hot* as a special field, and also to the deadening effect of the shallow emotionalisms of sweet (popular) jazz upon the public ear. — 1946 *Harvard Dictionary of Music*, p. 377. Largely under the influence of Armstrong there arose (c. 1925) the type known as "Hot Jazz" . . . as distinct from the conventional types thereafter known as "Sweet." — 1949 *A Treasury of the Blues*, p. 32. Their "improvisations" (like the "sweet jazz" orchestrations of Whiteman) come often to be carefully tailored in advance. — 1952 *Mademoiselle*, Dec., p. 120. . . . "sweet". . . was the "pop" tune, set in a treacly arrangement," played by a big band loaded with saxophones. And sweet meant *slow*, one of the qualities of the blues—although sweet had no more in common with the blues than swing did with the stomp. — 1956 *Guide to Jazz*. s.v. *sweet*: (1) gently played music. (2) commercial music played with a syrupy, insipid sweetness. Pejorative connotation in either case. — 1956 *Jazz: Its Evolution and Essence*, pp. 129–130. Both "straight" jazz and "sweet" music, which are commercial products, make use of a sonority and a melodic and harmonic language that are exaggeratedly sugar-coated.

swing, *n. & adj.* [cf. jazz etymologist Peter Tamony's article in 1960 *Jazz: A Quarterly of American Music*, Winter, tracing the semantic development of term to as far back as 1888, since which time the term has had some currency as a property of lively popular and/or jazz music; as a generic term for jazz, current c. 1935–c. 1945] See 1939, 1946, 1949, 1956, (esp.) 1960, 1961 quots. — 1899 *In the Hammock: Swing Song* (tune composed by Richard Ferber, copyright by Theo. Presser). With just the right swinging motion [Blurb]. — 1907 *Georgia Swing* (tune composed by Jelly Roll Morton, copyright 1928). — 1912 *The Trolley Car Song* (song). It's the cutest little thing,/Got the cutest little swing. — 1928 *Saratoga Swing* (tune recorded by The

Washingtonians on Cameo 9175). — 1932 *It Don't Mean
a Thing, If It Ain't Got That Swing* (song composed by
Duke Ellington and Irving Mills). — 1934 *Red Norvo
and His Swing Septet* (name of a small jazz group). —
1934 *Metronome*, June, p. 21. Director of their vaudeville
act apparently had no idea what good swing music was.
— 1936 *Harper's Magazine*, April, p. 567. The current
word "swing" is the latest attempt to name an art.
— 1936 *Hot Jazz: The Guide to Swing Music* (book
title). — 1937 *American Speech*, Feb., p. 48. *swing band:*
a dance orchestra specializing in swing music. — 1939
The Kingdom of Swing, pp. 174–175. In a word, swing is
a *property* of music played in a certain way, rather than
a definite kind of music itself. — 1946 *Harvard Dictionary of Music*, p. 378. From about 1935 on . . . the term
Swing (a word which seems to be of largely subjective
import referring to subtle and desirable rubato . . .)
comes into use to denote what appears to be a continuation of the Hot Jazz tradition. — 1949 *Music Library
Association Notes*, Dec., p. 52. *swing:* type of musical
performance popularized largely by Benny Goodman
(1935–1944) in which group-notated improvisation was
substituted for solo and ad lib improvisation. — 1955
Hear Me Talking to Ya, p. 40. Mutt had a very mellow
tone and a terrific swing. — 1956 *Guide to Jazz*. s.v.
swing: the rhythmic pulse vital to jazz; but also the
dominant jazz mode from c. 1934–c. 1945. — 1960 *Jazz:
A Quarterly of American Music*, Winter, pp. 6–7. Early
in 1935 *swing* was one of several terms used to describe
a dynamic of American jazz . . . By the middle of 1936
swing was almost solely employed to characterize a
suddenly-appreciated style that was getting daily, nation-
wide publicity as the new sound. — 1961 *Metronome*,
April, p. 12. Though Swing was largely a jazz-oriented
popular dance music, peak performances by Basie,
Goodman, Lunceford and a few others transcended

popular music entirely and many of these have survived, through recordings, as jazz for listeners.

v.i. & v.t. 1. [see note s.v. *n.:* Tamony traces the *v.t.* to as far back as 1897; however, widely current in a jazz sense only since c. 1935; current with *it* or *out* c. 1925–c. 1935, obs. since except historical] See 1935, 1958 quots. (for use with *out,* see 1951 quot.) — 1933 *Fortune,* Aug., p. 47. Returning to Trombonist Brown, he can . . . swing it . . . (. . . syncopate to beat the band). — 1935 *Stage,* Sep., p. 46. *swing:* play hot and rhythmically. — 1946 *Really the Blues,* p. 141. We would say he could swing or he couldn't swing, meaning what kind of effect did he have on the band. This word was cooked up after the unhip public took over the expression "hot" and made it corny by getting up in front of a band and snapping their fingers in a childish way, yelling "Get hot! Yeah man, get hot!" — 1949 *A Wreath for Rivera,* p. 10. "Then we switch to a cool funeral march and swing it to the limit." — 1951 *Esquire,* Dec., p. 209. *Potato Head Blues* was a tune they really did swing out with. — 1952 *Mademoiselle,* Dec., p. 118. "Oh, swing it, Chad!" — 1955 *Down Beat,* 5 Oct., p. 13. "How can you tell if a man's swinging? When you can pat your feet to what he's playing." — 1956 *Sideman,* p. 32. The band was swinging. — 1958 *Publication of the American Dialect Society,* Nov., p. 47. *swing:* to play well in all senses, technically and otherwise, but expecially to have the basic feel for jazz rhythms. A man can play well harmonically and rhythmically, but he will not swing without a feel for "the beat."

2. [by analogy with sense 1; widely current since c. 1955] As *v.i.:* see last 1959 quot.; also, by extension: to behave or live in such a way as to have a good time or be at peace with oneself. As *v.t.:* to provide enjoyment (for someone). — 1959 *Jazz for Moderns,* p. 21. *swing:* to have a ball—or some 2,000,000 other

things. — 1959 *The Holy Barbarians*, p. 78. Soon the air was filled with the sweet narcotic smell of pot and everybody was swinging. — 1959 *The Cool World*, p. 223. You gotta swing with the gang. — 1959 *Toronto Telegram*, 31 March, p. 3. *swing:* to get the feel of, to comprehend the truth or beauty of anything worth digging; to impart the same truth or beauty to others. — 1959 *Esquire*, Nov., p. 70J. *swing:* to have a good time, enjoy oneself. — 1961 *The Sound*, p. 66. "All reet, if that's the way you cats want to swing—!" — p. 155. "It's the way I swing, that's all." — 1961 *Down Beat*, 3 Aug., p. 26. I know groovy chicks swing *me* a lot faster than cute little Scottie dogs.

swinger, *n.* [current since c. 1950; see also SENDER] A person (frequently, a musician) or something (frequently, a piece of music) that provides pleasure or excitement. — 1959 *Jazz Poems*, p. 6. If you wish to be a swinger, drink and get high. — 1959 *Swinging Syllables*. s.v. *swinger:* hip, like a Satellite. — 1960 *Jazz Journal*, Nov., p. 14. The band are the number one swingers. — 1960 *Down Beat*, 24 Nov., p. 22. It is fast, furious, thunderous, and has nothing whatever to do with Bill Basie, Kansas City Swinger. — 1961 *Down Beat*, 19 Jan., p. 32. *Lover* is handled as a swinger and is one of the better tracks. — 1961 *Jazz Journal*, May, p. 31. Suffice it to say that they were a first class group, swingers all the way.

swinging, *adj.* [widely current since c. 1950] See quots. — 1958 *Publication of the American Dialect Society*, Nov., p. 47. *swinging:* the highest term of approval. May be applied to anything a jazzman likes, or any person. — 1959 *The Holy Barbarians*, p. 318. *swinging:* liberated, uninhibited.

Swing Street (or Alley), See s.v. STREET, THE.

T

✕✕✕✕✕✕✕✕✕✕✕✕✕✕

tag, *n.* [special application of standard term (i.e., an ornamental or familiar ending to a speech, song, etc.); current since c. 1925] See 1952, 1955 quots. — 1932 *Melody Maker*, June, p. 507. The tag . . . implies that this is a band record. — 1943 *Riverboat Jazz* (Brunswick Records pamphlet), p. 7. He comes in to play a tag— just a few notes. — 1952 *A History of Jazz in America*, p. 353. *tag:* final ending in a composition, scored or improvised; "coda" in traditional music terminology. — 1955 *The Encyclopedia of Jazz*, p. 347. *tag:* musical phrase added to the end of a chorus or performance. — 1960 *The Story of the Original Dixieland Jazz Band*, p. 59. The Dixieland Band's stock ending, the "dixieland tag," faithfully concluded every number. — 1961 *Metronome*, April, p. 18. "So many of the comical quotes and tags in jazz come out of different musical experiences, such as being in a little pit band."

tailgate, tail-gate, *adj.* [see 1947, 1957 quots. for explanation of semantic development and 1947 quot. for beginning date; very rare since c. 1945 except historical] See 1942, 1959 quots. — 1942 *The American Thesaurus of Slang*, p. 564. *tail gate:* New Orleans style of trombone playing. — 1947 *N.Y. Herald-Tribune*, 10 March. The term "tail-gate" originated in 1910 when jazz bands rode the streets of New Orleans in wagons. Because the trombone is such a cumbersome instrument its player was always assigned to the tail-gate of the wagon. — 1957 *The Book of Jazz*, p. 79. The expression "tailgate" trombone originated when brass bands playing ragtime or early jazz were loaded onto advertising trucks and the trombonist, in order to give free play to the full length of the slide, had to stand near the tailgate of the truck. — 1959 *Jazz: A Quarterly of American Music*, Fall, p. 284. *tailgate:* the style of trombone playing associated with New Orleans. Also **tail gate.**

take, *n.* [chiefly recording trade term, prob. derived from motion picture camera use, but some currency among jazzmen since c. 1925; see also MASTER] One of the several recordings made of a tune, from which is selected the one "take" (or *master,* q.v.) to be offered to the record-buying public. — 1942 *The American Thesaurus of Slang,* p. 569. *take:* phonograph record. — 1955 *Hear Me Talking to Ya.* p. 191. We ruined several takes that way. — 1958 *Playboy,* Nov., p. 66. "The first take, we knew we had it cold," he says. — 1960 *The Story of the Original Dixieland Jazz Band,* p. 68. LaRocca attributes this to nervousness on the part of his fellow musicians, who were inclined to play louder on the real "take." — 1961 *Down Beat,* 2 March, p. 32. Donaldson proves to be a soloist of greater-than-average interest on some of the takes in this album.

v.t. [special application of a standard meaning (i.e., to perform); according to jazzman Eubie Blake, current since c. 1900] To play (a piece of music). — 1940 *Take It!* (tune composed by Sy Oliver and Calvin Jackson). — 1961 *Down Beat,* 19 Jan., p. 31. *Sesame,* in particular, is swift-moving and taken up-tempo. — 1961 *The Sound,* p. 157. "Just flip one hundred of them singles and we'll take it from the top [i.e., play it from the beginning]."

take charge, [special application of a standard (esp. armed forces) phrase; also some sports use; according to jazzmen, some currency since c. 1915] To dominate a musical performance; also, attrib., capable of giving excitement and coherence to a musical performance: in this sense, oral evidence only. — 1955 *Hear Me Talkin to Ya*, p. 220. "Come on—let's take charge!" — 1959 *Cannonball Takes Charge* (LP album Riverside RLP 12–303).

take five, [short for *take a five-minute respite:* from theater slang; current since c. 1930] See second 1952 quot. —1942 *The American Thesaurus of Slang*, p. 564. *take five:* take a 5-minute rest. — 1952 *Music out of Dixie*, p. 50. "Take five, kid." — 1952 *A History of Jazz in America*, p. 353. *take five:* (said to musicians, usually at rehearsal) you are entitled to a five-minute intermission. — 1961 *The Feeling of Jazz*, p. 30. Man, I'm glad they said to take five, because this next arrangement looks rough.

take it slow (also take it light: oral evidence only), [cf. general colloquial "take it easy"; widely current c. 1935–c. 1945, very rare since; see also LATER] See 1938 quot.: used in place of "Farewell!" — 1937 *Metronome*, Nov., p. 11. " 'Nuff said, Savoy, so take it slow." — 1938 *Cab Calloway: Hi De Ho*, p. 16. *take it slow:* be careful. — 1952 *Who Walk in Darkness*, p. 13. "Take it slow."

take-off, takeoff, *n.* [by analogy with flight; some currency c. 1930–c. 1940, very rare since] An improvised solo. — 1935 *Vanity Fair*, Nov., p. 71. Breaks [jazz sense] are sometimes known as *get-offs* or *take-offs.* — 1959 *Blow Up a Storm*, p. 7. From his first takeoff, I knew that Woody was one of the finest trumpet players I had ever heard.

take off, [by analogy with flight; current c. 1925–c. 1945; see also GET OFF, GO TO TOWN, RIDE] See first quot. — 1938 *Cab Calloway: Hi De Ho*, p. 16. *take off:* play a solo. — 1938 *Collier's*, 25 June, p. 65. "Gosh,"

said Mr. Ketridge, "he's really taking off!" as Ding-Dong
hit a wild, weird pitch. — 1945 *Down Beat*, 1 July, p. 2.
Johnny Bothwell, star altoist and Raeburn's right hand
man, takes off on a solo.

taking care of business, [extension of the standard meaning
to the jazzman's "business"; current since c. 1955]   See
last quot. — 1957 *N.Y. Times Magazine*, 18 Aug., p. 26.
Who's takin' care of business?: Who's on the stand tonight? — 1960 *Down Beat*, 22 Dec., p. 42. It is, in fact, a
superior, hard-accented session, with all concerned taking care of business in an uncompromising and forth-
right manner. — 1961 *Down Beat*, 5 Jan., p. 16. "They're
not enough piano players out here taking care of business," he continued. — 1961 *The Jazz Review*, Jan., p. 31.
In the notes for Contemporary C–3551, Nat Hentoff tells
us that "if a musician is 'taking care of business' he is
playing very well." On the back of "Takin' Care of Business" (Jazzland 19), Orrin Keepnews explains that the
expression should be reserved "for those no-nonsense
occasions on which everything comes out just right and
the job at hand is done unusually and excitingly well."

talk, *v.i.* [by analogy with verbal communication: see
1961 quot. (see also LYING, MESSAGE, SAYING SOMETHING,
TELL A STORY); some currency since c. 1925]   In music,
to communicate significantly; also, rare: to attempt to
imitate the sounds of the human voice (see 1956, 1960
quots.). — 1929 *Heah Me Talkin' to Ya* (tune recorded
by the Louis Armstrong Orchestra). — 1947 *The Two
Worlds of Johnny Truro*, p. 24. "Listen, I'm talkin' to you,
boy, listen!" — 1955 *Hear Me Talkin to Ya*, p. 211. The
Box Back Boys used knife blades to keep their [i.e.,
musicians'] whining guitars talking all night long. —
1956 *The Heart of Jazz*, p. 36. The disregard of exact
pitch is a logical corollary of the effort of New Orleans
jazzmen to make their music "talk." — 1961 *Down Beat*,
30 March, p. 23. The jazz drummer also imitates the

cadence of speech, as do other instrumentalists. (It's no accident that the phrases, "Talk to me," "Shout," "Holler," "Now you're talkin'" and other speech references are a large part of jazz argot.)

taped, participle [perhaps by analogy with having successfully gotten music onto a tape recorder; also some general slang use; some currency among jazzmen since c. 1950] Mastered, understood, taken care of, under control. — 1952 *Who Walk in Darkness*, p. 68. "You really think you have everybody taped, don't you, Max?" I said. — 1959 *Blow Up a Storm*, p. 245. "Anyway, he had it taped."

taste, *n.* [old general slang: shortened form of *a taste of liquor;* current in its initial sense since c. 1945, and in its most general sense since c. 1955] Initially: liquor; also, since c. 1945: see 1951 quot.; also by extension, since c. 1955: see both 1959 quots. — 1951 *Esquire*, Dec., p. 210. He must have made a nice little "taste" (meaning) the tune made quite a bit of "loot" [i.e., money]. — 1959 *Newport Jazz Festival: 1959*, p. 46. *taste:* usually a drink or some money, but it can be a portion of anything. — 1959 *Esquire*, Nov., p. 70J. *taste:* usually a drink or some money. A portion of anything good. — 1960 *Down Beat*, 23 June, p. 28. "But baby, all I remember is Frank saying, 'Let's stop for a taste after the gig.'" — 1961 *The Sound*, p. 89. "'Bout time I had a little taste," he suggested. "Say a couple of big bills."

tea, tee, *n.* [prob. from the resemblance of the two types of leaves; current since c. 1925; see also BOO, GAGE, MARY JANE, POT] See 1958 quot. — 1930 *Tee Rollers Rub* (tune recorded by Freddie "Redd" Nicholson). — 1957 *On the Road*, p. 88. A couple of Negro characters whispered in my ear about tea. — 1958 *Southern Folklore Quarterly*, Sep., p. 134. *tea:* marihuana, a plant or weed. — 1959 *Mexico City Blues*, p. 61. Powerful Tea you gotta smoke/to believe that.

tea pad, [jazz slang *tea* + jazz slang *pad;* some currency c. 1930–c. 1940, obs. since except historical]   See quots. — 1939 *Jitterbug Jamboree Song Book*, p. 33. *teapad:* anyplace where they smoked weed. — 1940 *American Speech*, Oct., p. 337. *tea pad:* where marihuana is sold and smoked. — 1943 *Time*, 19 July, p. 54. Most tea pads are supplied with a juke box.

tear down, [hyperbole; current since the advent of the big hotel bands c. 1925; see also its antonym SET UP] To dismantle the music stands, etc., after a performance (also as *v.i.:* oral evidence only). — 1956 *Eddie Condon's Treasury of Jazz*, p. 462. He had no set way of tearing down and setting up a band.

tear (it) up, [by analogy with the finality of the effect; some currency since c. 1920; see also BREAK IT UP]   To play music excitingly, thrillingly. — 1955 *Hear Me Talkin to Ya*, p. 204. He had the first big colored band that hit the road and tore it up. — 1962 *Down Beat*, 30 Aug., p. 20. But once I heard Clifford, I wasn't leaving. He was really tearing up.

tear out, [special application of its general slang senses (i.e., to fight or to curse), poss. reinforced by *tear out into the street;* according to jazzman Eubie Blake, current c. 1900–c. 1935, obs. since]   To play an exciting improvised solo. Oral evidence only.

tell a (or **one's**) **story,** [by analogy with verbal communication (see also LYING, MESSAGE, SAYING SOMETHING, TALK); some currency since c. 1925]   In music, to communicate significantly—i.e., what one most profoundly feels. — 1934 *All About Jazz*, p. 144. He tells the simple, everyday story . . . to understand and appreciate which requires more than an average musical intelligence. — 1956 *Jazz: Its Evolution and Essence*, p. 168. A coherently developed chorus has a much better chance of being musically satisfying than one whose phrases are haphazardly thrown together. Jazz musicians have perfectly

well taken into account this necessity; when they compliment an improvisation by saying "It tells a story,"
don't they show that they recognize the value of good
development? — 1957 *The Charles Mingus Jazz Workshop: The Clown* (liner notes on LP album Atlantic
1260). "I think," says Porter, "that more jazz groups
should tell stories like Mingus does instead of just playing
notes and techniques." — 1961 *The Sound*, p. 177. "Lot
of other cats blow a mess of trumpet, high notes, fast
runs, and all, but Red always tells a story." — 1961
Jazz News, 2 Aug., p. 13. But the fact is that Lester was
irritated with people like, say, Allen Eager, because, as
he put it, they "aren't telling their own story; part of
their story is mine."

tenor (man), (note: similar forms exist for most instrumentalists—i.e., an alto saxophonist may be referred to
as "an alto," a bassist as "a bass," etc.—but the great
importance of the tenor saxophone since c. 1925 has
made this form the most common) [shortened form;
current since c. 1930] See 1942 quot. — 1942 *The
American Thesaurus of Slang*, p. 556. *tenor man:* a tenor
saxophone player. — 1958 *The Subterraneans*, p. 6. We
hear a new young tenorman come on. — 1959 *Jazz: A
Quarterly of American Music*, Summer, p. 182. Fletcher
did vow that he would bring in "that strange young
tenor man" at the first opportunity. — 1961 *Metronome*,
April, p. 30. With the release of this album we are
given a chance to take a long look at an important tenor.
— 1961 *The Jazz Life*, p. 34. "Like you'd hear about a
very good tenor in some night spot, and I'd have to go
down there and cut him."

terrible, *adj.* [one of several standard terms in which the
connotation has been reversed: see second 1959 quot. for
semantic explanation (see also BAD, HARD, MEAN, TOUGH);
current since c. 1955] See 1959 quots. — 1959 *Newport
Jazz Festival: 1959*, p. 46. *terrible:* great. — 1959

Nugget, Aug., p. 56. Normally cheerful and friendly, he can, when moved, become a regal and awesome figure—a "terrible" man in the jazz sense of the word, which connotes formidability. — 1959 *N.Y. Times,* 15 Nov., p. 2. Jazzmen often call a thing "terrible" or "bad" when they like it very much. — 1962 *Down Beat,* 7 June, p. 39. That old man's terrible! Four stars.

that's what I'm talking about!, that's right!, [both are fanciful expressions, since the speaker with premeditated and humorous inaccuracy implies that whatever he is approving of is what he himself had in mind all along; some currency esp. among Negro musicians since c. 1935 for the longer expression, c. 1958 for the shorter] I approve of that: see last quot. — 1961 *The Sound,* p. 45. "Yes!" Red cried softly. "That's what I'm talking about!" — 1961 *N.Y. Times Magazine,* 25 June, p. 39. *That's right!:* Bravo! (Improvised by saxophonist Cannonball Adderley after being knocked out [i.e., impressed] by a Miles Davis trumpet coda.)

there you go, [by favorable analogy with the kinetic; cf. 1956 *American Speech,* May, "Army Speech and the Future of American English," p. 108: *"There you go!* (Now you're talking sense)"; also some student and teenage use, but with esp. currency among jazzmen c. 1935–c. 1945, somewhat less since; see also SOLID, CRAZY] Expressions of approval or of assent. — 1956 *Sideman,* p. 100. "There you go," he grinned. — p. 296. "There you go!" Bill said happily.

thin, *adj.* [special application of standard term; according to jazzmen, some currency since c. 1935] Light (applied to a musician's tone): see last quot; also, by extension, since c. 1950: superficial (see the antonym HEAVY), not profound. — 1960 *Jazz: A Quarterly of American Music,* Winter, p. 20. He's a little thin, you know? — 1961 *Metronome,* Sep., p. 7. The thinness of much of his work becomes doubly apparent when contrasted with

Miles' deep probing. — 1961 *The Jazz Life*, p. 23. "Everyone, when he first started, thought: This man, his *tone*
is too *thin*, you know?"

thing, *n.* [understatement: somewhat special applications
of a term which also has many vague general colloquial
uses; current in its jazz senses since c. 1945] A musical
performance, composition, or conception (see also GET
ONE'S THING TOGETHER). — 1948 *Down Beat*, 19 May,
p. 13. *Sleeps* is an up tempo thing by Norvo. — 1955
Metronome, June, p. 22. We take some of the basic
ingredients of jazz and we intermingle them with some
of the new things that have been developed. —1956
Eddie Condon's Treasury of Jazz, p. 320. "Couple of
things—one original and a new arrangement of 'Man I
Love.'" — 1959 *Jazz: A Quarterly of American Music*,
Fall (inside front cover). "Ornette Coleman is doing the
only really new thing in jazz." — 1960 *The Jazz Review*,
May, p. 30. How about we tie up the Latin thing with a
college motif? — 1961 *Down Beat*, 5 Jan., p. 43. I loved
the Ray Nance thing.

(one's) own thing, [current since c. 1955; see also
GET (ONE'S) SHIT (or THING) TOGETHER] One's personal
musical style or idiom. — 1961 *Down Beat*, 2 March,
p. 43. He's been playing this way 15 years, and he's got
his own thing going. — 1961 *Jazz Journal*, July, p. 4. I
spent two years with him off-and-on, and he was the first
one to really push me into my own thing.

third stream, third-stream, thirdstream, [see first 1962
quot. for semantic explanation; current since 1960] See
first quot. — 1960 *N.Y. Times*, 17 May, p. 44. Gunther
Schuller . . . has been heralding the arrival of what he
calls a "third stream" of music—a music that is neither
jazz nor "classical" but that draws on the techniques of
both. — 1960 *New Yorker*, 24 Dec., p. 47. The steadily
increasing attempts made during the past several years
by such composers as Gunther Schuller, John Lewis,

George Russell and Charlie Mingus to establish a new
music midway between classical forms and jazz have at
last been blessed with a name—"third-stream" music.
— 1962 *Dinosaurs in the Morning,* p. 214. "What about the
third stream?" I asked. "I [Gunther Schuller] coined
the term as an *adjective,* not a noun. . . . This music is
only *beginning.* I conceive of it as the result of two
tributaries—one from the stream of classical music and
one from the other stream, jazz—that have recently flowed
out toward each other." — 1962 *Down Beat,* 10 May, p.
18. Hence the potential growth of a new music that is
not in the main stream but is a hybrid: the already
familiar Third Stream. — 1963 *Nugget,* Feb., p. 7. The
other is that curious amalgam of conservatory training
and jazz feeling known as "Thirdstream."

threads, *n. pl.* [synechdoche; current since c. 1935; see
also DRAPE, TOG, VINES] See 1938, 1959 quots. — 1938
Cab Calloway: Hi De Ho, p. 16. *threads:* suit, dress or
costume. — 1959 *Esquire,* Nov., p. 70J. *threads:* clothes.
Example: He's wearing a fancy set of threads. He's
wearing a good suit. — 1961 *The Sound,* p. 46. "It's just a
shame the way you treat your threads." — p. 109.
"How do you dig these threads?"

ticklers, ivory, See s.v. IVORY.

ticky, ricky-tick(y), *adj.* [onomatopoeic: the longer form
is an attempt to render phonetically the monotonous and
brittle regularity of the rhythm in such music, poss. reinforced by the tick-tock of a clock; long form current
since c. 1930, short form since c. 1935; see also CORNY,
MICKEY (MOUSE)] See 1952 quot.; also, by extension:
see 1959 quot. — 1937 *American Speech,* Feb., p. 48.
ticky: the placing of improper stress on some note-values
in the music, caused by incorrect phrasing and tonguing.
— 1942 *The American Thesaurus of Slang,* p. 563. *ricky-
tick:* of tempo and tone, gently, softly. — 1952 *A History
of Jazz in America,* p. 353. *ticky:* corny [jazz sense],

spec. applied to a mechanical beat. — 1953 *The American Thesaurus of Slang*, p. 55. *ticky:* with improper stress placed on some note values. — 1959 *Esquire*, Nov., p. 70J. *ticky:* stale, outmoded.

tight, *adj.* 1. [according to jazzmen, term developed semantically from an initially sexual use; also some general slang use; current esp. among Negro jazzmen since c. 1920] Intimate: see 1959 quot.; also, rare, noun: see second 1960 quot. — 1928 *It's Tight Like That* (tune copyright 1928 by Melrose Music Corp.). — 1956 *Lady Sings the Blues*, p. 32. He and Bub were real tight with the cops. — 1959 *Esquire*, Nov., p. 70J. *tight:* very friendly. — 1960 *Beat Jokes Bop Humor & Cool Cartoons*, p. 50. The Ham's tight ace, Horatio, had brought news of the ghost of The Big Ham. — 1960 *The Jazz Review*, Nov. p. 10. Drugs do tend to make a tightness—it is something in common. — 1961 *Down Beat*, 30 March, p. 21. "I really got tight with Max and learned great respect for him."

2. [relation, if any, to sense 1 unknown; some currency among jazzmen since c. 1925] Of people, formidable; of things, difficult or dangerous (see 1928 quot.). — 1928 *The Walls of Jericho*, p. 306. *tight:* tough; redoubtable; hard. — 1956 *Saturday Review*, 17 March, p. 30. "This is where it's tight, man." — 1960 *Hiparama of the Classics*, p. 16. He was a hard, tight, tough Cat. . . . Naturally Mark has got to put Cleo down [i.e., reject her], this was a tight move for him 'cause this Cleo was an early day Elizabeth Taylor.

time, *n.* [special application of the standard musical term; some earlier use, but with esp. currency only since c. 1945; see also BEAT] See 1959 quot. — 1949 *Metronome*, July, p. 17. That cat's blowing, man! His time is good. — 1957 *Down Beat*, 28 Nov., p. 14. "I think he's a fine musician, with a real jazz beat, or 'time,' as the modern boys say." — 1959 *Newport Jazz Festival: 1959*, p. 46.

time: sense and control of rhythm. — 1961 *Metronome,* April, p. 15. Little Jimmy Rushing, the man with the greatest time in jazz, came on for *Blue Skies,* and Gene settled back into a good groove. — 1961 *Down Beat,* 13 April, p. 22. "Zoot Sims is Mr. Time."

tipple, tiple, *n. & adj.* [relation to any of the standard meanings unknown; according to jazzmen, some currency c. 1920–c. 1930, during which time the instrument was sometimes used in jazz performances, obs. since except historical] See 1953 quot. — 1940 *Swing,* Jan., p. 24. Good tiple solos, solid bass plucking and jive singing. — 1953 *The American Thesaurus of Slang,* p. 549. *tipple uke:* a 12 stringed ukulele. — 1962 *High Fidelity,* Dec. p. 107. He plays both unamplified guitar and tiple, a ten-string instrument with double and triple strings tuned in octaves.

toddle, *n. & adj.* [from toddling movement of the dance; current c. 1920–c. 1930, obs. since except historical] A slow jazz dance in vogue c. 1920–c. 1930, and the slow tempo of the music to which it was danced. — 1926 *So This Is Jazz,* p. 25. A tune played doubly slow for a "toddle" is no less jazz than when performed at its original fox-trot tempo. — 1946 *The Jazz Record,* May, p. 10. Just before I left, the boss wanted us to play "toddle time" . . . four beats to the measure.

tog, *v.i.* [old slang and general colloquial term given wide currency by jazzmen since c. 1925] To dress (usually with *out* or some other adverbial modifier). — 1932 *The Inter-State Tattler,* 7 Jan, p. 9. Jimmy Ferguson . . . hit the stage togged strictly English. — 1938 *Cab Calloway: Hi De Ho,* p. 16. *togged to the bricks:* dressed to kill, from head to foot. — 1946 *Big Book of Swing,* p. 125. *togged out:* well-dressed. — 1946 *Really the Blues,* p. 29. I togged like a fashion plate. — 1961 *The Sound,* p. 44. "I dig the way you're togged out." — p. 109. "I mean, that cat can really tog out!"

together, get (or have) (one's) **self** (or shit, thing), be, [according to jazzmen, all forms have been current since c. 1955; see also (ONE's) OWN THING] To fit all of one's disparate creative and technical elements into a unified whole. — 1962 *Down Beat*, 12 April, p. 22. "I guess I was on my way in '57, when I started to get myself together musically." — 1963 *Down Beat*, 29 Aug., p. 30. I guess it's the regular rhythm section behind them because it sounds like everything is together.

togs, *n. pl.* [cf. 1925 *English Words & Their Background*, p. 52. "*togs* (Australian slang): clothing"; general colloquial use, but with esp. currency among jazzmen since c. 1925] Clothing. — 1946 *Really the Blues*, p. 41. A busted ragpicker would have given those togs the go-by.

Tom, (Uncle), [from Harriet Beecher Stowe's sympathetic but subservient Negro in *Uncle Tom's Cabin;* essentially a Negro slang term, but much in use among jazzmen, Negro and white, since c. 1945] As noun: see 1959 quot.; as *v.i.:* for a Negro to act in a servile manner in the presence of whites; for its gerund form, see last quot. — 1956 *Lady Sings the Blues*, p. 116. He'd bugged me [i.e., persisted] so and practically made me feel like a Tom for not sitting down with him. — 1956 *The Real Jazz Old and New*, p. 147. An *Uncle Tom* is one who caters to white taste. — 1959 *Esquire*, Nov., p. 70J. *Tom* or *Uncle Tom:* a Negro who does not try to maintain his complete dignity before whites. — 1960 *Monthly Review*, May, p. 24. As the late Billie Holiday once said, "Louis Armstrong Toms from the heart." — 1961 *Swank*, July, p. 60. "I called Howard a Tom (Uncle) to allow Lennie to talk like that." — 1961 *New Yorker*, 23 Sep., p. 101. The materials include offensive Uncle Tomming.

tonk, *n.* See s.v. HONKYTONK.

too much, [hyperbole (see 1946 quot.); widely current c. 1935–c. 1950, somewhat less since; see also OUT OF THIS WORLD, THE MOST] See 1944, 1959 quots. — 1937

Metronome, March, p. 55. That man's too much! — 1944
The New Cab Calloway's Hepsters Dictionary. s.v. *too
much:* term of highest praise. Example: "You are too
much!" — 1946 *Big Book of Swing,* p. 125. *too much:*
getting beyond belief. — 1954 *Down Beat,* 21 April, p. 22.
Stan plays too much [i.e., wonderfully] on that! — 1955
Bop Fables, p. 46. "I just dug your nose and it's too much."
— 1958 *Somewhere There's Music,* p. 155. "The City is
too much—and that's where I want to be." — 1959 *Esquire,* Nov., p. 70J. *too much:* remarkable. Excrutiating
in its sublimity.

top (down), from the, [by analogy with reading sheet
music; current since c. 1930] See 1936 quot.; also, by
extension, from the beginning of anything (to the end).
— 1936 *Metronome,* Feb., p. 21. *from the top down:* playing an orchestration right through. — 1956 *Eddie Condon's Treasury of Jazz,* p. 219. "Let's do this one more
time from the top, gentlemen."

top (of the beat), on, [according to jazzmen, current since
c. 1925; see also the antonyms DRAG, LAY BACK] In musical performance, ahead of the beat. Oral evidence only.

tore up, [nonstandard past participle applied in a special
way by jazzmen since c. 1950; see also RIPPED] See last
quot. — 1958 *Jive in Hi-Fi,* p. 27. In slang if you say
"tore up," it means something . . . disturbs or upsets
you. — 1959 *The Holy Barbarians,* p. 21. "He was no good
when he was all tore up." — 1959 *San Francisco Chronicle,* 4 June, p. 35. "Them people down there must be
plenty bugged if a book like this can get them so tore
up." — 1959 *Esquire,* Nov., p. 70J. *tore up:* extremely
distressed.

tough, *adj. & adv.* [one of several standard terms in which
the connotation has been reversed—i.e., because someone or something that's tough is also formidable, to be
reckoned with (see also BAD, HARD, MEAN, TERRIBLE);
widely current only since c. 1955] See 1959 quot.; as

adv.: much (see 1961 quot.). — 1959 *Esquire*, Nov., p. 70J. *tough:* great. — 1960 *Tough Tenors: Johnny Griffin & Eddie "Lockjaw" Davis* (LP album Jazzland J-45703). — (liner notes). The big news is that two of the toughest tenors in captivity are working *together*. — 1960 *Beat Jokes Bop Humor & Cool Cartoons*, p. 50. Had not the old man shown Little Ham how to make the toughest broads in the kingdom? — 1960 *The Jazz Review*, May, p. 30. "Like it's the cream of West Coast jazz with the toughest charts [i.e., arrangements] you ever . . ." — 1961 *Evergreen Review*, July-Aug., p. 25. "You really believe two chicks [i.e., women] could dig [i.e., love] each other that tough?"

toy band, [by analogy with their childlike instruments; some currency c. 1935–c. 1945; see also MICKEY (MOUSE), TICKY] See quot. — 1946 *Duke Ellington*, p. 126. The field was over-run with "Mickey Mouse" music, "cheese" or "toy" bands, as the jazzman calls orchestras which rely upon synthetic sounds rather than music for popular appeal.

track, *n.* 1. [by analogy with *racetrack:* that around which one moves; see 1960 quot. for beginning date; obs. since c. 1945 except historical] See 1944, 1946, 1960 quots. — 1944 *Dan Burley's Original Handbook of Harlem Jive*, p. 149. *track:* dance hall, a ballroom. — 1946 *Really the Blues*, p. 375. *The Track:* Savoy Ballroom in Harlem. — 1955 *Hear Me Talkin to Ya*, p. 194. When they opened at the "track," they were just a band without any particular leader. — 1960 *Dictionary of American Slang*, s.v. *track:* a dance hall. Some c. 1935 jive use. The Savoy Ballroom in New York City's Harlem was widely known as "The Track" to hepsters [sic].

2. [from the grooves in a phonograph record; initially a trade term; widely current among jazzmen since c. 1949] Any one of several performances on a long-playing phonograph record. — 1949 *Playback*, Oct.-Nov., p.

4. This took the form of a 10″ record with two "tracks" or "grooves" impressed on each side. — 1960 *Jazz: A Quarterly of American Music,* Winter, p. 19. Sometimes I squeeze a whole lp on one track. — 1961 *The Jazz Review,* Jan., p. 22. *Housewarming* is a good track. — 1961 *Down Beat,* 19 Jan., p. 40. LP? That came later, and you didn't say "track" then.

tram, *n.* [prob. a dialectal corruption of the first syllable of the standard term (cf. 1955 *Atlantic Monthly,* July, p. 55. "There would be no abrupt change in feeling simply because of the acquisition of cornets, clarinets, 'trambones.'") and a shortened form; current c. 1925–c. 1945, rare since; see also BONE] A trombone. — 1948 *Down Beat,* 1 Dec., p. 13. *This* is in a slower vein with good tram, fair tenor, and trumpet, and too much ensemble.

trick, (turn a), [prob. by analogy with the surprise element in magic; apparently a dialectal survival from Early Modern English: cf. 1948 *Shakespeare's Bawdy,* s.v. *trick:* "a bout of love-making"; prostitutes' slang but some currency among jazzmen since c. 1900] The sexual act or any of its variations (see 1926 quot.); also, see 1960 quot. — 1926 *Nigger Heaven,* p. 252. "I said, Now daddy, do you know any more tricks?" — 1946 *Really the Blues,* p. 30. "Turning a trick" was how they described one session with a john. — 1958 *Somewhere There's Music,* p. 127. Carl said he'd see if his old lady [i.e., wife] had turned any tricks for herself. — 1959 *Easy Living,* p. 54. "You ever have a habit? . . . You ever turn a trick for it?" — 1960 *Dictionary of American Slang.* s.v. *trick:* a prostitute's customer; a prostitute's "sale" or business transaction.

trim, *n. & v.t.* [relation to standard meaning(s), if any, unknown; cf. c. 1593 *Titus Andronicus,* V, i, 93–95. "They cut thy sister's tongue, and ravished her, And cut her hands, and trimm'd her"; rare since c. 1945] A woman sexually; to possess (a woman sexually). — 1952 *Flee the*

Angry Strangers, p. 429. "She was good trimmin, right
enough."

truck, *v.i.* [see 1945 quot. s.v. 2 for explanation of semantic
development; current c. 1900–c. 1945, obs. since except
historical] See 1938, 1939, 1942 quots. (usually with
on or *on down*) — 1937 *Metronome,* Nov., p. 11. "After
Louis boots, the cats truck on to their various domiciles."
— 1938 *Better English,* Nov., p. 51. *truck, truck on down:*
to go somewhere. — 1939 *Jitterbug Jamboree Song Book,*
p. 33. *truckin' on down:* to go somewhere, to leave. —
1942 *American Mercury,* July, p. 96. *trucking:* strolling.
2. *n. & v.i.* [by analogy with sense 1: see 1942, 1945
quots.; see 1944 quot. for beginning date; very rare since
c. 1945 except historical] See 1939, 1942, 1944, 1945
quots. — 1937 *N.Y. Amsterdam News,* 4 Sep., p. 12. The
new dance sensation [i.e., The Big Apple] . . . has
pushed "The Truck" out of the limelight. — 1939 *Jitterbug Jamboree Song Book,* p. 33. *truck:* to dance, the
dance itself. — 1942 *American Mercury,* July, p. 96.
trucking: dance step from the strolling motif. — 1944 (*Dan
Burley's Original Handbook of Harlem Jive,* p. 149. *trucking:* a dance introduced at Cotton Club in 1933. — 1945
Charm, Aug., p. 154. The shuffling rhythm which later
became a national dance craze called "Truckin'," for instance, was derived from the brass band funeral music
played by mourners on the return from the cemetery!

truth, *n.* [one of several terms derived by analogy with
verbal communication (see also LYING, MESSAGE, SAY
SOMETHING, TELL A STORY); some currency since c. 1945]
Music that is authentic, original or soulful. — 1959 *The
Horn,* p. 27. All who comped with funk . . . and blew
the truth. — p. 225 "I blew the truth for you sometimes,
didn't I?"

tub, *n.* (usually *pl.*) *& v.i.* (rare), [poss. from the shape
and poss. from the use of it as a homemade instrument
in some early jazz; some currency since c. 1935; see also

SKINS, HIDES] See 1942, 1955 quots.; as *v.i.:* to play drums
(see 1944 quot.) — 1942 *The American Thesaurus of
Slang,* p. 559. *tub:* a drum. — 1944 *Down Beat,* 15 Feb.,
p. 12. Wettling's Solid Tubbing Kicks Any Size Ork
(headline). — 1949 *Music Library Association Notes,*
Dec., p. 53. *tub:* swing term and now be-bop term,
for drum. — 1955 *Say,* 28 April, p. 53. *tubs:* drums. —
1961 *The Sound,* p. 99. "Yes, it's time that your boy Hass
packed his tubs and moved on."
tub, every, See s.v. EVERY.
tune, *n.* [analogical extension of standard meaning; some
currency since c. 1945] See 1963 quot.; also, by extension: a woman (oral evidence only). — 1960 *The Village
Voice,* 20 Jan., p. 1. "I don't dig the tune." [i.e., "I don't
comprehend what is being said."] — 1963 *Hiptionary,*
p. 8. *tune:* idea, story.
tuned out, [by analogy with turning off a radio; according
to jazzmen, some currency since c. 1950; see also TURNED
OFF] Uninterested; inattentive. Oral evidence only.
turkey trot, [dance designations frequently refer to animal
movements: cf. BUNNY HUG, CAMEL WALK, FOX-TROT;
term dates from at least mid-19th century, and was current
in the jazz milieu c. 1912–c. 1920, obs. since except his-
torical] A jazz dance (see note above). — 1914 *Modern Dancing* [1962 *Jazz: A History of the New York
Scene,* p. 37]. Drop the Turkey Trot, the Grizzly Bear,
the Bunny Hug, etc. — 1926 *Nigger Heaven,* p. 84. She
was good at the new ones too, the turkey trot and the
bunny hug. — 1934 *Metronome,* Jan., p. 30. We did
create the foxtrot which has outlasted a flock of other
forms as the turkey trot, Charleston, Black Bottom, etc.
turn a trick, See s.v. *trick.*
turned off, [by analogy with turning off a radio; some currency since c. 1950; see also TUNED OUT] Uninterested; inattentive. — 1961 *Metronome,* Feb., p. 30. I am
one of those who got turned off a couple of years ago

when Brookmeyer started recording albums that sounded like trumped-up dixieland.

turn on, 1. [from sense 2; current since c. 1946] To use marijuana or narcotics. — 1956 *Sideman,* p. 274. "If everybody starts turning on, you think they'll sell any lush [i.e., liquor]?" — 1959 *The Holy Barbarians,* pp. 171–172. When the marijuana head (vipers, we called them in the thirties) or the hype [i.e., narcotics addict] turns on, he has the feeling of setting something in motion inside himself.

2. [by analogy of the human being with a machine; current since c. 1945] See 1958 and first 1959 quots. — 1958 *American Speech,* Oct., p. 225. When he [i.e., a hipster] *turns* him [i.e., someone] *on* he supplies him with something—a smoke, a drink, or just a bit of information. — 1959 *The Beat Generation Dictionary,* p. 7. *turn on to:* introduce to. — 1959 *The Holy Barbarians,* p. 67. "It was Richard who turned me on to jazz." — 1959 *Jazz Poems,* p. 5. I want you babes to be turned on to the truth. — 1961 *The Sound,* p. 21. "Bernie, do you want me to turn you on?" Zaida said.

twisted, *adj.* [current since c. 1950] See 1960 quot. — 1949 *Twisted* (tune recorded by Wardell Gray). — 1959 *Newport Jazz Festival: 1959,* p. 46. *twisted:* confused, too far out [jazz sense]. — 1959 *Esquire,* Nov., p. 70J. *twisted:* confused. — 1960 *Metronome,* Sep., p. 16. *twisted:* obscure, confused, mentally disturbed.

two-beat, *adj. & n.* [see 1955 quot. for semantic explanation; current c. 1930–c. 1945, rare since except historical] See 1955 quot. — 1938 *Metronome,* Oct., p. 23. Just honest-go-goodness, two-beat, driving swing. — 1950 *Mister Jelly Roll,* p. 126. In his view "the light, two-beat jazz" which has come to be called "Dixieland" was the creation of the Keppard combination. — 1955 *The Encyclopedia of Jazz,* p. 347. *two-beat:* jazz in which two of the four beats in every bar are accented; usually asso-

ciated with Dixieland jazz. — 1962 *The New Jazz Book,*
p. 15. The older styles of jazz are grouped together under
the heading "two-beat jazz." — 1963 *Down Beat,* 14
Feb., p. 37. *Down Beat* came out with the new name
back in the '30s, calling it two-beat music.

two cents, See s.v. CENT.

uncool, un-cool, *adj.* [cf. narcotics use: 1953 *Junkie,* p. 13.
"*Un-cool:* liable to attract attention from the law"; some
currency since c. 1950] Not cool (q.v.); i.e., frenetic,
needlessly excited, unwise. — 1958 *Somewhere There's
Music,* p. 175. "Like buy my forthcoming book on what's
uncool in American education." — 1961 *The Sound,* p.
101. "I dunno, old man, to the average colored person
the average gray acts like he's in a sweat most of the
time. Hung up. Uncool." — p. 143. The ugly, un-cool,
four-cornered world of hang-ups, drags, and hard dues.
— 1962 *Jazz Journal,* June, p. 22. "It is uncool to let
anybody use your place as a forwarding address for
packages from Mexico."

unhip, un-hip, unhipped, *adj.* [current since c. 1935; see
also SQUARE, NOWHERE] See 1938, 1939 quots. — 1938
American Speech, Dec., p. 314. *unhipped:* opposite of
hipped. — 1939 *Jitterbug Jamboree Song Book,* p. 33.

unhip: not familiar, not wise. — 1946 *Really the Blues,* p. 69. Ray and Fuzzy were salty with our unhip no-playing piano player. — 1961 *The Sound,* p. 23. "That's all un-hip propaganda."

up a breeze, See s.v. BREEZE.

up-tempo, up, [originally prob. shortened form of *speed up; up-tempo* current since c. 1935, *up* since c. 1945] Of tunes, played at a fast tempo. — 1948 *Down Beat,* 19 May, p. 13. *Sleeps* is an up tempo thing by Norvo. — 1959 *Down Beat,* 28 Jan., p. 14. *Goof,* an up tempo original, tries hard but never really gets anywhere. — 1960 *The Jazz Word,* p. 30. On up tunes, particularly the scat songs, she improvises in a steady flow. — 1961 *Down Beat,* 19 Jan, p. 31. *Sesame,* in particular, is swift-moving and taken up-tempo. — 13 April, p. 36. *Moodsville,* which opens the second side, is a medium-up blues. — 1961 *The Sound,* p. 37. "Fast or slow?" "Up. 'Way up," Red said.

up tight, [cf. its underworld senses (i.e., impecunious; in difficulty); poss. sexual etym. (see note s.v. *tight,* sense 1); according to jazz dancer Leon James, some currency esp. among Negro jazzmen since c. 1958] Excellent (usually applies to music). — 1962 *Gene Ammons: Up Tight* (LP album on Prestige PRLP 7208).

uptown, *adj.* [prob. because New York City's largest Negro neighborhood, Harlem, is "uptown"; current c. 1930–c. 1945, rare since] See 1959 quot.; also, as applied to music, earthy (this is the sense in which the first two quots. are to be taken). — 1939 *Uptown Shuffle* (tune recorded by the Erskine Hawkins Orchestra on Bluebird 10506). — 1940 *Uptown Blues* (tune recorded by Jimmie Lunceford Orchestra on Vocalion 5362). — 1959 *Swinging Syllables.* s.v. *uptown:* an adjective, signifying one who is stylish, quite hip, or important. — 1962 *Uptown and Lowdown* (title of LP album of Dick Wellstood and Cliff Jackson on Prestige/Swingville 2026).

vibes, *n. pl.* [see 1954 quot.; current since c. 1937 when these instruments replaced the older xylophone in jazz] See 1954 quot. — 1940 *Swing*, July, p. 17. Lastly, some too-formal ensemble riffing with vibes. — 1954 *Esquire*, Nov., p. 82. Contrary to popular belief, the word "vibes" is not the nickname for the instrument; it is the word used to cover all instruments of which the manufacturing-company trade names are "Vibraphone," "Vibraharp," "Vibrabells," etc. — 1963 *Down Beat*, 3 Jan., p. 26. Two sides of almost continuous vibes solos gets to be a bit too much of one thing.

-ville, *suffix* [used to represent an extreme degree of the word to which it is appended; jazzman Emmett Berry prob. introduced it into jazz speech c. 1938, but it has been widely current only since c. 1945; see also -Crry] See note above and see first 1959 quot. — 1949 *Music Library Association Notes*, Dec., p. 41. Addition of the suffix *ville* is a common verbal procedure among song-pluggers. Origin of the device is perhaps Storyville in New Orleans, the area in which jazz reputedly had its birth. — 1955 *Bop Fables*, p. 10. "Weirdsville," said the baby bear. — p. 37. "Hangoversville, for all I know." — 1956 *American Jazz Festival*, p. 55. In fact the whole thing is strictly from Squaresville, U.S.A. — 1959 *Swinging Syllables*. s.v. *ville:* a suffix which can be added to any word to emphasize it, i.e. dictionary—wordville. — 1959 *The Holy Barbarians*, p. 126. The squares had discovered beatville. — 1961 *Down Beat*, 5 Jan., p. 23. Paul Desmond made a parallel observation, commenting wryly, "Diversityville—let a hundred flowers bloom."— 19 Jan., p. 22. The telephone rings and the gas and light company informs you that in 24 hours it's "candlesville." — 1961 *The Sound*, p. 32. Red had disembarked at the Los Angeles airport, taken one appraising look at Squaresville-on-the-Pacific, and immediately hopped the next plane back to the Apple [i.e., New York City].

vine(s), *n.* (usually *pl.*), [by analogy with the standard meaning—i.e., because it hangs on or clings to one; from underworld slang: cf. 1934 *A Dictionary of American Slang*, p. 43. "*vine*: a suit of clothes"; 1960 *Dictionary of American Slang*, s.v. *vine*: "orig. prison use = civilian or nonprison clothes, c. 1930; by c. 1935 in wide jive use and soon changed to 'vines' "; current among jazzmen since c. 1935; see also DRAPE, THREADS, TOG] See first two and 1957 quots. — 1944 *The New Cab Calloway's Hepsters Dictionary*. s.v. *vine*: a suit of clothing. — 1955 *Say*, 28 April, p. 53. *vines*: suits. — 1955 *Hear Me Talkin to Ya*, p. 106. I . . . bought her a lot of fine vines, a wardrobe with nothing but the finest. — 1957 *N.Y. Times Magazine*, 18 Aug., p. 26. *vines*: clothes.

viper, *n.* [since the term is self-imposed, it is prob., though Biblical in origin, a humorous self-castigation; widely current c. 1928–c. 1942, rare since] See 1940 quot. — 1930 *The Viper's Drag* (tune recorded by Cab Calloway Orchestra). — 1938 *N.Y. Amsterdam News*, 2 April, p. 17. "The thousands of . . . vipers . . . that are being hatched daily . . . are a peril." — 1940 *American Speech*, Oct., p. 337. *viper*: a marihuana user. — 1959 *The Holy Barbarians*, pp. 171–172. When the marijuana head (vipers, we called them in the thirties) or the hype turns on, he has the feeling of setting something in motion inside himself.

vocal, *n.* [from standard phrase *vocal music;* introduced as a distinguishing term c. 1935, somewhat less common since c. 1950] A musical arrangement which includes a part for voice (see last quot.); also, that vocal performance. — 1936 *Metronome,* Feb., p. 61. *vocal:* vocal arrangement. — 1948 *Down Beat,* 1 Dec., p. 10. We ran down [i.e., rehearsed] three new instrumentals and a vocal for Baubles Buxon! — 1950 *Metronome,* March, p. 25. I like everything about the vocal. — 1950 *Lingo of Tin-Pan Alley.* s.v. *vocal:* contrasts with instrumental. Song is sung.

voice, *v.t.* [special application of standard meaning (i.e., to harmonize voices); current since c. 1930] See 1961 quot. — 1933 *Metronome,* March, p. 34. Voicing ensembles should be considered entirely differently from voicing separate sax or brass trios. — 1937 *American Speech,* Feb., p. 47. It is voiced peculiarly in that the lead melody is carried lower than the clarinet. — 1956 *Sideman,* p. 36. The sax section played a chorus using Miller-voicing. — 1960 *Down Beat,* 8 Dec., p. 53. The arrangement was very good; I like the way it was voiced. — 1961 *Down Beat,* 18 Jan., p. 42. The word "voicing" is used—and misused—often enough in record reviews and liner notes. . . . Strictly speaking, voicing is the distribution on the keyboard or in the orchestra of the tones of a chord.

vonce, *n.* [etym. unknown: perhaps from Yiddish and German word for bedbug (hence, anything worthless; hence, anything); some currency esp. among Negro jazzmen since c. 1942; see also JAZZ, JIVE, SHIT] Thing(s) (may refer to a dance, sex organs—almost anything): see quots. — 1959 *Esquire,* Nov., pp. 70H–70I. *vonce:* marijuana. — p. 70J. *do the vonce:* make love.

wah-wah, wa-wa, wow-wow, *adj. & n.* [See 1933, 1956 quots. for etym.; current c. 1925–c. 1945, rare since except historical] See both 1942 and 1956 quots. — 1926 *Melody Maker*, March, p. 30. Secondly, I want to advise musicians of a new wow-wow glass mute modifier for trumpets which has recently been put on the market in this country [i.e., England]. — 1933 *Fortune*, Aug., p. 47. For example, it is now extremely *corny* to use the once popular wah-wah mutes which make brass instruments sound like crying babies. — 1939 *American Jazz Music*, p. 43. Such effects as the "laughing trombone" or the "baby cry" with the so-called "wah-wah" mute are novelties. — 1942 *The American Thesaurus of Slang*, p. 561. *wah-wah:* a bass effect obtained by favoring the bell of the horn with a mute. *wah-wah mute:* a rubber mute or plunger used on a trumpet or trombone to produce "wah-wah" effects. — 1955 *Hear Me Talkin to Ya*, p. 234. They were playing wah-wah music with plungers and things. — 1956 *Guide to Jazz*. s.v. *wa-wa:* a mute placed in the bell of a trumpet or trombone and constantly moved a little in order to produce sounds for which this name is onomatopoeic. — 1961 *New Yorker*, 16 Sep., p. 147. In "Dem Blues," Curson played two choruses of muted wa-wa trumpet, an unfashionable skill learned from Rex Stewart at Mingus' behest.

wail, *v.i.* [by analogy with loud lamentation; despite some occasional earlier use, widely current only since c. 1953; see also BURN, COOK, SMOKE] See 1955 and last three quots.; also, by extension: to be superb (see 1958 quot.). — 1955 *Vogue,* 15 Sep., p. 125. "Wailing" is the 1955 jazz word for playing superbly; the new equivalent of "really swinging." — 1955 *Hear Me Talkin to Ya,* p. 21. They'd put their music in their pockets and everybody started wailing. — 1956 *Sideman,* p. 24. "Man . . . like he ought to let us wail some tonight." — 1956 *Lady Sings the Blues,* p. 17. If I'd heard Pops and Bessie wailing through the window of some minister's front parlor, I'd have run free errands for him. — 1958 *Somewhere There's Music,* p. 32. "Those people, man, they had a culture that wailed." — 1958 *American Speech,* Oct., p. 224. Just now, the word *wailing* (meaning "playing exceptionally well," and analogically, "Having a very good time") seems destined for longevity. — 1959 *Newport Jazz Festival 1959,* p. 46. *wail:* to do anything very well. — 1959 *Esquire,* Nov., p. 70J. *wail:* to perform with inspiration.

wailer, *n.* [from jazz slang *wail;* some currency since c. 1955] A musician who plays well (see quot.); by extension: anyone who does anything well or simply is a superior person (see first 1959 quot. s.v. *wail*). — 1958 *Down Beat,* 16 Oct., p. 38. The whole story is right here in eight, eloquent preachments by as fine a quintet of wailers as can be assembled.

wail on him (or **'em**), [current esp. among Negro jazz-men since c. 1955; see also COOK ON 'EM, SMOKE ON 'EM] Best him (musically), play well. Oral evidence only.

wailing, adj. [from jazz slang *wail;* widely current since c. 1954] Superb, musically or otherwise. — 1956 *Sideman,* p. 98. "Coke's a wailing cat."

walk, *v.i. & adj.* [from earlier *adj., n.,* and *v.t.* use (see WALKING BASS, CAMEL WALK), reinforced by an old analogy—i.e., the 1900 practice of walking rhythmically (see also CAKE WALK, CAMEL WALK) to the post-funeral march music esp. in New Orleans; some currency since c. 1950] See 1955 quot. — 1952 *Mademoiselle,* Dec., p. 118. "And that's the basic jazz beat, that *walking* beat. Up here in the north all the jazzmen are playing too fast or too slow—nobody walks." — 1954 *Walkin'* (tune recorded by Miles Davis sextet on Prestige LP 7076). — 1955 *The Encyclopedia of Jazz,* p. 347. *walk:* establish a lively, four-beats-to-the-bar rhythm (usually said of bass players: "walking rhythm"). — 1956 *Enjoyment of Jazz* (EJ402). p. 3. In Basie's section . . . the bass and guitar "walk" with even stress on the four beats to the bar. — 1956 *It's Always Four O'Clock,* p. 99. I sure liked to hear him when he got in one of those walking moods. — 1957 *N.Y. Times Magazine,* 18 Aug., p. 26. *they really walk:* the rhythm section really swings [jazz sense]. — 1961 *The Sound,* p. 270. "Yes, man, we was *walking!"*

walk (the bass), walking (bass), [prob. by analogy with the progression (see 1950 quot.); current c. 1915– c. 1945, rare since except historical] See 1950, 1957 quots. — 1939 *American Jazz Music,* p. 51. *String bass,* more often plucked or slapped than bowed, usually playing two or four notes per bar or a "walking" (melodic) bass. — 1950 *Lingo of Tin-Pan Alley.* s.v. *walking bass:* type of bass piano progression in which movement is up or down by semitones, whole tones, or thirds—arranged in broken octaves. Progression may also be used orchestrally. — 1957 *The Book of Jazz,* p. 120. In rhythm section work these bass strings are usually "walked"; that is, played continuously, four notes to the bar. — 1959 *Jazz* (Hentoff & McCarthy), p. 93. The guitarists . . . "walked the basses" in eight-to-the-bar rhythms. — 1959 *Selected Poems,* p. 229. Down in the bass/That steady beat/Walking walking walking/Like marching feet.

walkin' the dog, [dance satirized this act, esp. the haughtiness which frequently characterized it; current c. 1916–

c. 1920, obs. since except historical] A jazz dance (see
note) in vogue c. 1916–c. 1920. — 1916 *Walkin' the Dog*
(tune copyright by Melrose Music Corp.). — 1943 *The
Jazz Record*, 15 April, p. 3. In 1917 . . . there were several dances in vogue, namely: "Walkin' the dog," "jazz
dance," and "ballin' the jack."

washboard *n.* [some currency c. 1910–c. 1935, obs. since
except historical] See quot. — 1956 *Guide to Jazz.* s.v.
washboard: literally; used as musical instrument by rub-
bing thimbles-on-fingers over it.

washboard band, [some currency c. 1910–c. 1935, obs. since
except historical] A band consisting wholly or partly
of washboards. — 1955 *Hear Me Talkin to Ya,* p. 50.
Even a washboard band was welcome.

waste, *v.t.* [by extension of standard *v.t.;* also some teenage use; current since c. 1955] See 1959 quot.; also: to
hurt (someone) badly or kill (someone). — 1959 *Esquire,* Nov., p. 70J. *to waste someone:* to do a person
bodily harm. — 1960 *Beat Jokes Bop Humor & Cool
Cartoons,* p. 50. "I think Pops got wasted." — p. 52. "One
minute you were balling, and the next you were stiff.
Who wasted you?" — p. 53. "Claudius stole my kingdom.
Revenge me, son. Waste that cat!" — p. 55. "Now might I
waste the cat."

wasted, *adj.* [see note s.v. *waste;* widely current since c.
1955] See 1956 quot. — 1956 *Tennessee Folklore Society Bulletin,* March, p. 22. *wasted:* tired or beat up. —
1958 *American Speech,* Oct., p. 225. If you are merely
tired . . . you are . . . wasted. — 1959 *Newport Jazz
Festival: 1959,* p. 46. *wasted:* boxed [jazz sense]. — 1959
Esquire, Nov., p. 70J. *wasted:* in bad physical shape. —
1961 *Down Beat,* 19 Jan., p. 22. You wake up at noon,
your wig [i.e., head] is aching, your stomach is completely wasted.

wax, *n. & v.t.* [from the substance from which records were
made; primarily a trade and writers' term, but also with

some currency esp. among white jazzmen c. 1925–c. 1950, obs. since except historical] A 78 rpm phonograph record; to record a piece of music. — 1935 *Metronome,* April, p. 45. Impressions in Wax (record review column title). — 1937 *American Speech,* Feb., p. 48. *wax:* a phonograph recording. — 1942 *The American Thesaurus of Slang,* p. 569. *wax:* make records. — 1948 *Down Beat,* 14 July, p. 13. Ventura's doubled up tenoring on *Body* is some of the best that he has set down on wax. — 1955 *Hear Me Talkin to Ya,* p. 232. On the second date I remember we waxed *Emigration Blues.*

way out, wayout, [from its remoteness from the conventional; some earlier use, but in wide currency only since c. 1950; see also FAR OUT, SOMETHING ELSE] See first quot. — 1958 *Publication of the American Dialect Society,* Nov., p. 47. *way out:* departing greatly from the norm; especially said of unusual (or unusually good) treatment of melody or harmony; now of anything that seems especially good—though still used in the original sense too.— 1958 *Somewhere There's Music,* p. 164. "I turn on [i.e., smoke marijuana] a little and I get way out." — 1959 *Esquire,* Nov., p. 70J. *way out:* intricate in nature, very advanced. — 1960 *The Jazz Word,* p. 123. How often I painted to wayout sounds.

wear them out, [by analogy with the effect; according to jazzmen, some currency c. 1920–c. 1935, obs. since except historical; see also BLOW DOWN, CARVE, CUT] To best another band in musical competition. — 1955 *Hear Me Talkin to Ya,* p. 25. Our band really wore them out.

weed, *n.* [metonymy — i.e., marijuana derives from a weed; current c. 1925–c. 1940, very rare since; see also BOO, GAGE, POT, TEA] See first 1938 quot. — 1931 *Chant of the Weed* (tune recorded by Don Redman Orchestra on Brunswick 80036). — 1933 *Chicago Defender,* 2 Dec., p. 5. The humble "reefer," the "weed," the marijuana, or

what you have by way of a name for a doped cigarette
has moved to Park Ave. from Harlem. — 1938 *Cab Calloway: Hi De Ho*, p. 16. *weed:* marijuana. — 1938 *N.Y.
Amsterdam News*, 2 April, p. 17. "He had learned to
smoke 'weeds' under the adept instruction of Sue."
weird, *adj.* [see 1958 quot. for explanation of semantic
adaptation; current since c. 1945]   Imaginative, interesting, delightfully surprising (note: occasionally the term
is used in the sense of *too* imaginative — consequently,
unintelligible; this is the sense in which its use in the
1959 quots. should be taken). — 1950 *Metronome*, Aug.,
p. 16. This is weird. — 1958 *Publication of the American
Dialect Society*, Nov., pp. 41–42. The adverse criticisms
of bop were taken over almost wholesale and made into
favorable ones. Such terms as *crazy, weird, wild,* and
nervous, all used to express favorable responses to music,
are adaptations of terms levelled against the bop musicians. Since they knew the music which people called
"crazy" was actually good, they took over the word in a
good sense. — 1959 *The Holy Barbarians*, p. 59. "This
Teena, she was a weird chick." — 1959 *The Horn*, p. 107.
"These weird cats are blowing weird . . . and . . .
everyone's a head."
weirdbag, *n.* [jazz slang *weird* + jazz slang *bag;* some currency since c. 1959]   The source of an unusually experimental musician's (or person's) inspiration or inventiveness. Oral evidence only (see BAG).
weirdie, weird-o, *n.* [from jazz slang *weird;* some currency
since c. 1950]   An interesting or imaginative musician
(or person)—sometimes, too imaginative: see second
1959 quot. — 1955 *The Encyclopedia of Jazz*, p. 347.
weird-o: a weird person. — 1959 *The Holy Barbarians*,
p. 86. Phil had an arrangement with the weirdie who
ran the shop. — 1959 *Down Beat*, 14 May, p. 20. Sonny
is no admirer of what he calls "weirdies," musicians

whose music is "too mysterious." — 1960 *Jazz Monthly*, Nov., p. 26. Everyone has had a go at . . . laying responsibility . . . on . . . weirdies.

went down, See s.v. GO DOWN.

West Coast jazz (or **school, sound**), [interchangeable with *cool jazz* (q.v.) as a generic term for a style of playing most of the practitioners of which came from the West Coast; current since c. 1952] The most popular jazz style c. 1950–c. 1957, characterized by restraint, intellectuality and a studied relaxation; its popularity has waned markedly (see FUNKY, HARD BOP) with the cognoscenti, though its practitioners remain legion, esp. on the West Coast. — 1955 *Hear Me Talkin to Ya*, p. 397. The West Coast restraint can be attributed then, I think, to Mulligan's influence. — 1957 *West Coast Ghost* (tune recorded by Charles Mingus on *East Coasting*, Bethlehem LP album BCP-6019). — 1961 *Commonweal*, 24 March, pp. 657–658. To the chagrin of those "cool" players who were Negro, a white adaptation of their style began to gain popularity in the comparatively anemic "West Coast" school of the first half of the 1950's.

Western style, [named for its place of origin; some currency c. 1925–c. 1935, obs. since except historical; see also its more common synonym CHICAGO (STYLE)] A jazz style c. 1925–c. 1935 differentiated from the earlier New Orleans style, q.v., on which it was based, though both together constitute "traditional" jazz: see s.v. CHICAGO STYLE. — 1928 *Melody Maker*, Dec., p. 1299. It . . . is known as the Western style, as pioneered in Chicago. — 1955 *Hear Me Talkin to Ya*, p. 234. The Western style was more open . . . open horns and running chords and running changes.

wheels, *n. pl.* [synechdoche; current since c. 1930; see also RUBBER, SHORT] See 1957 quot. — 1957 *N.Y. Times Magazine*, 18 Aug., p. 26. *wheels:* an automobile. — 1959 *Esquire*, Nov., p. 70J. *wheels:* car. — 1959 *Swinging Syl-*

lables. s.v. *wheels:* auto. — 1961 *The Sound,* p. 15. "Man
has wheels!" Zaida exclaimed.

where he's at, that's/you know [analogy of a state of being
with a place; according to jazzmen, current since c.
1960] (That is) where his essence lies; (that is) his passion or
concern; (that is) his nature. Oral evidence only.

whip that thing, [by analogy with inflicting pain or pun-
ishment and/or subduing; according to jazzman Eubie
Blake, current since c. 1900; very rare since c. 1940] See
quot.: frequently hortatory; also *whip it:* oral evidence
only. — 1939 *Jitterbug Jamboree Song Book,* p. 22. *whip
that thing:* play that instrument.

whipped (up), [by analogy with having been literally
whipped; some currency with *adv.* from c. 1935–c. 1945,
wide currency without *adv.* since c. 1945; see also BEAT,
HACKED] See 1938, 1939 quots. — 1938 *Cab Calloway:
Hi De Ho,* p. 16. *whipped up:* worn out, exhausted. —
1939 *Jitterbug Jamboree Song Book,* p. 33. *whipped up:*
beat [jazz sense], exhausted.—1958 *Somewhere There's
Music,* p. 36. "I'm whipped."

wig, *n.* 1. [fanciful synechdoche; in its initial sense (hair),
current since c. 1935, in its next sense (head), since c.
1938, and final (mind), since c. 1942] See note and
1944, 1958 and first 1959 quots. — 1944 *Dan Burley's
Original Handbook of Harlem Jive,* p. 150. *wig:* head,
brain, mentality. — 1944 *The New Cab Calloway's Hepsters Dictionary.* s.v. *blew their wigs:* excited with enthusiasm, gone crazy. — 1952 *Park East,* Dec., p. 30. My
queen in her scanties and I in my robe,/Had just fixed
our wigs for a long winter's load. — 1956 *Second Ending,*
p. 249. The mootah [i.e., marijuana] had snapped the
top of his wig. — 1956 *Lady Sings the Blues,* p. 221. I
straightened her wig right off [i.e., told her off]. — 1958
The Book of Negro Folklore, p. 488. *wig:* head, hair. —
1959 *The Holy Barbarians,* p. 318. *wig:* the mind. — 1959
The Horn, p. 153. The bandy-legged figure stood, with

wild wig that no pomade could subdue. — 1960 *Hipa-rama of the Classics*, p. 11. "Take it off you [i.e., your] wig, Naz, we've got it covered!" — p. 20. Nero's wig went straight up in the air. — p. 22. Them poo' Cats ain't had no place to lay their wigs. — 1961 *Down Beat*, 19 Jan., p. 22. You wake up at noon, your wig is aching.

2. (also **wigger**: see last quot.), [special application of the most recent meaning of sense 1; some currency since c. 1950] See quots. — 1959 *Newport Jazz Festival: 1959*, p. 46. *wig:* very crazy person. — 1959 *Jazz for Moderns*, p. 21. *wig:* a person who is very crazy. Sometimes called wigger.

3. [special application of the most recent meaning of sense 1; current since c. 1955] See 1959 quots. — 1958 *Saturday Review*, 11 Jan., p. 79. Musicians are now used to witnessing the unfulfilled innovator; they call these musicians "wigs." — 1959 *The Horn*, p. 132. Curny was a "wig" as primarily cerebral jazzmen are dubbed. — 1959 *Esquire*, Nov., p. 70J. *wig:* a person who is far-out [jazz sense] intellectually.

v.i. & v.t. 1. [formed from *n.*, sense 1—i.e., as a function or state of the mind; current since c. 1950; see also FLIP] As *v.i.:* see 1952 quot.; as *v.t.:* to provoke others to exasperation, enthusiasm or insanity (also used with *out*). — 1952 *A History of Jazz in America*, p. 350. *wig:* term expressing exasperation, enthusiasm, or insanity . . . describes the process of losing the hair or skin of the head. — 1955 *Solo*, p. 26. "He's got the idea jazz is still getting wigged and shutting your eyes and blowing up a storm." — 1955 *American Speech*, Dec., p. 305. "He wigged out at the prof's gag." — 1956 *Climax*, Summer, p. 22. "You wig me out, little man." — 1956 *Sideman*, p. 233. "When she found out I was dancing in nightclubs she wigged!" — 1959 *Toronto Telegram*, 31 March, p. 3. *wig:* to make others flip [jazz sense]. — 1959 *The Holy Barbarians*, p. 82. "Did you know So-and-So was wig-

ging?" — 1959 *San Francisco Chronicle*, 4 June, p. 35.
"Some real moldy [i.e., old-fashioned] cat in a library in
Alabama wigged out when she saw the white rabbits
and the black rabbits on the cover of the book together." — 1960 *The Jazz Review*, May, p. 30. "Baby,
there're a hundred car dealers that'd wig for th' opportunity." — 1961 *The Jazz Review*, Jan., p. 9. The guy was
about to wig. He told someone, "You gotta get this band
the hell outa here."

2. [formed from *n.*, sense 1—i.e., as a function or state
of the mind; current since c. 1955] See 1958 quot.; also,
as *v.t.*: to help someone else's thinking (i.e., to enlighten): see first 1959 quot. — 1958 *Publication of the
American Dialect Society*, Nov., p. 47. *wig*: to think; to
play extremely intellectual music. — 1959 *Diggeth
Thou?*, p. 43. Let me wig you to the deal that went down.
— 1959 *Esquire*, Nov., p. 70J. *to wig*: to think, to play.
Example: John wigged up this plan. — 1960 *Beat Jokes
Bop Humor & Cool Cartoons*, p. 22. "Don't be brought
down 'cause you didn't wig up this plan."

loose wig, [*wig, n.*, sense 1, in sense of the mind, *loose*
in sense of relaxed or uninhibited; some currency since
c. 1957] An imaginative person (usually, musician):
see both 1959 quots. (note: the phrase sometimes suggests a superfluity of imagination—i.e., unintelligibility:
see 1958 quot.) — 1958 *Jive in Hi-Fi*, p. 35. In slang, if
you say "loose wig" it means a person . . . talking in
circles. — 1959 *Jazz for Moderns*, p. 20. *loose wig*: a completely uninhibited really way-out [jazz sense] musician.
— 1959 *Esquire*, Nov., p. 70J. *loose wig*: one who is a
very advanced performer.

wild, *adj.* [see 1958 quot. for semantic explanation; current since c. 1948] Imaginative, unusual: see first two
1959 quots. — 1955 *Bop Fables*, p. 37. "I've fixed up a
real wild basket of ribs." — 1958 *Publication of the
American Dialect Society*, Nov., pp. 41–42. The adverse

criticisms of bop were taken over almost wholesale and made into favorable responses to music. Such terms as *crazy, weird, wild,* and *nervous,* all used to express favorable responses to music, are adaptations of terms levelled against the bop musicians. Since they knew the music which people called "crazy" was actually good, they took over the word in a good sense. — 1959 *Swinging Syllables.* s.v. *wild:* the greatest. — 1959 *Esquire,* Nov., p. 70J. *wild:* remarkable. — 1959 *The Horn,* p. 131. "Curn, it's wild, the greatest band you've ever had, but it'll bomb because it's too far out for the average ginmill owner." — 1959 *The Holy Barbarians,* p. 111. A maverick architect . . . used it as a hideaway workshop for some wild ideas. — 1960 *Hiparama of the Classics,* p. 8. They were blowin' so wild!

with it, (be or **get),** [in the sense of unification with life or reality; also some general colloquial use; current among jazzmen since c. 1940; see also DOWN WITH THE ACTION] See 1947, 1959 quots. — 1947 *Jive and Slang.* s.v. *git wit it:* enjoy yourself. — 1956 *It's Always Four O'Clock,* p. 39. "I'm not with it lately." — 1958 *Nugget,* Oct., p. 51. "You just ain't with it." — 1959 *Toronto Telegram,* 31 March, p. 3. *with it:* aware, digging [jazz sense]. — 1960 *Hiparama of the Classics,* p. 10. Now the Naz, was the kind of a Cat that came on so cool and so wild and so groovy and so *WITH IT,* that when he laid it down WHAM! It stayed there! — 1961 *The Sound,* p. 38. "Don't seem to be with it on tempo, though," Red commented.

wood pile, [from its shape: the instrument's keys were wooden; current c. 1933–c. 1940 when it was largely replaced as an instrument by the metal-keyed vibraphone and vibraharp (see VIBES), very rare since except historical] See 1936 quot. — 1936 *Metronome,* Feb., p. 61. *wood pile:* xylophone. — 1937 *This Thing Called Swing,* p. 9. *wood pile:* xylophone. — 1951 *Time,* 22 Oct., p. 69.

Red Norvo kept salting his half-hour stands with such tunes as . . . he used to rap out on his "woodpile" (xylophone) with Paul Whiteman's band 20 years ago.

wood-shed, woodshed, *v.i., v.t. & n.* [cf. 1960 *Dictionary of American Slang,* s.v. *woodshed:* "From the archaic and rural image of the woodshed where a boy could retire to smoke or otherwise occupy himself without detection"; current since c. 1930] To rehearse or practice (music) privately (see 1936, 1937 quots.); a period or a state of privately practicing (music). — 1936 *Swing That Music,* p. 71. We used to practise together, "wood-shed" as we say (from the old-time way of going out into the woodshed to practise a new song). — 1937 *This Thing Called Swing,* p. 9. *take it out in the woodshed,* or to *"woodshed" it:* try it out in private. — 1946 *Hollywood Note,* June, p. 4. T.D. [i.e., Tommy Dorsey] goes back to the woodshed. — 1955 *Hear Me Talkin to Ya,* p. 190. It was here that the term "woodshedding" originated. When one of the gang wanted to rehearse his part, he would go off into the woods and practice. — 1959 *The Horn,* p. 56. "I said I got to go, I got to woodshed for a while." — p. 59. That harrowing exile in the soul that jazzmen know as "woodshedding." — p. 242. Perhaps tomorrow he will begin his arduous woodshed. — 1961 *The Sound,* p. 28. "We gonna woodshed it tomorrow."

work, *v.i.* 1. [metonymy; cf. c. 1604 *Othello,* II, i, 116. "You rise to play, and go to bed to work"; according to jazzmen, current since c. 1945; see also TRIM] See first quot. — 1959 *The Holy Barbarians,* p. 156. "Work" means sexual intercourse. — 1959 *Esquire,* Nov., p. 70J. *work:* sexual intercourse. — 1961 *The Jazz Review,* Jan., p. 33. How about a new one called simply *Cojones,* or as the musicians would have it, *Work?*

2. [special application of the standard term; current since c. 1955; see also BLOW, GO, WAIL] To play (music) in earnest, energetically, excitingly. — 1956

Work! (tune composed by Thelonious Monk). — 1956
Workin: Miles Davis Quintet (LP album Prestige 7166).
— 1956 *Saturday Review,* 12 May, p. 34. Sims, along
with Stan Getz, is the most exciting of the young tenor
saxophonists, and when he is really working ("One to
Blow On"), he is irresistible. — 1961 *Metronome,* April,
p. 20. "The length is really determined by the way the
rhythm section is working and how everything is building
up."

   work out, [special application of its colloquial sense
(i.e., to exercise strenuously); current since c. 1958]
To play music intensely and energetically. — 1961
Workin' Out with The Barney Kessel Quartet (title of
LP album Contemporary M3585).

worst, the, [hyperbole: see also THE END, THE GREATEST,
LEAST, THE MOST; current since c. 1950] Anyone or
anything of poor quality, disappointing. — 1958 *Publication of the American Dialect Society,* Nov., p. 47.
the worst: opposite of *most, end,* etc.

wow, *interj.* [self-consciously childlike expression of
wonder; current since c. 1950; see also OOWEE] See
note: an expression of surprise or wonder (but in
contrast to its standard use, here it is a calculated
affectation). — 1961 *The Sound,* p. 113. "And, wow,
I should have thought of this before."

write, *v.i. & v.t.* [special application of standard meaning;
current since c. 1920] See 1958 quot. — 1926 *Melody
Maker,* Nov., p. 11. Now if you ever come to an instrument you are not sure about, there is only one way to
write his part. — 1933 *Metronome,* May, p. 39. I prefer
to transpose for the instruments as I write. — 1958
Publication of the American Dialect Society, Nov., p. 47.
write: to make an arrangement [i.e., musical].

writer, *n.* [current since c. 1935] See quot. — 1958
Publication of the American Dialect Society, Nov., p. 47.
writer: arranger.

wrong, *adj.* [standard term specially applied (i.e., to the
quality of music and, in an altered sense, to people);
prob. suggested by earlier underworld use: cf. 1934
A Dictionary of American Slang, p. 44. *"wrong:* un-
trustworthy; unreliable; deceitful"; current since c. 1950;
see also NOWHERE, RANK] Of poor quality; nasty. —
1959 *The Naked Lunch*, p. 226. In 1920s a lot of Chinese
pushers [i.e., narcotics sellers] found The West so unreliable, dishonest and wrong . . . when an Occidental
junky came to score [i.e., buy narcotics], they say, "No
glot . . . Clom Fliday . . . " — 1960 *The Jazz Review,*
Nov., p. 12. And they were so wrong until it was obnoxious to the average ear.

wrong riff, See s.v. RIFF.

Yard(bird), *n.* [see 1959 quot. for two contradicting ac-
counts of the origin of the nickname, a less common one
than its alternate, *Bird,* q.v.; current in any widespread
sense since c. 1945] Charlie Parker, 1920–1955, alto
saxophonist; most musicians and critics agree that he was
at once the most influential innovator and the greatest
instrumentalist in the history of jazz. — 1946 *Esquire's
1946 Jazz Book,* p. 43. One is altoist Charlie Parker,
familiar to jazzfans as "Yardbird." — 1950 *Yardbird*

Suite (tune composed by Charlie Parker). — 1959 *The Permanent Playboy*, p. 242. One friend says, "When he wasn't allowed in, he would stand outside in the alley with his ear to the wall, fingering his alto and playing— and that's how he got his name, they always found him in an an alley or a yard and they called him "Yardbird." (Parker's own version was different: he said people called him first "Charlie," then "Charl," the "Yarl," then "Yard," and finally "Yardbird.") — 1961 *Down Beat*, 25 May, p. 21. Yard had brought his horn with him.

yeah!, *interj.* [special use of colloquial term; reintroduced and widely current since c. 1950 after its use in the phrase *Yeah, man!*, q.v., had become passé among jazz-men c. 1940; see also THAT'S RIGHT, THERE YOU GO] See 1959 quot. — 1959 *Newport Jazz Festival: 1959*, p. 46. *yeah:* exclamation of approval. — 1961 *Charlie Rouse: Yeah!* (LP album Epic LA 16012).

yeah, man, *interj.* [see note s.v. *yeah;* current c. 1925–c. 1940, very rare since except historical (see 1946 quot.)] Exclamation of approval and/or ebullience. — 1932 *The Inter-State Tattler*, 7 Jan, p. 8. Still gatherin' dirt—yeah, man! — 1935 *His Hi De Highness of Ho De Ho*, p. 35. "Some jazz phrases . . . such as 'Yeah, man!' eventually have become part of the everyday language of all Americans." — 1938 *Cab Calloway: Hi De Ho*, p. 16. *yeah, man:* an exclamation of assent. — 1946 *Really the Blues*, p. 141. The unhip public took over the expression "hot" and made it corny by getting up in front of a band and snapping their fingers in a childish way, yelling "Get hot! Yeah man, get hot!"

you know?, [term has the same vague uses in general colloquial speech, but has been esp. common among jazzmen since c. 1945] See 1958 quot. — 1958 *Publication of the American Dialect Society*, Nov., p. 47. *you know:* means nothing (see like), but used as a question at the end of a statement. — 1959 *The Horn*, p. 68.

"Now pull yourself together, pops, you know?" — 1961 *Swank*, July, p. 4. On the way to L.A. we stopped at Hoover Dam stoned and peered over the edge! A MILE AND A HALF SHEER CONCRETE STRAIGHT DOWN! We wigged, you know? — 1961 *The Jazz Life*, p. 23. "Everyone, when he first started, thought: This man, his *tone* is too *thin*, you know?"

Z

zanzy, *adj.* [shortened form of *Zanzibar*, with whose predominantly Negro population many Negro jazzmen identify; adapted for some adjectival use esp. by Negro jazzmen c. 1945–c. 1950, obs. since] Authentic; splendid. Oral evidence only.

zonked, *adj.* [cf. comic strip attempt at onomatopoeic rendering of a blow: prob. by analogy with the effect; see also BOXED, HIGH, JUICED, STONED] See 1959 quot. — 1958 *Somewhere There's Music*, p. 85. "I think I got zonked on the beer." — 1959 *Esquire*, Nov., p. 70J. *zonked:* high, drunk. — 1961 *N.Y. Times Magazine*, 25 June, p. 39. *zonked:* one step past being stoned [jazz sense]. — 1963 *Nugget*, Feb., p. 21. This gentleman was so zonked he didn't remember a thing.

zoot(y), *adj.* [according to jazzman Zutty Singleton, the term was New Orleans patois for "cute" (a suggested

etym. differing from the one offered in 1943 quot., q.v.);
some currency c. 1925–c. 1945, obs. since except historical;
see also the much more widely current DAP, SHARP]
Initially: see second 1946 quot.; also, since c. 1935: see
1938, 1959 quots. — 1943 *New Yorker*, 19 June, p. 14. As
for the word "zoot," it is simply a corrupt form of "suit."
— 1944 *The New Cab Calloway's Hepsters Dictionary*.
s.v. *zoot:* overexaggerated as applied to clothes. — 1946
Really the Blues, p. 311. Colored kids . . . work on
their dungarees, pegging the legs till they're real sharp
and zooty. — p. 376. *zooty:* stylish, fashionable. — 1946
Time, 25 March, p. 52. No. 2 man is Bulee ("Slim") Gaillard, a skyscraping zooty Negro guitarist. — 1959 *Esquire*,
Nov., p. 70J. *zoot:* obsolete; exaggerated, ostentatious. —
1961 *Down Beat*, 13 April, p. 20. After World War II . . .
like the clothing it described, the word *zoot* faded from
use, except in satiric context—and as the nickname of a
very great tenor player [i.e., Zoot Sims].

zoot suit (with the reet pleat), [from rhyming slang
vogue c. 1935–c. 1940 (see also JACK THE BEAR, KILLER-
DILLER); though the phrase is originally jazz slang, its
currency was short and slight among jazzmen (c. 1938–
c. 1940), and it thrived primarily in non-jazz speech]
See first (only slightly exaggerated) quot. — 1942 *American Mercury*, July, p. 96. *zoot suit with the reet pleat:*
Harlem style suit, padded shoulders, 43-inch trousers at
the knee with cuff so small it needs a zipper to get into,
high waistline, fancy lapels, bushels of buttons, etc. —
1944 *The New Cab Calloway's Hepsters Dictionary*.
s.v. *zoot suit:* overexaggerated clothes. — 1959 *The
Jazz Scene*, p. 218. Before the vogue of the boppers'
costume it used to be the "zoot suit," with its epaulette
shoulders, its frock coat hanging almost to the pavement,
and its peg-bottom trousers.

Bibliography

A List of Works Cited

I. PERIODICALS

American Mercury
American Speech
American Weekly
Américas
Aramco World
Artesian
The Atlantic Monthly

Ballroom Dance
Bandleaders
Band Leaders and Record Review
The Billboard
Black Mask

Capitol News
Charm
The Chicago-Defender
Chicago Review
Clef
Climax
Coda
Commonweal
Confidential
Copper Romance
Cosmopolitan
Current History

Delineator
Disc
Down Beat

Ebony
Encounter
Escapade
Esquire
Evergreen Review

Flair
Fortune
Frontier

The Griffin

Harper's Magazine
Hi Fi & Music Review
High Fidelity
Hollywood Note

The Inter-State Tattler
Intro Bulletin

Jacobs' Orchestra Monthly
Jazz: A Quarterly of American
    Music

Jazz Forum
Jazz Journal
Jazz Monthly
Jazz News
Jazz Notes
Jazzology
The Jazz Record
The Jazz Review
The Journal of Abnormal and Social Psychology
Journal of Negro Education
Journal of Negro History

Life
Louisville Courier-Journal
The Lowdown

Mademoiselle
Melody Maker
Metronome
Modern Music
Monsieur
Monthly Review
The Musical Digest
The Music Quarterly
Music Library Association Notes
Music News

Neurotica
The New York Age
The New York Amsterdam News
New York Citizen-Call
New York Daily News
The New Yorker
New York Herald Tribune
New York Journal-American
New York Post
The New York Times
The New York Times Magazine

The New York Woman
Nugget

Oakland Tribune
Observer-Kaleidoscope

Park East
Partisan Review
Philadelphia Afro-American
Philadelphia Afro Magazine Section
Phylon
Pic
Play Back
Playboy
PM
Publications of the American Dialect Society

The Realist
The Record Changer
Record Research
Rhythm and Blues

Saga
San Francisco Chronicle
Saturday Review
Say
Scribner's Magazine
See
Show Business Illustrated
Sing Out!
Social Forces
Southern Folklore Quarterly
Spotlight
Stage
St. Louis Post-Dispatch
Swing

Tennessee Folklore Society Bulletin

This Week Magazine   Variety
Time   The Village Voice
Toledo Blade   Vogue
Toronto Daily Star
Toronto Telegram   The World

Vanity Fair   Zit's Theatrical Newspaper

II. Books, Miscellaneous Publications, etc.

(NOTE: *In order to facilitate reference from the citations to these works, the normal order of listing items has been reversed, the title here preceding the author.*)

After Hours Poetry: Jake Trussell. Kingsville, Texas: Trussell, 1958.
All About Jazz: Stanley R. Nelson. London: Health Cranton, 1934.
American Tramp and Underworld Slang: ed. by Godfrey Irwin. New York: Sears, 1930.
American College Dictionary. New York: Random House, 1959.
The American Jazz Festival: Louis R. Lawless. New York: International Jazz Associates, 1956.
American Jazz Music: Wilder Hobson. New York: W. W. Norton, 1939.
The American Language: H. L. Mencken. New York: Knopf, 1936–1948.
The American Thesaurus of Slang: A Complete Reference Book of Colloquial Speech: ed. by Melvin Van Den Bark & Lester V. Berrey. New York: Crowell, 1942; with new appendix, 1947; rev. 1953.
American Tramp and Underworld Slang: ed. by Godfrey Irwin. New York: Sears, 1930.
The Anatomy of Jazz: Leroy Ostransky. Seattle: University of Washington Press, 1960.
The Anatomy of Slang: Gilbert Highet. Book-of-the-Month Club transcript of WNYC radio talk, n.d.
The Angry Ones: John A. Williams. New York: Ace Books, 1960.
The Art of Jazz: ed. by Martin Williams. New York: Oxford, 1959.
The Autobiography of an Ex-Coloured Man: James Weldon

Johnson. New York: Hill & Wang reprint, 1960 (New York: Sherman, French, 1912).

Barefoot Boy with Cheek: Max Shulman. New York: Garden City, 1943.

Beale Street: Where the Blues Began: George W. Lee. New New: Robert O. Ballou, 1934.

The Beat Generation Dictionary: ed. by Albert Zugsmith. Hollywood, Calif.: M. G. M., n.d.

Beat Jokes Bop Humor & Cool Cartoons: ed. by Bob Reisner. New York: Citadel, n.d.

Big Bill Blues: William Broonzy & Yannick Bruynoghe. London: Cassell, 1955.

Big Book of Swing: ed. by Bill Treadwell. New York: Cambridge House, 1946.

Blow Up a Storm: Garson Kanin. New York: Random House, 1959.

Blues (Decca Records pamphlet, 1939).

The Book of Jazz: Leonard Feather. New York: Horizon, 1957.

The Book of Negro Folklore: Langston Hughes & Arna Bontemps. New York: Dodd, Mead, 1958.

Bop Fables: Steve Allen. New York: Simon & Schuster, 1955.

Cab Calloway: Hi De Ho. New York: Mills, n.d.

Call House Madam: Madam Beverly Davis & Serge G. Wolsey. New York: Paperback Books, 1963 (1942).

Chicago Documentary: Frederic Ramsey, Jr. London: Jazz Sociological Society, 1944.

The Collector's Jazz: Modern: John S. Wilson. Philadelphia: Lippincott, 1959.

The Collector's Jazz: Traditional and Swing: John S. Wilson. Philadelphia: Lippincott, 1958.

"A Compendium for the Teaching of Jazz History": Robert D. Fisher (unpubl. Master of Music thesis: U. of So. Cal., Jan. 1959).

Concerning Jazz: Sinclair Traill. London: Faber, 1957.

The Cool World: Warren Miller. Boston: Little, Brown, 1959.

The Country Blues: Samuel B. Charters. New York: Rinehart, 1959.

A Curtain of Green: Eudora Welty. Garden City, N.Y.: Doubleday, Doran, 1943.

Dan Burley's Original Handbook of Harlem Jive: Dan Burley. New York, 1944.

The Dead Ringer: Fredric Brown. New York: Bantam, 1949 (Dutton, 1948).

The Decca Book of Jazz: ed. by Peter Gammond. London: Frederick Muller, 1958.

The Dharma Bums: Jack Kerouac. New York: Viking, 1958.

A Dictionary of American English: Sir William Craigie. Chicago: University of Chicago Press, 1936–1942.

A Dictionary of American Slang: ed. by Maurice Weseen. New York: Crowell, 1934.

Dictionary of American Slang: ed. by Harold Wentworth & Stuart Berg Flexner. New York: Crowell, 1960.

Dictionary of American Underworld Lingo: ed. by Hyman E. Goldin. New York: Twayne, 1950.

A Dictionary of Slang and Colloquial English: ed. by John S. Farmer & W. E. Henley. New York: Dutton, 1905, rev. 1921.

A Dictionary of Slang and Unconventional English: Eric Partridge. New York: Macmillan, 1937.

A Dictionary of Slang, Jargon and Cant: ed. by Albert Barrere & Charles G. Leland. London: Ballantyne, 1890.

Diggeth Thou? Dan Burley. Chicago: Burley, Cross, 1959.

Dinosaurs in the Morning: Whitney Balliett. Philadelphia: Lippincott, 1962.

Down Beat Jazz Record Reviews 1956. Chicago: Maher, 1957.

Down Beat Jazz Record Reviews 1959. Chicago: Maher, 1960.

Down Beat Jazz Record Reviews 1961. Chicago: Maher, 1962.

Down Beat's Yearbook of Swing: ed. by Paul Eduard Miller. Chicago: Down Beat, 1939.

Down Memory Lane: Arthur Murray's Picture Story of Social Dancing: Sylvia G. L. Dannett & Frank R. Rachel. New York: Greenberg, 1954.

Duke Ellington: Barry Ulanov. New York: Creative Age, 1946.

Easy Living: Maitland Zane. New York: Dial, 1959.

Eddie Condon's Treasury of Jazz: ed. by Eddie Condon & Richard Gehman. New York: Dial, 1956.

The Encyclopedia of Jazz: Leonard Feather. New York: Horizon, 1955.

English Words & Their Background: George McKnight. New York: D. Appleton, 1925.

Enjoyment of Jazz (EJ 401, 402, 410). New York: American Recording Society [1956].

Esquire's 1944 Jazz Book. New York: Smith & Durrell, 1944.

Esquire's 1945 Jazz Book. New York: Smith & Durrell, 1945.

Esquire's 1946 Jazz Book. New York: Smith & Durrell, 1946.

Esquire's 1947 Jazz Book. New York: Smith & Durrell, 1947

Father of the Blues: An Autobiography: W. C. Handy. New York: Macmillan, 1941.

The Feeling of Jazz: George T. Simon. New York: Simon & Schuster, 1961.

Finnley Wren: Philip Wylie. New York: American, 1949 (Rinehart, 1934).

The First Book of Jazz: Langston Hughes. New York: Franklin Watts, 1955.

Flee the Angry Strangers: George Mandel. Indianapolis: Bobbs Merrill, 1952.

The French Quarter: Herbert Asbury. New York: Garden City, 1938.

From Spirituals to Swing (Carnegie Hall program: December 23, 1938).

Frontiers of Jazz: ed. by Ralph DeToledano. New York: O. Durrell, 1947.

Funk & Wagnalls New "Standard" Dictionary of the English Language. 1913, rev. 1960.

Gems of Jazz: Vol. I (Decca Records pamphlet, 1941).

Gems of Jazz: Vol. III (Decca Records pamphlet, 1941).

Gems of Jazz: Vol. IV (Decca Records pamphlet, 1942).

Giants of Jazz: Studs Turkel. New York: Crowell, 1957.

Go: John Clellon Holmes. New York: Scribner's, 1952.

Guide to Jazz: Madeleine Gautier & Hugues Panassie. Boston: Houghton, Mifflin, 1956.

Gutbucket and Gossamer: Fred Miller. Yonkers, N.Y.: Alicat, 1950.

Harlem Jazz, 1930 (Brunswick pamphlet, 1943).

Harvard Dictionary of Music: Willie Apel. Cambridge, Mass: Harvard University Press, 1946.

Hear Me Talkin to Ya: ed. by Nat Shapiro & Nat Hentoff. New York: Rinehart, 1955.

The Heart of Jazz: William L. Grossman & Jack W. Farrell. New York: New York University Press, 1956.

Hepcats Jive Talk Dictionary: ed. by Lou Shelly. Derby, Conn.: T. W. O. Charles, 1945.

The Hiparama of the Classics: Lord Buckley. San Francisco:
    City Lights, 1960.
Hiptionary: Elliot Horne. New York: Simon and Schuster, 1963.
His Hi De Highness of Ho De Ho!: Ned E. Williams. New
    York: Laurel, n.d.
A History of Jazz in America: Barry Ulanov. New York:
    Viking, 1952.
Hoagy Carmichael Songs (Decca Records pamphlet, 1939).
The Holy Barbarians: Lawrence Lipton. New York: Messner,
    1959.
The Horn: John Clellon Holmes. New York: Random House,
    1958.
The Hot and the Cool: Edwin Gilbert. New York: Doubleday,
    1953.
The Hot Jazz of Jelly Roll Morton: Charles Edward Smith.
    Camden, N.J.: R.C.A. Victor, n.d.
Inside Be-Bop: Leonard Feather. New York: J. J. Robbins,
    1949.
The International Cyclopedia of Music and Musicians: ed. by
    Oscar Thompson. New York: Dodd, Mead, 1939.
Invisible Man: Ralph Ellison. New York: Signet reprint, 1960
    (Random House, 1952).
It's Always Four O'Clock: James Updyke. New York: Random
    House, 1956.
Jam Session: An Anthology of Jazz: ed. by Ralph Gleason. New
    York: G. P. Putnam's, 1958.
Jazz: Paul Whiteman & M. M. McBride. New York: Sears, 1926.
Jazz: ed. by Nat Hentoff & Albert J. McCarthy. New York:
    Rinehart, 1959.
Jazzbook 1947. London: PL Editions, 1947.
Jazz for Moderns. New York: Associated Booking, n.d.
Jazz: A History of the New York Scene: Samuel B. Charters
    & Leonard Kunstadt. Garden City, N.Y.: Doubleday,
    1962.
Jazz: Hot and Hybrid: Winthrop Sargeant. New York: E. P.
    Dutton, 1946.
Jazz: Its Evolution and Essence: Andre Hodeir. New York:
    Grove, 1956.
The Jazz Life: Nat Hentoff. New York: Dial, 1961.
Jazzmen: ed. by Frederic Ramsey, Jr., & Charles Edward Smith.
    New York: Harcourt, Brace, 1939.

Jazz Poems: Ted Joans. New York: Rhino Review, 1959.
The Jazz Record Book: Charles Edward Smith. New York: Smith & Durrell, 1942.
The Jazz Scene: Francis Newton. London: MacGibbon & Kee, 1959.
Jazz Street: Dennis Stock. Garden City, N.Y.: Doubleday, 1960.
The Jazz Titans: Robert George Reisner. Garden City, N. Y.: Doubleday, 1960.
Jazzways: ed. by George S. Rosenthal & Frank Zachary. New York: Greenberg, 1946.
The Jazz Word: ed. by Dom Cerulli, Burt Korall, & Mort Nasatir. New York: Ballantine Books, 1960.
Jelly Roll Morton's New Orleans Memories: Jelly Roll Morton. New York: Consolidated Records, n.d.
Jitterbug Jamboree Song Book: Jean Herbert & Otis Spencer. New York: Marks Music Corp., 1939.
Jive and Slang: ed. by Marcus H. Boulware. Hampton, Va.: M. Boulware, 1947.
Jive in Hi-Fi: Willie Bryant. Los Angeles: Wilfern, 1958.
Junkie: William Lee (pseud., William Burroughs?). New York: Ace, 1953.
Just Jazz: Sinclair Traill & Gerald Lascelles. London: Peter Davies, 1957.
The Kingdom of Swing: Benny Goodman & Irving Kolodin. New York: Stackpole Sons, 1939.
King Oliver (Brunswick Radio Corp. pamphlet, 1946).
Lady Sings the Blues: Billie Holiday. New York: Doubleday, 1956.
Lingo of Tin-Pan Alley: Arnold Shaw. New York: Broadcast Music, 1950.
Mexico City Blues: Jack Kerouac. New York: Grove, 1959.
Mister Jelly Roll: Alan Lomax. New York: Duell, Sloan & Pearce, 1950.
Modern Dancing: Vernon & Irene Castle. New York: Harper & Bros., 1914 [as cited in *Jazz: A History of the New York Scene*, q.v.].
Murder on the Downbeat: Robert Avery. New York: Mystery House, 1943.
Music Out of Dixie: Harold Sinclair. New York: Rinehart, 1952.
The Naked Lunch: William Burroughs. Paris: Olympia Press, 1959.

The New Cab Calloway's Hepsters Dictionary: Language of Jive: Cab Calloway. New York: C. Calloway, 1944.

The New Edition of the Encyclopedia of Jazz: Leonard Feather. New York: Horizon, 1960.

The New Jazz Book: Joachim Berendt. New York: Hill and Wang, 1962.

Newport Jazz Festival: 1959 (program). Chicago: Down Beat, 1959.

New Short Novels: ed. by Mary Louise Aswell. New York: Ballantine, 1954.

New York Jazz Festival 1957. New York: n.p., 1957.

New York Jazz Festival: Vol. 3. New York: n.p., n.d.

Nigger Heaven: Carl Van Vechten. New York: Knopf, 1926.

Night Light: Douglass Wallop. New York: W. W. Norton, 1953.

Night Song: John A. Williams. New York: Farrar, Straus and Cudahy, 1961.

Nobody Knows My Name: James Baldwin. New York: Dial, 1961.

On the Road: Jack Kerouac. New York: Viking, 1957.

Oxford English Dictionary. 1884–1928; rev. ed., 1933.

Paris Blues: Harold Flender. New York: Ballantine, 1957.

The Permanent Playboy: ed. by Ray Russell. Chicago: Playboy, 1959.

A Pictorial History of Jazz: Orrin Keepnews & Bill Grauer, Jr. New York: Crown, 1955.

The PL Yearbook of Jazz: ed. by Albert McCarthy. London: PL Editions, 1946.

The Real Cool Killers: Chester Himes. New York: Avon, 1959.

The Real Jazz Old and New: Stephen Longstreet. Baton Rouge, La.: L.S.U. Press, 1956.

Really the Blues: Milton Mezzrow & Bernard Wolfe. New York: Random House, 1946.

Ride Out: Shelby Foote, in *New Short Novels* (ed. by Mary Louise Aswell). New York: Ballantine, 1954.

Riverboat Jazz (Brunswick Records pamphlet, 1943).

Salute to Fats Waller (Carnegie Hall program: April 2, 1944).

Satchmo: Louis Armstrong. New York: Prentice-Hall, 1954.

Second Ending: Evan Hunter. New York: Simon & Schuster, 1956.

Selected Poems: Langston Hughes. New York: Knopf, 1959.

Shakespeare's Bawdy: Eric Partridge. New York: Dutton, 1948.

Sideman: Osborn Duke. New York: Criterion, 1956.

Smaller Slang Dictionary: Eric Partridge. New York: Philo-
sophical Library, 1961.

So It Doesn't Whistle: Robert Paul Smith. New York: Harcourt,
Brace, 1941.

Solo: Stanford Witmore. New York: Harcourt, Brace, 1955.

Somewhere There's Music: George Lea. Philadelphia: J. B.
Lippincott, 1958.

So This Is Jazz: Henry O. Osgood. Boston: Little, Brown, 1926.

The Sound: Ross Russell. New York: Dutton, 1961.

The Sound of Surprise: Whitney Balliett. New York: Dutton,
1959.

The Story of Jazz: Marshall Stearns. New York: Oxford, 1956.

The Story of the Original Dixieland Jazz Band: H. O. Brunn.
Baton Rouge, La.: L.S.U. Press, 1960.

Strictly Ding-Dong: Richard English. Garden City, N.Y.:
Doubleday, 1941.

The Subterraneans: Jack Kerouac. New York: Grove Press, 1958.

Swinging Syllables. Memphis, Tenn.: Kimbrough, 1959.

Swing That Music: Louis Armstrong. London: Longmans,
Green, 1936.

They All Played Ragtime: Rudi Blesh & Harriet Janis. New York:
Knopf, 1950.

The Thin Man: Dashiell Hammett. New York: Permabooks
reprint, 1961 (Knopf, 1934).

This Is Jazz: Rudi Blesh. San Francisco: n.p., 1943.

This Thing Called Swing: ed. by Benny Goodman. Winston-
Salem, N.C.: R. J. Reynolds, n.d.

Toward Jazz: Andre Hodeir. New York: Grove, 1962.

Transatlantic Jazz: Peter Noble. London: Citizen Press, n.d.

A Treasury of the Blues: ed. by W. C. Handy. New York:
Boni, 1949.

Tremolo: Ernest Borneman. New York: Harper, 1948.

The Trouble with Cinderella: Artie Shaw. New York: Farrar,
Straus, & Young, 1952.

Trumpet on the Wing: Wingy Manone & Paul Vandervoort.
Garden City, N.Y.: Doubleday, 1948.

The Two Worlds of Johnny Truro: George Sklar. Boston: Little,
Brown, 1947.

The Walls of Jericho: Rudolph Fisher. New York: Knopf, 1928.

*Webster's New World Dictionary of the American Language:
    College Edition.* Cleveland: World, 1959.
Who Walk in Darkness: Chandler Brossard. New York: New
    Directions, 1952.
A Wreath for Rivera: Ngaio Marsh. Boston: Little, Brown, 1949.

Various song titles and lyrics, and various LP album titles and
liner notes—as indicated in the lexicon citations.

A Note on the Type

THE TEXT of this book is set in *Caledonia,* a Linotype
face designed by W. A. DWIGGINS, the man responsible
for so much that is good in contemporary book design
and typography. Caledonia belongs to the family of
printing types called "modern face" by printers — a term
used to mark the change in style of type-letters that
occurred about 1800. Caledonia borders on the
general design of Scotch Modern but is more
freely drawn than that letter.